THE SUFI ORDERS IN ISLAM

THE SUFI ORDERS IN ISLAM

J. SPENCER TRIMINGHAM

With a new foreword by
John O. Voll

Oxford University Press
New York Oxford

Oxford University Press

Oxford New York
Athens Auckland Bangkok Bogotá Bombay
Buenos Aires Calcutta Cape Town Dar es Salaam
Delhi Florence Hong Kong Istanbul Karachi
Kuala Lumpur Madras Madrid Melbourne
Mexico City Nairobi Paris Singapore Taipei
Tokyo Toronto

and associated companies in

Berlin Ibadan

First published by the Clarendon Press, 1971
First issued as an Oxford University Press paperback, 1973

Library of Congress Cataloging-in-Publication Data

Trimingham, J. Spencer (John Spencer), 1904–
The Sufi orders in Islam / J. Spencer Trimingham :
with a new foreward by John O. Voll.
p. cm.
Includes bibliographical references (p.) and index.

ISBN 0–19–512058–2
1. Sufism. I. Title.
BP189.68.T75 1998
297.4'8'09—dc21 97–46478

1 3 5 7 9 8 6 4 2

Printed in the United States of America

CONTENTS

FOREWORD

SUFISM is a significant part of the historical experience of Muslims. The simple, textbook definition of Sufism as "a mystical expression of the Islamic faith"[1] obscures the complexities of its nature and role. Most discussions of Sufism identify two dimensions as critical to understanding its nature and history. The first is the intellectual dimension, dealing with the content of Sufi teachings; the second is organizational, because Sufi teachings came to be manifested through associations with great significance within Muslim societies. Such an organization is called a *tariqa* ("path") and are often refered to as "brotherhoods" or "orders."

Many books have addressed Sufi teachings and their development,[2] and many others have examined specific *tariqas* or surveyed *tariqas* in specific regions and countries.[3] Few scholars, however, have attempted a comprehensive survey of the history and development of these organizations. It was an achievement of J. Spencer Trimingham to write such a broad survey, *The Sufi Orders in Islam*, which has been widely used since its first publication, in 1971.

When this book was published, reviewers emphasized that it "fills a notable gap in the literature."[4] One reviewer noted that for "the first time under one cover we have a comprehensive treatment of an important subject."[5] Of course, any attempt to cover such a broad and complex topic will have its problems, and everyone, including Trimingham, recognized that the book's coverage and analysis could be improved. The *Times Literary Supplement* suggested doubling the size of the book.[6] Another early review voiced a series of specific objections but concluded: "Until a more adequate historical account of the Sufi orders is written, this work is the most informative text available in English."[7]

The judgment of Trimingham's account has stood for more than two decades. Although specific topics have provoked disagreement or revision of Trimingham's analysis, no "more adequate account" of the whole spectrum of Sufi *tariqas* has yet been published. As a result, *The Sufi Orders in Islam* continues to be listed in most bibliographies as a "good historical survey of the orders,"[8] even though some sources note that it "has been severely criticized."[9]

Many studies have been published since Trimingham wrote this volume. These provide additionals and corrections to Trimingham's analysis, and sometimes suggest important new directions in the interpretation of the history of the Sufi orders. One excellent dissertation demonstrates the continuing importance of Trimingham's book in helping to fill the gaps. In a discussion of the later development of Sufi organization, Barbara Rosenow von Schlegell notes a number of important recent studies "of the Sufi elements in society . . . and in specific historical contexts"; however, she says, "with regard to organized Sufism, it is a great leap to make from the formation of Sufi orders to state regulation of Sufism in the nineteenth century, but, with few exceptions, literature on Sufism vaults, one might say, from Baha' al-Din al-Naqshband (d. 793/1390) to Frederick De Jong's *Turuq and Turuq-linked Institutions* (published in 1978), with only J. S. Trimingham to explain five hundred years of Sufi development."[10]

Trimingham provides a general schema of different modes of Sufi organization as they developed throughout Islamic history, tracing the development of *tariqas* through three stages. (One reviewer described this as "a rough-and-ready classification but . . . useful as a working hypothesis."[11]) The first stage is what he calls "the golden age of mysticism" (p. 103), when Sufism was basically an effort of individual devotional piety under the guidance of a spiritual master—the "*khanaqah*" stage, with the focus of Sufi life being the *khanaqah*, or small residential center that developed around a special teacher. The second stage is the "*tariqa*" stage, when more explicitly defined devotional paths were developed in the twelfth and thirteenth centuries as "ways" to be followed. The third stage, which began in the fifteenth century, involved a more rigid institutionalization of the orders; the *tariqas* become highly developed hierarchical associations. Although Trimingham identifies this as the "*ta'ifa*" stage of organizational development, he tends to follow the more common custom of speaking of the new, hierarchical associations as "*tariqas*," which, as one reviewer noted, can lead to ambiguity in his presentation.[12]

Trimingham (p. 103), his reviewers and scholars who work

within this framework have all referred to it as a three-stage schema. In fact, however, Trimingham adds a fourth stage, with a chapter on nineteenth-century revival movements. By the nineteenth century, Trimingham says, the orders had become "very decadent," and "the true Way of Sufi experience had weakened" within them (p. 106). As a result, some teachers within the Sufi tradition became activist reformers, working both to purify Sufism and to engage in the sociomoral reconstruction of Muslim societies. These efforts resulted in the creation of a number of renewalist *tariqas*.

Trimingham uses this grand outline to locate the main Sufi orders in both time and place, and it continues to be useful for scholars and students. *The Sufi Orders in Islam* serves as an historical dictionary for identifying hundreds of Sufi teachers and organizations. New research provides new information and perspectives, but it does not argue for rejecting the broader picture of the evolution of Sufi organizations from the *khanaqah* to the devotional paths to the more organized orders, even though the pace of this evolution varied from region to region of the Muslim world.

Some recent scholarship tends to confirm not only the sequence identified by Trimingham but the timing and nature of the shifts. A study of the development of Sufi organization in Khurasan, in eastern Iran, in the eleventh century emphasizes the importance of the transition from the *khanaqah* to the *tariqa* stage. Beginning with Sufis who had been "outside the mainstream of Islamic social life and institutions," Sufis developed the practices and organization "associated with membership in a Sufi order" during the eleventh century.[13] These developments provided the foundation for "the formation of the urban Sufi *tariqa* in the late twelfth and thirteenth centuries"[14] in a number of geographical areas.

A number of important subjects relating to the history of Sufism have been debated in recent years. Three of them have a direct relevance to the reassessment of Trimingham's analysis and should be reconsidered by interested scholars: "Neo-Sufism"; the middle centuries of Islamic history; and the role of Sufism in the modern era.

The term "neo-Sufism" was probably first used by Fazlur

Rahman in his discussion of the relationship between the historical development of Sufism and reform tendencies in premodern Muslim societies. As Sufi orders became widespread, some less-mystical mainstream scholars attempted to define a form of Sufism that moved away from popular religious practices and more ecstatic forms of Sufi devotions. The goal was "the strengthening of faith in dogmatic tenets and the moral purity of the spirit. This type of neo-Sufism, as one may call it, tended to regenerate orthodox activism and reinculcate a positive attitude to this world. . ., [instilling in Sufism] a puritanical, moral meaning and an orthodox ethos."[15]

Although Trimingham did not explicitly use the term "neo-Sufism," his works are seen as part of the school of thought that identified a new reformist style of Sufism as an important aspect of Islamic history in the eighteenth and nineteenth centuries.[16] Trimingham's description of the nineteenth-century revivalist movements is similar to Rahman's, and both scholars discuss the same *tariqas*. In many ways, Trimingham's analysis laid an important foundation for the analysis that named these revivalist movements "neo-Sufi," and many of his research materials found their way into the later discussions of Neo-Sufism.

In the early 1990s, some scholars reacted to Rahman, Trimingham, and others by developing a critique of what they called the "theory of Neo-Sufism." These critics grouped together the scholarship of a highly diverse group of scholars and presented it as if it were a coherent grand theory of a new phase of Sufism in the eighteenth and nineteenth centuries.[17] Trimingham was portrayed as a central figure in this so-called "neo-Sufi school of thought." The critics sometimes even portrayed him as if he had actually used the term "neo-Sufi," although it was not a term which he used, by inserting the term in brackets when quoting from his work.[18]

Lost in the enthusiasm of critiquing this so-called neo-Sufi school of thought, the ideas of *some* of these scholars were occasionally incorrectly attributed to *all* of the scholars in the group. For example, some scholars who wrote in the 1940s and 1950s *did* argue that Wahhabism inspired many of the revivalist movements of the eighteenth and nineteenth centuries. However, one critique of the so-called Neo-Sufism theory argued that "it is thus commonplace to speak of Wahhabi influences on the thought of the Indian Shah Wali Allah al-Dihlawi,"[19] citing an article that, in reality, suggested that the founder of the Wahhabi movement studied with some of the same teachers as Shah Wali Allah—in effect disproving Wahhabi influence upon that Indian scholar.[20] The scholar accused of speaking of such widespread "Wahhabi influences" had, in fact, written: "It has been common at times to assert that any teacher who happened to go to Arabia in the eighteenth century and who returned to his home full of fundamentalist enthusiasm was somehow influenced by the Wahhabis. . . . [M]any of the revivalist movements that emerged by the end of the century did so in the framework of Neo-Sufi thought and organization rather than by following the Wahhabi attitude."[21]

Analyses like Trimingham's made it possible to distinguish a broad spectrum of revivalist movements, and to go beyond the earlier simplistic identification of any revivalist as being somehow "Wahhabi-inspired." What Trimingham described were *two* developments that led to what he called "an intensified Islam—the Wahhabi movement and revival in the orders" (p. 105). This discussion of revivalism in the late eighteenth and early nineteenth centuries places Trimingham among those who believe that new Sufi orders inspired by a vision of Islamic renewal developed during this time. Despite a few excesses in the attempt to create a revisionist school rejecting the "theory of Neo-Sufism," most of the debate has constructively identified areas where the earlier scholarship was vague, oversimplified developments, or simply did not examine sources in depth. The result has been greater attention to the development of Sufi orders in the eighteenth and nineteenth centuries.[22]

Trimingham's analysis has an important place in the recent discussions on two of the important topics in the history of Sufism—the rise of early modern Islamic renewalism and the scholarly reassessment of the middle centuries of Islamic history. In these areas, his views are important, even if requiring some modification.

Trimingham was one of the first twentieth-century Western scholars to draw attention to Ahmad ibn Idris, a significant figure in the development of *tariqas* at the beginning of the nineteenth century. This teacher's students established some of the most important orders in the modern world, especially in Africa. In many ways, it was Trimingham's analysis of Ibn Idris that shaped his description of Islamic revivalism in the nineteenth century. Trimingham emphasized that Ibn Idris was a key figure in the development of a new type of *tariqa* that rejected extreme asceticism and stressed practical activities (p. 107).

The idea that this revivalism involved a reorganization of the *tariqa* is central to Trimingham's thinking. Even the strongest critics of the concept of Neo-Sufism agreed with Trimingham about organization.[23] R. S. O'Fahey, in his important study of Ahmad ibn Idris, distinguished between the organizational and intellectual aspects of what some called Neo-Sufism; with regard to *tariqas*, he identified "a new organizational phenomenon that appeared in certain areas of the Muslim world in the late eighteenth and early nineteenth centuries. In these areas, new orders were established that were relatively more centralized and less prone to fission than their predecessors; they introduced . . . new forms of social organization, . . . and later were politically active."[24] (In other words, whatever one chooses to call the general phenomenon, there were some significant developments in *tariqa* organization in the early nineteenth century, and Trimingham's description of nineteenth-century revivalism remains useful.)

Trimingham's description of the conceptual-theological dimension of nineteenth-century revivalism, especially in the thought of Ahmad ibn Idris, has also come under strong criticism. Many of those discussing Ibn Idris's role in Muslim revivalism have made generalizations and possibly inaccurate statements based on superficial analysis of his writings. Trimingham and others have suggested that this new Sufi thought brought a shift in the goal of Sufi devotional activities from "union with God" to "union with the spirit of the Prophet."[25] Critics have called this "an unsubstantiated assertion."[26]

In an analysis of Ibn Idris's position on this issue, O'Fahey concluded that in Ibn Idris's teachings, "Progress on the mystical path would bring the presence of Muhammad as a mentor and authenticator of the Koran and the Sunna, that the initiate would be able to learn Tradition directly from the Prophet," but that this "is by no means the same as the assertion that Ibn Idris advocated union with the spirit of the Prophet instead of union with God."[27]

However, this position makes it clear that the nature of the role of Muhammad in revivalist Sufi thinking in the nineteenth century is highly complex, and not as simple an issue as the first revisionist assertions seemed to indicate. Recent intensive research on the teachings of Muhammad Majdhub, a student of Ibn Idris, affirm that there was an important Prophet-centeredness in the thinking of at least some Sufi teachers of the time, and that much more research needs to be done on the meaning of Muhammad-oriented *tariqas.*[28] Thus, while Trimingham's description is outdated and oversimplified, it remains useful for identifying general trends of the times.

In his discussion of the middle centuries of Islamic history, Trimingham's presentation is more out of line with recent scholarship in perspective than in specific content. Trimingham maintains an older image of Islamic history wherein the early centuries of the great imperial caliphates were "the golden age," and the fifteenth and sixteenth centuries were an age of relative stagnation and intellectual obscurantism. Trimingham emphasized the increasingly structured nature of the Sufi experience, by the third stage of *tariqa* development, saying that although organization "arose naturally through the need for guidance and association with kindred aspirants," such organization "carried within itself the seeds of decay" (p. 103). With the completion of the development of the *tariqas* in the third stage, Trimingham felt that the "orders had now attained their final forms of organization and spiritual exercises. Innovations had become fully integrated and their spirit and aims were stereotyped. No further development was possible and no further work of mystical insight which could mark a new point of departure in either doctrine or practice was to make its appearance" (p. 104).

The image of the Islamic world as an intellectually stagnant and conservative region in the "dark centuries" following the end of the Abbasid caliphate in 1258 was relatively common in Orientalist scholarship, and Sufism was seen as an important determinant of this stagnation.[29] In terms of political history, Trimingham pays little attention to the great vitality and dynamism of the major Muslim empires of the sixteenth century—the Ottoman, the Safavid, and the Mughal—and the intellectual and economic life in their major cities. To broaden this perspective, one needs the portrayals of Muslim life in this era by such scholars as Marshall Hodgson and Ira Lapidus.[30]

We have many new perspectives on the impact of Sufism on Muslim life during Trimingham's "third stage." For example, although Trimingham mentions the Iranian teacher Sadr al-Din al-Shirazi, known as Mulla Sadra (pp. 99, 128), he does not indicate this scholar's importance; Mulla Sadra has been described as "the most impressive unifier of the ideas that were familiar to the Muslim world," having provided a major synthesis that demanded "a dramatic change of perspective."[31] Trimingham does not even mention Mulla Sadra in his chapter on the theosophy of the orders, even though many see Sadra as the key figure in the development of Transcendent Theosophy, with "a new perspective in Islamic intellectual life based on the synthesis and harmonization of nearly all the earlier schools of Islamic thought" and an influence that continues to this day.[32]

Trimingham does address most of the important people and movements in the era that he sees as a time of stagnation. It is his basic conceptualization of the intellectual and spiritual life of the times that requires significant modification in light of recent scholarship.

Trimingham diverges most sharply from recent scholarship in his coverage of Sufism in the modern era. He viewed *tariqas* as a last refuge for tradition-minded and possibly anti-modern people: "Though the orders can never regain their former influence in Islamic life they will continue to exist, for there are always some peasants, artisans, and intellectuals who need the type of spiritual solace they offer, or are ready to seek in them a way of escape or refuge from the anxieties of life in the modern world" (p. 257). This analysis makes it difficult to recognize the continuing strength of the *tariqas* in many different parts of the world.

The influence of Sufi Islam in the former Soviet Union was already visible in the 1960s. An important study of *tariqas* in the USSR affirmed that "Sufism is a fact, and a potent one, of Islamic reality in the Soviet Union. It has never been a negligible factor in the conduct of relations between Russians and the Muslims of the empire, and, given the domestic and foreign stimuli which affect it, it is unlikely to become negligible in the future."[33] Similarly, despite the official suppression of *tariqas* in Turkey after the establishment of the secularist republic in the 1920s, *tariqas* continued to play an important part in the lives of a significant number of Turks.[34]

Both the Soviet and the Turkish experiences might fit into some reformulation of the Trimingham model, but what Trimingham would have found incomprehensible is the growing strength of Sufism and *tariqas* among "modern" people who are not trying to escape modernity. The existence of an active *tariqa* in Vermont in the 1990s, and the International Association of Sufism—whose annual meeting in California was attended by 800 people in 1996[35]—are inconceivable in the perspective of *The Sufi Orders in Islam*, and probably would have been equally difficult for the former missionary and scholar to accept.

Trimingham's book remains the most useful and comprehensive guide to the Sufi orders of Islam in the premodern era. The spirit of the early reviews continue to apply more than a quarter of a century after the book was originally published: we may object to specific aspects of the book, but it remains the only one of its kind, and an essential reference.

JOHN O. VOLL

NOTES

1. John Renard, *Seven Doors to Islam: Spirituality and the Religious Life of Muslims* (Berkeley: University of California Press, 1996), p. 307.
2. One of the older standard works is A. J. Arberry, *Sufism: An Account of the Mystics of Islam* (New York: Harper and Row, 1970), while more recent coverage can be found in Julien Baldick, *Mystical Islam: An Introduction to Sufism* (London: I. B. Tauris, 1989); Annemarie Schimmel, *Mystical Dimensions of Islam* (Chapel Hill: University of North Carolina Press, 1975).
3. See, for example, country and regional surveys like Alexandre Bennigsen and S. Enders Wimbush, *Mystics and Commissars: Sufism in the Soviet Union* (Berkeley: University of California Press, 1985); F. De Jong, *Turuq and Turuq-linked Institutions in Nineteenth Century Egypt* (Leiden: Brill, 1978); B. G. Martin, *Muslim Brotherhoods in Nineteenth-century Africa* (Cambridge: Cambridge University Press, 1976); or, for specific *tariqas*, studies like Joseph Fletcher's study of the Naqshbandiyya in *Studies on Chinese and Islamic Inner Asia*, ed. Beatrice Forbes Manz (Aldershot: Variorum, 1995), or R. S. O'Fahey, *Enigmatic Saint: Ahmad Ibn Idris and the Idrisi Tradition* (Evanston: Northwestern University Press, 1990).

4. Paul J. Magnarella, review of *The Sufi Orders in Islam*, in *Ethnology* 74: 6 (December 1972), 1407.
5. Caesar E. Farah, review of *The Sufi Orders in Islam*, in *The Middle East Journal* 26: 1 (Winter 1972), 88.
6. *Times Literary Supplement*, no. 3612 (21 May 1971).
7. *Choice* 10: 8 (October 1973), 1222. [No author was listed.]
8. William C. Chittick, "Sufi Thought and Practice," in *The Oxford Encyclopedia of the Modern Islamic World*, ed. John L. Esposito (New York: Oxford University Press, 1995), 4: 109.
9. Baldick, *Mystical Islam*, p. 190.
10. Barbara Rosenow von Schlegel, "Sufism in the Ottoman Arab World: Shaykh 'Abd al-Ghani al-Nabulusi (d. 1143/1731)," unpublished dissertation, University of California, Berkeley, 1997, p. 15.
11. *Times Literary Supplement*, no. 3612, 21 May 1971.
12. F. De Jong, Review of *The Sufi Orders in Islam*, in *Journal of Semitic Studies* 17: 2 (Autumn 1972), 279.
13. Margaret Malamud, "Sufi Organizations and Structures of Authority in Medieval Nishapur," *International Journal of Middle East Studies* 26 (1994): 427–428.
14. Malamud, "Sufi Organizations," p. 438.
15. Fazkur Rahman, *Islam* (2nd ed.; Chicago: University of Chicago Press, 1979), p. 195.
16. See, for example, the critique of the "Neo-Sufism School" in R. S. O'Fahey and Bernd Radtke, "Neo-Sufism Reconsidered," *Der Islam* 70: 1 (1993): 52–87.
17. In addition to Fazlur Rahman and Trimingham, O'Fahey and Radtke's "Neo-Sufism Reconsidered" places in this "school" H. A. R. Gibb, B. G. Martin, Ira Lapidus, Edmund Burke, III, Nehemia Levtzion, possibly all of the late-nineteenth-century French Orientalists, and myself.
18. See, for example, O'Fahey and Radtke, "Neo-Sufism Reconsidered," p. 59.
19. Ahmad Dallal, "The Origins and Objectives of Islamic Revivalist Thought, 1750–1850," *Journal of the American Oriental Society* 113: 3 (July–September 1993), 342.
20. John Voll, "Muhammad Hayya al-Sindi and Muhammad ibn Abd al-Wahhab: An Analysis of an Intellectual Group in Eighteenth-Century Madina," *Bulletin of the School of Oriental and African Studies* 38, part 1 (1975). See especially the pages cited by Dallal, pp. 38–39.
21. John Obert Voll, *Islam: Continuity and Change*, p. 56. This statement was also in the first edition, published in 1982.
22. See, for example, the helpful discussion in Barbara Rosenow von Schlagell, "Sufism in the Ottoman Arab World," pp. 16–19.
23. See, for example, the concluding comments in O'Fahey and Radtke, "Neo-Sufism Reconsidered," p. 87.
24. O'Fahey, *Enigmatic Saint*, pp. 4–5.
25. Trimingham, *Sufi Orders*, p. 106. It should be noted that I made a similar generalization about tendencies in Sufi thought at the time; see Voll, *Islam Continuity and Change*, p. 27.
26. O'Fahey and Radtke, "Neo-Sufism Reconsidered," p. 56.
27. O'Fahey, *Enigmatic Saint*, p. 4.
28. Albrecht Hofheinz, "Internalising Islam: Shaykh Muhammad Majdhub,

Scriptural Islam and Local Context in the Early Nineteenth-Century Sudan," unpublished dissertation, University of Bergen, 1996. See especially p. 398 for "Prophet-centeredness" and pp. 550–551 for Tariqa Muhammadiyya.

29. See, for example, the conclusions in H. A. R. Gibb, "An Interpretation of Islamic History," in *Studies on the Civilization of Islam*, ed. Stanford J. Shaw and William R. Polk (Boston: Beacon Press, 1962), pp. 30–31.
30. Marshall G. S. Hodgson, *The Venture of Islam: Conscience and History in a World Civilization* (Chicago: University of Chicago Press, 1974); Ira M. Lapidus, *A History of Islamic Societies* (Cambridge: Cambridge University Press, 1988).
31. Baldick, *Mystical Islam*, p. 125.
32. Seyyed Hossein Nasr, *Sadr al-Din Shirazi and his Transcendent Theosophy* (Tehran: Imperial Iranian Academy of Philosophy, 1978), pp. 93–94.
33. Alexandre Bennigsen and S. Enders Wimbush, *Mystics and Commissars: Sufism in the Soviet Union* (Berkeley: University of California Press, 1985), p. 114.
34. See, for example, the discussion of the twentieth-century movement of Said Nursi in Serif Mardin, *Religion and Social Change in Modern Turkey* (Albany: State University of New York Press, 1989).
35. See, for example, Laurie Goodstein, "Sufi Faith Gains a Foothold in Vermont's Green Hills," *Washington Post*, 19 January 1997, p. A3.

PREFACE

WHILST Islamic mysticism has exercised a compelling attraction upon many Western scholars, its organizational aspect, the mystical orders, has been neglected. Yet a misleading impression of Islamic mysticism is conveyed if it is based exclusively upon the writings of its poets and theosophists, for mysticism is essentially a practical discipline based upon the insights of these illuminated seekers.

No modern study of the orders exists; the pioneer work of Louis Rinn, *Marabouts et Khouan*, published in Algiers in 1884, though concerned primarily with Algeria, still forms a valuable introduction, whilst its range was extended with the publication of A. le Chatelier's *Les Confréries musulmanes du Hedjaz* (Paris, 1887). Studies have appeared of particular orders or areas, especially north Africa, but nothing concerning their development through the centuries. The way in which my own views have changed since commencing this study has confirmed the need for a reassessment.

This study is primarily concerned with the historical development of the orders and seeks to trace the successive phases through which the practice of the Sufi spirit passed. This process took place within the Arabic and Persian spheres upon which the main emphasis is naturally placed. Other cultural spheres took over this development which continued to dominate, even though regional cultures made their own contributions and formed their distinctive practices.

The intellectual aspect is not ignored, but concern is restricted to the spiritual and intellectual movement which lay behind the practical working of the orders, their methods of organization and ritual. In terms of the wider setting within the Islamic culture we are concerned with a vast movement of the spirit which spread throughout the Islamic world, influencing the ordinary person no less than a mystical élite (which cannot be said of the mystical movement in Christendom), and which today faces a grave crisis through erosion by modern life and thought.

I wish to acknowledge the help given me by the Carnegie

Trust for the Universities of Scotland, when I was a member of the staff of Glasgow University, through a grant which enabled me to make a study tour in north Africa in 1960. My thanks are also due to my colleague, Professor Nicola Ziadeh, for his help in reading my draft and calling my attention to mistakes and to matters which needed clarification.

J. S. T

Beirut
September 1969

ABBREVIATIONS

A.I. E.O.	*Annales de l'Institut d'études orientales de l'Université d'Alger.*
Archiv. maroc.	*Archives marocaines.*
b.	ibn = son of.
B.I.F.A.O.	*Bulletin de l'Institut français d'Archéologie orientale du Caire.*
D. Isl.	*Der Islam*, Berlin.
E.I.[1], *E.I.*[2]	*Encyclopaedia of Islam*, 1st edition, 2nd edition.
E.R. E.	*Hastings' Encyclopaedia of Religion and Ethics.*
G.A.L.	Brockelmann, Carl, *Geschichte der arabischen Literatur.*
G.A.L.S	Supplement to *G.A.L.*
G.M.S	E. J. W. Gibb Memorial Series.
J. Asiat.	*Journal asiatique*, Paris.
J.R.A.S	*Journal of the Royal Asiatic Society*, London.
M.	Muhammad.
M. E.J.	*Middle East Journal, Washington, D.C.*
M.I.D. E.O.	*Mélanges de l'Institut dominicain d'Études orientales*, Cairo.
M.S.O.S.	*Mitteilungen des Seminars für orientalische Sprachen*, Berlin.
M.W.	*The Muslim World*, Hartford.
R. E.I.	*Revue des études islamiques*, Paris.
R.M.M.	*Revue du Monde musulman*, Paris.
R.S.O.	*Rivista degli studi orientali*, Rome.
Z.D.M.G.	*Zeitschrift der Deutschen Morgenländischen Gesellschaft*, Wiesbaden.

THE SUFI ORDERS IN ISLAM

I

The Formation of Schools of Mysticism

THE term *ṣūfī* was first applied to Muslim ascetics who clothed themselves in coarse garments of wool (*ṣūf*). From it comes the form *taṣawwuf* for 'mysticism'. There are excellent guides to Islamic mysticism and all that is necessary by way of introduction is to give some idea of how I am using the terms *ṣufī* and Sufism in the context of this study on the mystical Ways and their expression in orders.

I define the word *ṣūfī* in wide terms by applying it to anyone who believes that it is possible to have direct experience of God and who is prepared to go out of his way to put himself in a state whereby he may be enabled to do this. Many will not be happy about this definition, but I find it the only possible way to embrace all the varieties of people involved in the orders.

The term Sufism as used in this book is equally comprehensive. It embraces those tendencies in Islam which aim at direct communion between God and man. It is a sphere of spiritual experience which runs parallel to the main stream of Islamic consciousness deriving from prophetic revelation and comprehended within the *Sharīʿa* and theology. This contrast is the reason for the enmity legalists have always borne towards Sufism, for it means that the mystics are claiming a knowledge of the Real (*al-Ḥaqq*, their term for God) that could not be gained through revealed religion which in Islam became codified religion.

Mysticism is a particular method of approach to Reality (*Ḥaqīqa*, another special Sufi term), making use of intuitive and emotional spiritual faculties which are generally dormant and latent unless called into play through training under guidance. This training, thought of as 'travelling the Path' (*salak aṭ-ṭarīq*), aims at dispersing the veils which hide the self from the Real and thereby become transformed or absorbed into undifferentiated Unity. It is not primarily an intellectual process, though the experience of the mystic led to the formulation of various types of mystical philosophy, but rather a reaction against the external rationalization of Islam in law and systematic theology, aiming at spiritual freedom whereby man's intrinsic intuitive spiritual senses could be allowed full scope. The various Ways (*ṭuruq*, sing. *ṭarīqa*) are concerned with this process, and it is with the historical development, practical organization, and modes of worship of these Ways that this book is concerned.

Early Sufism was a natural expression of personal religion in relation to the expression of religion as a communal matter. It was an assertion of a person's right to pursue a life of contemplation, seeking contact with the source of being and reality, over against institutionalized religion based on authority, a one-way Master–slave relationship, with its emphasis upon ritual observance and a legalistic morality. The spirit of Qur'ānic piety had flowed into the lives and modes of expression, as in the form of 'recollection' (*dhikr*), of the early devotees (*zuhhād*) and ascetics (*nussāk*). Sufism was a natural development out of these tendencies manifest in early Islam, and it continued to stress them as an essential aspect of the Way. These seekers after direct experience of communion with God ensured that Islam was not confined within a legalistic directive. Their aim was to attain ethical perception (we shall see how this was to recur in later developments) and this was redirected or transformed to the aim of the Sufis to attain mystical perception.

Sufism was a natural development within Islam, owing little to non-Muslim sources, though receiving radiations from the ascetical–mystical life and thought of eastern Christianity. The outcome was an Islamic mysticism following distinctive Islamic lines of development. Subsequently, a vast and elaborate mystical system was formed which, whatever it may owe to neo-Platonism, gnosticism, Christian mysticism, or other systems, we may truly regard, as did the Sufis themselves, as 'the inner doctrine of Islam, the underlying mystery of the Qur'ān'.

Sufism has received much attention from Western scholars, yet the study of the development, writings, beliefs, and practices of the orders which are its objective expression has scarcely been attempted. Sufism in practice is primarily contemplative and emotional mysticism. As the organized cultivation of religious experience it is not a philosophical system, though it developed such a system, but it is a 'Way', the Way of purification. This practical aspect is our main concern. Sufi teaching and practice were diffused throughout the Islamic world through the growth of particular Ways which were disseminated among the people through the medium of religious orders, and as a religious movement displayed many aspects.

The foundation of the orders is the system and relationship of master and disciple, in Arabic *murshid* (director) and *murīd* (aspirant). It was natural to accept the authority and guidance of those who had traversed the stages (*maqāmāt*) of the Sufi Path. Masters of the Way say that every man has inherent within him the possibility for release from self and union with God, but this is latent and dormant and cannot be released, except with certain illuminates gifted by God, without guidance from a leader.

The early masters were more concerned with experiencing than with theosophical theorizing. They sought to guide rather than teach, directing the aspirant in ways of meditation whereby he himself acquired insight into spiritual truth and was shielded against the dangers of illusions. Sufism in practice consists of feeling and unveiling, since *maʿrifa* (gnosis) is reached by passage through ecstatic states. Consequently teaching succeeds rather than precedes experience. Abu Ḥāmid al-Ghazālī, a theorist of ethical mysticism, writes of his own realization that what is most peculiar to Sufis 'cannot be learned but only attained by direct experience, ecstasy, and inward transformation'. The drunken man knows nothing about the definition, causes, and conditions of drunkenness, yet he is drunk, whilst the sober man acquainted with the theory is not drunk.[1] Al-Ghazālī's own intellectual background, his inability to submit himself unreservedly to guidance, imposed too great a barrier for him to attain direct Sufi experience. Teaching about the state of *fanā'* (transmutation of self) will not help anyone to attain it, only guidance under an experienced director. Hence the great importance the guides attached to permission to recite *adhkār* (mystical exercises) and undertake retreats, for thereby the burden is adjusted to the capacity of the individual.

A *ṭarīqa* was a practical method (other terms were *madhhab*, *riʿāya*, and *sulūk*) to guide a seeker by tracing a way of thought, feeling, and action, leading through a succession of 'stages'

[1] Al-Ghazālī, *al-Munqidh min aḍ-ḍalāl*, Damascus edn., 1358/1939, pp. 124–5.

(*maqāmāt*, in integral association with psychological experiences called 'states', *aḥwāl*) to experience of divine Reality (*ḥaqīqa*). At first a *ṭarīqa* meant simply this gradual method of contemplative and soul-releasing mysticism. Circles of disciples began to gather around an acknowledged master of the Way, seeking training through association or companionship,[1] but not linked to him by any initiatory tie or vow of allegiance.

Two contrasting tendencies came to be distinguished as Junaidī and Bisṭāmī, or 'Irāqī and Khurasānī (but must not be taken too seriously or called schools of thought) after two men, Abu'l-Qāsim al-Junaid (d. 298/910) and Abu Yazīd Ṭaifūr al-Bisṭāmī (d. 260/874), who captured the imaginations more than any other of their contemporaries. These two are held to embody the contrasts between the way based on *tawakkul* (trust) and that on *malāma* (blame),[2] between intoxicated and sober, safe and suspect, illuminate and conformist, solitude and companionship, theist and monist, guidance under a this-world director (with a chain of transmitters to regularize in conformity with standard Islamic practice) and guidance under a spirit-shaikh.

'Alī al-Hujwīrī refers[3] to Bisṭāmī's teaching, which he calls Ṭaifūrī, as characterized by *ghalaba* (rapture, ecstasy) and *sukr* (intoxication); whereas that derived from al-Junaid 'is based on sobriety (*ṣaḥw*) and is opposed to that of the Ṭayfūrīs . . . It is the best-known and most celebrated of all doctrines, and all the Shaykhs have adopted it, notwithstanding that there is much difference in their sayings on the ethics of Ṣūfiism.'[4] Because he won the approval of orthodoxy as relatively 'safe', al-Junaid comes to be regarded as '*the* Shaikh of the Way', the common ancestor of most subsequent mystical congregations, even though many followed heterodox teaching; his inclusion in their genealogies

[1] *Li 'ṣ-ṣuḥba wa 'd-dars wa 'r-riwāya 'anhu.*

[2] See Appendix B.

[3] Abu 'l-Ḥasan 'Alī al-Jullābī al-Hujwīrī (d. *c.* 465/1072), *Kashf al-Maḥjūb*, tr. R. A. Nicholson, London, 1936, pp. 184–5.

[4] Ibid., p. 189. Junaid as the apostle of moderation (though he in fact held esoteric views) sought to tone down and explain away his ecstatic utterances, see Sarrāj, *Luma'*, pp. 380–90. On al-Bisṭāmī see 'Abd ar-Raḥmān Badawī, *Shaṭḥāt aṣ-Ṣūfiyya: I. Abu Yazīd al-Bisṭāmī*, Cairo, 1949, which includes (pp. 37–148) a biography entitled *An-Nūr min kalimāt Abī Ṭaifūr*, attributed to as-Sahlajī. The ideas of a far more significant contemporary, al-Ḥakīm at-Tirmidhī (d. *c.* 295/908), fell into oblivion until resurrected by the genius of Ibn al-'Arabī.

was a guarantee of orthodoxy, for a sound *isnād* can support a multitude of heresies.

These groups were very loose and mobile; members travelled widely seeking masters, some earning their way, others supporting themselves upon alms. But foundations came into being which served as centres for these wanderers. In Arab regions many were attached to frontier-posts or hostels called *ribāṭ*;[1] those in Khurasan were associated with rest-houses or hospices (*khānaqāh*[2]), whilst others were the retreat (*khalwa* or *zāwiya*) of a spiritual director. All these terms came to mean a Sufi convent. An early *ribāṭ* was found on ʻAbbādān island (the name itself is significant) on the Persian Gulf, which grew up around an ascetic called ʻAbd al-Wāḥid ibn Zaid (d. 177/793), survived his death, and became especially well known.[3] Other *ribāṭs* were found on the marches with Byzantium and in north Africa. Centres for devotees are mentioned at Damascus around 150/767, at Ramlah, capital of Palestine, founded by a Christian *amīr* before A.D. 800,[4] in Khurasan about the same time, whilst 'there appeared in Alexandria an organization (*ṭā'ifa*) calling itself aṣ-Ṣūfiyya' in the year A.H. 200.[5]

By the fifth/eleventh century organized convents of a quite different character had become numerous, though they still retained their character as collections of individuals pursuing their own way, even though they associated with and sought guidance from experienced men and ascribed themselves to such guides. The personnel of these places was still impermanent and migrant, and they adopted the bare minimum of institutional rules concerning their day-to-day life. Such Sufi 'companionship' (*ṣuḥba*) rules eventually became a religious obligation.[6]

Al-Maqdisī, whose range of interests was wider than that of

[1] On *ribāṭs*, see Chap. vi, pp. 167–8.

[2] *Khāne-gāh* (monastery, cloister).

[3] See Sarrāj, *Luma*ʻ, p. 429; al-Maqdisī, p. 118; Yāqūt, iii. 598; L. Massignon, *Lexique mystique*, p. 157.

[4] Jāmī, *Nafaḥāt al-uns*, Calcutta, 1859, p. 34; though this reference is too late to be of any value by itself (the book was written in A.H. 881 though based upon earlier material).

[5] Al-Kindī, *Quḍāt Miṣr*, ed. R. Guest, 1912, p. 162.

[6] The first such work, though concerned with general ethical relationships, appears to be *Ādāb aṣ-ṣuḥba*, by as-Sulamī (330/941–412/1021), edited by M. J. Kister, 1954. ʻAlī al-Hujwīrī refers to a number of treatises explaining the rules; see *Kashf*, p. 338.

most geographers, gives some information about Sufi groups. He says that in Shiraz 'Ṣūfis were numerous, performing the *dhikr* (*yukabbir*) in their mosques after the Friday prayer and reciting blessings on the Prophet from the pulpit'.[1] As an organized movement he shows that the Karrāmiyya[2] in his time (he is writing around A.D. 975) was more effective, having *khānaqāhs* all over Islamic Asia,[3] and it seems that it was from them that Sufis adopted the *khānaqāh* system. The only reference I have come across in al-Maqdisī to a *khānaqāh* where Sufi exercises take place is, 'There was a *khānaqāh* in Dabīl [Dwin, capital of Armenia] whose inmates were gnostics (*'ārifs*) in the system of *taṣawwuf*, living in the straitest poverty.'[4] Yet the Karrāmiyya was relatively short-lived (two centuries) whereas the Sufi movement went on from an individualistic discipline to change the whole devotional outlook of Muslims.

In the Syrian Jawlān mountains al-Maqdisī writes: 'I met Abu Isḥāq al-Ballūṭī with forty men, all wearing wool, who had a place for worship where they congregated. I found out that this man was a learned jurist of the school of Sufyān ath-Thawrī, and that their sustenance consisted of acorns (*ballūṭ*), a fruit the size of dates, bitter, which is split, sweetened, ground up and then mixed with wild barley.'[5]

Al-Maqdisī was assiduous in seeking new experiences as well as geographical information, and the following engaging account shows that organized congregations existed in his time and that you needed to belong to one to gain insight into Sufi experience, as

[1] Al-Maqdisī, *Aḥsan at-taqāsīm* (completed in Shiraz in 375/985), ed. de Goeje, 1906, p. 439, cf. p. 430. A non-Sufi usage of the term *dhikr* has to be looked for. Al-Maqdisī writes that in Jerusalem (Īliyā) were '*mudhakkirūn* who are [pious] story-tellers (*quṣṣāṣ*), and the followers of Abū Ḥanīfa have a *majlis dhikr* in the Aqṣā mosque where they recite from a book'; op. cit., p. 182, and cf. p. 327.

[2] Founded by Muḥammad ibn Karrām, d. 255/869. Al-Maqdisī calls them men of *zuhd* and *ta'abbud* (p. 365). It was a revivalist and ascetic school distinguished by a special mode of dress. They were by no means happy with the Sufis, especially with the quietists.

[3] And even outside, for they had their own section in Fāṭimid Fusṭāṭ; see al-Maqdisī, p. 202.

[4] Op. cit., p. 379. References like the following in the section on Khurasan are common: 'The Karrāmiyya have a group (*jalaba*) in Herāt and Gharch of the Shēr, and *khawāniq* in Ferghāna, Khuttal, and Gūzgānān, and in Marv ar-rūdh a *khānaqāh*, and another in Samarqand' (p. 323).

[5] Al-Maqdisī, op. cit., p. 188.

well as showing that it was as easy to be a false Sufi in those days as at any other:

When I entered Sūs [in Khūzistān] I sought out the main mosque, seeking a shaikh whom I might question concerning points of *ḥadīth*. It chanced that I was wearing a *jubba* of Cypriot wool and a Basran *fūṭa*, and I was directed to a congregation of Sufis. As I approached they took it for granted that I was a Sufi and welcomed me with open arms. They settled me among them and began questioning me. Then they sent a man to bring food. I felt ill at ease about taking the food since I had not associated with such a group before this occasion. They showed surprise at my reluctance and absention from their ceremonial.[1] I felt drawn to associate myself with this congregation and find out about their method, and learn the true nature [of Sufism]. So I said within myself, 'This is your opportunity, here where you are unknown.' I therefore threw off all restraint with them, stripping the veil of bashfulness from off my face. On one occasion I might engage in antiphonal singing with them, on another I might yell with them, and at another recite poems to them. I would go out with them to visit *ribāṭs* and to engage in religious recitals, with the result, by God, that I won a place both in their hearts and in the hearts of the people of that place to an extraordinary degree. I gained a great reputation, being visited [for my virtue] and being sent presents of garments and purses, which I would accept but immediately hand over intact to the Sufis, since I was well off, having ample means. Every day I used to spend engaged in devotions, and what devotions! and they used to suppose I did it out of piety. People began touching me [to obtain *baraka*] and broadcasting my fame, saying that they had never seen a more excellent *faqīr*. So it went on until, when the time came that I had penetrated into their secrets and learnt all that I wished, I just ran away from them at dead of night and by morning had got well clear.[2]

Whilst some centres of withdrawal, more especially the *ribāṭs* and *khānaqāhs* which were supported by endowments (*awqāf*), became permanent centres, those which were based upon the reputation of a particular master broke up after his death. Most masters were themselves migrants. There were no self-continuative orders, but groups of people possessing similar spiritual aspirations who had become disciples of an honoured master with whom the bond of allegiance was purely personal..

The eleventh century marks a turning-point in the history of

[1] Clearly not a question of accepting normal hospitality but a ritual meal.
[2] Al-Maqdisī, op. cit., p. 415.

Islam. Among other things it was characterized by the suppression of Shīʿism, which had attained political power in the dynasties of the Fāṭimids of north Africa and the Būyids of Persia, where even then it seemed likely to become the Persian form of Islam. The overthrow of political Shīʿism was brought about by the Seljuq rulers of Turkish nomads from central Asia. In A.D. 1055 they gained control of Baghdad and took over tutelage of the ʿAbbāsid caliph from the Būyids. In the Maghrib and Egypt the power of the Fāṭimids weakened[1] until finally they were overthrown by the Kurd Saladin in A.D. 1171.

The Turks were upholders of the Sunna and opponents of Shīʿite tendencies. The counter-revolution they accomplished in the Islamic sphere took the form of the reorganization of the *madrasa* from a private school, a circle around a learned master, to an official institution to which the Seljuqs ensured the recruitment of masters sympathetic to their religious policy. In these institutions the stress was placed on the religious sciences, whilst the profane sciences which had flourished equally under the early ʿAbbāsid and Shīʿite dynasties were discouraged or banned. The new form of *madrasa* soon spread from Iraq into Syria, Egypt, and eventually the Maghrib.[2]

But Islamic religious spirit could not be limited and confined within this institution alone and the cultivation of the deeper spiritual life took the form of the parallel institution of the organized, endowed, and supervised *khānaqāh* with which the Seljuqs were familiar from those of the Karrāmiyya in central Asia and Iran. The institution is a means of control, but it is to their credit that they encouraged the foundation of *khānaqāhs* and endowed them liberally.

The speculative Sufi spirit was viewed with suspicion. The dissociation of Sufis from recognized religious leaders had always been suspected and resented by the *ʿulamā'* (doctors of law), and provoked a reaction to which Shihāb ad-dīn Yaḥyā as-Suhrawardī

[1] The Zīrids of Ifrīqiya, Berber vassals of the Fāṭimids, repudiated their authority. Al-Muʿizz's recognition of the ʿAbbāsid caliph in the *khuṭba* is ascribed to various dates between 433/1041 and 437/1045. In far western Islam other nomads, the Murābiṭūn, ensured the triumph of Sunnism in its Mālikī form when Ṣanhāja from western Sahara overwhelmed Morocco (at the time the Seljuqs were taking Baghdad) and then Spain (Battle of Zallāqa in A.D. 1086).

[2] *Madrasas* did not increase greatly in the Maghrib until the thirteenth and fourteenth centuries under the Ḥafṣids, Marīnids, and ʿAbd al-Wādids.

fell victim.[1] But it was the formation of esoteric and mystical congregations outside the regular organization of Islam, together with the liturgical organization of the *samāʿ*, or spiritual concert for inducing ecstasy, which was more likely to provoke the reaction of the orthodox than suspect ideas.

By the end of the fifth century A.H. the change in the attitude of Islamic legalists towards a grudging and qualified acceptance of Sufism, begun by as-Sulamī and his disciple al-Qushairī, had been brought to a conclusion by al-Ghazālī, whilst the need for associations caring for religious needs other than the ritual sanctified and fixed by the Law was recognized. The association of Sufism in its *khānaqāh* form with the official favour of Nūr ad-dīn, Saladin, and their lieutenants and successors had made Sufi associations respectable. When the formation of separate congregations for liturgical 'recitals' became possible there began the development of an inner Islam with its own leaders, hierarchy, and forms of worship. But though accommodated in this way orthodoxy and mysticism followed not only separate but divergent paths. This is shown by the parallel institutional development of *madrasas* and *khānaqāhs*. The next stage is the formation of mystical schools consisting of circles of initiates. When this reconciliation or compromise was accomplished Sufism was still a Way which appealed only to the few, and the Sunnī doctors had no conception of what was to happen when it was mediated to the people in the form of a popular movement.

From the eleventh century the *zāwiyas* and *khānaqāhs* which provided temporary resting-places for wandering Sufis spread the new devotional life throughout the countryside and played a decisive role in the Islamization of borderland and non-Arab regions in central Asia and north Africa. By the twelfth century many *khānaqāhs* had become rich and flourishing establishments and Ibn Jubair, who travelled (A.D. 1183–5) in the near East in Saladin's time, writes of Damascus:

Ribāṭs for Sufis, which here go under the name of *khawāniq*, are numerous. They are ornamented palaces through all of which flow

[1] This Suhrawardī is to be distinguished from the *ṭarīqa* leaders bearing the same *nisba* by the epithet al-Maqtūl, 'the Martyr'. He taught in Anatolia at the court of Qilij Arslān II and his son, and wrote a number of remarkable theosophical works before he was tried and executed, martyr to the fanaticism of the orthodox *'ulamā'* of Aleppo, by al-Malik aẓ-Ẓāhir at the order of Saladin, at the age of 38 in 587/1191.

streams of water, presenting as delightful a picture as anyone could wish for. The members of this type of Sufi organization are really the kings in these parts, since God has provided for them over and above the material things of life, freeing their minds from concern with the need to earn their living so that they can devote themselves to His service. He has lodged them in palaces which provide them with a foretaste of those of Paradise. So these fortunates, the favoured ones among the Sufis, enjoy through God's favour the blessings of this world and the next. They follow an honourable calling and their life in common is admirably conducted. Their mode of conducting their forms of worship is peculiar. Their custom of assembling for impassioned musical recitals (*samā'*) is delightful. Sometimes, so enraptured do some of these absorbed ecstatics become when under the influence of a state that they can hardly be regarded as belonging to this world at all.[1]

However, it was not through such establishments that the next development in Sufi institutionalism took place but through a single master, sometimes settled in a retreat far from the distractions of *khānaqāh* life, sometimes in his *zāwiya* home in the big city, frequently a wanderer travelling around with his circle of disciples. Ibn Jubair occasionally mentions these humble ascetics of desert or mountain if something special calls them to his attention, such as when he finds Christians paying tribute to their dedication to the religious life.[2]

From the beginning of the thirteenth century certain centres (if we think of the centre as being a man, not a place) became the sees of *ṭarīqas*, mystical schools or teaching centres. This happened when a centre or circle became focused on one director in a new way and turned into a school designed to perpetuate his name, type of teaching, mystical exercises, and rule of life. Each such *ṭarīqa* was handed down through a continuous 'chain' (*silsila*), or mystical *isnād*.[3] The derivative shaikhs are, therefore, the spiritual heirs of the founder.

The link of a person with this *silsila* acquired an esoteric character, and initiation, whereby the seeker swore an oath of allegiance to founder and earthly deputy and received in return the secret *wird* which concentrates the spiritual power of the chain, was the means of gaining this link. Ibn Khallikān describes *fuqarā'* having

[1] *The Travels of Ibn Jubair*, ed. W. Wright and M. J. de Goeje, 2nd edn., 1907, p. 284.

[2] Ibid., p. 287.

[3] See Appendix A for some early *silsilas*.

such a tie (*ʿuqda, iʿtiqād*) with Ibn ar-Rifāʿī (d. A.D. 1182),[1] whose *silsila* is probably the earliest consciously maintained chain.[2]

The *silsila*-path was not intended to replace the formal Muslim religious organization which the Sufis regarded as a necessary concession (*rukhṣa*) to human frailty. This development can be regarded as the beginning of the process whereby the creative freedom of the mystic was to be channelled into an institution. These paths never developed sectarian tendencies. Their founders maintained careful links with the orthodox institution and did not repudiate the formal duties of Islam. One of their functions in Islamic life was to fill the gap left through the suppression of Shīʿī sectarianism. The difference between the paths lay in such aspects as loyalty to the head of the order and belief in a particular power-line, in types of organization, methods of teaching, peculiar practices and ritual. They differed considerably in their inner beliefs, but their link with orthodoxy was guaranteed by their acceptance of the law and ritual practices of Islam. All the same they formed inner coteries within Islam and introduced a hierarchical structure and modes of spiritual outlook and worship foreign to its essential genius.

How this process of ascription came about is not clear. Pupils had normally traced or ascribed[3] their *madhhab* (method), or *ṭarīqa* (course), to their revered teacher, for he was their guarantee of validity and training, but so far this had been primarily a direct personal link. It is true ʿAlī al-Hujwīrī (d. *c.* 467/1074) enumerates twelve schools of Sufism:

The whole body of aspirants to Ṣūfiism is composed of twelve sects, two of which are condemned (*mardūd*), while the remaining ten are approved (*maqbūl*). The latter are the Muḥāsibīs, the Qaṣṣārīs, the Ṭayfūrīs, the Junaydīs, the Nūrīs, the Sahlīs, the Ḥakīmīs, the Kharrāzīs, the Khafīfīs, and the Sayyārīs. All these assert the truth and belong to the mass of orthodox Muslims. The two condemned sects are, firstly, the Ḥulūlis, who derive their name from the doctrine of incarnation (*ḥulūl*) and incorporation (*imtizāj*), and with whom are connected the Sālimī sect of anthropomorphists; and secondly, the Ḥallājīs, who

[1] Ibn Khallikān, *Wafāyāt*, i. 95.

[2] See al-Wāsiṭī, *Tiryāq al-muḥibbīn*, Cairo, A.H. 1305, pp. 5–6, which gives three *silsilas* culminating in him. Most of the links linking him with al-Junaid are obscure figures, which implies that the chains were not invented as so many were later.

[3] *Intasaba*, *intamā*, and *tasammā* are the terms used.

have abandoned the sacred law and have adopted heresy, and with whom are connected the Ibāḥatīs and the Fārisīs.[1]

But these are theoretical ways, none of which developed into *silsila-ṭarīqas*. Their teaching was modified by their pupils in accordance with their own mystical experiences. In fact, al-Hujwīrī singles out as exceptional the transmission from Abū 'l-ʿAbbās as-Sayyārī whose 'school of Ṣūfiism is the only one that has kept its original doctrine unchanged, and the cause of this fact is that Nasā and Merv have never been without some person who acknowledged his authority and took care that his followers should maintain the doctrine of their founder'.[2]

The names of certain of these early masters were incorporated in the mystical *isnāds* of the *ṭarīqas*. The key figure in the lines of most *ṭarīqas* is Abu 'l-Qāsim al-Junaid (d. A.D. 910), yet Dhū 'n-Nūn al-Miṣrī, though continually quoted in support of mystical thought,[3] is missing from the *isnāds*. Similarly, Ḥusain ibn Manṣūr al-Ḥallāj is not normally found in them (though a Way was later attributed to him), whereas al-Bisṭāmī is found in the chains of many orders (for example, the Naqshabandiyya).[4] Al-Wāsiṭī, writing around A.D. 1320 when the Ways were fully established, says that there were two distinct primitive *sanads* to which all the then existing *khirqas* went back, the Junaidī and the Bisṭāmī,[5] and two extinct lines, the Bilāliyya and the Uwaisiyya.[6] The grounds for incorporation in the chains, or for their rejection, are not made clear. It is not a simple question of condemnation by orthodoxy. Some figure as founders of artificial *ṭarīqas*, and we have just mentioned that attributed to al-Ḥallāj;[7] that is, specific esoteric doctrines, *dhikrs*, and rules were ascribed to them in books of *khirqa* lines such as as-Sanūsī's *Salsabīl*, and certain masters would claim to initiate into the *dhikrs* of these figures. One of the earliest was Uwais al-Qaranī, a Yemeni contemporary of the Prophet.[8] The method (*ṭarīqa* or *madhhab*) of al-Junaid was

[1] *Kashf al-maḥjūb*, pp. 130–1. These schools are studied in the *Kashf* on pp. 176–266.

[2] *Kashf*, p. 251.

[3] Although most of these sayings may not be authentic it must be remembered that inspired inventions had to be in line with the Sufi's known genuine thought.

[4] As-Sanūsī, *Salsabīl*, p. 121.

[5] Al-Wāsiṭī, *Tiryāq*, p. 47.

[6] Ibid., p. 44.

[7] As-Sanūsī, *Salsabīl*, p. 57.

[8] He was unacquainted with the Prophet and is said to have been initiated after his death (traditionally in A.H. 37) by the spirit of the Prophet, hence

known to al-Hujwīrī,[1] and is mentioned in the thirteenth century in Ibn ʿAṭāʾ Allāh's treatise on the *dhikr*[2] which gives the eight stipulations of his Way. This method, though, was not confined to one line, but was inherited by all the Junaidī orders.[3]

The true *silsila-ṭarīqas* had a new element, not merely the teacher–pupil relationship which had prevailed so far, but the fuller one of director and disciple. A new aura emanates from the master as a *walī* (protégé) of God, which eventually, in the third stage, was to become belief in his mediumship and intercessory status with God. The Sufi life of recollection and meditation now becomes increasingly associated with a line of ascription so far as the majority of Sufi aspirants were concerned. *Murshids* (guide-initiators) bestowed the *ṭarīqa*, its *wird*, formulae, and symbols, as from their dead master and guided their own pupils along his Way in his name. This was primarily a consequence of the Islamic ideal of providing oneself with an *isnād* of guarantee and authority. The distinction within Sufism between Sufis and Malāmatīs now becomes defined, the Sufis being those who submit to direction and conformity and the Malāmatīs are those who retain their freedom.[4]

The change in the Sufis can be seen in the nature of the bond which unites them. The earlier groups had been linked by enthusiasm, common devotions, and methods of spiritual discipline, with the aim of stripping the soul and eliminating self to attain vision of Reality. They were, therefore, integrated by spirit and aim rather than by any formal organization, and were, in fact, very loose organizations. The change came with the development of such a *collegium pietatis* into a *collegium initiati* whose members ascribed themselves to their initiator and his spiritual ancestry, and were prepared to follow his Path and transmit it themselves to future generations.

dervishes who had no direct initiator were frequently called Uwaisīs. Such attribution is late (16th century?), though as a Sufi figure Uwais was known from an early date; see *Kashf al-Maḥjūb*, pp. 83–4. On his *dhikr* attribution see as-Sanūsī, *Salsabil*, pp. 49–50; and cf. D'Ohsson, *Tableau*, iv. 2, 619–21.

[1] See *Kashf*, p. 189.

[2] Ibn ʿAṭāʾ Allāh, *Miftāḥ al-Falāḥ*, margin of Shaʿrānī, *Laṭāʾif al-minan*, Cairo, 1357, ii. 144.

[3] At any time a Sufi might be told in a dream to convey al-Junaid's Way. We read, for example, that Yūsuf al-ʿAjamī al-Kūrānī (d. 768/1366) 'was the first to revivify the *ṭariqa* of al-Junaid in Egypt after its obliteration'; Shaʿrānī, *Lawāqiḥ*, Cairo, A.H. 1355, ii. 60.

[4] See Appendix B.

The transformation of Sufi companionships into initiatory colleges began with the Sunnī triumphs over Shīʿite dynasties (Būyids in Baghdad, A.D. 1055: Fāṭimids in Egypt, A.D. 1171), and was settled during the troubled time of the Mongol conquests (Baghdad, A.D. 1258), which were accompanied by considerable Sufi migrations whereby it became a rural, as well as urban, movement of the spirit. A significant feature of the change is that the groups, about the time of Saladin, took over the Shīʿite custom of *baiʿa*, initiation with oath of allegiance to the shaikh. There was also some linkage with and transmission from artisan *futuwwa* orders, another compensatory reaction against the suppression of open Shīʿism. *Futuwwa* orders were brought into prominence by Caliph an-Nāṣir's (A.D. 1219–36) attempt to create a knightly *futuwwa*, with whose patronage the great *murshid*, Shihāb ad-dīn Abū Ḥafṣ as-Suhrawardī, was associated, acting as an-Nāṣir's envoy in girding those grandees whom the Caliph wished to honour.

The *ṭarīqas* which became the most significant for the development of institutional Sufism were the Suhrawardiyya attributed to Ḍiyā' ad-dīn Abū Najīb as-Suhrawardī (d. A.D. 1168), but developed by his nephew, the just-mentioned Shihāb ad-dīn Abū Ḥafṣ (d. A.D. 1234); the Qādiriyya attributed to 'Abd al-Qādir al-Jīlānī (d. A.D. 1166), whose line of ascription did not extend before the fourteenth century; the Rifāʿiyya deriving from Aḥmad ibn ar-Rifāʿī (d. A.D. 1182); the nomadic Yasaviyya of Aḥmad al-Yasavī (d. A.D. 1166); the Kubrawiyya of Najm ad-dīn Kubrā (d. A.D. 1221); the Chishtiyya of Muʿīn ad-dīn M. Chishtī (d. A.D. 1236), mainly confined to India; the Shādhiliyya deriving from Abu Madyan Shuʿaib (d. A.D. 1197) but attributed to Abu 'l-Ḥasan ʿAlī ash-Shādhilī (d. A.D. 1258); the Badawiyya of Aḥmad al-Badawī (d. A.D. 1276) centred in Egypt; the Mawlawiyya inspired by the Persian Sufi poet, Jalāl ad-dīn ar-Rūmī (d. A.D. A.D. 1273), which was restricted to Anatolia; and the central Asian Naqshabandiyya, a mystical school, first called Khwājagān, which owes its initial insights to Yūsuf al-Hamadānī (d. A.D. 1140) and ʿAbd al-Khāliq al-Ghujdawānī (d. A.D. 1179), but was eventually associated with the name of Muḥammad Bahā' ad-dīn an-Naqshabandī (d. A.D. 1389). All subsequent *ṭarīqas* claim to be derivatives of one or more of these chains. An account of the founders of these lines and their principal characteristics will be given in the next chapter when other masters, such as Aḥmad al-Ghazālī and 'Alī al-Kharaqāni, who played an important role in founding lines but do not have a *silsila* named after them, will be given the recognition that is their due.

Many other groups continued for a time as family or localized orders, but unlike the Qādiriyya, which also was for long a restricted family order, did not lead to the formation of distinctive Ways such as those just mentioned. Such was the Rūzbihāniyya founded in Shiraz by Rūzbihān Baqlī (d. A.D. 1209), which became hereditary from the death of the founder[1] but did not spread outside Fars or even survive for very long. Ibn Khallikān mentions the Kīzāniyya founded in Cairo by Abu 'Abdallāh Mūḥammad, known as Ibn al-Kīzānī (d. 562/1167),[2] as such a *ṭarīqa manqué*. Of another he writes:

Yūnus ibn Yūsuf ibn Musā'id ash-Shaibānī, shaikh of the *fuqarā'* known after him as the Yūnusiyya, was a holy man. I asked a group of his followers who was his shaikh and they replied, 'He had no shaikh, he was a *majdhūb*.' By this word they designate one who has no shaikh but has been attracted (*judhiba*) to a life of piety and sanctity . . . He died in 619 (A.D. 1222–3) in his village of al-Qunayya in the province of Dāra [in the Jazīra], where his tomb is well known and attracts pilgrims.[3]

Yūnus's great-grandson, Saif ad-dīn Rajīhī b. Sābiq b. Hilāl b. Yūnus (d. 706/1306) went to live in Damascus where he was allotted the house of the *wazīr* Amīn ad-dawla for his *zāwiya* as well as a village in the Ghūṭa. From that time his line became a hereditary *ṭā'ifa*, with a branch in Jerusalem, and was still in existence in 1500.[4]

[1] The Rūzbihāniyya was a simple *ṭā'ifa*, a derivative of the Kāzerūniyya, a *ṭarīqa* which later changed its role into a religio-commercial guild. Accounts of the sons and grandsons of Rūzbihān (who were also invested with the Suhrawardī *khirqa*) are given by Abu 'l-Qāsim Junaid Shīrāzī, *Shadd al-izār fī khaṭṭ al-awzār 'an zuwwār al-mazār* (written 791/1389), ed. M. Qazwīnī and 'Abbās Iqbāl, Tehran, 1328/1910, pp. 227–39, 243–54. The tomb-centre in Shiraz was still famous when Ibn Baṭṭūṭa visited that city in 1325 (Paris edn., ii. 83), but after Junaid Shīrāzī's time it fell into oblivion.

[2] Ibn Khallikān, *Wafāyāt al-A'yān*, Cairo, A.H. 1199, ii. 391; tr. De Slane, iii. 158. Examples of his poetry are given in Ṣalāḥ ad-dīn Khalīl aṣ-Ṣafadī, *Al-Wāfī bi 'l-Wafāyāt*, ed. H. Ritter, Leipzig/Istanbul, 1931, i. 347–50.

[3] Ibn Khallikān, op. cit. iii. 522–3; tr. iv. 598; see also H. Sauvaire (ed.), 'Description de Damas', *J. Asiat.* sér. IX. v. 399–401. The *ṭā'ifa* still existed in Maqrīzī's time, see his *Khiṭaṭ*, Cairo, A.H. 1326, iv. 304–5, which gives his date incorrectly as 719/1319.

[4] Mujīr ad-dīn 'Ulaimī, *Al-Uns al-jalīl bi ta'rikh al-Quds*, extracts tr. by

There were many other small independent-lineage *ṭarīqas* which had only a restricted local influence,[1] but those mentioned above, together with the western Turkish Khalwatiyya,[2] were the foundation lines sponsoring distinctive Ways of mystical thought and spiritual exercises. Through these *ṭarīqas* the Sufi message was mediated to the Islamic world.

The *silsila*-founders belonged to two main schools of Sufi thought which may be designated as the Junaidī and Bisṭāmī schools, or the Mesopotamian and central Asian, though the exponents were not confined to these areas. Later, Maghribī Sufism, deriving from Abu Madyan (d. A.D. 1197), was to form a third area with its own special characteristics, but though the main *silsila*-founder, ash-Shādhilī, came from the Maghrib, he and his successors only received recognition and encouragement in Egypt and his line of attribution did not become popular in the Maghrib until much later.

Antinomian tendencies were stronger in Khorasan and central Asia, though by no means exclusive to these areas, but such elements are not seen in the *silsila*-founders, who were frequently men trained in the legal sciences. They were strong among the large numbers of vagrant dervishes (*malāmatīs* and *qalandarīs*) unattached to any recognized master or line, who were above the Law. But once *silsilas* were established and recognized as Sunnī they could incorporate all sorts of other elements.

Sufism had now become a profession and this period is characterized by a great growth of unspecialized Sufi establishments. The popularity of the Persian-type hospices in particular is associated with the Seljuq period as can be seen from any list of

H. Sauvaire, 1876, p. 159, mentions a *zāwiya*-Yūnusiyya in Jerusalem in his time (A.D. 1500).

[1] One such early family *ṭarīqa* which had great influence upon Islamic life in Hadramawt and has survived until the present day is the 'Alawiyya in south Arabia, founded by Muḥammad ibn 'Alī of the Bā 'Alawī tribe (574/1178–653/1255) who was initiated into the Way deriving from Abu Madyan Shu'aib, but developed his independent Way. He is said to have been the first to introduce Sufi discipline (*taḥkīm*) into Hadramawt (see F. Wüstenfeld, *Die Çufiten in Süd-Arabien*, Göttingen, 1883, p. 5; *E.I.*[2] i. 829). An example of a Damascene family *zāwiya* which survived for some time without expanding was the Qawāmiyya-Bālisiyya, founded by Abū Bakr ibn Qawām ibn 'Alī al-Bālisī (584/1188–658/1260). An account of his life is given in Ibn Shākir's *Fawāt al-Wafāyāt* (Bulaq, A.H. 1283, i. 101–2).

[2] Discussion of the Khalwatiyya has been reserved for the third chapter, see pp. 74–8.

the dates when these were founded,[1] and the tendency accelerated under the Ayyūbids. Saladin welcomed Asiatic Sufis to Egypt and he and his followers founded and endowed many *khānaqāhs*, *ribāṭs*, and *zāwiyas* of which al-Maqrīzī gives a long list.[2] Mujīr ad-dīn has accounts of these places in Jerusalem, Hebron, and Damascus.[3] Saladin in 585/1189 endowed a Khānaqāh Ṣalāḥiyya in Jerusalem,[4] diverting for this purpose the palace of the Latin patriarch.[5] His lieutenant in Egypt, Qarāqūsh ibn 'Abdallāh al-Asadi, 'erected a *ribāṭ* at al-Maqs',[6] whilst Muẓaffar ad-dīn Gökböri, Saladin's brother-in-law (d. 630/1233),

> built two *khānaqāhs* [at Irbil] for the Sufis, which housed a large number, both of residents and visitors. Festival days used to draw together so numerous a concourse that everyone marvelled. Both were well endowed to provide all that was needed by those staying there, each of whom must accept his expenses when he departed. Gökböri used to visit them frequently and associate himself with them in concerts.[7]

Ibn Khallikān then describes the pomp with which he celebrated the Prophet's birthday at Irbil in A.D. 1207 when he passed the nights listening to Sufi concerts. Gökböri also built a *khānaqāh* at Aleppo.[8]

The difference between the institutions mentioned seems to be that the *ribāṭ* was an Arab type of hostel or training-centre;[9] the

[1] The Seljuq conquest of northern Syria and Damascus was completed between A.D. 1071 and 1079, but the Ismā'īlī Fāṭimid state in Egypt survived until 1171. Khānaqāh al-Balāṭ, the first new-type convent in Aleppo, was built by Shams al-Khawāṣṣ Lu'lu', freedman of Riḍwān ibn Tutush, in 509/1115 when he was governor of that city; see Abū Dharr (d. 884/1479) in *Kunūz adh-dhahab*, quoted by M. Rāghib aṭ-Ṭabbākh, *I'lām an-nubalā' fī ta'rīkh Ḥalab*, Aleppo, 1923–6, iv. 218–21.

[2] Maqrīzī, *Khiṭaṭ*, ed. A.H. 1324–6, iv. 271–306.

[3] *Al-Uns al-jalīl*, already referred to, and for Damascus the translation of H. Sauvaire, 'Description de Damas', *J. Asiat.* sér. IX. v (1895), *khānaqāhs* (pp. 269–97), *ribāṭs* (pp. 377–81), and *zāwiyas* (pp. 387–403).

[4] See Ibn Khallikān, iii. 521, l. 12; tr. iv. 547.

[5] See Mujīr ad-dīn, tr. H. Sauvaire, 1876, pp. 77, 166.

[6] Ibn Khallikān, ii. 183; tr. ii. 520.

[7] Ibid. iii. 195; tr. ii. 538.

[8] See J. Sauvaget (tr.), *Les Perles choisies d'Ibn ach-Chiḥna*, Beirut, 1933, p. 100.

[9] M. ibn Aḥmad al-Fāsī (A.D. 1373–1429) in his *Shifā' al-Gharām fī akhbār al-Balad al-Ḥarām* (Cairo, 1956) names some fifty *ribāṭs* in Mecca (i. 330–7), many of which were founded about this time. For example, 'the *ribāṭ* of Rāmusht by the Ḥazwara Gate. Rāmusht, whose name was Shaikh Abū 'l-Qāsim Ibrāhīm ibn al-Ḥusain al-Fārisī [as-Sīrāfī, d. 534], gave it as a *waqf* in the year 529 [1135] for all male Sufis, exclusive of females, who wear the *muraqqa'a*, from the whole of Iraq'; i. 332, and cf. i. 232.

khānaqāh was the Persian non-training hostel type introduced into the cities of the Arab world; *zāwiya* was the term applied to smaller establishments where one shaikh dwelt with his pupils; whilst a *khalwa* designated the 'retreat' of a single dervish, frequently a cell situated around a mosque square. A more isolated 'hermitage' was sometimes called a *rābiṭa*.

Mysticism was the only religious sphere where women could find a place. There were many women Sufis, of whom Rābi'a al-'Adawiyya (d. A.D. 801) is the best known.[1] During this period there are references to convents for women. Al-Irbillī[2] uses the term *khānaqāh* for convents for men and *ribāṭ* for those of women. There were seven convents for women in Aleppo alone, all founded between A.D. 1150 and 1250.[3] Baghdad also had a number, of which the *ribāṭ* of Fāṭima Rāziya (d. 521/1127) was the best known. In Cairo there was Ribāṭ al-Baghdādiyya, built by a daughter of al-Malik aẓ-Ẓāhir Baibars in 684/1285 for a *shaikha* called Zainab ibnat Abī 'l-Barakāt, known as Bint al-Baghdādiyya, and her followers,[4] which still exists in ad-Darb al-Aṣfar.

Maqrīzī says that the first *khānaqāh* in Egypt was Dār Sa'īd as-Su'adā',[5] so called (its proper name was aṣ-Ṣalāḥiyya) from being situated in the confiscated house of Sa'īd as-Su'adā', a eunuch employed in the Fāṭimid palace who was enfranchised by al-Mustanṣir and put to death in 544/1149.[6] It was constituted a *waqf* in A.D. 1173. Its primary function was to serve as a hostel for foreign Sufis, but it expanded its functions to become the chief centre of Egyptian Sufism. Its shaikh had the official title of *shaikh ash-shuyūkh*,[7] which, however, was only honorific and did not imply any wider jurisdiction than that of his own establishment, and later the title was frequently given to heads of other *khānaqāhs*.[8]

[1] See Margaret Smith, *Rābi'a the Mystic and Her Fellow-Saints in Islam*, Cambridge, 1928.

[2] Al-Irbillī, *Madāris Dimishq*, ed. Dahman, Damascus, 1366/1947, pp. 15–16.

[3] See J. Sauvaget, *Les Perles choisies*, 1933, pp. 105–6.

[4] Maqrīzī, *Khiṭaṭ*, iv. 293–4.

[5] Ibid. 273–85; Ibn Khallikān, iii. 521, l. 6; Ibn Khaldūn, *Ta'rīf*, 1951, p. 121; as-Suyūṭī, *Ḥusn al-muḥāḍara*, ii. 141 f.

[6] Maqrīzī, *Khiṭaṭ*, Bulaq edn., ii. 415.

[7] Ibn Faḍl Allāh al-'Umarī (writing A.D. 1342–9) has preserved the directive (*waṣiyya*) that the chancellery of the Egyptian Mamlūk sultans gave to *shaikh ash-shuyūkh* at the time of his appointment; see *At-Ta'rīf bi 'l-muṣṭalaḥ ash-sharīf*, Cairo, A.H. 1312, pp. 127–30.

[8] Notably that of Siryāqūs on the outskirts of Cairo, founded by An-Nāṣir Muḥammad ibn Qalawūn; *Khiṭaṭ* of al-Maqrīzī, iv. 285.

The foundation of *khānaqāhs* continued under the Baḥrī (A.D. 1250–77) and other Mamlūk successors of the Ayyūbids. Ibn Khaldūn writes:

Since the old days of their masters, the Ayyūbid rulers, the members of this Turkish dynasty in Egypt and Syria have been erecting colleges for the teaching of the sciences, and monastic houses for the purpose of enabling the poor [Sufis] to follow the rules for acquiring orthodox Sufi ways of behaviour through *dhikr* exercises and supererogatory prayers. They took over that [custom] from the preceding caliphal dynasties. They set up buildings for [those institutions as mortmain gifts] and endowed [them] with lands that yielded income [sufficient] to provide stipends for students and Sufi ascetics . . . As a result, colleges and monastic houses are numerous in Cairo. They now furnish livings for poor jurists and Sufis.[1]

Ibn Baṭṭūṭa describes these *khānaqāhs* and their rules at the time of his visit to Cairo in A.D. 1326. He writes: 'Each *zāwiya*[2] in Cairo is assigned to a *ṭā'ifa* of dervishes, most of whom are Persians, men of culture and trained in the Way of *taṣawwuf*.'[3] This means an organized group, but it is unlikely that that means a group perpetuating a particular rule, certainly not in the government-sponsored *khānaqāhs*.

Al-Qalqashandī (d. A.D. 1418) describes briefly the relationship of the *khānaqāhs* of Egypt and Syria with the Mamlūk authority.[4] Since these institutions were in the gift of the Mamlūk rulers and often very lucrative to their heads, anyone whom the ruler wished to provide with a sinecure without affecting his own pocket was frequently given the appointment. None of the heads of the Sumaiṣatiyya (or Ṣalāḥiyya) *khānaqāh* in Damascus (founded *c.* 453/1061) seems to have been a Sufi.[5] The first to hold the post (which also carried the charge of *mashyakhat ash-shuyūkh*)[6] was

[1] Ibn Khaldūn, *At-Ta'rīf*, ed. Muḥammad aṭ-Ṭanjī (Cairo, 1370/1951), p. 279. The above translation is by F. Rosenthal, *Muqaddama*, ii. 435–6, n. 68.

[2] Ibn Baṭṭūṭa generally uses the word *zāwiya*, the term with which he was most familiar, but in regard to Cairo he has just specified that he is describing convents known under the term *khawāniq*.

[3] *Riḥla*, Cairo, 1939, i. 27.

[4] Al-Qalqashandī, *Ṣubḥ*, iv. 193, 221; xiii. 222–51. He is especially concerned with the oaths taken by the various groups.

[5] See the list of heads in H. Sauvaire, 'Description de Damas', *J. Asiat.* sér. IX, t. v. 279–80, 301–3; cf. Qalqashandī, *Ṣubḥ*, xii. 401, iv. 193. Ibn Jubair visited it (pp. 289–90).

[6] Al-Qalqashandī, *Ṣubḥ*, xii. 410.

a former *wazīr* of Khwarazm, Sa'īd ibn Sahl al-Falakī, who was detained in Damascus by Nūr ad-dīn Maḥmūd b. Zangī (A.D. 1146–73) and given the post to provide for his support, since all these were *waqf* foundations. In 791/1392 Ibn Khaldūn was appointed to the directorship of Khānaqāh Baibars.[1]

Whereas the *khānaqāhs* were little more than hostels for Sufis (and concert halls for the great) and *ribāṭs* had an indefinite character as the establishment of a teacher or preacher, not necessarily a Sufi, *zāwiyas* were centres for a genuine teaching shaikh, whose successors consciously carried on his particular teaching and method. Whereas appointments to the headship of *khānaqāhs* was made by the secular authorities, the superior of a *zāwiya* was elected by the *ikhwān* (brethren), and it was in these that hereditary succession began. In the accounts of the religious establishments of the great Muslim cities, their founders, pupils, and successors, only of the *zāwiyas* do the authors assert or imply continuity of teaching and a particular rule of life. Ibn Baṭṭūṭa lodged in many *zāwiyas* and eastern *khānaqāhs* distinguished by specific attributions: Suhrawardī in Isfahan (A.D. 1326), Mawlawī in Qonya, and numerous Rifā'ī establishments in Anatolia and Caucasus (A.D. 1332), in Damascus (Ḥarīrī branch), as well as the founder-centre in the Baṭā'iḥ of Iraq. Of Qonya he writes: 'In this city is the tomb of . . . Jalāl ad-dīn, known as Mawlānā. An organization (*ṭā'ifa*) exists in the land of Rūm whose members derive from him,[2] and are known by his name, being called the Jalāliyya, similar to the derivation of the 'Irāqian Aḥmadiyya [= Rifā'iyya], or the Khurasanian Ḥaidariyya. Around his tomb is a large *zāwiya* in which food is provided for all migrants.'[3] These, therefore, were Sufi *ṭā'ifas* in the full sense.

Ibn Baṭṭūṭa's narrative also demonstrates how important these establishments were in the expansion of Muslim commerce, in accommodation to their Hindu environment, and in the diffusion of Islam. For instance, all along the Malabar coast, which was under Hindu rulers, he was entertained in *khānaqāhs*: at Haunūr

[1] *At-Ta'rif*, ed. Ṭanjī, pp. 311–13. Ibn Khaldūn, though not a Sufi, was acquainted with the general theory of *taṣawwuf*. Apart from a short account in his *Muqaddama* he also has a work on the subject: *Shifā' as-sā'il li tahdhīb al-masā'il*, ed. Muḥammad aṭ-Ṭanjī, Istanbul, 1958, and I. A. Khalifa, Beirut, 1959.

[2] The verb used is *intamā ilā*.

[3] Ibn Baṭṭūṭa, *Riḥla*, Cairo edn., 1939, i. 234.

(near Bombay) at that of Shaikh Muḥammad an-Nājōrī,[1] at Ghogah (Bhaunagar) where he came across a company of *fuqarā'* Ḥaidariyya,[2] and in Kanbāya (Cambay in Gujarat), Calicut, and Kōlam (Travancore) where he lodged in the *khānaqāhs* of the Kāzerūnī Sufi insurance company.[3]

By Maqrīzī's day (A.D. 1364–1442) the lines of derivation were well established. Thus he writes of the *fuqarā' al-Aḥmadiyya ar-Rifā'iyya* in Cairo.[4] About the same time the Qādirī attribution begins to expand and a branch was formed in Damascus towards the end of the fourteenth century.[5] Sufis were frequently allowed the use of mosques for their exercises. Maqrīzī says that the Azhar was open to Sufis and *dhikrs* were performed there.[6] Some were even found in *madrasas*, Aqbuga's *madrasa* in the Azhar having a permanent group.[7]

Iranian regions do not seem to have developed the officially sponsored *khānaqāh* and the change of their Sufi hostels to representation of a holy line (stage three of change) was not marked by any change of name but by the addition of an honoured tomb, though more commonly the later *khānaqāhs* were new foundations in association with a tomb. Later Turk and Mongol rulers rebuilt the tombs of famous saints and associated convents on more magnificent lines.

Sufis trained in these institutions founded daughter lodges in

[1] Ibn Baṭṭūṭa, Cairo edn., 1928, ii. 109–10.

[2] Ibid. ii. 108. On the Ḥaidariyya, see below, p. 39.

[3] Ibid. ii. 106, 115–18.

[4] *Khiṭaṭ*, ed. A.H. 1326, iv. 294, referring to the *ribāṭ* known as the *Riwāq* of Aḥmad ibn Sulaimān al-Baṭā'iḥī (d. 691/1292), an introducer of the Rifā'iyya into Egypt. This building still exists outside Bāb Zuwaila.

[5] Zāwiya Da'ūdiyya founded by a Ḥanbalī, Abu Bakr ibn Da'ūd (d. 806/1403), about 800/1397, but developed by his son, 'Abd ar-Raḥmān (d. 856/1452); see H. Sauvaire, 'Description de Damas', *J. Asiat.* IX. v. 390–3: 'Il fit de cette zâwyeh une merveille: il y installa une roue à eau, une citerne, une grande grotte et une galerie où se trouvaient un *iwân*, une mosquée, des cellules, une bibliothèque pour les livres constitués en waqf en faveur de la zâwyeh, et des habitations pour les femmes. Il y établit un imâm, un mouaẓẓin, un gardien et un prédicateur . . . On y récitait les litanies (*dhikr*) chaque nuit du (lundi au) mardi. De toutes parts les gens y accouraient et il leur faisait préparer toutes sortes de mets.'
Many of these establishments functioned as pious night clubs, and this is an example. This 'Abd ar-Raḥmān was a Ḥanbalī who composed a number of books, none of them Sufi. After his death the sultan chose for his successor someone outside his family; subsequent disputes over the leadership were numerous, one superior being murdered in A.D. 1515.

[6] *Khiṭaṭ*, iv. 54.

[7] Ibid. iv. 225.

their own countries or in entirely new pasture grounds, especially in India. They rarely maintained direct contact with the mother institution[1] and became independent schools with their own characteristics and tendencies.

The thirteenth century was an age of disturbance and change as the Mongol hordes swept over central Asian Muslim states one after the other, Baghdad being conquered in A.D. 1258. Many refugees fled to those parts of the Muslim world which seemed more remote from the scourge. Among these were Anatolia in the north-west and Hindustan in the south-east. Many Sufis found a new home within the jurisdiction of the Turkish sultanate of Delhi.

Indian Islam seems to have been essentially a holy-man Islam. These migrants in the Hindu environment acquired an aura of holiness, and it was this which attracted Indians to them, rather than formal Islam. There were two categories of Sufis, those associated with *khānaqāhs* and the wanderers. The *khānaqāhs* were in a special sense focal points of Islam—centres of holiness, fervour, ascetic exercises, and Sufi training. Contrary to the Arab-world institutions bearing the same Persian name, the Indian *khānaqāhs* grew up around a holy man and became associated with his *ṭarīqa* and method of discipline and exercises. Two distinctive *ṭarīqas* were formed.

Muʿīn ad-dīn Chishtī of Sijistan (d. A.D. 1236), after a lifetime of wanderings, finally settled at Ajmer, capital of a powerful Hindu state. From him stemmed a *silsila* which won widespread popularity under his *khalīfa* and successor, Quṭb ad-dīn Bakhtiyār Kākī (d. A.D. 1235), to become eventually the leading Indian *ṭarīqa*. Of other *ṭarīqas* only the Suhrawardī gained a following in India. Shihāb ad-dīn himself designated *khalīfas* for India, the chief being Ḥamīd ad-dīn of Najore (d. A.D. 1274). Others were Nūr ad-dīn Mubārak Ghaznawī (d. 632/1234 at Delhi) and Bahā' ad-dīn Zakariyā (d. A.D. 1262 at Multan), probably the most effective organizer of the rule and chain in India, with whom the Persian *qalandarī* poet, ʿIrāqī,[2] 'associated' for some twenty years.

These shaikhs acquired such fame that they began to count in the calculations of the ruling authorities. The sultans of Delhi

[1] The Kāzerūniyya was one of the exceptions; see p. 236.

[2] His proper name is Fakhr ad-dīn Ibrāhīm b. Shahriyār; born Hamadan, A.D. 1213, died Damascus, 1289, and buried near his inspirer, Ibn al-ʿArabī.

paid honour to those within their sphere of rule, *khānaqāhs* sprang up everywhere, the majority without definite ascriptions. Wandering dervishes, for whom these *khānaqāhs* formed centres for training, meeting, and hospitality, were numerous and acted as cultural agents in spreading and stabilizing Islam.

The attractions of the Sufi Way declined from the time of Muḥammad ibn Tughluq (A.D. 1325–51), though not in consequence of the restrictions he imposed on leaders and convent activities. It seems rather that Sufism had not yet taken such form as would attract Indians, its outburst as a popular movement was to come later. The decline finds expression in the reflections of Naṣīr ad-dīn Maḥmūd (d. 757/1356), successor to the great shaikh Niẓām ad-dīn Awliyā';

Some *qalandars* had arrived and were staying as guests of Khwajah Shaykh Naṣīr ad-dīn for the night. (The Khwajah) said, 'These days the number of *darwishes* has decreased. In the days of the Shaykh [Niẓām ad-dīn Awliyā] *darwishes* used to come by twenties and thirties, and the Shaykh used to keep them as guests for three days . . . When there was an *'urs*, the Shaykh [Niẓām ad-dīn] would invite all *lashkardars* [men of the army] and *darwishes* would arrive from all sides . . . Nowadays there are neither such soldiers, nor such slaves, nor such armies. All have deteriorated. Men have to wait [in vain] for the *darwishes* to come.'[1]

In Anatolia the Seljuq period was significant in that the mystical movement was vitally linked with the spread of Islamic culture in that region. Both Persian refugees like Bahā' ad-dīn Walad,

[1] Translated by Riazul Islam in *J. Pakistan Or. Soc.* iii (1955), 204. Sufis at all times have voiced complaints about spiritual decline. Muḥammad ibn Tughluq was unpredictable and not opposed to Sufis as such. This Niẓām ad-dīn Awliyā was noted for his avoidance of courts and Tughluq's son, Muḥammad Shāh, used to visit him when he was in a state of *ḥāl* (trance), and when he died (725/1325) at the beginning of Tughluq's reign, the latter's grandson assisted in carrying his bier, much to Tughluq's annoyance (Ibn Baṭṭūṭa, iii. 211). Subservient *khānaqāhs* benefited from his patronage. Ibn Baṭṭūṭa reports that Rukn ad-dīn as-Suhrawardī of Multan, grandson of Bahā' ad-dīn Zakariyā, accepted a *jāgir* of 100 villages from Tughluq for the upkeep of his *khānaqāh* (iii. 324, see also pp. 101–2, 201). The hagiographers give accounts of his harshness to Naṣīr ad-dīn, successor of Niẓām ad-dīn, and other Sufis. The sultan was suspicious of the influence of some of these shaikhs and no doubt the close regulation and supervision he exacted led to measures of repression. Those who interfered in politics were dealt with severely, but one must remember that many of these leaders were frequently intriguers for position and power.

father of Jalāl ad-dīn Rūmī, and Turkish *bābās* from central Asia moved in considerable numbers into Anatolia during the thirteenth century, especially during the time of the Mongol invasions, but dervish activity was just as strong after the collapse of the Seljuq state of Rūm. The mystics, manifesting a fervour and spirit quite different from that of legalist Islam, a spirit which also expressed itself in practical social aspects such as hospitality to travellers and care for the sick and poor, were mediators of Islam to the Christians of the region. They had the support of the Seljuq authorities. Jalāl ad-dīn Rūmī was highly honoured by the court of Qonya and there are many references to official patronage at other courts, such as that of Mujāhid ad-dīn Bihrūz ibn ʿAbdallāh, Prefect of Iraq under Masʿūd ibn Ghiyāth, who founded a *ribāṭ* at Baghdad.[1]

It is important to distinguish between the mystical orders proper and such corporations as trade-guilds[2] and *futuwwa* orders of craftsmanship and chivalry,[3] which are known under the same term, *ṭāʾifa*, and have similar forms of organization and possess religious aspects. The difference between them is one of purpose and intent, rather than in types of organization and linkages. The *ṭarīqas* are purely religious organizations, but the purpose of the guilds was economic association, craftsmanship, or trade. A religious *ṭāʾifa* could not strictly be at the same time a trade or craft *ṭāʾifa*. This is true in spite of the fact that there are

[1] Ibn Khallikān, iii. 472.

[2] *Ṣinf* (pl. *aṣnāf, ṣunūf*), *ḥirfa* (pl. *ḥiraf*), and regional terms like Moroccan *hanṭa*, pl. *hanāṭi*. They are referred to more simply as *ṭāʾifas*. The *akhī* organization in Anatolia was a similar Turkish *futuwwa* craft corporation. The members were called *fityān* (pl. of *fatā*, 'youth', though not strictly a youth organization except in enrolment) and the head *akhī*, which term, originally Turkish, naturally became associated with Arabic *akhī*, 'my brother'. Ibn Baṭṭūṭa received hospitality from *akhīs* (*c.* 1333); see *Travels*, tr. H. A. R. Gibb, ii. 418 ff. On these see *E.I.*², art. 'akhi'. This type of organization disappeared during the 15th century with the full establishment of Ottoman power. But craft orders of a different type were an important aspect of the life of Ottoman Turkey. The Kāzerūniyya, though it took the name of an eminent Sufi, was developed rather as a religious-economic guild association; see below, p. 236.

[3] Similarly they are to be distinguished from the Anatolian *ghāzī* movements based on the *futuwwa* principle whose religious affiliations were with Turkish *darāwīsh*. Sufis used the term *futuwwa*, not for an organization, but in their own special sense of an ethical self-offering, as when Aḥmad ar-Rifāʿī is reported as saying, '*Futuwwa* means working for God's sake, not for any reward' (Al-Wāsiṭī, *Tiryāq*, p. 45). On *futuwwa* as understood by Sufis see, for example, ʿAbdallāh al-Anṣārī al-Harawī (A.D. 1006–89). *Manāzil as-Sāʾirīn*, ed. S. de Beaurecueil, Cairo, 1962, pp. 47–8; al-Qushairī, *Risāla*, p. 103.

apparent exceptions,[1] and that the initial organization of the religious orders owes much to that of the guilds, and that the *ṭarīqas* sanctify such secular associations. Every form of social life embodies itself in associations and in a religious culture the need for acting together for what we call secular purposes is given a sacred character by religion. A particular guild and its members tended to be linked with a particular *ṭarīqa* and saint. At initiations and other ceremonies, religious rites were the predominant feature, and it was behind the banner of that *ṭarīqa* that the guild members proceeded to and from the *ʿīd* prayer-ground. They were not secular associations, although centred on economic and social interests, but neither were they Sufi orders.

The organization of the orders, however, owes much to that of the guilds. These guilds had flourished under the Fāṭimid and other Shīʿite states and with the triumph of the Ayyūbids and Seljuqs over political Shīʿism the necessity for recognizing them was accepted by the Sunnī doctors. We have shown that the Ayyūbids encouraged the Sufi organization at the stage it had then reached—association in *khānaqāhs*. From then, when defined lines of mystical tradition had emerged, the organization of the *khānaqāhs*, which were also secular associations in some aspects of their relationship to the life of the community, drew more and more features from guild organization. As the latter had a grand-master (*ʿarīf*, *amīn*, or *shaikh al-ḥirfa*) and a hierarchy of apprentices (*mubtadiʾ*), companions (*ṣāniʿ*), and master-craftsmen (*muʿallim*), so the religious orders acquired a hierarchy of novices, initiates, and masters. Since legal Islam tolerated the secret character of the initiation and oath of the guilds, it had to accept the implications of the act of allegiance to the *shaikh aṭ-ṭarīqa* when Shīʿī practice was maintained. Medical doctors too, without necessarily belonging to a guild, would receive simple initiation into a Sufi chain as a possible source of spiritual aid to them in their work.[2]

[1] The sacred origins of the corporations are stressed, the Imām Jaʿfar being especially important in their traditions. Consequently, it may on occasion be difficult to distinguish which was the essential purpose of certain organizations of *akhīs* and central Asian Mongol-period *futuwwa* orders. The confusion is noticeable in Evliyā Chelebi's description (A.D. 1638) of the various guilds in Constantinople; see *Seyāḥat-nāme*, tr. von Hammer, I. ii. 90–100.

[2] See the chain acquired by Dr. Rashīd ad-dīn ʿAlī in A.D. 1218, given in Appendix A.

And now we find manifestations of spiritual power becoming associated with the orders. No clear distinction can henceforth be made between the orders and saint-veneration, since God's protégés (*awliyā' li 'llāh*) are within the orders. Sufism provided a philosophy of election which was diluted and adapted to the needs of the masses by the orders. Not merely the great shaikh but his successors who inherited his *baraka* (spiritual power) were mediums of his power. With this was associated *ziyāra* (visitation) to saints' tombs. As in other aspects of Sufi thought and practice there is an essential distinction between the way in which the genuine Sufi approached a saint's tomb and the practice of the people. The mystic carries out a *ziyāra* for the purpose of *murāqaba* (spiritual communion) with the saint, finding in the material symbol an aid to meditation. But the popular belief is that the saint's soul lingers about his tomb and places (*maqāms*) specially associated with him whilst he was on earth or at which he had manifested himself. At such places his intercession can be sought.

The state of sanctity (*wilāya*) is characterized by the manifestation of *karāmāt*, gifted spiritual powers. The earlier spiritual leaders dissociated themselves from the working of such powers, though they all accepted the principle that saints did perform them as gifts from God. Al-Qushairī remarks that though prophets needed miracles (*mu'jizāt*) to confirm the validity of their mission, saints were under no such necessity and ought rather to hide any they had involuntarily made. The extraordinary graces with which they were favoured are a confirmation of their progress and can nevertheless edify and confirm the faithful and serve to distinguish a real *walī* from an impostor.[1] Still, a true *walī* does not necessarily, or indeed probably, know that he is one.[2] The writings of Sufis contain a vast amount on this subject of the validity of *wilāya*, but we are mainly concerned with practical aspects.

[1] See al-Qushairī, *Risāla* (Cairo, 1319/1902), pp. 158–9. Ibn Khaldūn remarks, 'Among the Sufis some who are favored by acts of divine grace are also able to exercise an influence upon worldly conditions. This, however, is not counted as a kind of sorcery. It is effected with divine support, because the attitude and approach (of these men) result from prophesy and are a consequence of it' (*Muqaddama*, tr. Rosenthal, iii. 167).

[2] Cf. the *ḥadīth qudsī*: 'My saints are beneath my tents, none knoweth them but me.'

With this development is associated a new reverence for the Prophet, which not merely brought him into the category of wonder-workers at the popular level, but also led to the popular equivalent of the belief in the Spirit of Muḥammad as the Logos, guardian, and preserver of the universe. The celebration of the Prophet's birthday seems, at least in part, to be a compensation for the suppression of 'Alid demonstrations after the destruction of Shī'ite regimes. Ibn Jubair (travelled A.D. 1183–5) refers to it as an established practice.[1] It was fairly widespread in Ibn Taimiyya's time, for it comes under his condemnation,[2] but it was not yet an aspect of the people's religion. By the time of as-Suyūṭī (d. A.D. 1505) the *mawlid* had acquired its characteristic features.[3] These features and the writing of special recitations for performance at Sufi gatherings belong to the next stage, but the prophylactic poem, *Qaṣīdat al-Burda*, by al-Būṣīrī (d. 694/1295), was written during this time.

The blending of the saint-cult with the orders and a new reverence for the Prophet is one aspect of the change. The other is a change in the constitution of the body of adherents. Concern for his own spiritual welfare had led the devotee and early Sufi to isolate himself from the world, but the need for spiritual direction had necessitated the association of Sufis. Their congregation in hospices concerned for the welfare of travellers and care for the sick and unfortunate brought them back into the world. The hospices with their associated tombs became the foci of the religious aspirations of the ordinary man who sought the *baraka* of the saints. The dedicated disciples (*fuqarā'*, *darāwīsh*, or *ikhwān*) continued to devote themselves to ascetic practices and duties within the order, but membership was now extended to embrace tertiaries or lay adherents who 'took the *ṭarīqa*' from the shaikh or more usually his representative (*khalīfa*), but continued to follow their ordinary mode of life. This meant that they affirmed their belief in the ideals for which the *ṭarīqa* stood, especially valuing the link with the *baraka* of the saints, and accepted such rules and modes of worship as were compatible with the pursuit of a normal mode of life. In towns such association

[1] Ibn Jubair, *Travels*, 2nd edn., 1907, pp. 114–15.

[2] Ibn Taimiyya, *Majmū' fatāwī*, Cairo, A.H. 1326–9, A.D. 1908–11, i. 312.

[3] See as-Suyūṭī, *Ḥusn al-maqṣid fī 'amal al-mawlid*—a kind of *fatwā* on the festival which concludes that it is a *bid'a ḥasana*, an acceptable innovation.

was especially linked with membership of guilds. Whilst, on the one hand, new techniques for the individual *dhikr* were adopted, this broadening of membership led to changes in methods for the collective *dhikr*. The full development of this system of lay adherence belongs to the next stage, when the *ṭarīqas* come to be represented by local organizations throughout the whole Islamic world, wielding an immense influence throughout most strata of society.

Along with the development of new forms of devotion and their acceptance parallel to ritual prayer went the process of accommodating the sciences of astrology, divination, and magic—techniques which professed, not merely to reveal the secrets of the unseen world, but to control them. This development is especially associated with the name of Aḥmad ibn ʿAbdallāh al-Būnī (d. 622/1225), who put the seal to the work of his predecessors operating less openly by finally systematizing the sciences of divination, astrology, and magical invocation. Popular works brought all this within the range of the ordinary practitioner and became part of the equipment of the shaikhs and brethren.

It is easy to see why this aspect was so important and how easy it was to Islamize borrowed material. The orders stressed the power of the Word of God, and hundreds of booklets have been written on the virtues and properties of the names of God, of phrases like the *Basmala*, or Qur'ānic verses (*Āyat al-Kursī*), or chapters (*sūra* Yā Sīn). The association of these 'words', as in ash-Shādhilī's *Ḥizb al-Baḥr* or al-Jazūlī's *Dalā'il al-khairāt*, gives these magical properties. Power symbolism in Islam is, therefore, primarily based on words.

All the same, the ideals of the orders were maintained, however much they were compromised in practice. The honour which Islam accords to jurists is reflected by the fact that certain of the *silsila* founders were also professional jurists. They and their successors clung to the externals of Islamic practice and based their litanies solidly on the Qur'ān. They played an immense role in enriching the devotional life of the ordinary Muslim as well as adepts, within the sphere of the regular Islamic institutions. They invested orthodox ritual with esoteric significance, for 'every act commanded by the Law denotes a mystery'. Thus not merely does *wuḍū'* (ablution) signify the abandonment of profane actions, but every action within *wuḍū'* has its ethical and mystical meaning.

But apart from the deeper mysteries the effect of their stress upon the spirit instead of the letter of the Law was morally and spiritually stimulating.

Earlier Sufis had been concerned with ascetic-mystical theory, or, if they were poets, with illuminating their search and the states they experienced. The change towards greater systematization is seen in the manuals now being produced as guides for the director and his pupils. Whilst Najīb ad-dīn as-Suhrawardī wrote one of the earliest manuals of this nature,[1] *Ādāb al-murīdīn*, it was his nephew, Shihāb ad-dīn, who wrote what deservedly has been the most popular guide, *'Awārif al-ma'ārif*, the medieval vade-mecum for spiritual directors. Other manuals were Najm ad-dīn Kubrā's *Ṣifāt al-ādāb*[2] and Ibn al-'Arabī's *al-amr al-muḥkam*, suspect by many *'ulamā'* because of its author's reputation as an antinomian.

These manuals show that the ritual is now a traced-out Way, a rule of life, by following which the novice may attain union with God, founded upon a series of observances additional to the common ritual and duties of Islam. It involves a noviciate, during which he receives guidance from a shaikh, and it is now that the saying that the novice must be in the hands of his director like the corpse in the hands of the washer of the dead becomes popular.[3] This culminates in initiation, which includes investment with a *khirqa*, mantle, and headdress.

The Way under guidance implies a life in common (*mu'āshara*) for the dedicated group of aspirants and adepts in a convent under the direct supervision of a superior. Suhrawardī in the book just mentioned deals with the rules of behaviour in such an institution.[4] The superior allots various prayer tasks, supererogatory exercises, recitations of litanies, praises, and invocations (*adhkār*, *aḥzāb*, and

[1] An earlier manual on the rules of the noviciate was *Aḥkām al-murīdīn*, by Ṭāhir b. al-Ḥusain al-Jaṣṣaṣ, d. 418/1027. *Ādāb aṣ-ṣuḥba* by as-Sulamī (d. 1021) is a general treatise on manners, concerned especially with imitation of the prophet; it is not Sufi in content, though it has its place in as-Sulamī's work towards reconciling *taṣawwuf* with orthodoxy.

[2] Translated by F. Meier, 'Ein Knigge für Ṣūfi's', *R.S.O.* xxxii (1957), 485–524.

[3] The original, which is attributed to Sahl ibn 'Abdallāh at-Tustarī (d. A.D. 896), referred to God: 'The first stage in *tawakkul* (dependence upon God) is that the worshipper should be in the hands of God like a corpse in the hands of the washer, he turns it as he wills without impulse or initiative on its part'; al-Qushairī, *Risāla* (Cairo, A.H. 1319), p. 76.

[4] *'Awārif*, chapters 29–55.

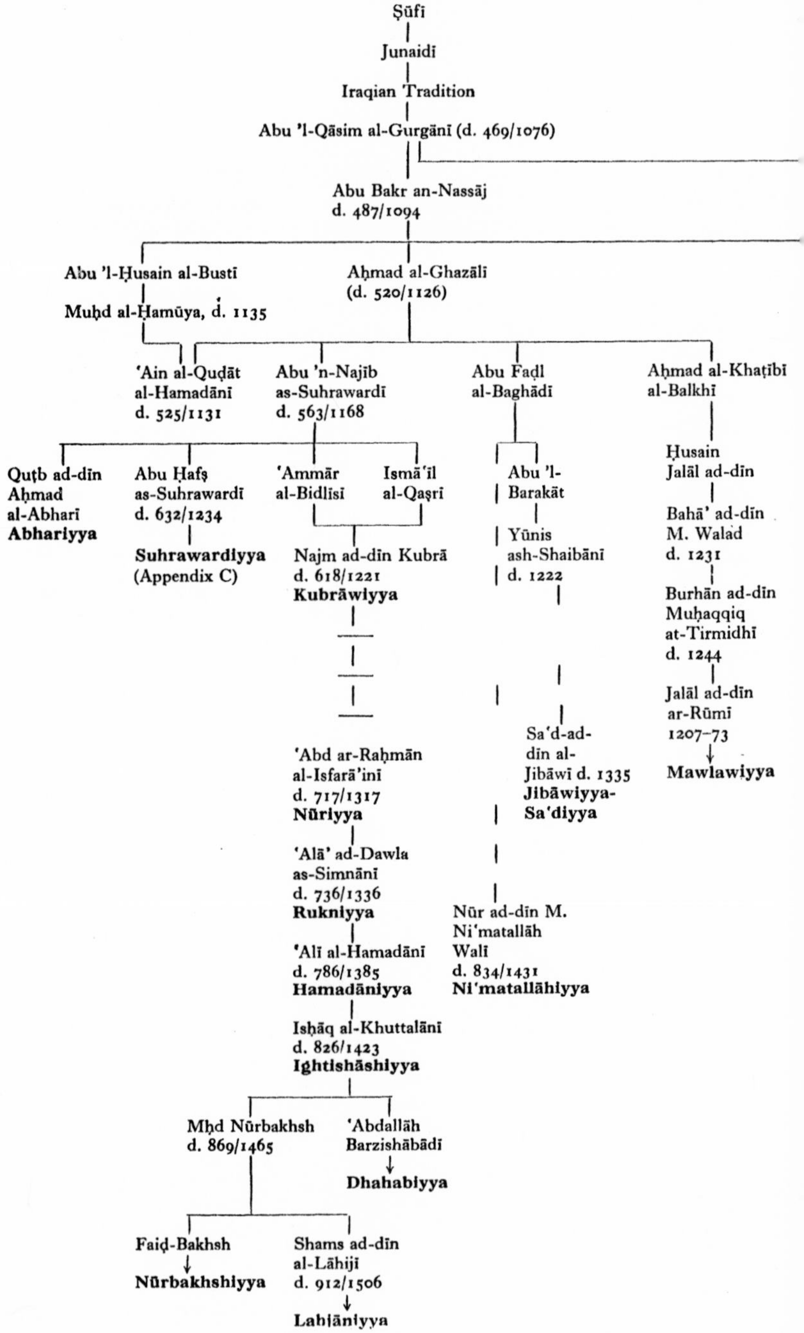

Ṣūfī
Junaidī
Iraqian Tradition
Abu 'l-Qāsim al-Gurgānī (d. 469/1076)
Abu Bakr an-Nassāj
d. 487/1094
Abu 'l-Ḥusain al-Bustī
Muḥd al-Ḥamūya, d. 1135
Aḥmad al-Ghazālī
(d. 520/1126)
'Ain al-Quḍāt
al-Hamadānī
d. 525/1131
Abu 'n-Najīb
as-Suhrawardī
d. 563/1168
Abu Faḍl
al-Baghādī
Aḥmad al-Khaṭībī
al-Balkhī
Quṭb ad-dīn
Aḥmad
al-Abharī
Abhariyya
Abu Ḥafṣ
as-Suhrawardī
d. 632/1234
Suhrawardiyya
(Appendix C)
'Ammār
al-Bidlīsī
Ismā'īl
al-Qaṣrī
Najm ad-dīn Kubrā
d. 618/1221
Kubrāwiyya
Abu 'l-
Barakāt
Yūnis
ash-Shaibānī
d. 1222
Ḥusain
Jalāl ad-dīn
Bahā' ad-dīn
M. Walad
d. 1231
Burhān ad-dīn
Muḥaqqiq
at-Tirmidhī
d. 1244
Jalāl ad-dīn
ar-Rūmī
1207–73
Mawlawiyya
Sa'd-ad-
dīn al-
Jibāwī d. 1335
Jibāwiyya-
Sa'diyya
'Abd ar-Raḥmān
al-Isfarā'inī
d. 717/1317
Nūriyya
'Alā' ad-Dawla
as-Simnānī
d. 736/1336
Rukniyya
Nūr ad-dīn M.
Ni'matallāh
Walī
d. 834/1431
Ni'matallāhiyya
'Alī al-Hamadānī
d. 786/1385
Hamadāniyya
Isḥāq al-Khuttalānī
d. 826/1423
Ightishāshiyya
Mḥd Nūrbakhsh
d. 869/1465
'Abdallāh
Barzishābādī
Dhahabiyya
Faiḍ-Bakhsh
Nūrbakhshiyya
Shams ad-dīn
al-Lāhijī
d. 912/1506
Lahijāniyya

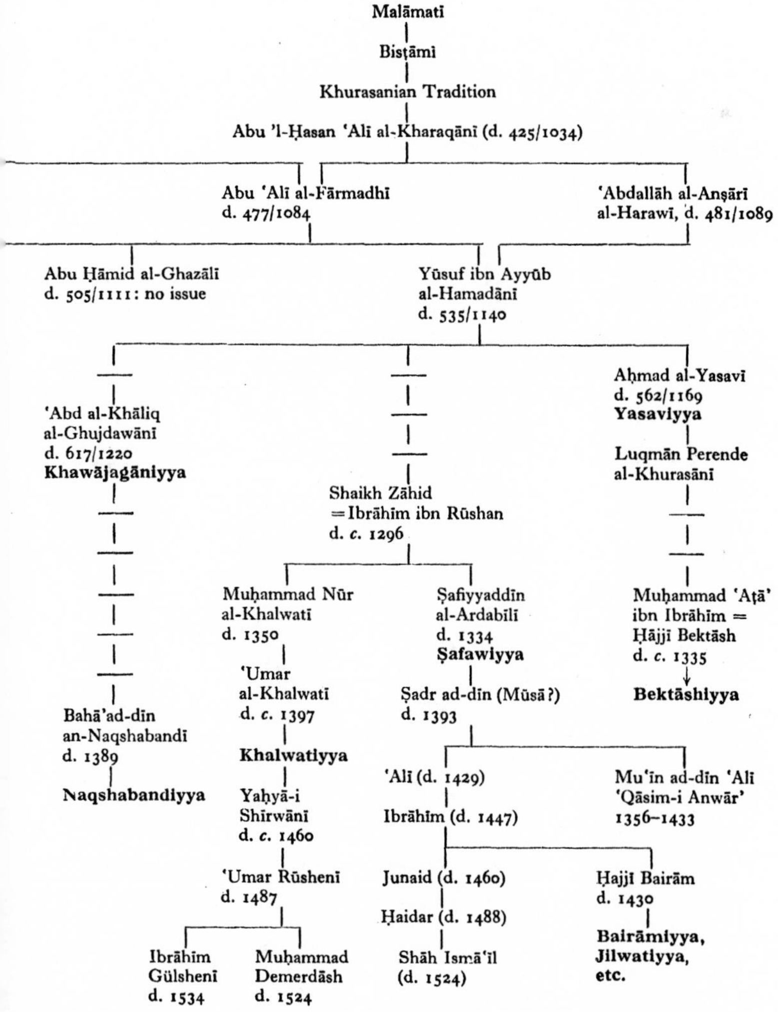
Malāmatī
Bisṭāmī
Khurasanian Tradition
Abu 'l-Ḥasan 'Alī al-Kharaqānī (d. 425/1034)
Abu 'Alī al-Fārmadhī d. 477/1084
'Abdallāh al-Anṣārī al-Harawī, d. 481/1089
Abu Ḥāmid al-Ghazālī d. 505/1111: no issue
Yūsuf ibn Ayyūb al-Hamadānī d. 535/1140
'Abd al-Khāliq al-Ghujdawānī d. 617/1220
Khawājagāniyya
Aḥmad al-Yasavī d. 562/1169
Yasaviyya
Luqmān Perende al-Khurasānī
Shaikh Zāhid = Ibrāhīm ibn Rūshan d. c. 1296
Muḥammad Nūr al-Khalwatī d. 1350
Ṣafiyyaddīn al-Ardabīlī d. 1334
Ṣafawiyya
Muḥammad 'Aṭā' ibn Ibrāhīm = Ḥājjī Bektāsh d. c. 1335
Bektāshiyya
'Umar al-Khalwatī d. c. 1397
Ṣadr ad-dīn (Mūsā?) d. 1393
Bahā'ad-dīn an-Naqshabandī d. 1389
Naqshabandiyya
Khalwatiyya
'Alī (d. 1429)
Mu'īn ad-dīn 'Alī 'Qāsim-i Anwār' 1356–1433
Yaḥyā-i Shīrwānī d. c. 1460
Ibrāhīm (d. 1447)
'Umar Rūshenī d. 1487
Junaid (d. 1460)
Ḥajjī Bairām d. 1430
Ḥaidar (d. 1488)
Bairāmiyya, Jilwatiyya, etc.
Ibrāhīm Gülshenī d. 1534
Muḥammad Demerdāsh d. 1524
Shāh Ismā'īl (d. 1524)

awrād), graded according to a person's stage, together with such mortifications as vigils (*sahr*) and fasts (*ṣiyām*). He is required to make periodic retreats (*khalwa*, *iʿtikāf*, *ʿuzla*, *iʿtizāl*, or *arbaʿīniyya* = quadragesima) individually in his cell or, if highly advanced, in the society of the convent.

But, as may be seen from these manuals, although the lines of the practice of the mystical Way had been worked out, the aims of the Sufis in association were still variable, confused, and limited. There were great variations too between the Sufi establishments. Some were rich and luxurious, favoured by authority, whilst others followed the strictest principles of poverty and unworldliness; some had no shaikh, others were under the authority of one leader and had become attached to one *silsila*; whilst others were governed by a council of elders. Then there were wandering dervishes such as the *qalandars*, who made use of these hostels, and had their own rules and linkages but no organization.[1]

[1] On *qalandars*, see Appendix B.

II

The Chief *Ṭarīqa* Lines

HAVING outlined the general stages in the development of the Sufi organization leading to the formation of schools of teaching and training we may now say something about the personalities from whom the great *ṭarīqas* derive and their subsequent development. We have shown that they came into existence through an outstanding director being succeeded by men who combined practical abilities along with spiritual qualities and insight, who made collections of his sayings and episodes from his life, and taught their own pupils in his name. The difficulty of utilizing the lives of the saints as historical sources is well recognized. Hagiographa is simply biography designed, and consequently distorted, to serve the cult of the saints. It forms an essential aspect of any study of the orders since these qualities, deeds, and manifestations are real to the believer, but they obscure the historical personality. At the same time, the historian is concerned with the effects, if not the reality, of such beliefs, since they account for the existence of the cult and help to elucidate its objective expression in an organization.

The main areas of Sufi thought and practice from the point of view of subsequent *ṭarīqa* development were Mesopotamia, Khurasan, and the Maghrib. Anatolian forms derive from central Asia, whilst Sufism in India, stemming originally from the first two, subsequently developed along lines of its own and its phases of growth, stagnation, and revival owed little to non-Indian influences.

1. MESOPOTAMIA

Here Sufism centred on Baghdad, embracing Syria and extending into Egypt. Lines of ascription go back through al-Junaid al-Baghdādī (d. 298/910) to Ma'rūf al-Karkhī (d. 200/815) and Sarī aṣ-Ṣaqaṭī (d. 251/865). It is here that Sufism won a qualified recognition from the doctors of Islamic legalism, on the one hand, through the work of 'Abd ar-Raḥmān as-Sulamī (d. 412/1021), the Khorasanian traditionalist and historian of early Sufism, his disciple al-Qushairī (d. 465/1072) who taught in Baghdad and wrote books on Ash'arite theology as well as *taṣawwuf*, and Abu Ḥāmid al-Ghazālī (d. 505/1111); and, on the other, through its association with the official favour of Nūr ad-dīn, Saladin, and their lieutenants and successors, who encouraged the development of parallel institutions of *madrasas* and *khānaqāhs*.

The Mesopotamian tradition is the nearest that we can get to an Arab Sufism and its objective expression, even though most of the leaders were not Arabs. We find two main lines, the Suhrawardī and the Rifā'ī. Both stand squarely in the Junaidī tradition. The Rifā'ī, with its family antecedents centred on the Basran marshes, haunt of outlaws, stressed strongly the Arab ancestry of Aḥmad ar-Rifā'ī and his standing in direct succession to Arab Sufis. It was the only *ṭarīqa* in this tradition which gained any great following in the Seljuqid empire. The Suhrawardī school was distinctively urban and orthodox Shāfi'ī. The Ḥanbalī Qādiriyya is also included since 'Abd al-Qādir, of Persian origin, was a contemporary of the other two; but he does not count in any of the *ṣuḥba* and *silsila* Sufi ascriptions and the *ṭarīqa* which carries his name only came into existence later, and even then it was some time before it became a universal *ṭarīqa*.

The key figure in this tradition is Aḥmad al-Ghazālī. The way in which he, and his equally important master, al-Fārmadhī,[1] combined the lines of Sufi devotional expression is shown:

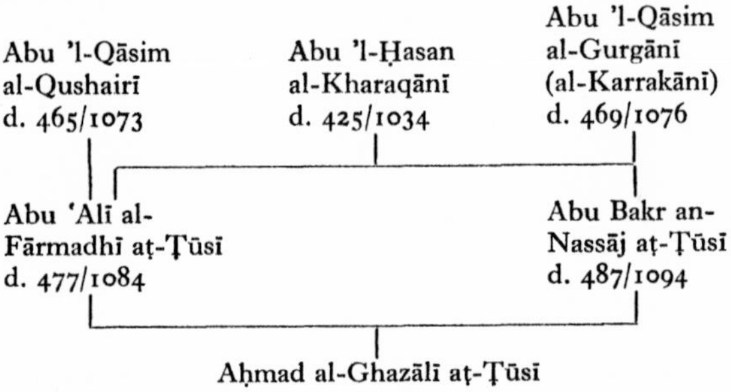

Abu 'l-Futūḥ Aḥmad ibn Muḥammad al-Ghazālī[2] (d. at Qaswīn

[1] See as-Subkī, *Aṭ-Ṭabaqāt ash-Shāfi'iyya*, Cairo, A.H. 1324, iv. 9, for his training under al-Qushairī.

[2] Not much is known about his life for he attracted no hagiographer. Ibn Khallikān (writing *c.* A.D. 1256) has only a short account (*Wafāyāt al-A'yān*,

520/1126), younger brother of the ethical theologian Abu Ḥāmid, was early attracted to the Sufi life, serving his apprenticeship with Sufis and then wholly devoting himself to the Way. Abu ʿAlī al-Fārmadhī, also a Ṭūsī but teaching at Nisapur, was his *shaikh aṣ-ṣuḥba*.[1] He was at one and the same time withdrawn from and active in the world, no *khānaqāh* Sufi but a vagrant evangelist, 'visiting villages and the countryside, and even preaching to bedouins the way of approach to God'.[2] He spent a period in Baghdad, where his sincerity immediately won people's hearts, and he taught for a time at the Niẓāmiyya, deputizing for his brother when the latter was in the throes of his spiritual crisis (488/1095). The part that he played in his brother's life during this period can only be conjectured. According to M. al-Murtaḍā, the final straw

'which caused Abu Ḥāmid to break the bonds with this world . . . came one day when his brother Aḥmad entered while he was preaching and recited:

> You lent a hand to them when they hung back, and you yourself have been kept behind, whilst they went ahead of you.
> You have taken the role of guide, yet you will not be guided; you preach but do not listen.
> O whetstone, how long will you whet iron, but will not let yourself be whetted?'[3]

(*a*) *Suhrawardiyya*

This *ṭarīqa* may be regarded as going back to Ḍiyā' ad-dīn

Cairo, A.H. 1299, i. 49; tr. de Slane, i. 79). As-Subkī (A.D. 1327–70) brings together what material he could find in his *Ṭabaqāt* (iv. 54–5), but he was much more interested in his elder brother.

[1] Abu Ḥāmid also studied under him as well as under Yūsuf an-Nassāj; see Subkī, iv. 109, and the account of his friend, ʿAbd al-Ghāfir b. Ismāʿīl al-Fārisī (d. 529/1134), quoted in M. al-Murtaḍā's introduction to his commentary on the *Ihyā'* in *Itḥāf as-Sāda*, Cairo, 1911, i. 19. Although he engaged under al-Fārmadhī's guidance in a course of Sufi discipline he received no enlightenment at this stage of his career. That came later through Yūsuf an-Nassāj, *murshid* of his brother Aḥmad. Abu Ḥāmid told Quṭb ad-dīn M. b. al-Ardabīlī: 'I was at first sceptical about the reality of the ecstatic states of the Sufis and the stations of the gnostics until I put myself under the guidance of my shaikh Yūsuf an-Nāssaj in Ṭūs. He persevered in the task of refining me with soul-cleansing disciplines until I was vouchsafed revelations (*wāridāt*) and saw God in a dream.' Then follows an account of the dialogue between God and himself (*Itḥāf*, i. 9).

[2] As-Subkī, iv. 55.

[3] M. al-Murtaḍā az-Zabīdī, *Itḥāf as-Sāda*, i. 8.

Abu 'n-Najīb as-Suhrawardī (490/1097–563/1168)[1] owing to his influence upon his nephew Shihāb ad-dīn. He belonged to a family with initiatory filiation (*nisbat al-khirqa*). He left Suhraward as a youth for Baghdad where he followed the customary courses of *uṣūl* and *fiqh*. He taught for a while at the Niẓāmiyya, 'then left it in order to associate with Shaikh Aḥmad al-Ghazālī who wafted upon him the breath of felicity and guided him along the Sufi Path.[2] He cut himself off from ordinary society in order to lead a life of seclusion and retreat. *Murīds* came to put themselves under him and the fame of his *baraka* spread widely.'[3] He built a *ribāṭ* on a ruined site on the Tigris, which also became a place of refuge. He was the author of *Ādāb al-murīdīn*, a manual for Sufi aspirants. Among his disciples were Abu Muḥammad Rūzbihān Baqlī of Shiraz (d. 606/1209),[4] Ismā'īl al-Qaṣrī (d. 1193), and 'Ammār al-Bidlīsī (d. *c.* 1200), the last two of whom were masters of the great Khwarizmian mystic, Najm ad-dīn Kubrā, from whom stems the Kubrāwiyya line of mystical ascription.[5]

The man regarded as the founder of the Way was Abu 'n-Najīb's nephew, Shihāb ad-dīn Abu Ḥafṣ 'Umar (539/1145–632/1234), who received his early training in his uncle's *ribāṭ*.[6] He was no ascetic living withdrawn from the world, though he passed periods in retreat, but associated with the great. The caliph an-Nāṣir li dīni 'llāh realized the importance of the influence of Sufi leaders and showed Shihāb ad-dīn great favour. He associated him with his aristocratized *futuwwa* and sent him as ambassador to 'Alā' ad-dīn Kaiqubād I, Seljuq ruler of Qonya (A.D. 1219–36),[7] the Ayyūbid al-Malik al-'Ādil, and the Khwārizm-

[1] Accounts of his life are found in Ibn Khallikān, i. 535–6; as-Subkī, *Ṭabaqāt*, iv. 256–7; Yāqūt, *Mu'jam*, s.v. 'Suhraward'; as-Sam'ānī, *Ansāb*, G.M.S. xx.

[2] Ḥammād ad-Dabbās (d. 525/1131) also gave him some Sufi training, but Aḥmad al-Ghazālī was his true guide.

[3] As-Subkī, *Ṭabaqāt*, iv. 256.

[4] See Junaid Shīrāzī, *Shadd*, pp. 243–7. Rūzbihān Baqlī travelled seeking initiations, but his true *silsila*, the one he himself passed on, was the Kāzerūniyya of Abu Isḥāq Ibrāhīm al-Kāzerūnī (d. 426/1034), through Junaid and Ibn Khafīf, into which he was initiated by Sirāj ad-dīn Maḥmūd ibn Khalīfa (d. 1166), head of the *khānaqāh* in Shiraz. The Rūzbihāniyya as a branch order was restricted to Fars, but a later-stage Kāzerūniyya became widespread; see below, p. 236.

[5] See the Kubrāwī table of spiritual *nisbas*.

[6] Ibn Khallikān says (tr. ii. 382) that one of Shihāb ad-dīn's masters was 'Abd al-Qādir al-Jīlī, but the subject of study was *uṣūl ad-dīn*, not *taṣawwuf*, according to al-Wāsiṭī, *Tiryāq al-muḥibbīn*, Cairo, A.H. 1305, p. 61.

[7] J. von Hammer, *Histoire de l'Empire Ottoman*, tr. J. J. Hellert, 1844, i. 41.

shāh.[1] An-Nāṣir built for him a *ribāṭ*, associated with a large establishment which included a bath-house and a garden for himself and his family.[2] He was no theoretical exponent of Sufism and his association with the *futuwwa* may have encouraged the introduction of certain initiatory practices, such as the *shadd* (girding), into Sufi associations. He was a great teaching shaikh, whose influence, not only through his pupils, but through his work, *'Awārif al-ma'ārif*, has extended to almost every Sufi leader to this day. Sufis from all over the world came to him for training, and he himself made extended stays at *khānaqāhs* in various towns, including Damascus and Aleppo. They also sent to him seeking mystical 'opinions', as is seen from this account by Ibn Khallikān:

I met a number of those who had attended his courses and sojourned in his *khalwa*, training under his direction according to Sufi custom. They would give me an account of the strange sensations which overcame them during those occasions when they experienced ecstatic states (*aḥwāl*). He came to Irbil as an envoy from the government in Baghdad and held assemblies for spiritual counsel, but I had not the opportunity of seeing him since I was too young. He performed the pilgrimage frequently and sometimes resided near the House for a time. Contemporary Sufi leaders in other lands used to write to him putting to him problems, seeking advice in the form of *fatwās*.[3]

The spiritual insight of Shihāb ad-dīn was deeper than that of the founders of the Qādiriyya and Rifā'iyya. The Suhrawardiyya was a mystical school and his pupils introduced his teaching into

[1] W. Barthold, *Turkestan Down to the Mongol Invasion*, 1928, pp. 373–4.

[2] Ibn al-Fuwaṭī, *Al-Ḥawādith al-jāmi'a*, ed. H. Jawād, Baghdad, 1351/1932, p. 74.

[3] Ibn Khallikān, ii. 95; tr. ii. 383. Correspondence became a regular feature of the activities of many of these mystics. In the Arab world few collections were made. The earliest include the *Rasā'il* of al-Junaid, edited and translated with an introduction on his thought and work by Dr. Ali Hassan Abdel-Kader, *The Life, Personality and Writings of Al-Junaid* (London, 1962). *Ar-Rasā'il aṣ-ṣughrā* of the western mystic Ibn 'Abbād of Ronda (A.D. 1332–90) have been edited by P. Nwyia (Beirut, 1958), who has also written a study of Ibn 'Abbād based on this and his larger collection (Beirut, 1956). The Persian *Maktūbāt* of 'Ain al-Quḍāt al-Hamadānī still exist only in manuscript. The letters of Jalāl ad-dīn Rūmī have been edited by Ahmed Remzi Akyürek, Istanbul, 1937.

Collections were more common in India. *Fawā'id al-fu'ād*, the letters of Niẓām ad-dīn Awliyā', were collected by Amīr Ḥasan Sijzī; *Khair al-majālis* of Naṣīr ad-dīn Maḥmūd (d. A.D. 1356) were collected by Ḥamīd Qalandar. There are also *maktūbāt* by Aḥmad ibn Yaḥyā Manīrī (d. A.D. 1381), Aḥmad al-Fārūqī as-Sirhindī (d. A.D. 1624), his son, Muḥammad Ma'ṣūm, and the Chishtī, Gīzū Darāz (d. 825/1422).

all parts of the Muslim world. From him only a few regularly organized *ṭā'ifas* stemmed. His son, 'Imād ad-dīn M. (655/1257) succeeded him as warden of Ribāṭ al-Ma'mūniyya in Baghdad, and he by his son, 'Abd ar-Raḥmān,[1] but it only survived as a family *ṭā'ifa*. 'Abd ar-Raḥmān al-Wāsiṭī, writing about A.D. 1325, says[2] that the Suhrawardiyya had more branches (*furū'*) than any other *ṭarīqa*, but it is difficult to get confirmation of the existence of many distinct *ṭā'ifas* as compared with the large numbers of Sufis claiming to belong to the Suhrawardī *silsila*.

Shihāb ad-dīn maintained a careful orthodoxy and this was continued by his more immediate followers, among whom may be mentioned the well-known Shirazi shaikh, Najīb ad-dīn Buzghūsh (d. 678/1279),[3] and his son and successor, Ẓahīr ad-dīn 'Abd ar-Raḥmān. Many who could hardly be called Sufis received the *khirqa* from him,[4] such as Abū Bakr M. ibn Aḥmad al-Qasṭallānī (614/1218–686/1287), who founded a school of traditionalists.[5] Similarly, the great Persian poet Sa'dī of Shiraz (A.D. 1208–92), who came under his influence when he was in Baghdad, was not a follower of the Sufi Path, though his wide range of understanding embraced Sufism and the ways of dervishes, and in his *Būstān* he refers to Shihāb ad-dīn's piety and love for his fellow men.[6] Ibn Baṭṭūṭa was another who loved to collect these affiliations and he was invested with a Suhrawardī *khirqa* at Isfahan in A.D. 1327,[7] and with another at Outch.[8] This shows what little meaning was sometimes to be attached to these initiations. Later leaders claiming a Suhrawardī ascription included all types of Sufis, men of such distinctive characteristics as Nūr ad-dīn 'Abd aṣ-Ṣamad

[1] Ibn al-Fuwaṭī, *Ḥawādith*, p. 323.

[2] *Tiryāq*, p. 49, cf. p. 61.

[3] See Mu'īn ad-dīn Abu 'l-Qāsim Junaid, *Shadd al-izār fī khaṭṭ al-awzār 'an zuwwār al-mazār*, ed. M. Qazwīnī and 'Abbās Iqbāl, Tehran, 1328/1950, pp. 334–8, and Ẓahīr ad-dīn, pp. 338–9.

[4] Such references are incomplete unless one knows what type of *khirqa* is involved. We have to distinguish between the *khirqa* of teaching (*ta'līm*), companionship (*ṣuḥba*) which includes training, and guidance (*tarbiya*).

[5] *G.A.L.S.* i. 809. Al-Qasṭallānī attacked his fellow Andalusian emigré, Ibn Sab'īn, Aristotelian gnostic philosopher, then enjoying favour in Mecca. He was expelled from Mecca but welcomed in Cairo by Baibars, who put him in charge of Dār al-Ḥadīth al-Kāmiliyya in 667/1268; see L. Massignon, *Opera Minora*, ii. 53, 409–10.

[6] Sa'dī, *Būstān*, ed. Graf, p. 150.

[7] Tr. H. A. R. Gibb, ii. 297.

[8] French edition, iii. 116.

an-Naṭanzī, 'Abd ar-Razzāq al-Kāshānī (d. 730/1329), and Sa'īd ibn 'Abdallāh al-Farghānī (d. *c.* 700/1300).[1]

(*b*) *Rifā'iyya*

The Way of Aḥmad ibn 'Alī ar-Rifā'ī (A.D. 1106–82) is no derivative from the Qādiriyya as has been claimed. On the contrary, he himself inherited a family *silsila* and his order came into prominence as a distinctive Way from his lifetime, whereas the Qādiriyya did not emerge as a *khirqa* line until much later. The Rifā'iyya was distinguished by peculiar practices deriving from Aḥmad himself, and his centre in the Baṭā'iḥ counted as a focus of attraction for Sufis in a way that 'Abd al-Qādir's *ribāṭ* in Baghdad did not.

Little is known about the life of Ibn ar-Rifā'ī,[2] but sufficient to show its contrast to the careers of as-Suhrawardī and 'Abd al-Qādir. He was born into an Arab family and spent the whole of his life in the Baṭā'iḥ, the marshlands of southern Iraq between Baṣra and Wāsiṭ, leaving it only once (A.D. 1160) to go on pilgrimage. Little learned in either *fiqh* or *taṣawwuf*, he wrote nothing; the few *awrād* attributed to him are probably not genuine. The Baṣra–Kūfa region was the nurture centre for Arab Sufism. From it came Ma'rūf al-Karkhī (d. A.D. 813) whose parents were Ṣābians (=Mandæans). His *shaikh aṣ-ṣuḥba*, who invested him with his first *khirqa*, was 'Alī Abī 'l-Faḍl al-Qāri' al-Wāsiṭī, but he also inherited a religious community called ar-Rifā'iyya from his maternal uncle, Manṣūr al-Baṭā'iḥī (d. 540/1145).[3] Manṣūr gave him the *khirqa* in his 27th year and established him in Umm 'Abīda; then, just before his death, he invested him with the *mashyakha* (spiritual jurisdiction) and *sajjādat al-irshād*, or throne of spiritual direction. Ibn Khallikān writes (around 654/1256):

Abu 'l-'Abbās Aḥmad ibn Abī 'l-Ḥasan 'Alī, commonly known as Ibn ar-Rifā'ī, was a holy man and a *faqih* of the Shāfi'ī school. By origin

[1] Jāmī, p. 651; *G.A.L.S.* ii. 807, 812. The Indian Suhrawardī school is discussed subsequently (pp. 65–6) and the chief affiliations are given in Appendix C.

[2] The earliest life of Aḥmad ar-Rifā'ī is *Tiryāq* [*thēriakē*] *al-muḥibbīn fī sīrat . . . A. b. ar-Rifā'ī*, by Taqī ad-dīn 'Abd ar-Raḥmān al-Wāsiṭī (A.D. 1275–1343), published in Cairo 1305/1888. Subsequent *manāqib*-type works have little sound material to add. Sha'rānī's account in *Lawāqiḥ* (Cairo, A.H. 1355, i. 121–5) consists mainly of sayings.

[3] Sha'rānī gives the biographies of Manṣūr and other members of the group drawn from the books of the order in *Lawāqiḥ*, i. 114–16.

he was an Arab and lived in the Baṭā'iḥ, at a village called Umm 'Abīda. A large concourse of *fuqarā'* attached themselves to him, taking the full compact of allegiance and following him [as their guide]. The dervish order (*aṭ-ṭā'ifa min al-fuqarā'*) deriving from him is known as Rifā'iyya or Baṭā'iḥiyya. His followers experience extraordinary states during which they eat living snakes and enter ovens blazing with fires which are thereupon extinguished. It is said that in their own country [the marshlands] they ride on lions and perform similar feats. They hold festival gatherings (*mawāsim*) at which uncountable numbers of *fuqarā'* congregate and are all entertained. Ar-Rifā'ī died without issue but the spiritual and temporal succession[1] was maintained in that region through his brother's children until this day.[2]

Although Aḥmad was no original thinker, the fame of his marshland retreat spread widely, a focus of attraction for migrant Sufis, four of whom founded independent *ṭarīqas*: Badawiyya, Dasūqiyya, Shādhiliyya, and 'Alwāniyya.[3] In the time of Ibn Baṭṭūṭa Rifā'ī *zāwiyas* were clearly differentiated; he refers to them frequently in his travels, as well as to the extravagant practices for which they were notorious. When his caravan stayed at Wāsiṭ in A.D. 1327 for three days he writes:

This gave me the opportunity of visiting the grave of the saint Abu 'l-'Abbās Aḥmad ar-Rifā'ī, which is at a village called Umm 'Ubaida, one day's journey from Wāsiṭ . . . It is a vast convent in which there are thousands of poor brethren . . . When the afternoon prayers have been said drums and kettle-drums were beaten and the poor brethren began to dance. After this they prayed the sunset prayer and brought in the repast, consisting of rice-bread, fish, milk and dates. When all had eaten and prayed the first night prayer, they began to recite their *dhikr*, with the shaikh Aḥmad sitting on the prayer-carpet of his ancestor above-mentioned, then they began the musical recital. They had prepared loads of fire-wood which they kindled into a flame, and went

[1] *Al-mashyakha wa 'l-wilāya.*

[2] Ibn Khallikān, Cairo, 1299, i. 95–6. He was in fact succeeded by his sister's son, 'Alī ibn 'Uthmān. Ibn Khallikān also reports that the Rifā'ī dervishes memorized the poems of the local poet, Ibn al-Mu'allim (d. 592/1196), and sang them at their concerts in order to excite themselves to ecstasy (op. cit. ii. 400). Aḥmad tried to get him to compose religious poetry; *Tiryāq*, p. 24.

[3] The first three are discussed subsequently; see pp. 45–51. The 'Alwāniyya was a Yemenite *ṭarīqa* founded by Abu 'l-Ḥasan Ṣafī ad-dīn Aḥmad ibn 'Aṭṭāf ibn 'Alwān (d. 665/1266), who took the *ṭarīqa* from Aḥmad al-Badawī and Aḥmad aṣ-Ṣayyād, *khalīfa* of Ibn ar-Rifā'ī; al-Wāsiṭī, *Tiryāq*, p. 18. A list of attribute-*ṭā'ifas* is given in Appendix H, most of them small nineteenth-century family groups.

into the midst of it dancing; some of them rolled in the fire, and others ate it in their mouths, until finally they extinguished it entirely. This is their regular custom and it is the peculiar characteristic of this corporation of Aḥmadī brethren. Some of them will take a large snake and bite its head with their teeth until they bite it clean through.[1]

Elsewhere Ibn Baṭṭūṭa mentions the related Ḥaidarī group centred in Khurasan south of Mashhad, derived from Quṭb ad-dīn Ḥaidar,[2] 'who place iron rings in their hands, necks and ears, and even their male members so that they are unable to indulge in sexual intercourse'.[3] These Rifā'ī exercises signify the victory of the spirit over the flesh and its temporary annihilation in absolute Reality. Rifā'ī dervishes are still noted for their fire-resistant and snake-charming properties.[4] The Ḥaidariyya spread into Iran, Syria, Anatolia,[5] and India[6] where it was linked with and finally absorbed in the qalandarī trend. A notable *khānaqāh* was that of Abu Bakr Tūsī Qalandarī, situated on the banks of the river Jumna.[7]

The Rifā'iyya spread into Egypt through the agency of Abu 'l-Fatḥ al-Wāsiṭī (d. 632/1234) and into Syria through Abu Muḥammad 'Alī al-Ḥarīrī (d. at Buṣrā, capital of the Ḥawrān, in 645/1248), whence this branch was known as the Ḥarīriyya.[8]

[1] *The Travels of Ibn Battuta*, tr. H. A. R. Gibb, ii. 273–4.

[2] He was a disciple of the qalandarī, Muḥammad ibn Yūnus Jamāl ad-dīn as-Sāwajī, a refugee fleeing before the Mongol invasion who settled in Damascus (A.D. 1221) and died in 630/1232.

[3] French edition, iii. 79–80.

[4] An Egyptian Rifā'ī gave the writer a demonstration of snake- and scorpion-charming which was simply jugglery. He also offered to teach for a consideration the formula of Ibn ar-Rifā'ī, which he guaranteed to ensure infallible protection against snake-bite. Lane (*Modern Egyptians*, Everyman edn., p. 460) refers to members of the Sa'diyya branch eating snakes, but this would be a similar process of disappearance into the mouth.

[5] Aflākī gives an account (tr. Huart, i. 196–7) of the installation in Qonya of a Ḥaidarī named Ḥājjī Mubārak, as shaikh of an establishment called Dār adh-Dhākirīn, when there were present, besides *fuqarā'* and *akhīs*, the dignitaries of the state. On this occasion Jalāl ad-dīn Rūmī excelled himself in the dance of the spheres.

[6] Ibn Baṭṭūṭa, tr. Gibb, ii. 274–5, and French edn., iii. 439 (Tibet).

[7] K. A. Nizami, *Religion and Politics in India during the Thirteenth Century*, Bombay, 1961, pp. 286–7.

[8] See H. Sauvaire, 'Description de Damas', *J. Asiat*, sér. IX, v. 387–9, 404. A notable disciple of al-Ḥarīrī, Najm ad-dīn M. b. Isrā'īl (A.H. 603–77), who is given a notice in *Fawāt al-Wafāyāt* (ii. 269), received his *khirqa* from Shihāb ad-dīn as-Suhrawardī. Ḥasan al-Jawālīqī, a Persian qalandarī who founded a *zāwiya* just outside Cairo, later went to 'Alī al-Ḥarīrī's *zāwiya* in Damascus and died there in 622/1225; Maqrīzī, *Khiṭaṭ*, ed. Cairo, A.H. 1326, iv. 301.

He was a noted Malāmatī who was imprisoned under al-Ashraf (A.D. 1228–37), but was released by Aṣ-Ṣāliḥ Ismā'īl on condition that he kept away from Damascus. Another branch in Damascus (Zāwiya Ṭālibiyya) was founded by Ṭālib ar-Rifā'ī (d. 683/1284).[1] Other Syrian branches were the Sa'diyya or Jibāwiyya[2] and the Ṣayyādiyya.[3] There was a *zāwiya* in Jerusalem.[4] It spread into Anatolia among Turks and Ibn Baṭṭūṭa lodged frequently in Aḥmadī (as he calls the Rifā'īs) establishments.[5] One *zāwiya* he visited in Machar, had seventy *fuqarā'*, of varied origins, Arabs, Persians, Turks, and Greeks.[6] A group was even found in the Maldive island of Mahal.[7]

It is probably true to say that until the fifteenth century the Rifā'iyya was the most widespread of all *ṭarīqas*, but from that century it began to loose its popularity in favour of the Qādiriyya, which expanded as a *ṭarīqa*, though never to the extent that is so often claimed.

(*c*) *Qādiriyya*

It is difficult to penetrate through the mists of legend which formed even during the lifetime of 'Abd al-Qādir ibn Abī Ṣāliḥ Jangīdōst and thickened rapidly after his death,[8] and to discern

[1] See *J. Asiat.* IX. v. 394.

[2] See below, p. 73.

[3] Founded by 'Izz ad-dīn Aḥmad aṣ-Ṣayyād (*ḥafid* A. b. ar-Rifā'ī), d. 670/1273. On him and his successors see Muḥammad Abu 'l-Hudā aṣ-Ṣayyādī (1850–1909), *Tanwīr al-abṣār fī ṭabaqāt as-sādat ar-Rifā'iyya*, Cairo, A.H. 1306.

[4] Mujīr ad-dīn, *Uns*, tr. Sauvaire, 1876, p. 167.

[5] See *Travels*, tr. Gibb, ii. 436, 445, 449. Aflākī has an account (tr. Huart, ii. 203) of how Tāj ad-dīn, great-grandson of Aḥmad ar-Rifā'ī, visited Qonya accompanied by a group of dervishes who intrigued the whole population with their extraordinary performances. Tāj ad-dīn it seems settled in Anatolia, since Ibn Baṭṭūṭa reports on his coming to Umm 'Abīda to receive the investiture; tr. Gibb, ii. 273. Taqī ad-dīn al-Wāsiṭī says that he accompanied Tāj ad-dīn Abū Bakr ar-Rifā'ī, shaikh Riwāq Umm 'Abīda, on the pilgrimage in the year 720/1321; *Tiryāq al-muḥibbīn*, p. 72.

[6] Tr. H. A. R. Gibb, ii. 479; 1928 edn., i. 211.

[7] Paris edn., 1879, iv. 141.

[8] The most elaborate biography of 'Abd al-Qādir, which completely obscures his personality and presents him as a great miracle-monger, *Bahjat al-Asrār* by 'Alī ibn Yūsuf ash-Shaṭṭanawfī (d. 713/1314), was written over a hundred years after his death (A.D. 1166). The shorter and still later notice of adh-Dhahabī (d. 748/1348), but based on Ibn an-Najjār, edited and translated by D. S. Margoliouth (*J.R.A.S.* 1907, 267–310), is more valuable because he adopts a critical attitude and is sceptical of the more extravagant type of miracles ascribed to 'Abd al-Qādir. Of the former treatise adh-Dhahabī writes: 'The Shaikh Nūr ad-dīn al-Shaṭṭanaufī the Mukri composed a lengthy work in three volumes on

why he, out of the hundreds of saintly figures of the period, survived in a unique way to become the inspirer of millions, a heavenly receiver of petitions and bestower of benefits, right up to the present day. Vast numbers have accorded him a devotion which evoked the condemnation of orthodoxy, yet he himself was a strict Ḥanbalī, who would never have made such claims. He is acclaimed as a great preacher, but his reputation was certainly not gained from the content of his sermons.[1] And as for his Sufi reputation there is not the slightest indication that he was a Sufi at all or that he struck any new note, and it seems likely that his reputation for soundness was used by others who were responsible for such developments as paved the way for ordinary people to participate in the insights and experiences of Sufis.

'Abd al-Qādir was born in Jīlān,[2] where Ḥanbalism was strong, in 470/1077. He came to Baghdad in A.H. 488 and pursued a legalistic course of Ḥanbalī training, refusing to study at the Niẓāmiyya where the Sufi, Aḥmad al-Ghazālī, had succeeded his brother Abū Ḥāmid. He received the *khirqa* of first investiture at the hands

his life and work, wherein he has produced milk with the cud equally, and has mixed with truth statements that are groundless and false, being told on the authority of persons of no worth. So they assert that the Shaikh took thirteen steps in the air off his pupil at a meeting; and that once when the Shaikh was discoursing and no-one was moved, he said, "You are not moved, and feel no pleasure. Ye lamps, manifest *your* delight!", whereupon the lamps moved about and the dishes danced' (tr. D. S. Margoliouth, loc. cit., p. 310).

A contemporary, Taqī ad-dīn 'Abd ar-Raḥmān al-Wāsiṭī (d. A.D. 1343), also attacks Shaṭṭanawfī's book as a tissue of lies. He mentions the names of authorities who claimed that he was a *kadhdhāb muttahim*, an indicted liar. Even though al-Wāsiṭī is an interested party since Ibn ar-Rifā'ī is his hero, his criticisms seem fair and sound enough. He shows that Shaṭṭanawfī's book has led to a distorted estimate of 'Abd al-Qādir himself, whose undoubted qualities are not enhanced by claiming that he was a Sufi subject to *aḥwāl* and a miracle-worker (*Tiryāq*, p. 51).

Still later works include al-Yāfi'ī (d. 768/1367), *Khulāṣat al-mafākhir fi 'khtiṣār manāqib ash-Shaikh 'Abd al-Qādir* and the notice in his *Mir'āt al-jinān*, iii. 347–66. Ibn Khallikān (d. A.D. 1282) did not consider him important enough to include in his 'Obituaries' and M. ibn Shākir's (d. A.H. 764) account in his 'Omissions from the Obituaries' (Bulaq, 1283/1866, ii. 2–3) contains nothing of interest.

[1] See *al-Fatḥ ar-Rabbānī*, a collection of 62 sermons delivered in A.H. 545–6. His most important works are the collection of 78 of his discourses under the title of *Futūḥ al-Ghaib* (tr. W. Braune, Leipzig, 1933) and a treatise on legalistic ethics and theology entitled *Al-Ghunya li ṭālibī ṭarīq al-Ḥaqq*, Cairo, 1322/1905.

[2] He was a Persian and when he visited the Baṭā'iḥ during his wanderings he was known as al-'Ajamī. Al-Wāsiṭī says that none of the genealogists supported his claim to a Ḥasanī nasab (*Tiryāq*, p. 50).

of the Ḥanbalī *faqih*, Abu Saʿd ʿAlī al-Mukharrimī, 'by order of al-Khaḍir', but there is no indication that he received any Sufi training until he attended the school of Abu 'l-Khair Ḥammād ad-Dabbās (d. 525/1131),[1] to the disgust of Dabbās's other pupils who resented the intrusion of this Hanbalī. After this he seems to have spent some twenty-five years as a wandering ascetic in the deserts of Iraq. Only in 521/1127 when he was over fifty years old did he suddenly come into prominence as a popular preacher in Baghdad.[2] From that date his reputation grew, but as a Ḥanbalī preacher, not as a Sufi. He dressed like an *ʿālim*, not like a Sufi. A *madrasa* with an attached *ribāṭ* as a residence for himself, his large family, and pupils was specially built for him (A.H. 528), but there is no evidence that he ever claimed to have a Path or guided anyone or initiated anybody. No Sufis ascribed themselves to him but to such men as Aḥmad al-Ghazālī, Abu Najīb as-Suhrawardī, and Abu Yūsuf al-Hamadānī. Taqī ad-dīn al-Wāsiṭī wrote:

> ʿAbd al-Qādir was renowned during his lifetime for his sermons and courses of religious instruction, but he never at any time propagated any *khirqat at-taṣawwuf*. However, after his death, with the passage of time, certain people were given his *khirqa*, then it grew through his *baraka* and expanded through highland and lowland . . . The only two of his children who did not pursue a secular career were ʿAbd ar-Razzāq [A.H. 528–603] and ʿAbd al-ʿAzīz [d. A.H. 602]. These two shaikhs set to work to propagate their father's Way in all sincerity, temperance and modesty, and in that movement they were assisted by certain godly and sympathetic associates of their father.[3]

Because it was suspect ʿAbd al-Qādir's *silsila* rarely figures in other than Qādirī lines, for instance, in the attributions in Sanūsī's *Salsabīl*.[4] The order attributed to him produced few famous Sufis

[1] Ibn al-Athīr, xi. 80; M. b. Shākir, *Fawāt al-wafāyāt*, ii. 3; al-Wāsiṭī, *Tiryāq*, p. 54; al-Yāfiʿī, *Mirʾāt al-jinān*, iii. 242.

[2] It is noteworthy that his biographers give no indication that he had any contact, let alone training, with any of the great Sufis of the day, except for one story of his appealing to Yūsuf al-Hamadānī (visited Baghdad in 506/1112; Ibn al-Athīr, x. 496–7), and this very account shows his lack of Sufi training. The story goes that ʿAbd al-Qādir, troubled by inner voices ordering him to go out and preach, consulted Yūsuf al-Hamadānī, 'the Quṭb of the Age'. Yūsuf told him: 'Since you possess the light of *fiqh* and the Qur'ān, you can now preach to the people. Hesitate no longer! Mount the pulpit!'

[3] Al-Wāsiṭī, *Tiryāq*, pp. 53–4.

[4] We read in Ibn Khallikān (ii. 440) of *fuqarā'* tracing themselves (*al-muntasibūn ilaihi*) to Aḥmad ar-Rifāʿī, but no such attributions to ʿAbd al-Qādir.

or Sufi works; the *awrād*, teaching and other material found in Qādirī manuals, being largely borrowed. His later followers attributed to him a line of mystery teaching he could not possibly have taught. An inspired Qādirī would attribute to his master the miracles he ought to have done and the overflowings he experienced when in a state of *jadhb*; things like the interesting divine questionnaire called *al-Ghawthiyya* or *al-Mi'rājiyya*.[1]

According to Shaṭṭanawfī[2] 'Abd al-Qādir's pupils taught his *madhhab* (system) in various parts of the Islamic world, 'Alī al-Ḥaddād in Yemen, Muḥammad al-Baṭā'iḥī in Syria, and Muḥammad ibn 'Abd aṣ-Ṣamad in Egypt. This is unlikely since 'Abd al-Qādir left no system, let alone Path, to be introduced, and even the *Bahja*, as Margoliouth has pointed out,[3] does not support the claim that his sons propagated his Way throughout the Muslim world. Although Qādirī centres existed in Iraq and Syria in A.D. 1300, nothing indicates that it spread at all widely or rapidly before the fifteenth century. In the course of time a body of rules, teaching, and practice was formed,[4] and some shaikhs began to initiate their pupils into his name because his fame as an intercessor was spreading. In Iraq it remained a local Baghdadi *ṭā'ifa*,[5] centred upon his tomb-mosque which suffered a number of destructions until Ottoman patronage restored the local influence of the family. It gained greater influence at a later period among Kurds.

Although 'Abd al-Qādir became the most universally popular *saint*, to whom many *maqāms* were erected, we must stress that the Qādirī *ṭarīqa* never became popular. Its spread as a Way belongs to the *ṭā'ifa* stage discussed in the next chapter, but it might be useful to bring together here some references to propagators. The foundation of the first Qādirī *zāwiya* (Da'ūdiyya) in Damascus in the early fifteenth century has been mentioned.[6]

[1] See Ismā'īl ibn M. Sa'īd, *Al-Fuyūḍāt ar-Rabbāniyya*, Cairo, A.H. 1353, pp. 4–12.

[2] Shaṭṭanawfī, *Bahja*, Cairo edn., 1304, pp. 101, 109–10.

[3] *E.I.*[1] ii. 609.

[4] According to tradition music and the rhythmic dance were not introduced until the time of 'Abd al-Qādir's great-grandson, Shams ad-dīn.

[5] There are references to the family in the chronicles of Baghdad, such as al-Mustanṣir's appointment of one of them as shaikh of a newly-built *ribāṭ* in 626/1229; Ibn al-Fuwaṭī, *al-Ḥawādith al-jāmi'a*, Baghdad, A.H. 1351, pp. 2, 86–7, but few references to its influence elsewhere. The Mongol conquest put an end to any fame the tomb had acquired and when that assiduous tomb visitor Ibn Baṭṭūṭa went to Baghdad in 727/1326 he makes no mention of it.

[6] See above, p. 21, n. 5.

In Egypt it has never been a popular order. In India it did not become an established order until the arrival of Muḥammad Ghawth (d. A.D. 1517), who claimed descent from ʿAbd al-Qādir, and even then it remained localized. The author of *Ā'īn-i Akbarī*,[1] writing about A.D. 1600, does not include the *ṭarīqa* among the orders represented in India. Around A.D. 1550 it was introduced from Hijaz into the Funj state of the two Niles by Tāj ad-dīn al-Bahārī al-Baghdādī.[2] During the Turkish expansion in Asia Minor there is no evidence that the Qādirī as a distinct line of ascription was represented among the multitudes of dervishes carving out their niches of holiness within the religious eclecticism of that region. The order was only introduced in any definitive fashion into Istanbul through the energetic initiative of Ismāʿīl Rūmī (d. 1041/1631 or 1053/1643), who founded a *khānaqāh* at Tōp-khāneh. He is called *Pīr Thānī* (second master), which implies that he was the first to introduce it (the first master, of course, was ʿAbd al-Qādir), and he is said to have founded some 40 (or 48) *tekkēs* in the region.[3]

2. EGYPT AND THE MAGHRIB

Egypt and the Maghrib constitute a special zone, since most orders founded in these regions, mainly in the next phase when in the Maghrib they underwent a unique development, did not spread far beyond their confines, or at least outside Africa. Further, the Sufis of the region contributed little during the formative period to the doctrines and method of *taṣawwuf*.

A number of eminent Sufis were Egyptians, at least by adoption: Dhū 'n-Nūn (d. A.D. 860), whose father came from the Nubian stretch, the greatest Arab Sufi poet, ʿUmar ibn al-Fāriḍ (d. A.D. 1234), of Syrian parentage but born and lived in Egypt,[4] and al-Būṣīrī (d. A.D. 1296), important because of his influence

[1] Abu 'l-Faḍl al-ʿAllāmī, *Ā'īn-i Akbarī*, tr. H. S. Jarrett, new edition, 1948, iii. 398.

[2] *Ṭabaqāt* of Wad Ḍaif Allāh, ed. Mandīl, pp. 42–3; ed. Ṣidaiq, pp. 44–5.

[3] J. von Hammer-Purgstall, *Histoire de l'Empire Ottoman*, ed. J. J. Hellert, Paris, 1835–43, xviii. 77. Among the hundreds of convents mentioned by Evliya Chelebi very few are Qādirī; references in von Hammer's translation under the title of *Narrative of Travels in Europe, Asia and Africa by Evliya Effendi*, London, 1834–50, I. ii. 59, 81; II. 8, 213.

[4] Some of Ibn al-Fāriḍ's poems were composed for singing at Sufi ecstasy concerts; see C. A. Nallino, *Raccolta di Scritti*, ii. 205–6.

upon popular piety. Though few schools of mystical insight had their origin in Egypt, the cities abounded with *khānaqāhs* which welcomed Sufis from both East and West. Such *khānaqāhs*, however, were urban and professional institutions and had little effect upon the spiritual life of *fallāḥīn*.

Egypt became the elected home of ash-Shādhilī, the chief centre from which his teaching spread, to become eventually one of the great Ways. Two Egyptian *ṭarīqa* founders whose orders survived were Aḥmad al-Badawī and Ibrāhīm ad-Dasūqī. Aḥmad al-Badawī (b. 596/1199) was an Egyptian by adoption, for he belonged to an Arab family which had emigrated to Fez and then returned to the Hijaz.[1] He was originally a Rifāʿī and received his training at the centre in the Baṭā'iḥ of Iraq. On the death in 632/1234 of Abu 'l-Fatḥ al-Wāsiṭī, *khalīfa* of Aḥmad ar-Rifāʿī, former *murshid* of ash-Shādhilī and from A.H. 620 Rifāʿī representative in Egypt, the ʿIrāqī brethren sent Aḥmad to take his place.[2] He settled in Ṭanṭa, won great renown, and received divine authority to found his own Way. He died in 675/1276 and his tomb at Ṭanṭa was to become the most famous sanctuary and place of *ziyāra* in Egypt. His order, known as the Aḥmadiyya but better referred to as the Badawiyya to avoid confusion with other orders of the same name, gave rise to a number of branches,[3] not confined to Egypt, for it spread into Hijaz, Syria, Turkey, Tripolitania, and Tunisia.

Ibrāhīm ibn Abī 'l-Majd ad-Dasūqī (*c.* 644/1246–687/1288) was no *khānaqāh* Sufi but came from the soil of the Nile banks, being born in a village into a *baraka*-inheriting family and deriving his *nisba* from another village with which he was associated. Ash-Shaʿrānī's considerable notice on him[4] consists mainly of quotations from his *Jawāhir*, a book of instructions to *murīds*, and little is known about his life. He is shown to have been initiated into the Suhrawardī,[5] Rifāʿī, and Badawī chains, and then received

[1] Ash-Shaʿrānī gives an account of his life and *dicta* transmitted by his brother Ḥasan; *aṭ-Ṭabaqāt al-kubrā*, Cairo, A.H. 1355, i. 158–63.

[2] He received his *nisba* of al-Badawī through having arrived in Egypt wearing Arab dress. Later he was called *al-Mulaththam*, 'the Muffled', but it is unlikely that he was a Ṣanhājī Berber. Ash-Shaʿrānī (op. cit. i. 160, l. 16) says he wore the two *lithāms* (of the eastern Arabs) from childhood.

[3] A list of these branches is given in Appendix E.

[4] Ash-Shaʿrānī, *aṭ-Ṭabaqāt al-Kubrā*, A.H. 1355, i. 143–58.

[5] Association with Najm ad-dīn Maḥmūd al-Iṣfahānī? al-Wāsiṭī, *Tiryāq*, p. 61.

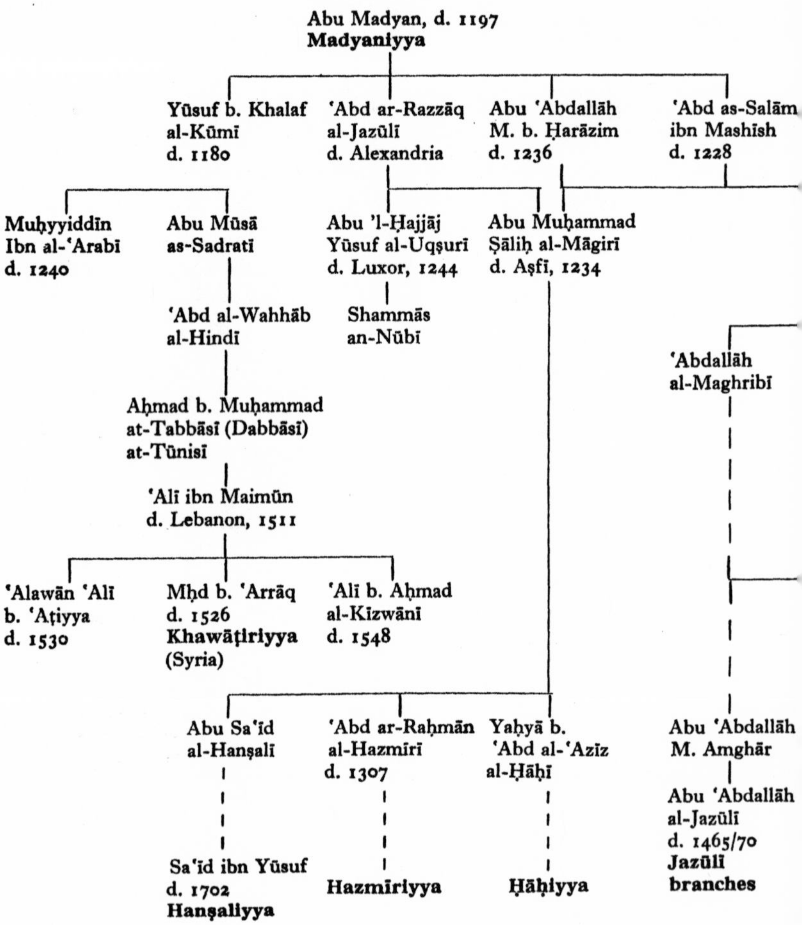
Abu Madyan, d. 1197
Madyaniyya
Yūsuf b. Khalaf al-Kūmī d. 1180
ʿAbd ar-Razzāq al-Jazūlī d. Alexandria
Abu ʿAbdallāh M. b. Ḥarāzim d. 1236
ʿAbd as-Salām ibn Mashīsh d. 1228
Muḥyyiddīn Ibn al-ʿArabī d. 1240
Abu Mūsā as-Sadratī
Abu ʾl-Ḥajjāj Yūsuf al-Uqṣurī d. Luxor, 1244
Abu Muḥammad Ṣāliḥ al-Māgirī d. Aṣfī, 1234
ʿAbd al-Wahhāb al-Hindī
Shammās an-Nūbī
ʿAbdallāh al-Maghribī
Aḥmad b. Muḥammad at-Tabbāsī (Dabbāsī) at-Tūnisī
ʿAlī ibn Maimūn d. Lebanon, 1511
ʿAlawān ʿAlī b. ʿAṭiyya d. 1530
Mḥd b. ʿArrāq d. 1526 **Khawāṭiriyya** (Syria)
ʿAlī b. Aḥmad al-Kīzwānī d. 1548
Abu Saʿīd al-Hanṣalī
ʿAbd ar-Raḥmān al-Hazmīrī d. 1307
Yaḥyā b. ʿAbd al-ʿAzīz al-Ḥāḥī
Abu ʿAbdallāh M. Amghār
Abu ʿAbdallāh al-Jazūlī d. 1465/70 **Jazūlī branches**
Saʿīd ibn Yūsuf d. 1702 **Hanṣaliyya**
Hazmīriyya
Ḥāḥiyya

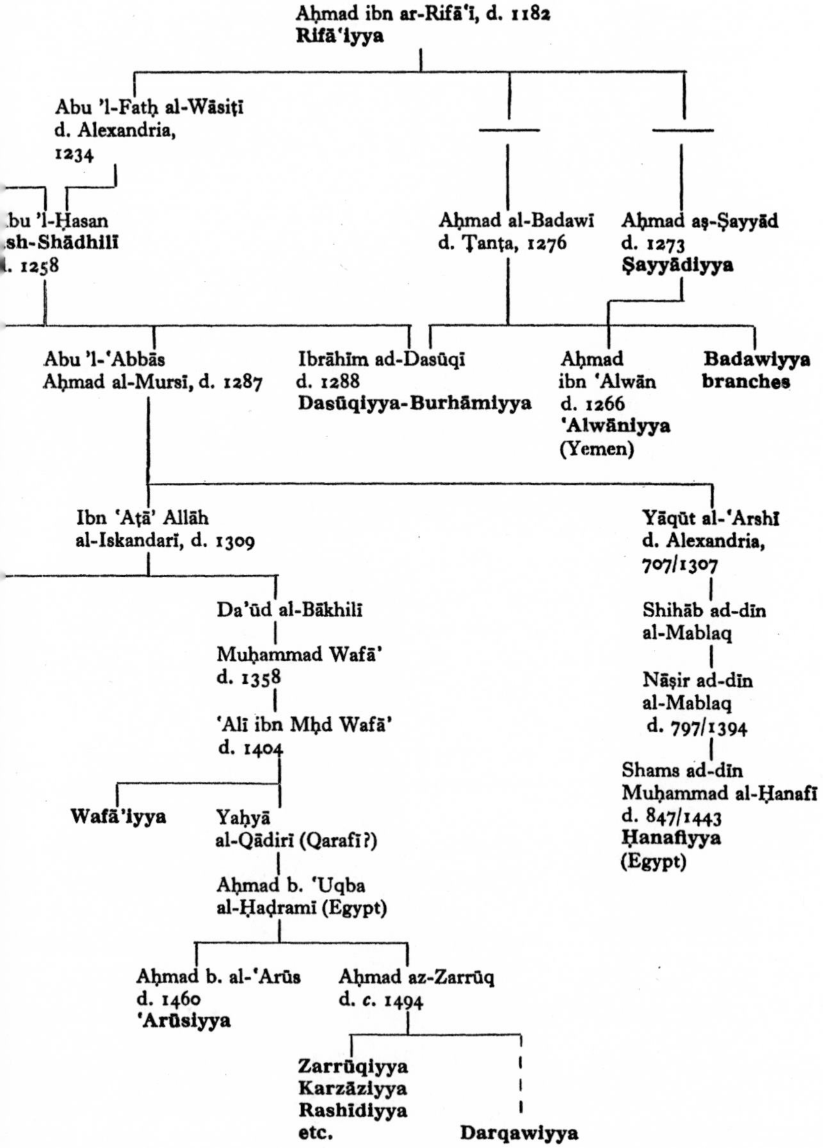
Aḥmad ibn ar-Rifā'ī, d. 1182
Rifā'iyya
Abu 'l-Fatḥ al-Wāsiṭī
d. Alexandria,
1234
.bu 'l-Ḥasan
.sh-Shādhilī
.. 1258
Aḥmad al-Badawī
d. Ṭanṭa, 1276
Aḥmad aṣ-Ṣayyād
d. 1273
Ṣayyādiyya
Abu 'l-'Abbās
Aḥmad al-Mursī, d. 1287
Ibrāhīm ad-Dasūqī
d. 1288
Dasūqiyya-Burhāmiyya
Aḥmad
ibn 'Alwān
d. 1266
'Alwāniyya
(Yemen)
Badawiyya
branches
Ibn 'Aṭā' Allāh
al-Iskandarī, d. 1309
Yāqūt al-'Arshī
d. Alexandria,
707/1307
Da'ūd al-Bākhilī
Shihāb ad-dīn
al-Mablaq
Muḥammad Wafā'
d. 1358
Nāṣir ad-dīn
al-Mablaq
d. 797/1394
'Alī ibn Mḥd Wafā'
d. 1404
Shams ad-dīn
Muḥammad al-Ḥanafī
d. 847/1443
Ḥanafiyya
(Egypt)
Wafā'iyya
Yaḥyā
al-Qādirī (Qarafī?)
Aḥmad b. 'Uqba
al-Ḥaḍramī (Egypt)
Aḥmad b. al-'Arūs
d. 1460
'Arūsiyya
Aḥmad az-Zarrūq
d. c. 1494
Zarrūqiyya
Karzāziyya
Rashīdiyya
etc.
Darqawiyya

permission to found an independent *ṭarīqa*. This was known as the Ibrahīmiyya until the ninth century A.H. when adherents began calling themselves Dasūqīs. It was also known as the Burhāniyya from his *laqab* Burhān ad-dīn. Like the Badawiyya it split into independent groups and spread outside Egypt to Syria, Hijaz, Yemen, and Hadramawt.

Sufism was slow in spreading into the Maghrib,[1] but in spite of the kind of Mālikī and official obscurantism which had led to the promulgation of a *fatwā* condemning and banning al-Ghazālī's works (503/1109) it gained a foothold during the Almoravid period (A.D. 1056–1147) and even flourished under the Almohades (A.D. 1130–1269). In Spain, although there was the brief flowering associated with Ibn Masarra (A.D. 883–931) and his pupils, Sufism could not thrive openly in the atmosphere of intolerance and suspicion that prevailed there. Eminent Sufis of the age were the Ṣanhājī Abu 'l-'Abbās Aḥmad, known as Ibn al-'Arīf (A.D. 1088–1141), whose disciple, Abu 'l-Qāsim ibn Qasiyy, demonstrated how easily spiritual power can aspire to mundane power when he rose from his *ribāṭ* of Silvas (A.D. 1141) and subjected a large section of Algarves region (southern Portugal) before he was killed in 546/1151. The greatest Sufi to come out of Spain was, of course, Ibn al-'Arabī (A.D. 1165–1240), but he was of Arab origin and a universal figure, against whose doctrines Mālikī literalism imposed, successfully for the most part, a barrier of condemnation.

In enduring influence in relation to subsequent *ṭarīqa* development the greatest of the early Sufis was Abu Madyan Shu'aib b. al-Ḥusain (A.D. 1126–98).[2] Born near Seville he moved as a young man to Fez, where he was attracted to the pursuit of the mystic Way and was initiated by Muḥammad ad-Daqqāq and Abu Ya'azza (d. A.D. 1176), the latter a crude non-Arabic-speaking Berber. He went on pilgrimage and travelled to Iraq, where he

[1] Al-Maqdisī (ed. de Goeje, 1906, p. 238) says that there was not a single *khānaqāh* of the Karrāmiyya in the Maghrib in his time (about A.D. 970) and assuredly none of the Ṣūfiyya.

[2] Biographies of the Maghribī mystics of this period are given in the collections of Ibn az-Zayyāt at-Tādilī, *At-Tashawwuf ilā rijāl at-Taṣawwuf*, written around 617/1220, and 'Abd al-Ḥaqq al-Bādisī, *Al-Maqṣad*, written *c.* 711/1311, tr. G. S. Colin in *Archives Marocaines*, xxvi (1926). Colin points out (p. 11 and n.) that only one of the holy men mentioned in the *Maqṣad* and none of the 260 in the *Tashawwuf* is qualified by the title of *sharif*, a title without which holiness was impossible to achieve in the Maghrib at a later date.

met Aḥmad ar-Rifā'ī, ties of fraternity and extrasensory contact being established between them.[1] On his return he settled at Bougie (Bijāya). His teaching and reputation stirred the envy and opposition of the Almohade *'ulamā'*; he was summoned to the capital Marrākush to give an account of himself and died on the way at the village of 'Ubbād (presumably a centre of 'devotees') near Tilimsān.

Although a distinctive Madyanī Way derives from him and he was the master of the twelfth-century Sufis of western Islam, relatively few Madyanī *ṭā'ifas* came into being. A number of Abu Madyan's spiritual sons and grandsons went to Egypt and gained great fame there.[2] These included Abu 'l-Ḥajjāj Yūsuf, a former customs officer, who founded a *zāwiya* at Luxor in the ruins of the Temple of Amun where he died (642/1244) and whose *mawlid* there became the most famous in upper Egypt.[3] Another was Abu 'l-Ḥajjāj's master, 'Abd ar-Razzāq al-Jazūlī, who went to live in the *zāwiya* ascribed to Dhū 'n-Nūn at Akhmīm and then Alexandria where he is buried. Other western Sufis who found a more congenial spiritual home in the East were the Andalusians Ibn al-'Arabī (d. Damascus 638/1240), Ibn Sab'īn (d. Mecca 669/1270), and the latter's disciple the poet Shushtarī (d. 668/1269 near Damietta), a Madyanī by mystical ascription, who wrote short *muwashshaḥāt* poems which have continued to be popular in Shādhilī *ḥadras* to this day.[4] In Jerusalem there is a *zāwiya* founded by a grandson of Abu Madyan situated near Bāb as-Silsila of the Ḥaram ash-Sharīf which still survives.

Abu Madyan's Way was perpetuated through his pupil, 'Abd as-Salām ibn Mashīsh (d. 625/1228), and the latter's most eminent disciple, Abu 'l-Ḥasan 'Alī ash-Shādhilī, whose Way, called the Shādhiliyya, was to become the most important in north Africa

[1] See Ibn Baṭṭūṭa, *Riḥla*, Cairo edn., 1928, i. 59.

[2] Sha'rānī says (*Lawāqiḥ*, ii. 19, l. 27) that Abu Madyan himself sent many of his followers to Egypt. These included the son, Madyan, from whom he derives his *kunya*. The site of his tomb is mentioned; op. cit., i. 133.

[3] On Abu 'l-Ḥajjāj al-Uqṣurī see al-Bādisī, *Maqṣad* (pp. 153–7), where his successor, a Nubian of Christian origin, Shammās an-Nūbī, and other 'companions' are named. Sha'rānī has a notice on him in *Lawāqiḥ* (i. 136–7), and Ibn Baṭṭūṭa visited his tomb (i. 107). Another immigrant Berber was 'Abd ar-Raḥīm at-Targhī (d. at Qena, 592/1196), master of Abu 'l-Ḥasan 'Ali b. aṣ-Ṣabbāgh al-Qūsī (d. at Qena, 613/1216).

[4] Commentaries on these poems have appeared in Madyanī circles, e.g. the Syrian, 'Alawān 'Alī b. 'Aṭiyya (d. A.D. 1530), *an-Nafaḥat al-qudsiyya fi sharḥ al-abyāt ash-Shushtariyya*; see Ibn al-'Imād, *Shadharāt*, viii. 218.

from Morocco to Egypt and also to gain a following in Syria and Arabia.

This Abu 'l-Ḥasan, born in the village of Ghumāra in the far West in 593/1196, received his first *khirqa* from Abu 'Abdallāh M. b. Ḥarāzim (d. 633/1236), a pupil of Abu Madyan. He went east in A.H. 615, where he was drawn to the Rifā'ī school, accepting Abu 'l-Fatḥ al-Wāsiṭī as his shaikh (A.D. 618). He became obsessed with the search for the *Quṭb* (Pivot) of the universe[1] and Abu 'l-Fatḥ told him to return to the West where he would find him. He returned and eventually found him in 'Abd as-Salām ibn Mashīsh of Fez who 'prepared him for the *walāya*'.[2] Later, on the advice of 'Abd as-Salām, he left Morocco to go into retreat in a cave near a village of Ifrīqiya called Shādhila, whence derives his *nisba*. Periodically he went out on preaching and teaching tours, thereby incurring the hostility of the Tunisian '*ulamā*'. So bitter did the persecution become that, in spite of the support of the sultan, Abu Zakariyyā al-Ḥafṣī, he was driven to take refuge in Egypt, where he won great renown, not only among the populace, but surprisingly enough even with '*ulamā*'. He made a practice of going on *ḥajj* every year and he died at Ḥumaithrā on the Red Sea coast whilst on the way back from one of them in 656/1258.[3]

We have said that it is usually impossible to pierce through the mists of pious legend to the real men beneath. A few letters of Abu 'l-Ḥasan have survived which show him as a very human shaikh, a leader of pilgrimages, whose personal dedication did not weaken his concern for the welfare of his followers. But in addition they enable us to discern how he and other *ṭarīqa* leaders were able to become the inspirers of enduring systems. This correspondence is inaccessible to me but here is a testimony to its value from P. Nwyia:

> This correspondence shows not only that Shādhilī had a deep knowledge of the Sufi teaching of the eastern doctors, but a personal experience of spiritual realities. If Shādhilī knew how to inspire his disciples it was not so much that he preached to them a simple Sufism as because he had the qualities of a spiritual master as is revealed by his letters. He certainly formed no intellectual system, but he had qualities of

[1] See Aḥmad b. M. b. 'Abbād, *Al-Mafākhir al-'Aliyya*, Cairo, A.H. 1327, p. 10; and for the *Quṭb* see below, pp. 163–5.

[2] *Walāya* used in this way has the sense of 'spiritual office or jurisdiction'.

[3] See Ibn Baṭṭūṭa, 1939 edn., i. 42.

spiritual discernment and knew how to extract from his personal experiences what was valuable to others.[1]

Abu 'l-Ḥasan as a shaikh *sā'iḥ* or 'vagabond ascetic' did not himself initiate his pupils into any special rule or ritual, but his teaching was maintained by his disciples. One disciple in particular, Abu 'l-'Abbās Aḥmad al-Mursī (616/1219–686/1287), Andalusian in origin, who joined his circle in Alexandria, was regarded as his successor, and a *ribāṭ* with a mosque was built for him. The existence of any Shādhilī *ṭarīqa* at all is due to al-Mursī and his successor, Tāj ad-dīn ibn 'Aṭā' Allāh 'Abbās (d. Cairo 709/1309),[2] who wrote an account of the life and sayings of both Abu 'l-Ḥasan and Abu 'l-'Abbās[3] and collected their *awrād*. Pupils carried on the Way of ash-Shādhilī in scattered *zāwiyas* having little connection with each other. In Ifrīqiya his name was kept alive by a small group of pupils with whom Abu 'l-Ḥasan had kept up a correspondence after he had been forced to leave the country.[4] An Egyptian derivative was the Wafā'iyya, founded by Shams ad-dīn M. ibn Aḥmad Wafā' (701/1301–760/1359),[5] whose son 'Alī (761/1357–807/1404) is one of the great names in Egyptian Sufism. The Wafā'iyya spread into Syria[6] and survived in Egypt into the present century.

[1] P. Nwyia, *Ibn 'Abbād de Ronda*, Beirut, 1958, p. 124.

[2] At least one Egyptian line, the Ḥanafiyya, came directly from al-Mursī; see Maghribī table of spiritual genealogies. On the founder, Muḥammad al-Ḥanafi (d. 847/1443), see Sha'rānī, *aṭ-Ṭabaqāt al-Kubrā*, ii. 81–92 (the ascription is on p. 82); 'Alī Mubārak, *Khiṭaṭ Jadīda*, iv. 99–102.

[3] *Laṭā'if al-minan*, by Tāj ad-dīn Aḥmad ibn 'Aṭā' Allāh al-Iskandarī, composed in A.D. 1284, printed on margin of ash-Sha'rānī, *Laṭā'if al-minan*, Cairo, A.H. 1357.

[4] Two of these wrote short lives of their master, which also include selections from his correspondence: Muḥammad ibn aṣ-Ṣabbāgh, *Kitāb durrat al-asrār wa tuḥfat al-abrār* (ed. Tunis), compiled about 720/1320; and 'Abd an-Nūr ibn M. al-'Imrānī, *Fī manāqib Abū 'l-Ḥasan ash-Shādhilī*, composed about 745/1344.

[5] On Muḥammad Wafā' (also known as M. Baḥr aṣ-Ṣafā) and his son 'Alī, well known for his *aḥzāb*, see Sha'rānī, *Aṭ-Ṭabaqāt al-kubrā*, ii. 19–60. He took the *ṭarīqa* from Da'ūd ibn Bākhilī and he from Ibn 'Aṭā' Allāh.

[6] Mujīr ad-dīn mentions a *zāwiya* in Jerusalem in his time (he died in 927/1521); see *al-Uns al-jalīl*, ii. 389; tr. Sauvaire, p. 147. He is to be distinguished from Abu 'l-Wafā' called Kākish (417/1026–501/1107). This Abu 'l-Wafā' was connected with the *khirqa* line founded by Abu Muḥammad 'Abdallāh Ṭalḥa ash-Shunbukī (tenth century), hence the double name given to it of Shunbukiyya-Wafā'iyya, which is one of the *silsilas* to which Ibn ar-Rifā'ī was connected. This 'Abdallāh converted the former highway robber Abu 'l-Wafā', who became so famous in the Baṭā'iḥ that he was nicknamed Tāj al-'Ārifīn,

Through the circulation of Ibn ʿAṭā' Allāh's works the Shādhilī Way began to spread in the Maghrib, which had rejected the master. But it remained an individualistic tradition, almost Malāmatī, though this term was not used, placing strong stress upon the cultivation of the interior life. Shādhilīs wore no habit (references to investment with the *khirqa* now begin to disappear), and no popular form of devotions was encouraged. It was made clear that *faqr* (poverty) meant no life of mendicity or complete withdrawal from normal life, rather the term refers to the interior life. This is brought out in order to point the contrast with the fifteenth-century Shādhilī movement to which the diffusion of Abu 'l-Ḥasan's *silsila* is largely due, a devotional movement which affected every family in the Maghrib.[1]

The period of the early Marīnids of Morocco (full dynastic span, 1195–1470) and early Ḥafṣids of Ifrīqiya (A.D. 1228–1534) was important for the flowering of western Sufism. Like the Seljuqs in the East, the Marīnids and Ḥafṣids paralleled the foundation of *madrasas* with patronage of Sufi leaders and their *zāwiyas*. The Marīnid, Abu 'l-Ḥasan, after his capture of Tilimsān in A.D. 1337, sponsored the development of a large establishment around the tomb of Abu Madyan by building a mosque, *madrasa*, public baths, and ancillary buildings. Thus *fiqh* and *taṣawwuf* became mutually tolerated companions. Sufism in the Maghrib, as also in Nilotic Sudan, became a subject for regular teaching compatible with the acquisition of legal sciences. This contrasts with their relationship in Arab Near East in general, where classical Sufism was just tolerated.

It is clear that a basic, continuative Madyanī tradition was maintained in the Maghrib quite distinct from the Shādhilī which was then more Egyptian than Maghribī, being known only

'Crown of the Gnostics'. On him see especially al-Wāsiṭī, *Tiryāq*, pp. 41–4; later accounts are found in collections like Shaʿrānī, *Lawāqiḥ*, A.H. 1355, i. 116. 'Abd al-Qādir al-Jīlānī is said 'to have frequented his *majlis* and benefited from his *baraka*', but was not initiated by him (*Tiryāq*, p. 42), nor was he regarded as one of Abu 'l-Wafā's star pupils: 'Someone said to Shaikh Baqā' ibn Baṭū, "O my lord, was there among the disciples of Abu 'l-Wafā' any man so carried away by the flashings of ecstasy as 'Abd al-Qādir al-Jīlī?" He replied, "By God's glory! there were ranged under the banner of Abu 'l-Wafā' seventeen sultans, everyone of them more perfect in ecstatic progression than 'Abd al-Qādir" ' (*Tiryāq*, p. 44).

[1] This is not to deny the existence of popular, even extravagant, *dhikr* devotions practised in common, but these seem to be localized when contrasted with their later profusion.

in Tunisia, and spreading only slowly westwards, not becoming popular until the fifteenth-century revival. Al-Wāsiṭī, writing in Iraq about A.D. 1320, calls the Madyanī tradition the Tilimsāniyya,[1] and *zāwiyas* associated with it provided the nuclei from which the popular movement began. Ibn Qunfudh in his *Uns al-faqīr*, composed in A.D. 1385 and principally concerned with the life of Abu Madyan, mentions[2] six *ṭā'ifas* in western Morocco. The Māgiriyyūn deriving from Abu Muḥammad Ṣāliḥ ibn (Yanṣāran) Sa'īd al-Māgirī (*c.* 550/1155–631/1234), a disciple of Abu Madyan, who spent twenty years in Alexandria and, on his return to Morocco to found a *ribāṭ* at Aṣfī, intensified the movement of pilgrims to the holy places. He wrote a *Talqīn al-wird* and had much to endure from the enmity of the *fuqahā'*.[3] At the end of the seventh/thirteenth century his order was in a state of confusion and a descendant, Aḥmad ibn Ibrāhīm al-Māgirī, wrote a life called *al-Minhāj al-wāḍiḥ* in order to preserve the name of the master from the charge of *bid'a* cast upon it by the Mālikī bigots, as well as to recount his *karāmāt* or manifestations of God's favour.

Other defined Berber groups included: the Shu'aibiyyūn, deriving from Abu Shu'aib Ayyūb b. Sa'īd, patron saint of Azammūr (d. A.D. 1165) and one of the masters of Abu Ya'azza; the Ḥāḥiyyūn, from Abu Zakariyā Yaḥyā al-Ḥāḥī; the Ghammātiyyun (or Aghmātiyya) or Hazmīriyya, from Abu Zaid 'Abd ar-Raḥmān al-Hazmīrī (d. A.D. 1307); a group of Banu Amghār known as Ṣanhājiyyūn, centred on the *ribāṭ* of Tīṭ-an-Fiṭr, founded around A.D. 1140; and a Ḥujjāj group, whose members were restricted to those who had accomplished the pilgrimage to Mecca.

3. IRANIAN, TURKISH, AND INDIAN SPHERES

In the Iranian world Sufis blended the two traditions of interior religion: that which came to be linked with the name of al-Junaid (Sufi: Mesopotamian), and that associated with Abu Yazīd

[1] Al-Wāsiṭī, *Tiryāq*, p. 49.

[2] References to these groups will be found in G. S. Colin's translation of the *Maqṣad* of al-Bādisī, *Archiv. Maroc.* xxvi (1926), 207–8; see also P. Nwyia, *Ibn 'Abbād de Ronda*, Beirut, 1958, pp. xxx–xxxi; A. Faure, art. 'Hazmīriyyūn', *E.I.*[2] iii. 338–9.

[3] See al-Bādisī, *Maqṣad*, pp. 92–3, 196.

al-Bisṭāmī (Malāmatī: Khurasanian).[1] Iranian Sufis tended to express greater individualism, divergent tendencies, and heterodox doctrines and practices, and consequently it was here that such tendencies are reflected in later orders. Many Sufis were strongly drawn towards 'Alī as the source of esoteric teaching, and Imāmī-Twelver (and to a lesser degree Ismā'īlī) ideas survived under the cloak of Sufism. Later, these were to come into the open and consolidate themselves in new orders (Dhahabiyya, Nūrbakhshiyya, Ni'matullāhiyya, and Bektāshiyya), or as with the Ṣafawiyya, whose head in the early sixteenth century became the master of Iran, actually change from a Sunnī to a Shī'ī order.

The accompanying tree of spiritual genealogies, which shows some aspects of the merging of the two traditions, serves at least to introduce the names of famous Sufis whose leadership and ideas were deeply to influence subsequent orders. Two significant figures in central Asian Sufi history were Abu 'l-Ḥasan 'Alī al-Kharaqānī (d. A.D. 1034 at the age of 80), who regarded himself as the spiritual heir of al-Bisṭāmī,[2] and Abu 'Alī al-Farmadhī (d. A.D. 1084). Two of the latter's pupils, important in that from them the chief lines of mystical ascription are derived, are Aḥmad al-Ghazālī (d. 520/1126), younger brother of the better-known Abu Ḥāmid, and Yūsuf al-Hamadānī (441/1049–535/1140). The name of Abu Ḥāmid al-Ghazālī has been inserted in the tree to show why he counts so little in the teaching as well as the ascriptions of the orders. He comes fully within our definition of a Sufi, but, though his mysticism of intellectual insight and understanding is acknowledged, he is not regarded as being a practising Sufi by the ecstatics and gnostics. Aflākī reports Jalāl ad-dīn Rūmī as commenting:

L'imām Moḥammed Ghazālī a nettoyé la mer de la science dans le monde des anges; il en a levé l'étandard; il est devenu le guide de l'univers et le savant des mortels. S'il avait eu un atome d'amour

[1] See al-Wāsiṭī, *Tiryāq*, p. 47. Other early Khurasanian shaikhs with strong Malāmatī tendencies included Yūsuf ibn al-Ḥusain ar-Rāzī (d. 301/913), Abu Ḥafṣ al-Ḥaddād (d. 265/879), and Abu 'Uthmān al-Hairī (d. 298/911).

[2] On al-Kharaqānī see E. Berthel's article in *Islamica*, iii. 5 ff.; Farīd ad-dīn 'Aṭṭār, *Tadhkirat al-awliyā'*, ed. R. A. Nicholson, 1905–7, ii. 201–55. De Beaurecueil has pointed out (*Khawādja 'Abdullāh Anṣārī*, Beirut, 1965, pp. 65–6) a number of traits which Kharaqānī and Bisṭāmī had in common; apart from the fact that they came from the same district, they were both illiterates who, on their own, without the supervision of any *murshid*, sought to follow the Way to God by direct divine guidance.

mystique comme Aḥmed Ghazālī, cela aurait mieux valu, et il aurait connu le mystère de la proximité mahométane, comme Aḥmed l'a connu, car il n'y a rien de pareil, dans l'Univers, à l'amour d'un maître, d'un directeur spirituel, d'un introducteur [des profanes auprès de la Divinité].[1]

The twelfth century was a period of transition in these regions towards a distinctively Persian Sufism, for which the way had been prepared by Sufi poets like Abu Sa'īd ibn Abī 'l-Khair (A.D. 967–1049).[2] With this movement Abu Ya'qūb Yūsuf al-Hamadānī al-Būzanjirdī (A.D. 1049–1140) is especially associated. He left his native Lūr-Kurd village in Hamadān province for Baghdad, where he studied *fiqh* under the famous Shāfi'ī jurist, Abu Isḥāq ash-Shīrāzī (d. A.D. 1083). He did brilliantly, especially devoting himself to *'ilm an-naẓar* (rationalism), and was put in

[1] Cl. Huart, *Les saints des derviches tourneurs*, 1918, i. 200. See also Ibn Sab'īn's very shrewd assessment of Abu Ḥāmid; Arabic text given by L. Massignon, *Recueil de textes inédits relatifs à la mystique musulmane*, Paris, 1929, pp. 129–31.

The most remarkable of Aḥmad's pupils, 'Abdallāh ibn M., commonly known as 'Ain al-Quḍāt al-Hamadānī, regarded the *Iḥyā'* as primarily a treatise on practical ethics. Although his reading of the *Iḥyā'* marks his transition from formal learning into Sufism 'Ain al-Quḍāt owed his release from spiritual impasse and subsequent Sufi training to Aḥmad al-Ghazālī. Enthusiastically indiscreet he ignored the Sufi injunction *Ifshā' sirr ar-rubūbiyya kufr* (it is impiety to reveal [to the commonalty] the secret of divine power), and after Aḥmad's death taught his inner doctrine openly. This led to his joining (in 525/1131 at the early age of 33) al-Ḥallāj and preceding as-Suhrawardī 'al-Maqtūl' of Aleppo on the roll of Sufi martyrs. It was for him that Aḥmad wrote his treatise 'Intuitions of the Lovers' (*Sawāniḥ al-'ushshāq*) which he (='Ain) paraphrased in Persian under the title *Lawā'iḥ* (ed. H. Ritter, *Aphorismen über die Liebe*, Istanbul/Leipzig, 1942: Bibliotheca Islamica, Bd. 15). 'Ain al-Quḍāt's remarkable defence in Arabic called *Shaqwā 'l-gharīb*, addressed to his friends whilst in prison, has been edited and translated by M. 'Abd al-Jalīl in *J. Asiat.* ccxvi (1930), 1–76, 193–297.

[2] Other early Sufi writers in Persian include the Hujwīrī to whose *Kashf* (composed around A.D. 1050) we have referred frequently, the *qalandarī* known as Bābā Ṭāhir (d. A.D. 1010), Abu 'l-Majd Sanā'ī (d. *c.* A.D. 1141) ,and Abu Ismā'īl 'Abdallāh al-Anṣārī al-Harawī (d. Herat, A.D. 1089). Harawī's Ḥanbalism was tempered and his outlook modified through his coming under the influence of Abu 'l-Ḥasan al-Kharaqānī. He headed a teaching circle in Herat; one who studied under him being Yūsuf al-Hamadānī. Strictly he should not have been included in the table of spiritual genealogies since he does not appear to have been a transmitting *murshid* and his name does not appear in *silsilas*. As well as his famous Sufi guide-book in Arabic, *Manāzil as-sā'irīn* (ed. and tr. S. de L. de Beaurecueil, Cairo, I.F.A.O., 1962), he wrote *Munājāt*, meditations in Persian *saj'* and verse, which is supposed to have influenced the composition of Sa'dī's *Būstān*.

charge of a class of students. Then suddenly 'he abandoned all the theoretical speculation to which he had been devoted and took himself off into retreat to prepare to dedicate himself to the things which really mattered—the personal life of devotion in God's service, to calling people to God, and to guiding his contemporaries along the right Path'.[1] He returned to Hamadān, then to Merv, dividing his time between there and Herāt. Many famous Sufis ascribed themselves to him, but from two of his *khalīfas* in particular spring two major lines of ascription, one Persian, derived from 'Abd al-Khāliq al-Ghujdawānī, the other Turkish, derived from Aḥmad al-Yasavī.

The Paths of these great central Asian Sufis, after taking root among Iranians, also took hold of the expanding Turks, and were an important factor in facilitating their adjustment to Islam. These ascriptions and tendencies spread with their dispersion, a process accelerated by the Mongol conquests, and became especially influential at the far extremes, in Anatolia and India. Aḥmad al-Yasavī stands as the prototype of all the Turkish Sufis, and from him derives Ḥājjī Bektāsh[2] as a kind of mythical symbol of hundreds of migrating Turkish *bābās*,[3] whose name served as the eponym of a famous *ṭarīqa*. The Yasavī tradition was strongly Turkish from the beginning. Aḥmad began his training under a Turkish shaikh, Arslān Bābā, after whose death he went to Bukhara, at that time still largely Iranian, to join Yūsuf al-Hamadānī's circle, becoming his *khalīfa* number four.[4] Later, he resigned his position to return to Turkestan to become the head of a group of Turkish-ascribed shaikhs (*sar-i silsila-i mashā'ikh-i Turk*).[5] A long line of Turkish mystics derive from his inspiration which, with the migration of *bābās*, spread among the Turks of Anatolia. Whereas the Mawlawiyya, which thrived in certain

[1] Ibn Khallikān (*Wafayāt*, Cairo, A.H. 1299, iii. 426) quoting Ibn an-Najjār (d. 643/1245), who in turn is quoting Abu Sa'd as-Sam'ānī (d. 562/1166), historian of Merv.

[2] Al-Wāsiṭī shows (*Tiryāq*, p. 47) that the derivation of the *khirqa* of Sayyid Bektāsh al-Khurasānī, *nazil bilād ar-Rūm*, from Aḥmad al-Yasavī was accepted in Iraq *c.* 1320.

[3] *Bābā* is the Turkish term for a missionary or popular preacher. *Ata* is an equally common designation and title for a holy man.

[4] His first *khalīfa* was 'Abd al-Khāliq, the second 'Abdallāh Barqī, and the third Abu Muḥammad Ḥasan al-Andāqī (d. A.D. 1157). It is highly unlikely that Aḥmad succeeded to the leadership of the Bukharan circle as Yasavī tradition asserts.

[5] 'Alī ibn Ḥusain al-Wā'iẓ, *Rashaḥāt 'ain al-ḥayāt*, pp. 8–9.

circles in Anatolia, belonged to the Iranian tradition, the Khalwatiyya derived from this central Asian Turkish tradition, but its treatment has been reserved for the next chapter.

Having inserted a genealogical table it may be well to remark that the lines of ascription up to this age do not imply the descent of *one rule*. Sufis still wandered about seeking masters, many did not transmit any one tradition, but formed their own Ways from their various sources of enlightenment. This is particularly the case with the order-founders. The difference after their establishment is that they become true *silsila-ṭarīqas*, that is to say, the line traced back through certain figures is consciously maintained. These chains of authority are often very complicated. Whilst that from the founder to the ancestor tends to become stable, the lines of each individual *khalīfa* back to the founder varied.

The main *ṭarīqas* emerging from the central Asian tradition which survived in some form were the Kubrāwiyya, Yasaviyya, Mawlawiyya, Naqshabandiyya, Chishtiyya, and Bektāshiyya. We will give a short account of the founder and the development of the tradition, with the exception of Ḥājjī Bektāsh, whose relationship to the order attributed to him is tenuous, whilst the order itself comes more appropriately into the next stage of development.

(*a*) *Kubrāwiyya*

From Najm ad-dīn Kubrā (540/1145–618/1221)[1] stem many chains of mystical ascription or derivative orders, mostly now defunct but important for the historical range of the orders and for their *sanads* of *dhikr* practices. Although born in Khīva (Khwārizm) Najm ad-dīn followed a course of ascetic discipline in Egypt under the Persian *shaikh-sā'iḥ*, Rūzbihān al-Wazzān al-Miṣrī (d. 584/1188), disciple of Abū Najīb as-Suhrawardī, from whom he received his first *khirqa*, but it was not until his search led him to Bābā Faraj of Tabrīz that he adopted the full Sufi life. Another teacher was ʿAmmār ibn Yāsir al-Bidlīsī (d. *c*. A.D. 1200), but his real training took place under Ismāʿīl al-Qaṣrī (d. 589/1193), who gave him the *khirqa* of *tabarruk*. He settled eventually in his native Khwārizm and built a *khānaqāh* in which he trained a number of remarkable men, including Majd ad-dīn al-Baghdādī[2]

[1] On Najm ad-dīn Kubrā see F. Meier's edition of his *Fawā'iḥ al-jamāl wa fawātiḥ al-jalāl* (Wiesbaden, 1957) which contains a valuable study of his life and thought.

[2] The *nisba* probably relates to Baghdādak in Khwārizm.

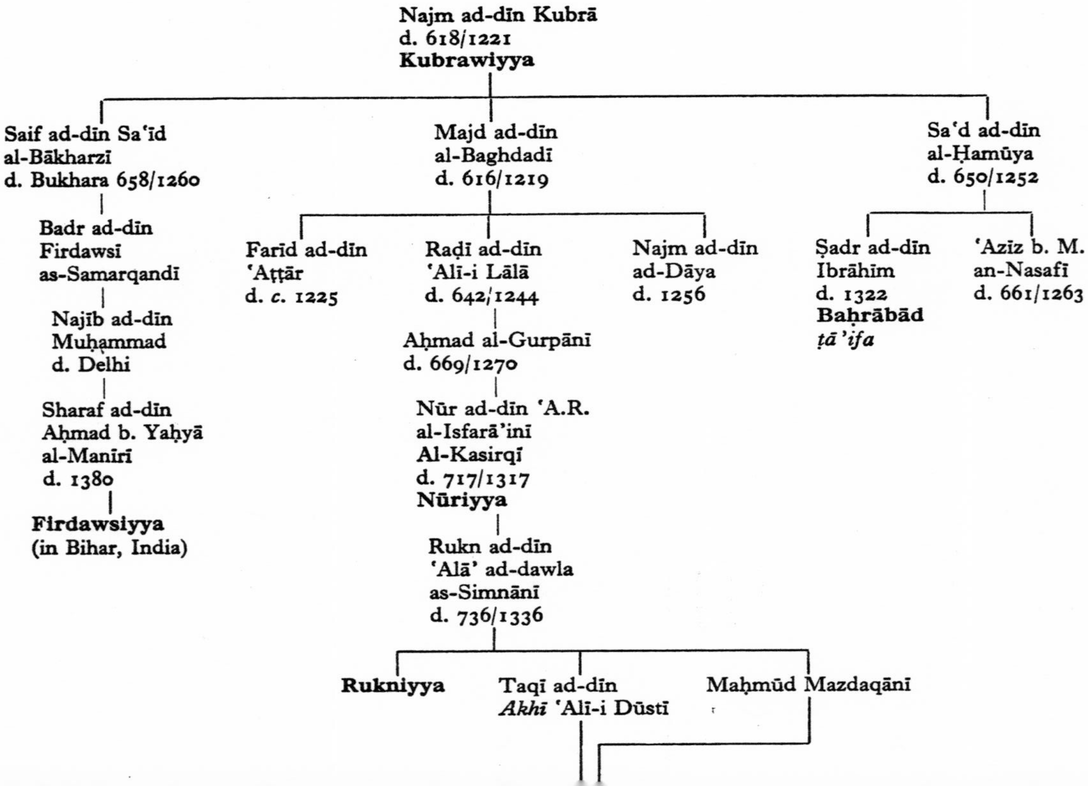

Najm ad-dīn Kubrā
d. 618/1221
Kubrawiyya
Saif ad-dīn Sa'īd
al-Bākharzī
d. Bukhara 658/1260
Badr ad-dīn
Firdawsī
as-Samarqandī
Najīb ad-dīn
Muḥammad
d. Delhi
Sharaf ad-dīn
Aḥmad b. Yaḥyā
al-Manīrī
d. 1380
Firdawsiyya
(in Bihar, India)
Majd ad-dīn
al-Baghdadī
d. 616/1219
Farīd ad-dīn
'Aṭṭār
d. c. 1225
Raḍī ad-dīn
'Alī-i Lālā
d. 642/1244
Aḥmad al-Gurpānī
d. 669/1270
Nūr ad-dīn 'A.R.
al-Isfarā'inī
Al-Kasirqī
d. 717/1317
Nūriyya
Rukn ad-dīn
'Alā' ad-dawla
as-Simnānī
d. 736/1336
Rukniyya
Taqī ad-dīn
Akhī 'Alī-i Dūstī
Maḥmūd Mazdaqānī
Najm ad-dīn
ad-Dāya
d. 1256
Sa'd ad-dīn
al-Ḥamūya
d. 650/1252
Ṣadr ad-dīn
Ibrāhīm
d. 1322
Baḥrābād
ṭā'ifa
'Azīz b. M.
an-Nasafī
d. 661/1263

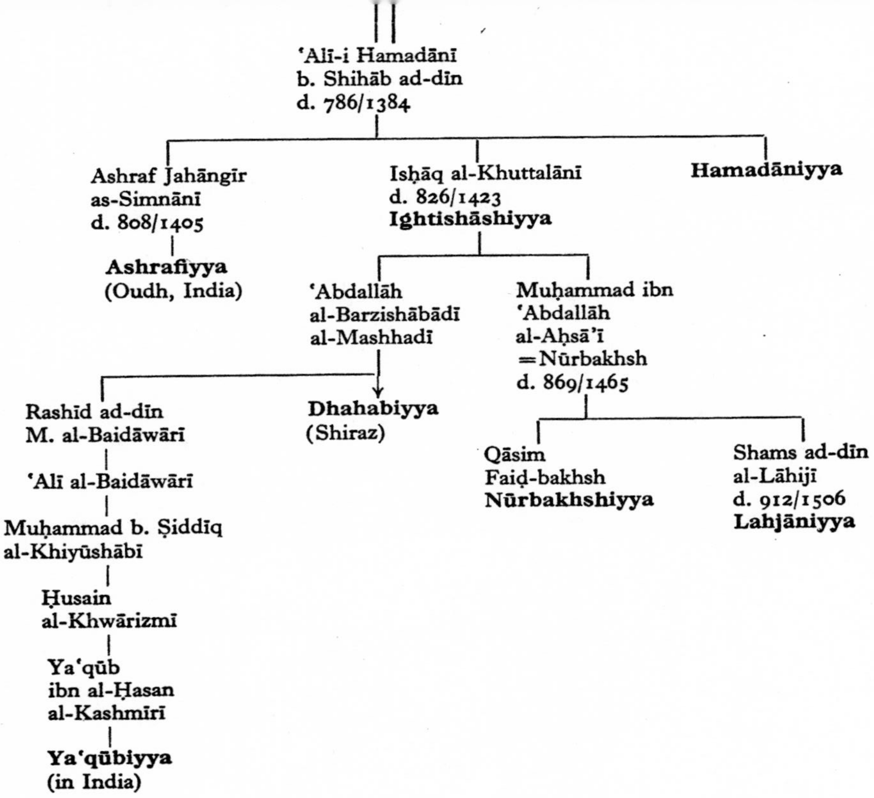
'Alī-i Hamadānī
b. Shihāb ad-dīn
d. 786/1384
Ashraf Jahāngīr
as-Simnānī
d. 808/1405
Ashrafiyya
(Oudh, India)
Isḥāq al-Khuttalānī
d. 826/1423
Ightishāshiyya
Hamadāniyya
'Abdallāh
al-Barzishābādī
al-Mashhadī
Muḥammad ibn
'Abdallāh
al-Aḥsā'ī
=Nūrbakhsh
d. 869/1465
Rashīd ad-dīn
M. al-Baidāwārī
Dhahabiyya
(Shiraz)
Qāsim
Faiḍ-bakhsh
Nūrbakhshiyya
Shams ad-dīn
al-Lāhijī
d. 912/1506
Lahjāniyya
'Alī al-Baidāwārī
Muḥammad b. Ṣiddīq
al-Khiyūshābī
Ḥusain
al-Khwārizmī
Ya'qūb
ibn al-Ḥasan
al-Kashmīrī
Ya'qūbiyya
(in India)

(d. A.D. 1219), who was the shaikh of the great Persian poet, Farīd ad-dīn 'Aṭṭār (d. *c.* A.D. 1225), author of *Manṭiq aṭ-Ṭair* ('Speech of the Birds'), an allegorical *mathnawī* which traces the spiritual pilgrimage through 'Seven Valleys' (stages) with deep insight. Najm ad-dīn fell victim to the Mongol sack of Khwārizm in A.D. 1221. Although most of his works are in Arabic he wrote in Persian a *Ṣifat al-ādāb* (rules of conduct) for the guidance of neophytes, which forms an important landmark in the trend towards the Iranization of Sufism.

From many of Najm ad-dīn's *khalīfas* no defined branch orders stemmed but rather a Kubrāwī *ṭā'ifa* localized around the *khalīfa's* tomb, to which were attached a convent and ancillary buildings. Many establishments of this kind were visited by Ibn Baṭṭūṭa in A.D. 1333. These included that of Najm ad-dīn himself outside Khwārizm[1] and that of Saif ad-dīn al-Bākharzī (d. 658/1260), who received the adherence of Berke, Khān of the Golden Horde, to Islam,[2] and whose tomb and convent in Bukhara were built under Timur's patronage.[3] Another *khalīfa* was the Shī'ī, Sa'd ad-dīn M. al-Ḥamūya (or Ḥamūyī, d. *c.* 650/1252), whose descendants maintained a localized *ṭā'ifa* around his tomb at Baḥrābād in Khurasan.

The main orders deriving from Najm ad-dīn were:[4]

Firdawsiyya, an Indian branch of the line from the Bākharzī of Bukhara who has just been mentioned. It derives its name from a *khalīfa* of his called Badr ad-din Firdawsī, whose *khalīfa*, Najīb ad-dīn Muḥammad (d. Delhi *c.* A.D. 1300), introduced the order into India.[5]

Nūriyya, a Baghdadi branch, founded by Nūr ad-dīn 'Abd ar-Raḥmān al-Isfarā'inī (d. 717/1317), master of as-Simnānī.

Rukniyya, a Khurasani branch, deriving from Rukn ad-dīn Abu 'l-Makārim Aḥmad ibn Sharaf ad-dīn, generally known as 'Alā' ad-Dawla as-Simnānī, d. 736/1336.

Hamadāniyya, a Kashmiri branch of the Rukniyya, founded by

[1] Ibn Baṭṭūṭa, Paris edn., iii. 5–6.

[2] Ibn Khaldūn, *'Ibar*, Bulaq, 1867, v. 534.

[3] Ibn Baṭṭūṭa (iii. 27), who attended a *samā'* at the convent when songs were sung in Turkish and Persian.

[4] Most derivatives branched out from one line, that of Najm ad-dīn's most forceful and independent pupil, Majd ad-dīn al-Baghdādī; see Kubrāwī table.

[5] According to *Ā'īn-i Akbarī*, 1948 edn., iii. 407–8.

Sayyid 'Alī ibn Shihāb ad-dīn b. M. al-Hamadānī, b. Hamadān 714/1314, d. in Pakhli 786/1385, and buried at Khotlan in Tājikistān. The definitive establishment of Islam in Kashmir is ascribed to three visits of this vagrant Sufi in A.D. 1372, 1379, and 1383. He was associated with a migration of seven hundred Sufis seeking a haven from the Mongols under Timur, followed by another three hundred under 'Alī's son, Mīr Muḥammad.[1]

Ightishāshiyya,[2] a Khurasani branch founded by Isḥāq al-Khuttalānī (assassinated by emissaries of Shāh Rukh in 826/1423), a pupil of 'Alī al-Hamadānī. From him through his pupil, 'Abdallāh Barzishabādī Mashhadī, came the Shī'ī order of *Dhahabiyya* (centred today in Shiraz), the term by which Najm ad-dīn's line is frequently and confusingly denominated.

Nūrbakhshiyya, a Khurasani branch, deriving from Muḥammad ibn 'Abdallāh, called Nūrbakhsh (d. 869/1465), a pupil of Isḥāq al-Khuttalānī, who developed his own distinctive Shī'ī beliefs. From him again stemmed two lines: that through his son, Qāsim Faiḍ-bakhsh, carried on the Nūrbakhshī, and the other through Shams ad-dīn M. al-Lāhijī (or Lāhjānī, d. 912/1506–7), who had a *khānaqāh* in Shiraz, branched out independently.

As-Simnānī was a most important influence in the intellectual development of central Asian and Indian orders, even though his own order was of no great importance. Born in 659/1261 in the Khurasanian village of Simnān into a family with a civil service tradition he entered the service of the Buddhist Ilkhān Arghūn (reg. A.D. 1284–91); then, as a result of experiencing an involuntary *ḥāl*, he adopted the mystical life. After surmounting initial difficulties with Arghūn he was allowed to pursue his new course, and was initiated into the Kubrāwī *silsila* by al-Kasirqī al-Isfarā'inī. After accomplishing the pilgrimage and spending some training spells in his master's *khānaqāh* in Baghdad, he settled in his native place of Simnān, founded his own *khānaqāh*, Ṣūfiyābād-i Khudādād, and lived there tranquilly until his death in 736/1336.

He was the author of numerous works,[3] and followed an

[1] *Ta'rīkh-i Rashīdī*, tr. E. Denison Ross, London, 1895, pp. 432–3.

[2] To be distinguished from the Ighit-bāshiyya, a Khalwatī order in Anatolia.

[3] For his works in Arabic see *G.A.L.* ii. 263; *G.A.L.S.* ii. 281. On as-Simnānī see F. Meier's art. in *E.I.*², i. 346–7, and for his ideas, with references to unpublished MS. material, see A. A. Rizvi, *Muslim Revivalist Movements in Northern*

orthodox line, advocating a literal interpretation of the Qur'ān, and strict adherence to the *sharī'a* as the essential foundation for progress along the Path. He deprecated current corruptions (*bida'*) in Sufi thought, though not in practice. He condemned ideas concerning *wilāya* and saints' miracles. He disputed the theosophical theories of Ibn al-'Arabī, teaching that the world is a reflection, not an emanation, of Reality. Later, his approach, taken up by the Indian Naqshabandī, Aḥmad as-Sirhindī, came to be known as *waḥdat ash-shuhūd* (Unity of the witness or phenomena) in contradistinction to the *waḥdat al-wujūd* (Unity of the Being) of Ibn al-'Arabī.

Although such an orthodox Sufi in the intellectual sphere, he was a thorough-going ecstatic and adopted and popularized *dhikr* practices derived from the methods of the Yogis, in addition to a particular form of head-jerks developed by his initiator al-Kasirqī. He also taught that form of 'confrontation' (*tawajjuh*) which aimed at contact, through concentration, with the spirits of dead Sufis; and in particular made a unique contribution to Najm ad-dīn's vision-pattern and colour-scheme associated with the Sufi stages of progressive enlightenment.

(*b*) *Yasaviyya*

Aḥmad ibn Ibrāhīm ibn 'Alī of Yasī (a town later called Turkestan) we have said was formed in the tradition of Yūsuf al-Hamadānī but returned to his homeland in Turkestan and died there in 562/1166. Although little is known about his life, Aḥmad's significance in the formation of a Turkish Islamic tradition is undisputed.[1] The Yasavī tradition has many ramifications, religious, social, and cultural; it played a role in the Islamization of Turkish tribes, in the adaptation of Islam to a Turkish nomadic milieu,[2] and

India in the Sixteenth and Seventeenth Centuries, Agra, 1965, pp. 36–42. There is also a valuable study by M. Molé, 'Les Kubrawiya entre Sunnisme et Shiisme aux huitième et neuvième siècles de l'hégire', *R.E.I.* xxix (1961), 61–142.

[1] See Köprülüzade Mehmed Fuad, *Türk edebiyatenda ilk mutesavviflar* ['The First Mystics in Turkish Literature'], Pt. 1, Istanbul, 1919; summarized by L. Bouvat in *R.M.M.* xliii (1921), 236–82.

[2] Turkish customs incorporated into ritual and practice gave an ethnical colouring to the *ṭariqa*—types of dress, the saw-*dhikr*, women's participation in seances, and methods of cattle sacrifices which survived among derivatives like the Bektāshiyya. Turkish was used in worship outside ritual prayer. Ibn Baṭṭūṭa says (iii. 36) that 'Alā' ad-dīn Ṭarmashīrīn, sultan of Transoxiana (A.D. 1326–34), whose winter camp he visited, recited his *dhikr* after morning prayer until sunrise in Turkish.

in linguistic reconciliation through the poems of Aḥmad and his successor dervishes like Yūnus Emre (d. *c.* 740/1339).

The following gives some names in direct succession, famous in central Asian Turkish folklore:

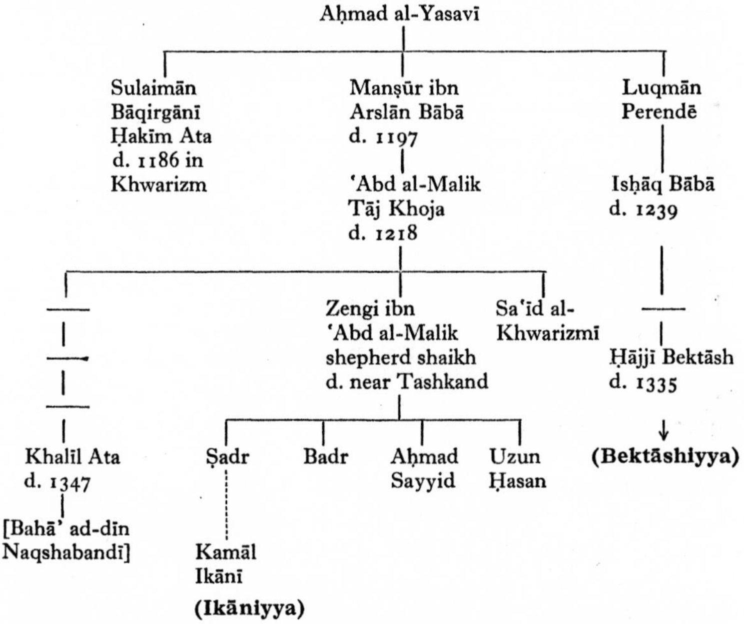

The Yasaviyya was a *ṭarīqa* of wanderers; there were few distinctive branches or permanent settlements, except those associated with the tombs of these shaikhs to which pilgrimage became a permanent feature of central Asian Islam. The Yasavī Way was a Way of holiness and a method of religious practice which displaced the ancient religion of the Turks, rather than a mystical Way. These wanderers spread the tradition throughout Turkestan and among the Kirghiz, from eastern Turkestan northwards into Transoxiana (and the region of the Volga), southwards into Khurasan, and westwards into Azerbaijan and then Anatolia, where they contributed in the persons of men like Yūnus Emre to the formation of the popular side of the new Islamic Turkish civilization, but where the Yasavī as a distinctive tradition did not establish itself. The strength of the cult of Ḥaḍrat-i Turkestān, as Aḥmad was called, in the eighth century A.H. is shown by Tīmūr's readiness to erect an edifice (completed in 801/1398)

on the Sīr-Darya consisting of a two-domed structure, one over Aḥmad's grave and the other over the mosque.

The order stressed the retreat (*khalwa*), and the Khalwatiyya which developed in the Azerbaijan region and spread into Anatolia may be regarded as its western Turkish extension. It also claimed Bahā' ad-dīn an-Naqshabandī as a descendant through the dervish-sultan Khalīl.[1] A definite order-descendant was the Ikāniyya, deriving from Kamāl Ikānī, fifth in spiritual descent from Zengi Ata. Yasavī shaikhs are still mentioned in the sixteenth century in central Asia and even in Kashmir.[2]

(*c*) *Mawlawiyya*

This order falls into a special category, since it derives from a Persian immigrant into Anatolia who belonged to the Khurasanian rather than to the Baghdadian tradition. It is also a localized order, its influence being restricted to Asia Minor and the Ottoman European provinces; such *tekkes* as were founded elsewhere, as in Damascus, Jerusalem, and Cairo, being chiefly for Turks.

Jalāl ad-dīn[3] was born in Balkh in A.D. 1207 to a father, Bahā' ad-dīn Walad (1148–1231), steeped in the Khwarizmian mystical tradition. Local difficulties and the Mongol advance set the family upon wanderings (1217) which eventually brought them into the region governed by the Seljuqs of Rūm (hence Jalāl ad-dīn's *nisba* Rūmī) in 1225. They stayed for a time at a place called Lāranda (now Qaramān) until invited by Kaiqubād I to his capital of Qonya, where Jalāl ad-dīn was to spend the rest of his life. His Sufi training, begun under his father, proceeded along stereotyped lines under another Balkhī refugee called Burhān ad-dīn Muḥaqqiq at-Tirmidhī (d. A.D. 1244). But his life was then transported into a new dimension which turned him from a sober follower of tried paths into an ecstatic whose visions he transmuted into inspired Persian poetry. This came about in 1244, through his fifteen

1 See below, p. 63.

2 See *Ta'rīkh-i Rashīdī*, pp. 369, 371.

3 The book about Jalāl ad-dīn and his more immediate successors written under the title of *Manāqib al-'Ārifīn* by Shams ad-dīn Aḥmad al-Aflākī, begun in A.D. 1318, forty-five years after Jalāl ad-dīn's death, and finished in 1353, is not a biography but a hagiography. Part of the *Manāqib* was translated by J. W. Redhouse in the introduction to his translation of Book I of the *Masnawī* (London, 1881), and there is a complete translation by C. Huart, *Les saints des derviches tourneurs*, Paris, 1918–22. The best edition is that by T. Yaziji, Ankara, 1959–61.

months' association with a wandering dervish called Shams ad-dīn of Tabrīz. So obsessed with Shams ad-dīn did Jalāl ad-dīn become and his life so disrupted that his *murīds* plotted against the dervish. To Jalāl ad-dīn's dismay he disappeared as mysteriously as he had appeared. In fact, he had been murdered by the *murīds* with the connivance of one of Jalāl ad-dīn's sons.[1]

This experience released Jalāl ad-dīn's creative powers and set him upon a new Way which derives its name from the title *mawlānā* (our master), given to its founder. Ibn Baṭṭūṭa, whose visit to Qonya in 1332 we have mentioned earlier, refers to the Way as the Jalāliyya.[2] The Way developed as a self-perpetuating organization immediately after Jalāl ad-dīn's death in 1273.

This order is so well known owing to the publicity given to its mystical exercises and the fame of the master's mystical poem, the *Mathnawī*, that we need only refer to its place in the general context of the *ṭarīqas*. The famous *Mathnawī* is a somewhat incoherent accumulation of Jalāl ad-dīn's outbursts, anecdotal ruminations, and above all parables, expressed in poetical form. Mawlawīs regard it as a revelation of the inner meaning of the Qur'ān, and it was in fact called by Jāmī 'the Qur'ān in Persian' (*hast Qur'ān dar zabān-i Pahlavī*).

From the close association of the founder with the Seljuq ruling authority the order developed aristocratic tendencies and became a wealthy corporation. It played a considerable cultural role in Turkey and helped in the reconciliation of certain types of Christians to Islam. Almost from the beginning it was an hereditary order. Jalāl ad-dīn was succeeded by his vicar, Ḥasan Ḥusām ad-dīn, the inspiring genius of the *Mathnawī*,[3] but after his death (683/1284) the succession passed to Jalāl ad-dīn's son, Bahā' ad-dīn Sulṭān Walad, and thereafter rarely was the dynastic succession broken. The development of the principles and organization of the order around the name of Mawlānā took place under Sulṭān Walad. His works gave solidarity to the aesthetic and emotional mysticism of the master, and when he died at an advanced age (712/1312) the order had spread widely throughout Anatolia and a number of daughter centres had been founded.

[1] See the article by H. Ritter in *E.I.*[2] ii. 393–6.

[2] *Travels*, tr. H. A. R. Gibb, ii. 431.

[3] See Aflākī, quoted in J. W. Redhouse's translation of the first book of the *Mathnawī*, p. 113.

His successor Jalāl ad-dīn Amīr 'Ārif (d. A.D. 1320) travelled widely, consolidating these centres, and in his time the principles, ritual, and organization solidified, though its creative inspiration survived into the age of Selīm III when the order produced its last great poet in Ghālib Dede (Meḥmed Es'ad: A.D. 1758–99). The order remained centralized and was not subject to the splitting process which so typified the Khalwatiyya, but this also meant that its influence was restricted to Turkey.[1]

The members of this order became famous for their devotion to music and the nature of their *dhikr* exercises, whence they were known to Europe as the 'whirling dervishes'. The dance, which is symbolic of the universal life of the spheres, infinitely complex in form yet essentially a unity, is frequently referred to in Jalāl ad-dīn's lyrical poems known under the title of the *Dīwān* of Shams ad-dīn Tabrīzī.[2]

(*d*) *Khawājagān-Naqshabandiyya*

Naqshabandī tradition does not regard Bahā' ad-dīn an-Naqshabandī as the founder of the *ṭarīqa* which bears his name and the lines of ascription (*silsilat at-tarbiya*) do not begin with him. Fakhr ad-dīn 'Alī b. Ḥusain, who wrote a history of the *ṭarīqa* called *Rashaḥāt 'Ain al-Ḥayāt*, begins it with Abū Ya'qūb Yūsuf al-Hamadānī (d. A.D. 1140),[3] whilst his *khalīfa* (by spiritual appointment), 'Abd al-Khāliq al-Ghujdawānī (d. A.D. 1220), may be regarded as the organizer of its special tendencies.[4] He is responsible for the stress placed upon the purely mental *dhikr*, and he also formulated the eight rules[5] which governed *Ṭarīqat al-Khawājagān*, the name by which the *silsila* was known. 'Abd al-Khāliq was taught the *ṭarīqa*'s special form of *ḥabs-i dam*,

[1] Outside Turkey the Mawlawīs had *tekkes* only in Damascus, Aleppo, Nicosia, Cairo, and a few other towns where there was a Turkish population; see Murādī, *Silk ad-durar*, Cairo, 1874–83, i. 329, iii. 116; and for Jerusalem Mujīr ad-dīn, *al-Uns al-jalīl*, tr. H. Sauvaire, 1876, p. 181.

[2] R. A. Nicholson, *Selected Odes from the Diwan-i-Shams-i-Tabriz*, Cambridge, 1898, and his edition of the *Mathnawī*, iv. 734.

[3] The main account of Yūsuf al-Hamadānī is found in the *Rashaḥāt*. Short notices are given by Ibn Khallikān (*Wafāyāt*, vi. 76–8), Sha'rānī (*Ṭabaqāt*, i. 116–17), and Jāmī (*Nafaḥāt al-uns*, Tehran edn., pp. 375–7).

[4] The reference in al-Wāsiṭī's *Tiryāq* (p. 47) records it as a distinctive line whose founder was al-Ghujdawānī. A reference to an-Naqshabandī may have been added by a later hand.

[5] These rules, which Bahā' ad-dīn expanded to eleven, are given below, pp. 203–4.

or 'restraint of the breath', by al-Khaḍir, the spirit of Islamic gnosis. The succession from him is as follows:[1]

> 'Ārif Riwgarī, d. 657/1259
> Maḥmūd Anjīr Faghnawī, d. 643/1245 (or 670/1272)
> 'Azīzān 'Alī ar-Rāmitanī, d. 705/1306 (or 721/1321)
> Muḥammad Bābā as-Sammāsī, d. 740/1340 (or 755/1354)
> Amīr Sayyid Kulalī al-Bukhārī, d. 772/1371
> Muḥammad ibn M. Bahā' ad-dīn an-Naqshabandī, 717/1318–791/1389.

Bahā' ad-dīn, who was a Tājīk, served his apprenticeship under both as-Sammāsī and Kulalī ('the Potter'). But he also had Turkish links and there is a romantic story of his encounter with a Turkish dervish called Khalīl whom he had first seen in a dream, and his subsequent association with him until this dervish eventually (A.D. 1340) became Sultan Khalīl of Transoxiana.[2] Bahā' ad-dīn served him for six years, but after Khalīl's fall (747/1347) Bahā' experienced a revulsion against worldly success, returned to his Bukharan village of Rewartūn, and resumed his interrupted spiritual career. Like most of the men after whom *ṭarīqas* have been named, Bahā' ad-dīn did not found an organization (whilst his *ṭarīqa* he had inherited), but gathered around himself like-minded devotees prepared to strive towards a quality of mystical life along Malāmatī lines without show or distracting rites, for, as he said, 'the exterior is for the world, the interior for God' (*aẓ-ẓāhir li 'l-khalq al-bāṭin li 'l-Ḥaqq*). Though modified through the corruptions of time this Way never lost the stamp of 'Abd al-Khāliq's genius in the quality of its leadership and teaching and the purity of its ritual. From the Islamic point of view it was especially important in ensuring the attachment of Turkish peoples to the Sunnī tradition. Bahā' ad-dīn's mausoleum and the attached convent (a magnificent structure was erected in A.D. 1544 by Amīr 'Abd al-'Azīz Khān) became one of the most

[1] Most of these come from the neighbourhood of Bukhara as is evident from their *nisbas*. Riwgar, Faghna, and Rāmitan are, like Ghujdawān, villages near that city. Apart from the Naqshabandī books the *silsila* is given in al-Wāsiṭī, *Tiryāq*, p. 47.

[2] Ibn Baṭṭūṭa describes the rise to power of Khalīl (-Allāh Qazan), French edn., 1877, iii. 48–51. He knows nothing of any dervish upbringings and says that he was the son of the Chagatai prince Yasavur.

important places of pilgrimage in central Asia. The great Persian mystical poet Jāmī derives from Bahā' ad-dīn through an intermediary. Outside central Asia, the order spread into Anatolia and the Caucasus, among mountain peoples in Kurdistan (where it became a factor in Kurdish nationalism), and southwards into India, but never became popular in the Arab world.

(*e*) *Chishtiyya*

From the sixth (thirteenth) century central Asian Sufis had been migrating southwards into India as well as westwards into Anatolia. The formation of various kinds of *khānaqāhs* and small associations coincided with the foundation of the Sultanate of Delhi. Apart from the Baghdadian Suhrawardiyya, the only other order to become defined and influential in India during this formative age was the Chishtiyya. Orders which were introduced later, like the Shaṭṭāriyya ('Abdallāh ash-Shaṭṭār, d. A.D. 1428), Naqshabandiyya (with Bāqī Bi'llāh d. A.D. 1563), and Qādiriyya (by M. Ghawth of Uchch, d. A.D. 1517), never attained the range of allegiance and influence of these two lines.

The Chishtiyya[1] is one of the 'primitive' lines. Mu'īn ad-dīn Ḥasan Chishtī, born in Sijistan about 537/1142, was attracted early to the errant Sufi life and served his master, 'Uthmān Harvanī, during some twenty years of wanderings, and then continued them on his own. Nothing reliable is known about his life. His biographers (late and untrustworthy) claim that he met and was given initiatory authority by most of the celebrated Sufis of this formative age, including not only 'Abd al-Qādir al-Jīlānī but others who were dead before he was born.[2] The *ṭarīqa* is not regarded as linked with the Suhrawardī line though *'Awārif al-ma'ārif* was adopted as the basic textbook of the order. He came across Quṭb ad-dīn Bakhtiyār Kākī (d. 633/1236), who was later to become his *khalīfa* in Delhi.[3] Mu'īn ad-dīn went to Delhi in

[1] On the order and its founder see the articles 'Čishtī' and 'Čishtiyya' in *E.I.*[2] ii. 49–56, by K. A. Nizami.

[2] Until one gets as far back as Ibrāhīm ibn Adham no well-known names appear in his *silsila* (see Sanūsī, *Salsabīl*, pp. 151–2) which was invented later, for it would never have occurred to a rootless wandering dervish like Mu'īn ad-dīn that such a thing was of any importance, as it did to a lineage-conscious Arab like Ibn ar-Rifā'ī.

[3] Quṭb ad-dīn Kākī's *Hisht Bahisht* or 'Eight Paradises', a collection of the sayings of eight of his Chishtī predecessors, was most important in giving a distinctive line to the doctrinal outlook of the order.

589/1193, then to Ajmer, seat of an important Hindu state, where he finally settled and died (633/1236), and where his tomb became a famous centre for pilgrimage.

One of Quṭb ad-dīn Bakhtiyār's initiates called Farīd ad-dīn Mas'ūd, known as Ganj-i Shakar (1175–1265), is regarded as being the person most responsible for the definition and wider diffusion of this line, since he initiated many *khalīfas* who moved to different parts of India, and after his death maintained their *khānaqāhs* as independent institutions in which the succession became hereditary. Important figures in the Chishtī *silsila* are Niẓām ad-dīn Awliyā' (d. 725/1325) and his successor, Naṣīr ad-dīn Chirāgh-i Dihlī (d. 757/1356), who opposed the religious policy of Muḥammad ibn Tughluq. From the Niẓāmiyya many branches diverged. A separate line was the Ṣābiriyya derived from 'Alā' ad-dīn 'Alī b. Aḥmad aṣ-Ṣābir (d. 691/1291).

(*f*) *Indian Suhrawardiyya*

In the Arab and Persian spheres few shaikhs attributed themselves directly to as-Suhrawardī, as, for example, adherents of the hundreds of *ṭā'ifas* in the Shādhilī tradition claim that they are Shādhilī. But the Suhrawardī *silsila* spread in India as a distinctive school of mystical ascription to become one of the major *ṭarīqas*.[1] Outstanding figures were Nūr ad-dīn Mubārak Ghaznawī, a disciple of Shihāb ad-dīn, whose tomb at Delhi is famous, and Ḥamīd ad-dīn of Najore (d. 673/1274), Shihāb ad-dīn's chief Indian *khalīfa* until he transferred his allegiance to the Chishtī, Quṭb ad-dīn Bakhtiyār Kākī.[2] The chief propagandist in Sind and Punjab was another disciple, Bahā' ad-dīn Zakariyā (A.D. 1182–1268), of Khurasanian origin, who worked in Multān and was succeeded by his eldest son, Ṣadr ad-dīn M. 'Ārif (d. A.D. 1285), the succession continuing in the same family. But also from him diverged a large number of independent lines, some becoming known in India as *Bī-Shar'* (illegitimate orders). One orthodox line, the *khānaqāh* of Jalāl ad-dīn Surkhposh al-Bukhārī (A.D. 1192–1291) at Uchch, became an important diffusion centre. Contrary to the Chishtī shaikhs of the only other order active in India, Bahā' ad-dīn pursued a worldly policy, associating freely

[1] See Appendix C for the various branches.
[2] See Ibn Baṭṭūṭa, iii. 156.

with princes, accepting honours and wealth, and building up a large fortune. He and his associates also followed a rigid orthodox line, pandering to the *'ulamā'* and rejecting *samā'* (public recital) in the form which prevailed among Chishtīs.

III

The Formation of *Ṭā'ifas*

WHILST *ṭarīqa* is the method, *ṭā'ifa* is the organization, and though the *khānaqāhs* were correctly described as *ṭawā'if* (plural of *ṭā'ifa*), since they were organizations of separate groups,[1] they were still not the orders as we know them. The completion of their development as *ṭā'ifas* or orders in this specialized sense during the fifteenth century coincided with the growth of the Ottoman Empire. In the Maghrib this stage coincided with the appearance of Sharifism and what the French call *maraboutisme*. There are, in fact, four areas of significant change: Persia and central Asia, Anatolia (Rūm), India, and the Maghrib.

The fullest development of the variegated robe of Sufism had taken place in Iranian regions. In the same regions its linkage with the lives of ordinary people had come about through the wandering dervishes, Iranian and Turkish. Then had come the Mongol conquests. From around A.D. 1219, when the first Mongol movements into Khurasan began, to A.D. 1295 Muslim Asia was subjected to the domination of non-Muslim rulers and Islam was displaced from its position as the state religion. With the accession of Ghāzān Khān (A.D. 1295–1304) Islam once again became the imperial religion in western Asia. But there was this difference from its position under previous regimes in that Sufis replaced the *'ulamā'* class as the commenders of Islam to Mongols and as the significant representatives of the religion. During this period the Sufis became for the people the representatives of religion in a new way and after their death they continued to exercise their influence. The shrine, not the mosque, became the symbol of Islam. The shrine, the dervish-house, and the circle of *dhikr*-reciters became the outer forms of living religion for Iranians, Turks, and Tatars alike. And this continues. Timur, who swept away the remnant and successor states which had

[1] There are many early references to these organizations as *ṭā'ifas*. Ibn Khallikān, we have shown, refers to the Kīzāniyya *ṭā'ifa* (ii. 391). But for our purpose it is simply a convenient term for the completed organization.

formed after the decline of Mongol power, was a Sunnī, but showed a strong veneration for saints and their shrines, many of which he built or restored.

Anatolia, where Islam's spread followed the westward movement of the Turks from the thirteenth century until the Ottomans became a world power and regulated the religious life of the regions they controlled, was the scene of religious interaction and confusion, and it is not easy to tell what was happening there. The Ghāzī states of Anatolia in the thirteenth and fourteenth centuries, in order to supply the religious cement, linked themselves with the only Islamic organization available in the marches which possessed any dynamic element—the wandering Turkish *darāwish*, the *bābās* from central Asia who accompanied, followed, and fortified the warriors. The orders, with their borrowed symbolism and formulae for initiation, provided the means of consecrating the *ghāzī* as a dedicated warrior in the cause of Islam. Paul Wittek writes:

> We find in the biographies of the Mevlevī shaikhs, by Eflākī, written about the middle of the fourteenth century, clear traces of a ceremony of granting the title of Ghāzī, comparable to that of investiture with knighthood in the West. We are told how one of the emirs of the house of Aydın was designated as 'Sultan of the Ghāzīs' by the shaikh of the Mevlevī darvish order. From the hands of the shaikh he received the latter's war-club, which he laid on his own head and said: 'With this club will I first subdue all my passions and then kill all enemies of the faith.' This ceremony means that the emir accepted the shaikh as his 'senior' [*seigneur*], and his words show that the quality of Ghāzī also involved ethical obligations.[1]

During the Seljuq and early Ottoman periods heterodoxy was the evident characteristic of many representatives of Islam, especially in eastern and southern Anatolia. Many of the wandering *bābās* were Shīʿī *qizil-bāsh* and Ḥurūfīs, others were *qalandarīs* and *abdāl*, both cover-terms. The Yasaviyya, dispersing from Turkestan, was a *ṭarīqa* of wanderers, whose link with Aḥmad al-Yasavī gave them a distinctively Turkish spiritual ancestry. Out of the diverse heritages of heterodox Islamic tendencies and Christian Anatolian and Turkish superstitions came the Bektāshī

[1] P. Wittek, *The Rise of the Ottoman Empire*, 1938; reprint, 1958, p. 39; and see the account in Aflākī, tr. C. Huart, ii. 391–2; ed. T. Yāzijī, Ankara, 1959–61, ii. 947–8.

order: very nebulous at first, it became highly organized and centralized, yet parochial, providing a village religion, a system of lodges, and a link with a *futuwwa* military order. Another Turkish tendency arising out of the haze from the Tabriz region, displaying strong *malāmatī* inspiration, became distinguished as the Khalwatiyya and Bairāmiyya. These remained decentralized and fissiparous, spawning many distinctively Turkish orders, but also spreading widely through the Arab world in localized orders.

We have said that this final stage of organization coincided with the foundation of the Ottoman Empire (by A.D. 1400 the Ottomans were masters of Anatolia and they triumphed over the Syrian and Egyptian Mamlūks in 1516–17). In Turkey under the Ottomans relative harmony was achieved through toleration of three parallel religious strands: official Sunnī legalism, the Sufi *tekke* cult, and the Folk cult. Shī'ism, which was not tolerated, was forced to seek asylum within Sufi groups, among whom the Bektāshiyya gave it its fullest expression. The Ottomans in their task of building up a stable administrative system came to rely upon the regularly constituted *'ulamā'* body as the backbone of the whole order. The foundation of *madrasas* became a feature of this allegiance. They were set up in Bursa and Nicaea, for example, immediately after their conquest in A.D. 1326 and 1331.[1] But the orders also had their place, and *tekkēs* and *zāwiyas* became more ubiquitous than *madrasas*. The essential difference was that whereas the *madrasas* were alike except in size and reputation and catered for the formal requirements of Islam, the convents were of all kinds, catering for every religious need. In Arab lands there was a clear distinction between *khānaqāhs* and other Sufi institutions. *Khānaqāhs*, which from the beginning had been defined and regulated by the state—the price they paid for official recognition and patronage—were weakening and dying out wherever they had failed to become integrated with a saint-cult. Consequently, Sufi organizations tended to absorb popular movements since this was the only way whereby the ideals for which such movements of the spirit stood could survive. Throughout the history of this empire, whose power embraced almost the whole Arab world (for Tunis and Algiers were vassal states, only Morocco remaining outside its organization), the orders played an important

[1] See P. Wittek, op. cit., p. 42.

role in religious, social, and even political life, and when it fell they also were destroyed.

At the same time as the Ottoman state was becoming a world power a Sufi order was providing Persia for the first time since its conquest by the Arabs with a dynasty whose state religion was Shī'ite. It is interesting that the region where the movement arose, Azerbaijan and Gilan, was the nurturing place for the movement of Turkish *bābās* professing every known type of Islam which flooded Anatolia (this was quite distinct from the Persian Sufi current, out of which came the Mawlawiyya affecting the Iranized class), and which also provided the impulse and manpower supporting the great Shī'ite movement of the Ṣafawids. The Ṣafawid order continued to be a largely Turkish order for long after it became a military movement, and it had a strong following in the Turkish provinces of Asia Minor. Even the Baghdadian tradition affected the *bābās*, but through an alternative stream deriving from the Kurdish saint Abu 'l-Wafā' Tāj al-'Ārifīn[1] through Bābā Ilyās Khurāsānī.

This development into orders, and the integral association of the saint cult with them, contributed to the decline of Sufism as a mystical Way. Spiritual insight atrophied and the Way became paved and milestoned. From this period, except in Persia. Sufi writings cease to show real originality. They become limited to compilations, revisions and simplifications, endless repetition and embroidery on old themes, based upon the writings of earlier mystics. They produced variations on their poems in the form of *takhmīs*, *mawlids* or nativities in rhymed prose, invocation series like Jazūlī's *Dalā'il al-khairāt*, and manuals dealing with technical aspects of the orders, details concerning the relationship between shaikh and disciple, rules for the disciplinary life and for the recitations of litanies and liturgies. Numerous biographical collections of saints (*ṭabaqāt al-awliyā'*) or pure hagiographies (*manāqib al-'ārifīn*) were produced, together with *malfūẓāt* or *majālis*, collections of their table-talk, and *maktūbāt* (correspondence). Among the few original writers within the Arab sphere we may mention 'Abd al-Ghanī an-Nābulsī (d. 1143/1731). Initiated into many lines,[2] his primary Way was the Naqshabandiyya and he was strong on the catholistic side of Sufism.

[1] On Abu 'l-Wafā' (died 501/1107) see above, pp. 49–50.
[2] See al-Murādī, *Silk ad-durar* (Cairo, 1874–83), iii. 30–8.

Whilst it may be true, as theologians assert, that spiritual expression is closely linked with the development and vigour of dogmatic values and that the hardening of *fiqh* and *kalām* in the ninth–tenth centuries A.H. led or at least contributed to the decline of *taṣawwuf*, yet both are probably symptoms rather than causes of a deeper spiritual malaise.

The *ṭarīqas*, we have shown, were essentially source-schools. During this third stage men who linked themselves with these older traditions developed new orders, with *isnāds* stretching both ways from themselves as the central point. As Abu 'l-Faḍl al-'Allāmī put it: 'Any chosen soul who, in the mortification of the deceitful spirit and in the worship of God, introduced some new motive of conduct, and whose spiritual sons in succession continued to keep alight the lamp of doctrine, was acknowledged as the founder of a new line.'[1]

At no particular point can it be stated that here the Way deriving from Shaikh Fulān hardens into a *ṭā'ifa* any more than we can state that 'here the Way of ash-Shādhilī begins', except in so far as it begins with ash-Shādhilī. But we know when most of the fifteenth-century *ṭā'ifas* began. Many branched out into hundreds of derivative *ṭā'ifas*. The Rifā'iyya *zāwiya* visited by Ibn Baṭṭūṭa was already a fully developed *ṭā'ifa*. One aspect of the change, even if not an integral one, was the tendency for the headship of many orders to become hereditary. Formerly, the superior designated a disciple to succeed him, or failing this, he might be elected by the initiates, but now his successor was increasingly designated or elected from within his own family.

The orders became hierarchical institutions and their officials approached nearer to a clergy class than any other in Islam, whilst the *zāwiya* was the equivalent of the local church. The

[1] Abu 'l-Faḍl al-'Allāmī, *Ā'īn-i Akbarī*, tr. H. S. Jarrett, 1894, iii. 357; second edn., Calcutta, 1948, iii. 397.

There are references to *ṭā'ifas* bearing the names of famous early Sufis. These may sometimes have arisen through a teacher bearing the same *nisba*, or more commonly through the desire of a master to relate himself with a particular tradition of the past, receiving confirmation in a dream. *Zāwiyas* of Bisṭāmī dervishes were found in Jerusalem and Hebron in the 8/14th century derived from 'Alī aṣ-Ṣafī al-Bisṭāmī (d. 761/1359); see Mujīr ad-dīn, tr. Sauvaire, pp. 118, 166, 223. This order claimed the Ṭaifūrī Bisṭāmī as its original shaikh, by spiritual investiture through a vision; see the account of two derivative *zāwiyas* in Aleppo founded by Muḥammad b. Aḥmad al-At'ānī (d. 807/1405) in M. Rāghib aṭ-Ṭabbākh, *I'lām an-nubalā' fi ta'rīkh Ḥalab*, Aleppo, 1923–6, v. 144–7.

shaikh ceased to teach directly but delegated authority both to teach and initiate to representatives (*khulafā'*, sing. *khalīfa*). A special cult surrounded the shaikh's person, associated with the power emanating from the founder-saint of the *ṭā'ifa*; he becomes an intermediary between God and man. If we characterize the first stage, as affecting the individual, as surrender to God, and the second as surrender to a rule, then this stage may be described as surrender to a person possessing *baraka*, though of course embracing the other stages.

The difficulties of reconciling these ideas with the dogma and law of Islam had long been evident; the orders had been bitterly attacked by zealots like Ibn Taimiya, but now a parallel developed in practice. The founder and his spiritual heirs affirmed their loyalty to the *sunna* of the Prophet as a necessary first stage in their code of discipline. But this is regarded as only the minimum stage for the vulgar. The orders linked their daily 'tasks' (*dhikr al-awqāt*) with ritual prayer by requiring their recitation immediately following the completion of the ritual, though in fact regular ritual prescriptions had less power and binding force than those of the orders. To justify their teaching and practices, the leaders derived it from the Prophet himself or his immediate companions to whom their chains are traced back. In addition, the founders of all orders from the fifteenth century, when they acquired their definitive form, claim to have been commanded by the Prophet in a dream to found a new Way, an actual *ṭarīqa*. Such a *ṭarīqa* acknowledges its dependence upon the parent *silsila* and is distinguished from it in only minor aspects, a different way of carrying out the *dhikr*, and, more important, a new *wird* delivered to the founder by the Prophet. Beginning as a single organized group, a *ṭā'ifa*, it might or might not expand into a wider system of dependent centres. The Prophet himself being their supernatural authority, the historical revelation is in practice relegated to a secondary place, however much they use it in their *aḥzāb*. The shaikhs of each *ṭā'ifa* claim to be depositaries of divine power (*baraka*) which enables them to discern truth supernaturally, as well as work miracles—the function which is most prominent, but not necessarily the most important.

Whilst inheritance of the *baraka* of the founder by son, brother, or nephew began with some groups even as early as the fourteenth century it did not become widespread until the sixteenth, and has never become universal. In the Maghrib it became associated with a peculiar reverence for hereditary holiness, so that groups acquire a new genealogical point of departure from a saint or sayyid eponym. The Maghribīs in a sense reorientated their past, a transformation in many instances also associated with Arabization.

Succession in the Mawlawiyya has normally been hereditary. The Yūnusiyya became an hereditary *ṭā'ifa* in Damascus from about 1250.[1] Another hereditary Damascene *ṭā'ifa* is the Sa'diyya or Jibawiyya[2] which still exists. The Qādiriyya began as a localized *ṭā'ifa* in Baghdad with family branches in Damascus and Ḥamā. In Hadramawt leadership of the 'Alawiyya and of its family offshoots was hereditary in the Bā 'Alawī family from its foundation by Muḥammad ibn 'Alī ibn Muḥammad (d. A.D. 1255); such a group can only be regarded as an expanded family *ṭarīqa*. Another derivative of the 'Alawī line is the 'Aidarūsiyya *ṭā'ifa* of Tarīm, founded by Abu Bakr ibn 'Abdallāh al-'Aidarūs (d. in Aden 914/1509), who acquired a Kubrāwī *silsila*, and whose order spread through the movement of members of the family into India, Indonesia, and the east African coast, but always remained a restricted lineal *ṭarīqa* with little influence.[3] Throughout the sphere of the Ottoman Empire hereditary succession was becoming widespread in the eighteenth century, but it was still not a universal practice.

[1] See above, p. 15.

[2] The Sa'diyya is a family *ṭā'ifa* claiming Sa'd ad-dīn al-Jibāwī ibn Yūnus ash-Shaibānī (d. near Jiba a few miles north of Damascus in 736/1335) as its founder, who took the *ṭarīqa* from the Yūnisī and Rifā'ī lines. It is mentioned around A.D. 1320 as the Khirqa Sa'diyya by al-Wāsiṭī (Tiryāq, p. 49). It came into prominence with Muḥammad ibn Sa'd ad-dīn (d. 1020/1611) who, after being miraculously converted at Mecca, returned to Damascus to exploit his *baraka* so successfully that he became very rich. He became shaikh in 986/1578 (Al-Muḥibbī, *Khulāṣat al-Athar*, iv. 160–1). He was succeeded by his son Sa'd ad-dīn (d. 1036/1626), during whose tenure of the *sajjāda* Syria was convulsed by a notorious scandal concerning the arrest in a brothel of his *khalīfa'* in Aleppo, Abu 'l-Wafā' ibn M. (A. le Chatelier, *Confréries*, pp. 213–15; al-Muḥibbī, i. 152–4, 298–9). Although the order did not spread widely it was active in Turkey and was introduced into Egypt by Yūnus ibn Sa'd ad-dīn (not to be confused with the Egyptian, Yūnus ash-Shaibānī) where it acquired notoriety through the celebrated biannual *dawsa* (*dōsa*) ceremony in Cairo, when the shaikh rode on horseback over the prostrate dervishes (frequently described, see E. W. Lane, *Modern Egyptians*, chap. x), suppressed in 1881 in the time of Khedive Tawfīq.

[3] For an account of the leaders see O. Löfgren, art. ''Aydarūs', in *E.I.*[2] i. 780–2.

In Turkey proper the most important orders were the Khalwatiyya, Bektāshiyya, Mawlawiyya, and the Naqshabandiyya, though, since '"the ways to God are as manifold as the souls", there are many thousand ways and religious orders'.[1] The Mawlawiyya was an aristocratic, intellectual, and cultural fraternity, finding its following and patronage in the classes corresponding to these terms. We have said earlier that it was a centralized order and did not spread outside Asia Minor. The Qaramān-oğlu dynasty which succeeded that of the Seljuqs (*c.* 1300) tended to favour the *bābās*, but with the success of the Ottomans the Mawlawiyya came into its own.

The Khalwatiyya was a popular order, based on reverence for the leader with power, a reputation for strictness in training its dervishes, and at the same time its encouragement of individualism. Consequently, it was characterized by a continual process of splitting and re-splitting. It is regarded as one of the original *silsilas*, or source-schools. Its origins are obscure, for it had no original teaching personality behind it like the other Ways, but rather an ascetic association in the Malāmatī tradition. It traces its origin to semi-mythical Persian, Kurdish, or Turkish ascetics, in succession Ibrāhīm az-Zāhid (al-Gīlānī), Muḥammad Nūr al-Khalwatī,[2] and (Ẓāhir ad-din) 'Umar al-Khalwatī.[3] If the first was the *pīr* of Ṣafiyyaddīn (d. 1334), founder of the Ṣafawiyya, the history of the order[4] provides a little information. His real name was Ibrāhīm ibn Rūshan as-Sanjānī and he died between A.H. 690 and 700 (A.D. 1291 and 1300). He was a wandering dervish connected with the Suhrawardī *silsila* and it took Ṣafiyyaddīn, who had been directed to seek his guidance, four years before he finally tracked him down among the hills of Gīlān. However, the last named, 'Umar (said to have died about 800/1397 at Caesarea in Syria), is regarded as the founder, in the sense of one who formulated rules for Sufis who carried this designation.[5] There is also reference to one Yaḥyā-i Shīrwānī (d. *c.* 1460, author of the

[1] Evliya Chelebi, *Narrative*, tr. von Hammer, 1846–50, I. ii. 29.

[2] Karīm ad-dīn M. al-Khwarizmī, known as *Akhī* Meḥmed ibn Nūr al-Halveti.

[3] See the *silsila* of al-Bakrī aṣ-Ṣiddīqī given by al-Jabartī, *'Ajā'ib*, Cairo edn., 1959, ii. 271.

[4] Hagiography of Ṣafiyyaddīn called *Ṣafwat aṣ-ṣafā'* by Ibn Bazzāz (d. 773/1371); see E. G. Browne, *Lit. Hist. Persia*, iv. 32 ff. The tradition of the Bairāmiyya also connects with Ibrāhīm Zāhid Gīlānī through Ṣafiyyaddīn.

[5] D'Ohsson, *Tableau*, IV. ii. 624.

Khalwatī *Wird as-Sattār* and master of ʿUmar Rūshanī) being the *pīr-i thānī* (the second master), that is, the founder of the Khalwatī order.

This *ṭarīqa*, therefore, never had a founder or single head or centre, but certain Sufis or lodges in the Ardabīl region noted for their ascetic discipline became associated with this name. In this way there came into existence a mystical school which placed its main emphasis on individual asceticism (*zuhd*) and retreat (*khalwa*). As a distinctive Way it spread first in Shīrwān and among the Black Sheep Türkmens in Azerbaijan, then expanded into numerous *ṭā'ifa*-convents in Anatolia, then into Syria, Egypt, Hijaz, and Yemen, following the triumphs of the Ottomans.

One early introduction of the Khalwatī line into Anatolia was by Muḥammad Shams ad-dīn, known as 'Amīr Sulṭān' (d. A.D. 1439), who had migrated from Bukhara to Bursa, and was the initiator of Sulaimān Chelebi (ibn Aḥmad b. Maḥmūd, d. A.D. 1421), author of a famous Turkish metrical *mawlid*. The chief propagators in Turkey, from whom stemmed distinctive derivatives, were Ḥajjī Bairām (d. 1429) manifesting a strong Malāmatī tradition, and *Dede* ʿUmar Rūshanī of Tabrīz (d. 1487). The Khalwatī tradition initially had strong links with the cult of ʿAlī[1]—the Ithnāʿasharī or Twelver form, as is shown by the legend that ʿUmar al-Khalwatī instituted the twelve-day fast in honour of the twelve Imāms—but finding their strongest support in Anatolia the leaders had to reconcile themselves to a Sunnī dynasty and their ʿAlid teaching was modified or relegated to their body of secret teaching. The following were the principal Anatolian Khalwatī *ṭā'ifas*:

Aḥmadiyya: Aḥmad Shams ad-dīn of Manissa (Marmara village), d. 910/1504.

Sünbüliyya: Sünbül Sinān Yūsuf (d. 936/1529), head of the *tekkē* of Qoja Muṣṭafā Pasha in Istanbul. He was succeeded by Muṣliḥ ad-dīn Merkez Mūsā (d. 959/1552), whose tomb-mosque (near Yeni-Kapū), with its miraculous well, became famous.

Sināniyya: Ibrāhīm Umm-i Sinān, d. 958/1551 or 985/1577.

Ighit-Bāshiyya: Shams ad-dīn Ighit-Bāshī, d. 951/1544.

[1] See ibid. IV. ii. 659–60.

Sha'bāniyya: Sha'bān Walī, d. 977/1569 at Qasṭamūnī.

Shamsiyya: Shams ad-dīn Aḥmad Sīwāsī, d. 1010/1601 (other sources: d. 926/1520). Also called Nūriyya-Sīwāsiyya after 'Abd al-Aḥad Nūrī Sīwāsī, d. 1061/1650 in Istanbul.

Miṣriyya or Niyāziyya: Muḥammad Niyāzī al-Miṣrī of Bursa, d. in exile on Isle of Lemnos in 1105/1694. *Tekkēs* in Greece and Cairo as well as Turkey.

Jarrāḥiyya: Nūr ad-dīn M. al-Jarrāḥ, d. 1146/1733 (or 1133/1720) in Istanbul. Also called Nūraddīnīs.

Jamāliyya: Muḥammad Jamālī b. Jamāl ad-dīn Aqsarā'ī Edirnewī. b. in Amasya, d. 1164/1750 in Istanbul.[1]

The first Khalwatī *zāwiya* in Egypt was founded by Ibrāhīm Gülshenī. Of Turkish origin (from Āmid, Diyarbakr) he was a disciple of 'Umar Rūshenī of Aydin (d. 892/1487), an exponent of Ibn al-'Arabī's theosophy, against whom condemnatory *fatwās* were promulgated. Ibrāhīm succeeded to his chair[2] and also to the opprobrium under which his master had laboured; then after the Ṣafawid occupation of Tabrīz he became a refugee and eventually (A.D. 1507) settled in Egypt, where he was well received by Qanṣawh al-Ghawrī. After the Ottoman occupation he became a popular figure among the Turkish soldiers.[3] His enemies intrigued against him in Istanbul and he was summoned to the capital to clear himself of charges of heresy. Not only did he do this successfully but left behind him three *tekkēs* in Turkey. He died in Cairo in 940/1534 in his *zāwiya* outside Bāb Zuwaila.[4] Another disciple of 'Umar Rūshenī who founded a *zāwiya* at 'Abbāsiyya on the outskirts of Cairo was Shams ad-dīn Muḥammad Demerdāsh (d. *c.* 932/1526).[5] A famous ascetic, a converted Circassian Mamlūk, initiated by 'Umar Rūshenī in Tabrīz who

[1] D'Ohsson, *Tableau* IV. ii. 626.

[2] According to some sources Ibrāhīm's successor at Baku was Yaḥyā-i Shīrwānī, but Evliya Chelebi writes (I. ii. 29) that 'Umar Rūshenī and Gülshenī were successors of Yaḥyā.

[3] Sha'rānī, *Ṭabaqāt*, ii. 133.

[4] An account of his *zāwiya*-tomb is found in 'Alī Mubārak, *Khiṭaṭ Jadīda*, Bulaq, A.H. 1306, iv. 54.

[5] Brief mention in Sha'rānī, *Ṭabaqāt*, ii. 133; also 'Abd al-Ghanī an-Nabulsī, *Riḥla*, p. 139, 'Alī Mubārak, *Khiṭaṭ*, iv. 112–13.

lived in the Muqaṭṭam hills for forty-seven years, was Shāhīn ibn ʿAbdallāh al-Jarkasī (d. 954/1547).[1]

Khalwatī adherents in Egypt had so far come mainly from Turkish milieux, but during the twelfth/eighteenth century a Khalwatī revival spread the order among Egyptians and extended into Hijaz and the Maghrib. A Syrian Khalwatī who was a frequent visitor to Egypt, named Muṣṭafā ibn Kamāl ad-dīn al-Bakrī,[2] sought a more closely linked grouping by binding various groups together in his own Bakriyya. However, the bond was personal and his chief disciples set up their own orders after his death. These were Muḥammad ibn Sālim al-Ḥafnīsī or Ḥafnāwī (d. 1181/1767),[3] ʿAbdallāh ash-Sharqāwī, and Muḥammad ibn ʿAbd al-Karīm as-Sammānī (A.D. 1718–75), whose orders were known respectively as the Ḥafnawiyya (or Ḥafniyya), Sharqawiyya,[4] and Sammāniyya. From these came other branches:

Raḥmāniyya (Algeria and Tunisia). Founded by Abu ʿAbdallāh M. b. ʿAbd ar-Raḥmān al-Gushtulī al-Jurjūrī (A.D. 1715/28–1793), disciple of al-Ḥafnīsī.[5] Its distinctive development took place under his successor, ʿAlī ibn ʿĪsā (d. 1837), but afterwards the various *zāwiyas* became independent.

Dardīriyya: Aḥmad ibn M. al-ʿAdawī ad-Dardīr, 1127/1715–1201/1786.[6] Author of a prose *mawlid*. The *ṭā'ifa* is also called Sibāʿiyya after his successor, Aḥmad as-Sibāʿī al-ʿAyyān. Both are buried in the same mosque-mausoleum.[7]

Ṣāwiyya: Aḥmad ibn M. aṣ-Ṣāwī (d. in Madina 1241/1825), pupil of ad-Dardīr and of Aḥmad ibn Idrīs.[8] Localized in the Hijaz.

[1] Shaʿrānī, *Ṭabaqāt*, ii. 166; Ibn al-ʿImād, *Shadharāt*, viii. 302; Karl Baedeker, *Egypt and the Sudan*, eighth edn., 1929, p. 126.

[2] His dates are 1099/1688–1162/1749, see Murādī, *Silk ad-durar*, iv. 190–200. He is to be distinguished from another Muṣṭafā al-Bakrī (d. 1709), also a Khalwatī, who founded the Bait Ṣiddīqī or Bait Bakrī, whose head functioned as *Shaikh Mashā'ikh aṣ-Ṣūfiyya* until 1926 when someone outside the family was elected.

[3] Murādī, *Silk ad-durar*, iv. 50; al-Jabartī, *ʿAjā'ib*, Cairo, ii (1959), 257–81.

[4] To be distinguished from the Sharqāwa, a Moroccan branch of the Jazūliyya at Būjād, deriving from Muḥammad ash-Sharqī, d. 1601.

[5] L. Rinn, *Marabouts et Khouan*, Algiers, 1884, pp. 452–80.

[6] Al-Jabartī, ii. 157–8; works given in *G.A.L.* ii. 353, *G.A.L.S.* ii. 479.

[7] ʿAlī Mubārak, *Khiṭaṭ Jadīda*, vi. 27.

[8] Shams ad-dīn b. ʿAbd al-Mutaʿāl, *Kanz as-Saʿādati wa 'r-rashād*, Khartoum, 1939, pp. 12–13.

Ṭayyibiyya: Sammānī offshoot in Nilotic Sudan. Founder Aḥmad aṭ-Ṭayyib b. al-Bashīr (d. 1239/1824), pupil of as-Sammānī. From this order came the Mahdī of the Sudan.

Other small Egyptian branches included the Ḍaifiyya, Masallamiyya, and Maghāziyya.

The Bairāmiyya, though nurtured within the same tradition as the Khalwatiyya, is a separate *ṭarīqa*, since Ḥājji Bairām al-Anṣārī[1] derives from the line of Ṣafiyyaddīn Ardabīlī. His spiritual descendants included:

Shamsiyya: Āq Shams ad-dīn M. ibn Ḥamza, *khalīfa* of Ḥājji Bairām, 792/1390–863/1459. His long search for a charismatic leader led him eventually to Bairām Walī, who gave him the power, and he became a famous worker of miracles. He had a Suhrawardī *silsila* from Zain ad-dīn al-Khʷāfī (d. 838/1435), initiator of a Turkish Suhrawardī line, the Zainiyya. One of Shams ad-dīn's sons was the poet Ḥamdī (Ḥamdallāh Chelebī, A.D. 1448–1509) who, besides a Nativity (*mevlīdi*), wrote a *mathnawī*, Yūsuf u Zelīkha, a common Sufi theme, which became very popular.

Eshrefiyya: 'Abdallāh ibn Eshref ibn Meḥmed (d. 874/1470 or 899/1493 at Chin Iznik). He was a famous poet and is generally known as Eshref Oghlu Rūmī.

'Ushshāqiyya: Ḥasan Ḥusām ad-dīn 'Ushshāqī, d. Istanbul 1001/1592.

Malāmiyya-Bairāmiyya: Dede 'Umar Sikkīnī of Bursa, d. A.D. 1553?

Bairāmiyya-Shaṭṭāriyya: History of the branch has been written by La'lizāde 'Abd al-Bāqī, d. 1159/1746.

Jilwatiyya: 'Azīz Maḥmūd Hudā'ī (950/1543–1038/1628) was the organizer of this order, which is attributed to Muḥammad Jilwatī 'Pīr Üftāde' (d. Bursa 988/1580) and consequently is frequently called the Hudā'iyya. Other derivatives from

[1] The date 833/1430 seems to be the most reliable for his death. According to D'Ohsson (*Tableau*, IV. ii. 624) it took place in 876/1471, which is unlikely in view of the known dates of his spiritual descendants. One of his teachers, Ḥāmid Walī, died in 815/1412. Ḥājjī Bairām's tomb stands beside the ruined temple of Roma and Augustus in Ankara.

Muḥammad Jilwatī were the Hāshimiyya (Hāshim Bābā, d. 1773) and the Fanā'iyya (?).

The Bairāmiyya was carried to Egypt by Ibrāhīm ibn Taimūr Khān ibn Ḥamza, nicknamed al-Qazzāz, d. 1026/1617. Originally from Bosnia he travelled extensively and eventually settled in Cairo as a tomb-haunting ascetic. He took the *ṭarīqa* from Muḥammad ar-Rūmī, from Sayyid Ja'far, from 'Umar Sikkīnī (d. 1553), from Sulṭān Bairām, so there are two names missing between the last two.[1]

Leaders ascribing themselves to other *ṭarīqa* lines branched out into their own *ṭā'ifas*. When Aḥmad al-Badawī died in A.D. 1276 he was succeeded by his *khalīfa*, Ṣāliḥ 'Abd al-'Āl (d. 1332), who was responsible for building the tomb-mosque in Ṭanṭa and fostering the already existing cult which quickly attracted to itself Egyptian customs. Various groups ascribing themselves to the Badawiyya came into existence, though they were each independent and generally localized.[2] As a *ṭarīqa* the Badawiyya lacked any distinctive characteristic such as that shown by the Shādhiliyya. It produced no teaching personalities or writers, but was rather a people's cult, whose manifestations at Ṭanṭa have at all times been subject to the censure of the *'ulamā'*, though with little effect until the modern age.[3] The most distinctive among the later Egyptian succession lines in importance and width of spread was the Bayyūmiyya.[4]

Born in the village of Bayyūm in lower Egypt in 1108/1696–7, 'Alī ibn Ḥijāzī ibn Muḥammad went to live in the Khalwatī *zāwiya* of Sīdī Demerdāsh in Cairo, but at about the age of thirty he became affiliated to the Ḥalabiyya branch of the Badawiyya, then under the grandson of 'Alī al-Ḥalabī (d. 1044/1634–5).[5] He became famous as an illuminate, leading the noisy Badawī *ḥaḍra* which took place on Wednesdays in the mosque of Sīdnā

[1] See his biography as given in al-Muḥibbī, *Khulāṣat al-Athar*, i. 16–17.

[2] See Appendix E.

[3] The *'ulamā'* were quite ineffective unless they could enlist the support of the political authority, and that they could very rarely do since the rulers relied on the saints and their representatives to provide them with spiritual support. See, for example, the references to Badawī shaikhs in Ibn Iyās, *The Ottoman Conquest of Egypt*, tr. W. N. Salmon, 1921, pp. 7, 41, 84.

[4] The best account of the origins of the Bayyūmiyya is A. le Chatelier, *Les Confréries Musulmanes du Hedjaz*, 1887, pp. 182 ff.

[5] 'Alī al-Ḥalabī was the author of one of the few Badawī writings, *an-Naṣīḥat al-'Alawiyya fī bayān ḥusn Ṭarīqat as-sāda al-Aḥmadiyya.*

al-Ḥusain in Cairo, and consequently incurring the enmity of the *'ulamā'*, who tried to stop him using the mosque.[1] He was able to hold his own and later the Shaikh al-Islām even offered him a chair at the Azhar.

'Alī's aim was the reform of the Badawī order by return to its supposed original purity, but the ritualistic changes he made[2] and his personal ascendancy was such that his followers regarded him as the initiator of a new Way, and he himself decided that this was more likely to succeed than attempting to reform an old fissiparous order. At the same time he retained the red *khirqa* (=bonnet) of the Badawiyya with its *silsila* and other characteristics to show his filiation.

During his frequent journeys to Mecca he preached his *ṭarīqa* and won a following among both citizens and *badāwīn* in Hijaz. After his death (1183/1769) the order spread into Yemen, Hadramawt, Persian Gulf, lower Euphrates, and the Indus valley. The death of the third *shaikh as-sajjāda*, Muḥammad Nāfi' (time of Muḥammad 'Alī), caused a split in the order and its weakening.

Whilst the Khalwatiyya was characterized by fissiparous tendencies, the headship of each *ṭā'ifa* becoming hereditary, the Bektāshiyya maintained a strong central organization, with affiliated village groups, and was limited to Anatolia and its European provinces. The Bektāshiyya claimed to be a Sunnī order, though in fact very unorthodox and having so strong a reverence for the House of 'Alī that it might well be called a Shī'ī order. The practical recognition of the order as Sunnī seems to be due to the fact that when, after the early association of Turkish Sufis with the *ghāzī* and *akhī* movements which assisted the Ottoman surge to conquest, when the Ottoman authority came more and more under the influence of orthodox Ḥanafīs, the early *ghāzī* association was not repudiated but found new vigour and a powerful organization in the Bektāshiyya.

1 See al-Jabartī, *'Ajā'ib*, i. 339; account also in 'Alī Mubārak, *Khiṭaṭ Jadīda*, A.H. 1305, x. 26.

2 'Alī al-Bayyūmī elaborated the simple handclasp of the Badawiyya to one of interlaced fingers (*talqīn mushabbaka*) and hung the *tasbiḥa* around the neck of the *murid*. He also changed the movements of the *ḥaḍra*. Whereas the Badawīs confined themselves to bending the body to the waist whilst keeping the arms stretched out, the Bayyūmīs cross them on the breast at each inclination of the head, and then in straightening swing them up to clap them above the head; see Le Chatelier, op cit., p. 184; E. W. Lane, *Modern Egyptians*, Everyman edn., pp. 461–2.

This organization was associated with the name of a semi-legendary Turkish Sufi called Ḥājjī Bektāsh of Khurasan, who emigrated to Anatolia[1] after the Mongols had destroyed the Seljuq state and the remains of the Caliphate. He probably died about 738/1337, for Taqī ad-dīn al-Wāsiṭī (1275–1343) mentions the *Khirqa Bektāsh* (deriving from Aḥmad al-Yasavī, al-Ghujdawānī, etc.) without adding *rāḍī Allāh 'anhu* after his name, so he was still alive about 1320 and known in Iraq.[2] However, the organization of the Bektāshiyya did not develop until the fifteenth century and the Janissary corps, instituted by Murād I, was associated with it from the end of the sixteenth century. One consequence of this association with the Janissaries and so with Ottoman authority was that the Bektāshīs were rarely attacked on grounds of doctrine or innovations. Ottoman authorities sometimes took severe measures against leaders, but that was through their involvement in the numerous Janissary revolts, not on account of their beliefs and practices. But immediately the Janissary corps was abolished in 1826 the Bektāshīs fell with them. The orthodox 'ulamā' then castigated them as heretics.[3] Some were killed, their *tekkēs* destroyed, and their properties handed over to Naqshabandīs. However, because they were not a military order but had deep roots in the life of the people, they survived underground, some groups within other orders, and when circumstances became more propitious they began once more to expand.

The heretical and Shī'ī doctrines and ritual of the Bektāshiyya do not derive from Ḥājjī Baktāsh, though there is no need to assume that he was any more orthodox than other *bābās*. His name is simply a term to provide a point of identity. The order grew out of saint-veneration and the system of convents into a

[1] For legends of his investiture by one Luqmān, disciple of Aḥmad Yasavī, and his migration see Evliya Chelebi [A.D. 1611–79], *Narrative*, ii. 19–21. He appeared in Anatolia after Jalāl-ad-dīn Rūmī was well established (d. A.D. 1273) and was recognized by a group there who called him the *khalīfa* of one Bābā Rasūl Allāh. This it seems was the Isḥāq Bābā who led his dervishes against the Seljuq sultan, Ghiyāth ad-dīn Kay-Khusrau II in 1240 (see J. K. Birge, *The Bektashi Order of Dervishes*, 1937, pp. 32, 43–4). He does not need to be a direct *khalīfa*. Aflākī says of Bektāshī that he was 'un mystique au cœur éclairé, mais il ne s'astreignait pas à suivre la loi apportée par le prophète' (tr. C. Huart, *Les Saints des derviches tourneurs*, i. 296).

[2] Al-Wāsiṭī (d. 1343), *Tiryāq al-muḥibbīn*, p. 47.

[3] See Assad-Éfendi Mohammed, *Précis historique de la destruction du corps des Janissaires par le Sultan Mahmoud, en 1826*, tr. A. P. Caussin de Perceval, Paris, 1833, pp. 298–329.

syncretistic unity, combining elements from many sources, vulgar, heterodox, and esoteric; ranging from the popular cults of central Asia and Anatolia, both Turkish and Christian Rūmī, to the doctrines of the Ḥurūfīs. When the inspirer of the Ḥurūfī movement, Faḍl Allāh ibn 'Alī of Astarabad, was executed by Mīrān Shāh in 796/1394 (or 804/1401) his *khalīfas* dispersed widely. One of these, the great Turkish poet Nesīmī, went from Tabriz to Aleppo, where he made numerous converts, but the *'ulamā'* denounced him to the Mamlūk sultan, Mu'ayyad, who had him executed in 820/1417.[1] It has been suggested that another *khalīfa*, al-'Alī al-A'lā (executed in Anatolia 822/1419), went to Anatolia and there fostered certain Ḥurūfī doctrines upon a local saint buried in central Anatolia called Ḥājjī Bektāsh.[2] But he was only one among many, for the propaganda of the Ḥurūfīs spread widely, even though they were persecuted, especially under Bayazīd II. Bektāshīs themselves do not refer Ḥurūfī ideas back to Bektāsh, but this organization, tolerated by the authorities, became their depository and assured their perpetuation. The actual role of the Ahl-i Ḥaqq during the Bektāshī formative period is unknown. At any rate, during this fifteenth century when the Bektāshiyya was developing into a comprehensive organization, it incorporated other beliefs besides Ḥurūfī from the new environment and beyond some were Christian in origin and others came from such sources as the *qizilbāsh* (red-heads)[3] of eastern

[1] On Nesīmī, whose full name is Nesīm ad-dīn Tabrīzī, see E. J. W. Gibb, *History of Ottoman Poetry*, i. 343 ff.

[2] An important, though hostile, account is Isḥāq Efendi's *Kāshif al-Asrār*, published in 1291/1874–5. This relates how, after the execution of Faḍl Allāh, 'his *Khalīfas* (vicars or lieutenants) agreed to disperse themselves through the lands of the Muslims, and devoted themselves to corrupting and misleading the people of Islam. He of those *Khalīfas* who bore the title of al-'Alī al-A'lā ('the High, the Supreme') came to the monastery of Ḥājjī Bektāsh in Anatolia and there lived in seclusion, secretly teaching the *Jāwidān* to the inmates of the monastery, with the assurance that it represented the doctrine of Ḥājjī Bektāsh the saint (*walī*). The inmates of the monastery, being ignorant and foolish, accepted the *Jāwidān*, . . . named it "the secret"; and enjoined the utmost reticence concerning it, to such a degree that if anyone enters their order and afterwards reveals "the secret", they consider his life as forfeit' (tr. E. G. Browne, *Literary History of Persia*, iii. 371–2; cf. 449–52). The *Jāwidān-nāma* mentioned was written by Faḍl Allāh after his revelation of 788/1386.

[3] The Turks applied the term *qizilbāsh* to *fuqarā'*, chiefly Turkish at first, who wore red turbans. Later, after Shaikh Ḥaidar of the Ṣafawiyya was divinely instructed in a dream to adopt a scarlet cap distinguished by twelve gores, the term especially designated his followers.

Asia Minor and Kurdistan. Many of these were the later affiliated nomadic and village groups (alevīs, takhtajīs, etc.) initiated into allegiance to Ḥājjī Bektāsh as the spiritual factor in communal life.[1] The Bektāshīs proper are those who were fully initiated into a lodge. Probably the first leader of any true Bektāshī organization was Bālim Sultan (d. 922/1516), whose title of *Pīr Sānī*, the Second Patron Saint, implies that he is the founder.[2] According to tradition he was appointed to the headship of the Pīr Evi, the mother *tekkē* at Ḥājjī Bektāsh Koy (near Qirshehir) in 907/1501. A rival head was the *chelebi*, whose authority was recognized by many of the village groups. Claiming descent from Ḥājjī Bektāsh, he is first heard of in connection with a rising of Kalenderoglu, supported by various dervishes and Turkmans, which began in A.D. 1526.[3] This office became hereditary (at least from 1750), whereas the Dede, the head deriving from Bālim Sultan, was an apostolic head chosen by a special council.

This confusion of origins and complexity of groupings supports the supposition that various groups which would have been regarded as schismatic and liable to be persecuted in the type of Sunnī state towards which that of the Ottomans was moving,[4] gained the right of asylum under the all-embracing and tolerant umbrella of the Bektāshī organization. From Bālim Sultan derives the organized Bektāshī initiatory system, with initiates living in *tekkēs* situated near, but not within, towns, and to be distinguished from the village groups. Yet the whole organization composed of such diverse elements blended in time to express loyalty to a common ideal and purpose. Similarly, the unification of the basic ritual and symbolism, together with the custom of celibacy practised by a class of their dervishes, are ascribed to Bālim Sultan.

North Africa also experienced new developments. The mystical movement, which passed through its classical period in the twelfth and thirteenth centuries, had flagged. This movement of

[1] The *tekkē* of Hājjī Bektāsh was at one time supported by the revenues of 362 villages whose inhabitants were affiliated to the order; see F. W. Hasluck, *Christianity and Islam under the Sultans*, 1929, ii. 503.

[2] See J. K. Birge, *The Bektashi Order of Dervishes*, 1937, pp. 56–8.

[3] J. von Hammer, *Histoire de l'Empire Ottoman*, ed. J. J. Hellert, 1844, i. 489.

[4] The decisive date after which these organizations in the Ottoman dominions had to profess a surface Sunnī allegiance was Sultan Salīm's victory at Čaldiran over Shāh Ismā'īl in A.D. 1514.

the spirit had appealed only to a religious élite, but from the middle of the fourteenth century the Way had lost even this appeal and a mystic such as Ibn 'Abbād stands out simply because of the spiritual aridity of the age. At the same time, a popular form of devotion based on the *dhikr* had spread, though as yet practised only by urban and *zāwiya* groups.

> Shaikh Abū Isḥāq ash-Shāṭibī [d. 790/1388] was asked about the position (legitimacy) of a *ṭā'ifa* ascribing itself to Sufism and self-discipline whose members would get together on many a night at the house of one of them. They would open the proceedings with some ejaculating in unison. Then go on to engage themselves in singing, hand-clapping, and making ecstatic utterances, carrying on until the night was over. During the course of the evening they would partake of food prepared by the owner of the house.[1]

But something more was needed, and this came with the generalized *baraka* movement which, beginning in the west in the early fifteenth century, spread throughout the Maghrib in such a way that it was able to permeate and transform the very consciousness of ordinary people, not merely in the urban slums but in the countryside of plain, mountain, and desert. This process of social change, also associated with a strong surge to Arabization, except in Morocco, changed the attitude of the Berbers towards Islam. The influence of the shaikhs was such that whole tribes came to regard themselves as their descendants. All holy men had now to call themselves *sharīfs*, and *baraka* became, not just a gift, but something that could be passed down and inherited. The popular fame of Abū Madyan, for example, derives, not from his maintained Sufi tradition, but through the fostering of tomb-veneration by the Marīnid sultans. Many other establishments grew up around tombs of early shaikhs, like that associated with Abū Muḥammad Ṣāliḥ, buried in the *ribāṭ* of Aṣfī (Ṣafi) on the Atlantic coast.

Abū 'Abdallāh Muḥammad ibn Sulaimān al-Jazūlī, author of the famous 'Proofs of the Blessings' (*Dalā'il al-khairāt*), is more than anyone else linked with this new aspect which so changed Islamic life in the Maghrib. Initiated into the Shādhiliyya at Tīṭ in southern Morocco by Abu 'Abdallāh M. b. Amghār aṣ-Ṣaghīr, he manifested the gift of miracle, was recognized as a *walī*, and affiliated followers indiscriminately, without novitiate,

[1] Aḥmad ibn Yaḥyā al-Wansharīsī, *Al-Mi'yar*, lith. Fez, A.H. 1314, xi. 31.

into his Way. The Sufi Path was henceforth eclipsed by this easy way of attachment to the power of those honoured by God. Such was the success of al-Jazūlī that the governor of Aṣfī, which he had made his centre, had him expelled, and he died, poisoned according to report, in either 869/1465 or 875/1470.

Al-Jazūlī formed neither *ṭarīqa* (his Way was Shādhilī) nor *ṭā'ifa*, but from him came something much more universal, a devotional school with new aims and drive, based on intense concentration upon the Prophet and the acquisition of power through recitation of *Dalā'il al-khairāt*. From him, however, derive many *ṭawā'if* founded by his disciples and their disciples, and the allegiance diffused so rapidly that many older orders (really *zāwiya*-centres) were absorbed or eclipsed.[1] The subsequent Islamic revival derived force from other causes. It was directed against both the Portuguese occupation of coastal places (between 1415 and 1514) and the imperialism of the Makhzan, whose energies were for long to be directed towards containing the new *ṭā'ifas* by winning the allegiance of the great shaikhs and balancing one against the other.[2] At the same time, this shows how much temporal power had to depend upon the new religious movement.[3] No section of Maghribi life escaped their influence, though it was only too often to be at the expense of their spirituality. The idea of sanctity lost its integrity and became a mechanical attribute. In the very broadest terms, we may say that, whilst in the East Sufism remained basically an individual pursuit, in the West it only became popular when it became collectivized.

[1] See *Mumatti' al-asmā fi dhikr al-Jazūlī wa 't-Tabbā'*, tr. in *Arch. Maroc.* xix. 278. A *ṭā'ifa* did in fact stem from his successor, 'the inheritor of his *baraka*', Abu Fāris 'Abd al-'Azīz at-Tabbā', known as al-Ḥarrār (d. 914/1508), in the Jamā'at at-Tabbā'iyya in Fez.

[2] Two prominent Jazūlī derivatives in the Jebala region were that of 'Allāl al-ḥājj al-Baqqāl at Harā'iq, and that of Muḥammad ibn 'Alī Ber-Raisul at Tazerut. These drew some of their influence and prestige from the struggle against the Portuguese.

Towards the end of the seventeenth century the Filāla dynasty encouraged the development of the *zāwiya* of Wazzān. By astute policy the *makhzan* ensured that no *zāwiya* in north-west Morocco was capable of stimulating any effective movement; see E. Michaux-Bellaire, 'Les Derqaoua de Tanger', *R.M.M.* xxxix (1920), 98–100.

[3] The Sa'dī dynasty in Morocco came to power (930/1523) through reliance upon the followers of al-Jazūlī, and one of the first acts of Aḥmad al-A'raj was to have his father buried beside the tomb of al-Jazūlī. Later, in 1529, he had both bodies transferred to Marrakush to consecrate the new dynastic connection with that city; see *Mumatti' al-asmā*, in *Arch. Maroc.* xix. 288.

The Maghrib was a *ṭarīqa* zone to itself and the orders derivative from al-Jazūlī[1] did not spread outside that zone, but in the Maghrib itself they, together with a parallel line, express the religious history to the present day. An important derivative was the ʿĪsāwiyya. Its founder, Muḥammad ibn ʿĪsā (A.D. 1465–1524), received his authority from Aḥmad al-Ḥārithī (d. between 1495 and 1504), a disciple of al-Jazūlī, whom he succeeded as head of the *zāwiya* of Miknāsa az-Zaitūn. He adopted ecstatic practices, whereby the dervishes became immune to sword and fire, from the Rifāʿiyya or an offshoot, either when on pilgrimage or from his Syrian companion, Beghān al-Maḥjūb al-Ḥalabī, who shares the same tomb. After his first successor the succession has continued in the founder's family,[2] but the centre moved to Ouzera near Médéa where the founder's grandson established what has remained the chief *zāwiya* to this day.

The way the religious revolution revived old *baraka* lines may be illustrated by the Hanṣaliyya. This derived from a thirteenth-century Abu Saʿīd al-Hanṣalī, disciple of Abū Muḥammad Ṣāliḥ (d. A.D. 1234), patron saint of Ṣafī, which was revived as a distinct *ṭā'ifa* by Abū Ayman Saʿīd ibn Yūsuf al-Hanṣalī. He served many shaikhs but his inspiration-shaikh was an Egyptian Shādhilī, ʿĪsā al-Junaidī ad-Dimyāṭī, who gave him the poem called ad-Dimyāṭiyya on the ninety-nine names of God, composed by Abū ʿAbdallāh Shams ad-dīn Aḥmad b. M. ad-Dīrūṭī ad-Dimyāṭī (d. 921/1515),[3] which became the *wird* of the Hanṣaliyya. One day when he was praying beside the tomb of Abū 'l-ʿAbbās al-Mursī in Alexandria he received the call which determined his apostolic vocation, but the *ijāza* to propagate and initiate into the Shādhilī Way came from ʿAlī ibn ʿAbd ar-Raḥmān at-Tazemūtī, *muqaddam* in the distinctive Jazūlī tradition. He constructed his *zāwiya* at Ait Metrif and died there in 1114/1702.[4] Under his son and successor, Abū ʿImrān Yūsuf, the order expanded considerably among the Berbers of the Atlas ranges, but weakened after Yūsuf was killed by Mūlay Ismāʿīl (A.D. 1727).

The linkage of the movement of change with al-Jazūlī may well have been exaggerated, for in addition to the Hanṣaliyya many

[1] Appendix F gives a list of the principal orders.

[2] On the ʿĪsāwiyya see R. Brunnel, *Essai sur la confrérie religieuse des ʿAîssaoua au Maroc*, Paris, 1926.

[3] See ash-Shaʿrānī, *Ṭabaqāt*, ii. 164–5.

[4] On Saʿīd ibn Yūsuf see especially Rinn, *Marabouts*, pp. 385–98.

independent orders were reconstituted from older maraboutic families. Tomb-cults of early Sufis, such as 'Abd as-Salām ibn Mashīsh, which become single *zāwiya* orders, also begin at this time. But the most important sphere of ascription derives from Abū 'l- 'Abbās al-Mursī and the Egyptian Wafā'iyya.[1] The following are the main orders:

Wafā'iyya. Founder: Muḥammad b. M. b. Aḥmad Wafā' (d. A.D. 1358), deriving from Ibn 'Aṭā' Allāh al-Iskandarī (d. 709/1309). This order is mentioned to show the continuance of the strong Egypto-Syrian tradition, older than and quite distinct from the Maghribī.[2]

'Arūsiyya. Founded *circa* A.D. 1450/60 by Abū 'l-'Abbās Aḥmad ibn 'Arūs (d. 1463 at Tunis), who claimed also a Qādirī chain. Libyan branch (Salāmiyya) founded (*c*. 1795) by 'Abd as-Salām ibn Salīm *al-Asmar* al-Fitūrī of Zliten.

Zarrūqiyya. Moroccan order founded by Abū 'l-'Abbās Aḥmad b. 'Īsā al-Burnusī, known as az-Zarrūq. Born in Morocco 845/1441 and died at Mezrata in Tripolitania in 899/1494 (or between 921/1515 and 930/1524).[3] He studied for a time in the *zāwiya* of Abu 'l-'Abbās Aḥmad b. al-'Uqba al-Ḥaḍramī on the Nile. His numerous teachers included Aḥmad ibn 'Arūs.[4]

Rashīdiyya or *Yūsufiyya*. Founded by a disciple of Aḥmad az-Zarrūq called Aḥmad ibn Yūsuf al-Milyānī ar-Rashīdī, d. 931/1524–5, tomb at Milyana.

Among the numerous derivatives we may mention:

(*a*) *Ghāziyya*. Abu 'l-Ḥasan b. Qāsim al-Ghāzī (commonly known as Ghāzī Bel Gāsim), d. A.D. 1526, pupil of Aḥmad ar-Rashīdī.

(*b*) *Suhailiyya*. M. b. 'Abd ar-Raḥmān as-Suhailī, originally from Yanbu' on the Red Sea, also a pupil of Aḥmad ar-Rashīdī. Among his order-founding pupils were:

(i) 'Abd al-Qādir ibn Muḥammad (d. 1023/1614), founder of the *Shaikhiyya* or Awlād Sīdī Shaikh of Orania. About A.D. 1780 it split into two groups: Sheraga and Geraba.

[1] See Maghribī genealogical table.
[2] See Appendix G for list of Syrian and Egyptian Shādhilī orders.
[3] According to Ibn 'Askar, *Dawhat an-Nāshir*, *Arch. Maroc*. xix. 93.
[4] For his many writings see *G.A.L.* ii. 253, *G.A.L.S.* ii. 360–2.

(ii) Aḥmad ibn Mūsā al-Karzāzī (d. 1016/1607), founder of the *Karzāziyya*.

(*c*) *Nāṣiriyya*. Founder: Muḥammad ibn Nāṣir ad-Dar'ī, d. 1085/1674. Centred at Tamghūt in Wādī Dar'a. From it derives the *Ziyāniyya* of M. b. 'Abd ar-Raḥmān b. Abī Ziyān (d. 1145/1733), commonly known as Mulay Bū-Ziyān, who founded the *zāwiya* of Qenādhā.

Once the new conceptions had taken root in the Maghrib the Berbers inhabiting Mauritania and the Sudan-belt Sahil came within their influence. 'Umar ash-Shaikh (d. A.D. 1553) of the Arab Kunta tribe who is regarded as the initial propagator, however, was initiated into the Qādirī,[1] not the Shādhilī–Jazūlī tradition, and this accounts for the almost exclusive prevalence of the Qādiriyya in west Africa until the nineteenth-century Tijāniyya was introduced.

The complete integration of saint-veneration with the orders characterizes this stage. The *ṭā'ifa* exists to transmit the holy emanation, the *baraka* of its founder; the mystical tradition is secondary. Though Muḥammad ibn 'Īsā, for example, is in the Shādhilī–Jazūlī line, his power, a contagion transmissible through his posterity, is essentially his own. But it is by no means exclusively a saint-cult, for the link with Sufism remains important and is shown in the teaching and throughout the ritual, personal and communal, as in the *aḥzāb* and *adhkār* of the ritual *ḥaḍra* sessions. Another aspect of this stage is that it provided a means of embracing within Islam all the extra-mural aspects of popular religion—belief in *baraka*, materialized in the form of touch, amulets, charms, and other mechanical means of protection and insurance.

In the Maghrib the new tendency coincides with the development of the characteristic 'maraboutism', which is wider than the *ṭā'ifas*. Sharīfism took its special form[2] after the discovery in

[1] The Qādirī line was introduced into Fez about A.D. 1466 by refugees from Spain after the reconquest.

[2] We first hear of the *baraka* of royalty in the late thirteenth century in relation to the *amīr* 'Abd al-Ḥaqq. 'His *baraka* was famous and his requests to God always granted. His skull-cap and trousers were greatly venerated by the Zanāta who took them to women in travail and their labours were alleviated': Ibn Abī Zar' (726/1326), *Rawḍ al-Qirṭās*, tr. A. Baumier, Paris, 1860, p. 406; Ibn al-Aḥmar, *Rawḍat an-Nisrīn*, ed. and tr. Gh. Bouali and G. Marçais, Paris, 1917, tr. p. 56.

A.D. 1437 of the tomb of Mūlay Idrīs II at Fez in the reign of the last Marīnid, ʿAbd al-Ḥaqq ibn ʿAlī Saʿīd (d. A.D. 1465), and eventually brought the Saʿdian dynasty to power. Henceforth, in this region no one could hope to fill any role, religious or otherwise, unless recognized as a descendant of the Prophet. The Sharīfian dynasty of Banū Saʿd, founded by Muḥammad ash-Shaikh al-Mahdī (d. 1557), whose bid for power began in 1524, succeeded with the help of these religious leaders.

The Maghribī revival had little effect in Egypt and the Arab lands, where the trend was towards greater and greater conformity towards legalistic tradition, at least in the recognized orders subject to governmental supervision and approval. What really happened is that the clamp placed on the exercise of the mind was effective in suppressing speculative Sufism, so that little genuine insight is to be expected from Sufi writings, but official condemnations had no effect upon popular practices of the orders and especially the cult of saints. There was certainly no blank uniformity; we have men like Shāhīn, the hermit on Jabal al-Muqaṭṭam, on the one hand, and ash-Shaʿrānī,[1] on the other, and the most extravagant forms of *dhikr* and *mawlid* celebrations.

Although the Shādhilī order had come into existence in Alexandria, it did not take root in Syria until the beginning of the sixteenth century. The man most responsible for its definitive planting was a Moroccan Sufi called ʿAlī ibn Maimūn ibn Abī Bakr (854/1450–917/1511).[2] After a varied career, which included a period engaged in fighting the Portuguese, he experienced a conversion and was initiated into the Madyanī line in Tunisia. In 901/1495 he travelled east, to Cairo, Mecca, Syria, Brūsa, back to Ḥamāt, and then Damascus. Essentially of a Malāmatī type, he refused to keep *khalwa* or wear or confer the *khirqa*. He forbad his followers to take part in normal social life, especially to seek favours from the great of this world. He did not achieve celebrity in the Syrian world until after his return from Rūm (=Brūsa) to Ḥamāt in 911/1505. He went to Damascus; there his fame as a guide and revivalist attracted vast numbers, until one day 'He was overcome by a "contraction"[3] whilst in the Ṣāliḥiyya [khānaqāh] in Damascus

[1] A notice on ash-Shaʿrānī is given in chapter viii, pp. 220–5.

[2] An account of his life is given by Ibn al-ʿImād, *Shadharāt adh-dhahab*, viii. 81–4.

[3] *Qabḍ* in Sufi, especially Shādhilī, terminology refers to the spiritual state

which persisted in sticking to him until he abandoned the lecture-hall and began inquiring about places situated in the depths of valleys and on the tops of mountains, until, at the suggestion of Muḥammad ibn 'Arrāq he went to Majdal Ma'ūsh' [Lebanon],[1] where after a few months he died.

'Alī's companion during his time of trial, Muḥammad ibn 'Arrāq,[2] is mainly responsible for the spread of the Madyaniyya in Syria, where the new approach brought a breath of new life to its decadent Sufism. Ibn 'Arrāq had been a Circassian officer of some wealth who, under the influence of 'Alī ibn Maimūn, left all to follow his Way. After the death of his master he developed the organization which came to be known as the Khawāṭiriyya or 'Arrāqiyya.[3]

In central Asia the two-century period separating the Mongol invasion from the foundation of the Ṣafawid regime in Persia was a time of ferment, crucial for the future of Islam in the region. The immediate consequences of the Mongol conquests had been the displacement of Islam as the state religion throughout the region. Islam had now to prove itself and accommodate itself to non-Muslim rulers, Shamanist, Buddhist, or crypto-Christian. It was a time pregnant with possibilities, and the outcome was the triumph of Islam as the dominant religion of central Asia. Sufism's role was of considerable significance, not as a Way, but

associated with the alternation *basṭ/qabḍ*, 'dilation/contraction'; see A. b. 'Abbād, *al-Mafākhir al-'aliyya*, Cairo, A.H. 1327, pp. 58–60. Here it is probably used in a more general sense as a state of spiritual dereliction, and a reaction against popularity.

[1] Ibn al-'Imād, op. cit. viii. 83.

[2] His full name was Shams ad-dīn Abū 'Alī Muḥammad b. 'Alī, known as Ibn 'Arrāq; 878/1473–933/1526. An account of his life is given by Ibn al-'Imād, op. cit. viii. 196–9.

[3] Ibn 'Arrāq wrote a book on his Way deriving from 'Alī ibn Maimūn called *as-Safinat al-'Arrāqiyya fī libās khirqat aṣ-Ṣūfiyya*, and a *qaṣīda Lāmiyya* on the Beautiful Names which was sung at all their *ḥaḍras*. As-Sanūsī gives the *dhikr* and *sanad* in *Salsabīl*, pp. 144–5. The line is carried back to Abu Ya'qūb Yūsuf al-Kūmī al-Qaisī (d. A.D. 1180), the initiator of Ibn al-'Arabī. It is, therefore, Madyanī and not Shādhilī, and is regarded as a distinct *ṭarīqa*. Ibn 'Arrāq's son, Sa'd ad-dīn 'Alī (d. in Medina, A.D. 1556) is responsible for the limited propagation of the order in Hijaz.

Others in Syria who took the *ṭarīqa* from 'Alī ibn Maimūn were 'Alawān 'Alī ibn 'Aṭiyya (d. A.H. 936: Ibn al-'Imād, *Shadharāt*, viii. 217–18), Zain ad-dīn Abu Ḥafṣ 'Umar b. Aḥmad (d. A.H. 936: ibid., pp. 218–19), and Abu 'l-Ḥasan 'Alī b. Aḥmad al-Kīzawānī (d. A.H. 955: ibid., p. 307; Sha'rānī, *Ṭabaqāt*, ii. 163). Both 'Alawān and al-Kīzawānī trained under 'Alī ibn Maimūn in Brūsa.

through its men of power, manifested also after their death from their tombs, many of whose structures were raised by Mongol rulers. It is significant that two of the first Mongol princes to adopt Islam, Berke of the Golden Horde and Ghāzān of Tabriz, sought out a Sufi rather than a Sunnī *'ālim* before whom to make their public declaration of adhesion to Islam. Berke (reg. A.D. 1257–67), Khān of the Golden Horde, went specially to Bukhara to acknowledge Islam at the hands of the Kubrāwī, Saif ad-dīn Sa'īd al-Bākharzī (d. 658/1260);[1] whilst Ghāzān Khān son of Arghūn sent for the Shī'ī Sufi, Ṣadr ad-dīn Ibrāhīm, from his *khānaqāh* at Baḥrābād[2] in Khorasan to act as officiant at the ceremony on the pasture grounds in the Alburz mountains in 694/1295 at which the Khān acknowledged before the Mongol, rather than the Muslim, world his adoption of Islam as the western Mongol cult,[3] symbol of his independence of the confederacy of the Gur Khan of Peking.

Central Asia, therefore, was an area of mission, and here the wandering dervishes were all-important.[4] At the same time, Muslim sentiment acquired everywhere fixed centres of devotion in the tombs. These had their guardian dervishes and became the centre of a shaikh and his circle of devotees. Ibn Baṭṭūṭa is a valuable witness to their widespread diffusion, for these places

[1] See the discussion by Jean Richard, 'La conversion de Berke et les débuts de l'Islamisation de la horde d'or', *R.E.I.* xxxv (1967), 173–84.

[2] Ṣadr ad-dīn was the son of Sa'd ad-dīn al-Ḥamūya, on whom see pp. 99, 261.

[3] Dawlatshāh, *Tadhkirat ash-Shu'arā'*, ed. E. G. Browne, 1901, p. 213; Rashīd ad-dīn, *Geschichte Gāzān Khāns*, ed. K. Jahn, Leiden, 1940, p. 79.

[4] It is surprising that the western Turkish Khalwatī tradition made so little impact upon the eastern Turks. The order spread into eastern Iran from the Tabriz region with the wandering dervishes. Rude and unlettered, they were despised by the Naqshabandīs and Kubrāwīs and were probably absorbed by the Yasavīs, for, though a few as individual thaumaturgists gained fame, the Khalwatī lines eventually died out. The following are a few names associated with a semi-legendary:

- Muḥammad al-Khalwatī al-Khwārizmī d. 751/1350?
  - —
    - Nūr ad-dīn Aḥmad al-Khwārizmī
  - Niẓām ad-dīn d. 'Ishqābād (Jām) 775/1374
  - Saif ad-dīn d. Herat 783/1381
    - Ẓāhir ad-dīn d. 800/1398
    - Abū Sa'īd al-Ḥabashī d. 820/1418

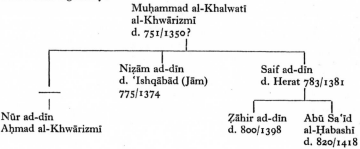

with their open hospitality were the stopping-places for parties of travellers. In Bisṭām, for example, he stayed in the *khānaqāh* attached to the tomb of Abū Yazīd al-Bisṭāmī, where he also visited that of Abū 'l-Ḥasan al-Kharaqānī.[1] Many of the tombs to which *khānaqāhs* became attached were not those of Sufis, since the possession of *baraka* has nothing to do with Sufism. Ibn Baṭṭūṭa wrote:

Outside Samarqand is the domed tomb of Qutham ibn al-'Abbās ibn 'Abd al-Muṭṭalib who was martyred during the conquest of that city. The people of Samarqand go on visitation to his tomb on the nights of Monday and Friday. The Tatars do the same, making vows to him on a large scale, bringing cattle and sheep as well as money, offering them for the support of travellers, the inmates of the *khānaqāh*, and the blessed tomb.[2]

Other non-Sufi tombs he visited include those of 'Alī ar-Riḍā (d. A.D. 818 near Tus) situated inside a *khānaqāh*,[3] and 'Akāsha ibn Miḥṣan al-Asadī, a companion of the Prophet, outside Balkh,[4] whose shaikh took Ibn Baṭṭūṭa on a tour of the many tombs of that city, which included that of the Prophet Ezekiel and the house of the Sufi, Ibrāhīm ibn Adham, then used as a storehouse for grain. His narrative shows that the nomad Turks and Mongols shared with Muslims the belief in the *baraka* of the saints.

The Islamic movement took varied forms within the two traditions of Sunnī and Shī'ī. The Ilkhānid states were officially Sunnī, but Shī'ī ideas and loyalties were very much alive as historical sources show, by demonstrating the relative ease with which the Ṣafawid revolution was accomplished. In the Sunnī tradition the Naqshabandiyya played a distinctive role. We have shown[5] how Bahā' ad-dīn an-Naqshabandī, who gave Silsilat al-Khawājagān its name and form, simply carried on one of the most strongly established Sufi traditions. Although so clearly Iranian and urban, it was adopted by many Tatar tribes as a kind of tribal religious linkage, and had its place in their triumphs following the death of Shāh Rukh (850/1447). During this century the rapid progress of the order, from central Asia westwards into Anatolia and southwards into the Indian subcontinent, led to its division into three main branches:

[1] Ibn Baṭṭuṭa, Paris edn., iii. 82.
[2] Ibid. iii. 52–3.
[3] Ibid. iii. 77–9.
[4] Ibid. iii. 62.
[5] See above, p. 62.

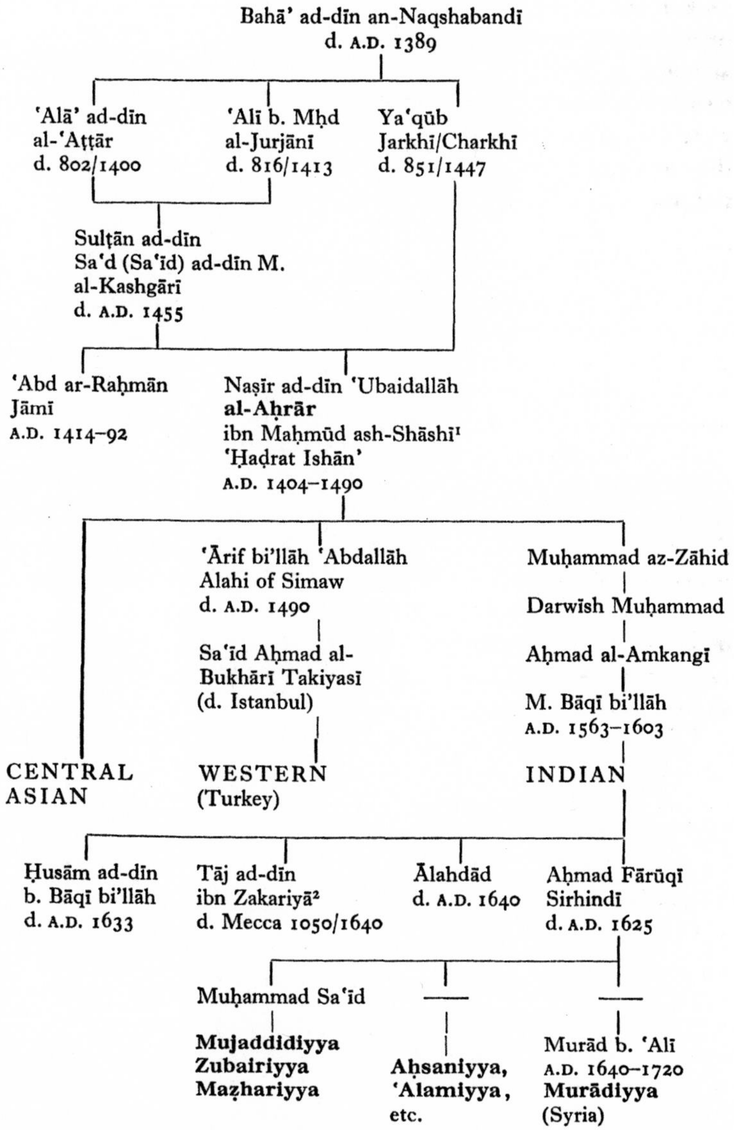

[1] Tashkand was then called Shāsh.

[2] Tāj ad-dīn had an interesting career and eventually found a niche in Mecca away from the rivalries which ensued after the death of Muḥammad Bāqī bi'llāh. From this vantage point he had much to do with commending the Naqshabandī Way to Arabs. He translated books like Jāmī's *Nafaḥāt* and

Jāmī has been included in this tree, not for any significance in the *silsila*, but for his influence upon Persian, Turkish, and Indian Sufism, as well as for his biographies of Sufis, *Nafaḥāt al-uns*, finished in 881/1476. Though not an initiating shaikh, Jāmī is said to have given the Naqshabandī *ṭarīqa* to Mīr 'Alī Shīr Nawā'ī (A.D. 1441–1501) when this minister to the Timurid sultan, Abu 'l-Ghāzī Ḥusain, undertook a period of retreat in 881/1476. 'Alī Shīr was famous as a patron of the arts and as a writer of distinction in prose and poetry, especially as a pioneer poet in Chagatay Turki. He founded and endowed a Khānaqāh Ikhlāṣiyya in Herāt (as Shāh Rukh had also done) as well as some 90 *ribāṭs*, this term here meaning 'resthouses'.[1]

The most influential figure after Bahā' ad-dīn was Khwāja Aḥrār, popularly known as Ḥaḍrat Īshān, from whom all the three regional lines derive—central Asian, western Turkish, and Indian. Members of the order were largely responsible for the spread of Islam among the Özbegs, among whom Khwāja Aḥrār wielded great spiritual power, and among whom he consequently played a political role.[2] The heads of all the independent states which succeeded the Mongols (except in Persia) favoured this great Sunnī order, honouring its leaders during their lifetimes and building mausoleums over their graves and *khānaqāhs* to house their dervishes. Although it weakened in time, it remained the dominant regional order, with great centres at Samarqand, Merv, Khiva, Tashkand, Herat, as well as Bukhara. There were also significant groups in Chinese Turkestan and Khokand, Afghanistan, Persia, Baluchistan, and India.

The order was first introduced into India during the time of Bābur (d. A.D. 1530), but its real propagator was M. Bāqī bi'llāh Berang (A.D. 1563–1603) who finally settled in Delhi. His spiritual

'Alī al-Kāshifī's *Rashaḥāt 'Ain al-Ḥayāt* into Arabic, and we have referred to a *risāla* of his on Naqshabandī practices. Al-Muḥibbī devotes a long article to him in his *Khulāṣat al-Athar* (i. 464–70) and also to his other master Ālah-Bakhsh (i. 423–4), *khalīfa* of Sayyid 'Alī ibn Qiwām of Jaunpur. Tawfīq al-Bakrī has a note on the Tājiyya as he calls the order; *Bait aṣ-Ṣiddīq*, p. 384.

[1] See the study of 'Alī Shīr by M. Belin in *J. Asiat.* v. xvii–xviii (1861), 192.

[2] For example, during the attack of the Timurid Abu 'l-Qāsim Bābur (d. A.D. 1457), grandson of Shāh Rukh, on Samarqand, al-Aḥrār's exhortations were effective in strengthening the resistance of another Timurid, Abu Sa'īd Mīrzā (reg. A.D. 1451–68), of Mā' Warā 'n-Nahr. When Mīrzā Bābur offered a truce (1454) it was to al-Aḥrār that his emissaries addressed themselves; see *Rashaḥāt 'Ain al-Ḥayāt*, which is especially concerned with al-Aḥrār.

descent from al-Aḥrār was Muḥammad az-Zāhid, a darwīsh Muḥammad, then Aḥmad al-Amkangī who sent him to India. Another propagator who settled in Lahore was Khwand Māḥmūd (d. 1052/1642), whose son spread his allegiance. Of the various lines diverging from Bāqī bi'llāh two, which contrasted greatly in outlook, were that through his son, Ḥusām ad-dīn Aḥmad (A.D. 1574–1633), following a pantheistic line, and a somewhat bigoted Sunnī movement inspired by Bāqī's pupil, Aḥmad Fārūqī Sirhindī (A.D. 1563–1624), nicknamed *Mujaddid-i Alf-i Thānī* (Reformer of the Second Millennium), who, within his sphere of influence, attacked the link of Sufism with antinomian mysticism and advocated what came to be known as the Shuhūdiyya doctrine derived from as-Simnānī. His reaction against Akbar's tentatives towards religious syncretism earned him the Emperor's disfavour, but his reformist outlook won the support of subsequent Mogul emperors.

In the Ottoman empire the Naqshabandī *silsila* was of significance only in Syria and Anatolia. Introduced into Syria in the seventeenth century it did not begin to expand until propagated by Murād ibn 'Alī al-Bukhārī.[1] Born in fact in Samarqand in A.D. 1640 he went to India, where he was initiated by Muḥammad Ma'ṣūm, son of Aḥmad Sirhindī. He eventually made Damascus his centre, but continued to travel extensively in Arab lands and Anatolia, training and initiating *khalīfas* indiscriminately, and died in Istanbul in 1132/1720. From Murād stemmed a number of minor branches, 'Abd al-Ghanī an-Nābulsī (A.D. 1641–1731), one of the few Arab Sufis of the age who possessed any insight, belonged to the Naqshabandiyya. The order was introduced into Egypt by Aḥmad al-Banā' ibn M. ad-Dimyāṭī (d. 1127/1715) who was initiated and given the *khilāfa* in Yemen by Aḥmad ibn 'Ujail and 'Abd al-Bāqī al-Mizjājī.[2]

In Turkey the Naqshabandiyya was strong in towns; there being fifty-two *tekkés* in Istanbul in the 1880s. Evliya Chelebi

[1] D'Ohsson refers to him (*Tableau*, IV. ii. 626) as Murād Shāmī, founder of the Murādiyya. Muḥammad Khalīl al-Murādī, a descendant, gives many biographies of Murād ibn 'Alī and members of the family in his *Silk ad-durar*.

[2] Al-Jabartī, *'Ajā'ib*, Cairo, 1958, i. 226–9. Aḥmad Abū 'l-Wafā' ibn 'Ujail (d. 1664) took the *ṭarīqa* from Tāj ad-dīn b. Zakariyā in Zabīd and Mecca and became the regional Naqshabandī *khalīfa* in Yemen; on him see al-Muḥibbī, *Khulāṣat al-Athar*, i. 346–7, 464. He was succeeded by his son Abū 'z-Zain Mūsā. 'Abd al-Bāqī was also a local Yemeni *khalīfa* (d. 1663: Muḥibbī, ii. 283).

wrote: 'Well informed men know that the great shaikhs may be classed in two principal orders—that of Khalveti and that of Nakshbendi.'[1] Like the eastern, the western branch was divided into many separate and frequently isolated groups, each distinguished by its own *ṭā'ifa* name.[2]

The only *ṭarīqa* of the Kubrāwī *silsila* to achieve any widespread fame was the Hamadāniyya. 'Alī al-Hamadānī had conducted large movements of his followers into Kashmir where they formed a number of branches, one of the best-known being the Ashrafiyya, deriving from Ashraf Jahāngīr Simnānī (d. 1405) who settled at Kichhauchha in Oudh. The order continued to exist among Iranians, and towards the end of the fifteenth century made its appearance in Syria. One Sharaf ad-dīn Yūnus b. Idrīs al-Ḥalabī (d. 923/1517) is reported to have taken it from 'Ubaid Allāh at-Tustarī al-Hamadānī. 'He acquired many followers who practised the authentic *awrād* in al-Madrasat ar-Rawāḥiyya in Aleppo. Then he moved to Damascus setting himself up in Dār al-Ḥadīth near the citadel.'[3] And there were other visitors. 'Abd al-Laṭīf b. 'Abd al-Mu'min al-Khurasānī al-Jāmī, on his way to carry out the pilgrimage with a large following of *murīds*, stayed in Istanbul for some time, eulogized Sultan Sulaimān and gave him the *dhikr* of the order (the *talqīn*), then went on to Aleppo where he taught *al-awrād al-fatḥiyya*,[4] and after carrying out the *ḥajj* returned to his own country, dying in Bukhara in 956/1549 (or 963/1555–6).[5]

In India a characteristic of this period is the widening of allegiance to the established Suhrawardī and Chishtī lines and the more restricted spread of the Naqshabandī, Qādirī, and Shaṭṭārī orders—each expressed in hundreds of local establishments surrounding a living or dead holy man. The success of the orders was based on this mystique of saint-intercessors and adaptation to deep-rooted Indian religious instincts. The Suhrawardī and Chishtī *ṭarīqas* were fortunate in having inspired leaders, but

[1] Evliya Chelebi, tr. von Hammer, I. ii. 29.

[2] The names of some of the western offshoots are given by A. le Chatelier, *Les Confrèries musulmanes du Hedjaz*, 1887, p. 155 n.

[3] Ibn al-'Imād, *Shadharāt*, viii. 128.

[4] The cycle of prayers called *al-awrād al-fatḥiyya* were given to 'Alī al-Hamadānī by the Prophet. They are the pivot of the order and specially intended for recitation at the group *ḥalqa*; see As-Sanūsī, *Salsabīl*, p. 107.

[5] Ibn al-'Imād, op. cit. viii. 282–3.

the Qādirī had so far lacked both leaders and any clear attractive Sufi doctrine.

Muḥammad Ghawth, claiming to be tenth in succession from 'Abd al-Qādir, is responsible for the definitive introduction of his order into India. Born in Aleppo, he settled (A.D. 1482) in Uchch in Sind, long conditioned as a strong Suhrawardī centre, gained the patronage of the Sultan of Delhi, Sikandar Lodī, and died in 1517, to be succeeded by his son, 'Abd al-Qādir (d. 1533). The Baghdad centre of the order gained the favour of the Ottoman dynasty because of its orthodoxy.[1] Other members of the family moved also to India, and finding it to be fruitful were followed by more members, who formed independent branches. In the seventeenth century it took on a new lease of life and a surprising change took place in its teaching (so far *ẓahirī* and non-mystical) and practices. It expanded under various leaders, including Shāh Abu 'l-Ma'ālī (d. 1615), Miyān Mīr (d. 1635), and Mulla Shāh Badakhshī (d. 1661). The last two were teachers of Dārā Shikōh, during his earlier and more orthodox period.[2] The Indian Qādirī shaikhs now extend very far the process of compromise with Hindu thought and custom.

Naturally in as diversified a region as India regional orders were formed.[3] The most important was the Shaṭṭāriyya. Its origins are obscure. It claims to be in the Ṭaifūrī tradition, but is attributed to a descendant of Shihāb ad-dīn as-Suhrawardī called 'Abdallāh

[1] When Shāh Ismā'īl the Ṣafawid took Baghdad in A.D. 1508 his troops destroyed tombs, including that of 'Abd al-Qādir (rebuilt after Hulagu's destruction of 1258), and expelled the family, some of whom took refuge in India. Sulaimān the Great, after conquering the former 'Abbāsid capital, made donations towards its restoration in 941/1534, and (after Shah 'Abbās's destruction in 1623) Murād IV did the same in 1048/1638. Increasing prosperity enabled the family to build the present mosque.

[2] On this remarkable son of Shāh Jahān see B. J. Hasrat, *Dārā Shikūh: His Life and Works*, Visvabharati, Santiniketan, 1953.

The names of a few of the more important Qādirī *ṭā'ifas* in India are given in Appendix D.

[3] A distinctive order founded in India a little earlier, but with a narrow outreach, was the Madāriyya. Nothing certain is known about its founder, Badī' ad-dīn Shāh Madārī, an immigrant (Syrian?) who settled in Jaunpur where he died *circa* 1440, his tomb at Makanpūr (near Cawnpore) becoming the focus of a remarkable festival and fair. This occasion also acquired notoriety through the rite of fire-walking performed by the Madārī *faqirs* (see J. A. Subhan, *Sufism*, 1938, pp. 305–6; *'Ā'īn-i Akbarī*, 1948 edn., iii. 412). This group is regarded as a *bi-shar'* order, but it is more of a syncretistic sect than an order. As-Sanūsī includes it among his forty *ṭarīqas* and describes its aims and practices (*Salsabīl*, pp. 152–4), but he knew nothing about it at first hand.

ash-Shaṭṭār. His *pīr*, Muḥammad 'Ārif (attribution unknown?), sent him to India. He was at first at Jawnpur, capital of Ibrāhīm Shāh Sharqī (reg. A.D. 1402–40); then difficulties caused him to go on to Mandu, capital of the small Muslim state of Mālwa (Multan), where he died in 1428/9. His Way was spread by his pupils, especially the Bengali, Muḥammad 'Alā', known as Qazan Shaṭṭārī, but owes its full development as a distinctive order to Shāh Muḥammad Ghawth of Gwalior (d. 1562/3),[1] fourth in succession from the founder, and to be distinguished from the Muḥammad Ghawth of Uchch (d. 1517), propagator of the Qādiriyya in India. His successor Shāh Wajīh ad-dīn (d. 1018/1609), should be mentioned, since he was the author of many books, founded a long-lived *madrasa*, and was honoured as a great saint in Gujerat. Since the Shaṭṭāriyya does not regard itself as an offshoot of any order (though its chain links with the Suhrawardiyya), it may be regarded as a distinct *ṭarīqa* with its own characteristics in beliefs and practices.[2] It was known as the 'Ishqiyya in Iran and Turan, and as the Bisṭāmiyya in Ottoman Turkey, the name in both instances deriving from the name of a propagator called Abu Yazīd al-'Ishqī.[3]

None of the orders in India could escape being influenced by their religious environment. Many branches became very syncretistic, adopting varieties of pantheistic thought and antinomian tendencies. Many practices were taken over from the Yogis—extreme ascetic disciplines, celibacy, and vegetarianism. Wanderers of the qalandarī type abounded. Local customs were adopted; for example, in the thirteenth century the Chishtīs paid respect to their leaders by complete prostration with forehead on the ground.[4]

[1] Muḥammad Ghawth was the author of a *mi'rāj* in which he describes his progress along the path of spiritual ascension. The pantheistic expressions he used caused the *'ulamā'* of Gujerat to call for his condemnation for heresy, from which he was vindicated by 'Shāh' Wajīh ad-dīn who became his disciple and then successor. Other books he wrote include *Jawāhir-i Khamsa* and *Awrād-i Ghawthiyya*. As-Sanūsī describes the *dhikrs* of the order, including the Jūjiyya = Yoga; *Salsabīl*, pp. 126–35.

[2] Besides the works of Muḥammad Ghawth and his successor, an account of its doctrines is given in *Irshādāt al-'Ārifīn* by Muḥammad Ibrāhīm Gazur-i Ilāhī, a contemporary of Awrangzaib (1659–1707).

[3] The 'Ishqiyya is one of the orders given by as-Sanūsī (he calls it 'a *ṭā'ifa* of the Shaṭṭāriyya'), but he has 'Ishqī's *sanad* muddled up; see *Salsabīl*, pp. 135–6.

[4] The custom is referred to frequently in Amīr Ḥasan 'Alā Sijzī's *Fawā'id*

Shī'ite Orders. The orders were closely involved with the in-increasing Shī'ī movement in Iranian regions. This is seen in the leaders deriving from the Kubrāwiyya movement of Sufi thought;[1] and even the Naqshabandī order, so definitely Sunnī, made great concessions to the cult of 'Alī without in any way becoming Imāmī Shī'ite. Of course, most orders trace their origin to 'Alī and accord him a special position as the medium through which their esoteric teaching had been transmitted, but in any case remaining Sunnī.

A continuous 'Alid Sufi chain had been maintained for a long while, certainly since the prohibition on the open profession of Ismā'īlī Shī'ism in Egypt (A.D. 1171), Syria (Maṣyaf A.D. 1260, triumph of Baibars A.D. 1272), and the fall of Alamūt (A.D. 1256), when many Shī'īs found a home within Sufi orders. One of the earliest surviving chains[2] which shows the double gnostic procession from 'Alī (both hereditary and initiatory) is that of Ṣadr ad-dīn M. ibn Ḥamūya (d. 617/1220), belonging to a family of Persian origin, whose most famous Sufi member was the Shī'ī, Sa'd ad-dīn ibn Ḥamūya.

Shī'ism under a Sufi cloak formed a powerful undercurrent within the Kubrāwī, Khalwatī, Bektāshī, and Bairāmī orders. In the Ottoman Empire it had to remain under cover, but in Persia there were various Shī'ī Sufi movements, though with the formation of Shī'ī states Sufi orders and their shaikhs did not in fact fare very well. Sunnī orders were naturally resented by the Shī'ī *mujtahids* as having abandoned the Imām for the *murshid/quṭb*, but Shī'ī Sufis also suffered. Shī'ī thought flourished during the Ṣafawid period in a renaissance heralded by men like the Sufi Mīr M. Bāqir Dāmād (d. 1631), Qāḍī Sa'īd Qummī (d. 1691), and Mullā Ṣadrā Shīrāzī (d. 1642).

The most interesting Shī'ī–Sufi movement from the historical point of view was the Ṣafawiyya, which began as a Sunnī order. The founder, Ṣafiyyaddīn (647/1249–735/1334),[3] who claimed

al-fu'ād, a record of the conversations of Shaikh Niẓām ad-dīn Awliyā', see K. A. Nizami, *Religion and Politics in India during the Thirteenth Century*, 1961, p. 94.

[1] For example, as-Simnānī; see M. Molé, 'Les Kubrawiyya entre Sunnisme et Shiisme aux huitième et neuvième siècles de l'hégire', *R.E.I.* xxix (1961), 61–142.

[2] See Appendix A.

[3] On Shaikh Ṣafī see the account in E. G. Browne, *Persian Literature in Modern Times*, 1924, pp. 3–44, which utilizes the *Ṣafwat aṣ-ṣafā'*, written by

descent from the seventh Imām, Mūsā Kāẓim, was born in Ardabīl in eastern Azerbaijan. He experienced difficulty in finding a director, but eventually discovered a Shaikh Zāhid[1] with whom he remained for twenty-five years until his death (694/1294), when he succeeded him. From Ṣafiyyaddīn the succession was hereditary: (2) Ṣadr ad-dīn, d. 1393, (3) Khwāja 'Alī, d. 1429, (4) Ibrāhīm Shāh, d. 1447/8, (5) Junaid, killed in battle in 1460, (6) Ḥaidar, also killed in battle in 1488, and (7) Shāh Ismā'īl (d. 1524), founder of the Ṣafawī dynasty.

It is not clear when the order became Shī'ī. Khwāja 'Alī showed Shī'ī tendencies and when Shaikh Junaid, with whom its militant role began, fled to Ūzūn Ḥasan, chief of the White Sheep dynasty, with his ten thousand Sufi warriors (*ghuzāt-i Ṣūfiyya*) 'who deemed the risking of their lives in the path of their perfect Director the least of the degrees of devotion',[2] he visited the shrine of Ṣadr ad-dīn al-Qonawī,[3] whose incumbent, Shaikh 'Abd al-Laṭīf, denounced him as a heretic. Shaikh Ḥaidar was responsible, in answer to divine revelation, for instructing his followers to adopt the scarlet cap of twelve gores[4] signifying the twelve Imāms, which led to their being known by the Turkish term *qizil-bāsh* (Redheads). Shāh Ismā'īl's battle-cry was '*Allāh! Allāh! wa 'Alī waliyyu 'llāh!*',[5] and he made Twelve-imām Shī'ī belief the state religion, in fact the only tolerated religion in his dominions. The Ṣafawids eventually gained the adherence of groups like the descendants of Nūrbakhsh and the Musha'sha'.

The Ṣafawiyya, as a strongly Turkish order, had considerable repercussions upon Anatolia both religiously and politically.

Tawakkul ibn al-Bazzāz around 760/1359, but subsequently revised and augmented. The book has been analysed by B. Nikitine in *J. Asiat.* 1957, 385–94.

[1] His proper name was Tāj ad-dīn Ibrāhīm ibn Rūshan of Ḥilyakirān in the Khānbalī district of Gīlān. His link, and so that of Ṣafī, was with the Suhrawardī *silsila*, but it is better attached to the Khurasanian rather than the Baghdadian tradition. It is interesting that Shāh 'Abbās (1588–1629) appointed Shaikh Abdāl, a descendant of Shaikh Zāhid, custodian of his shrine at Shaikhānbar in Ardabīl in 1600. So the shrine reverted to the original line (cf. E. G. Browne, *J.R.A.S.* 1921, 395 f.).

[2] E. G. Browne, *Lit. Hist. Persia*, iv. 47.

[3] Ṣadr ad-dīn al-Qonawī (d. A.H. 1273), a famous commentator on the thought of Ibn al-'Arabī, whose lectures on the *Fuṣūṣ* inspired the Persian poet 'Iraqī to compose his *Lama'āt*.

[4] *Tāj-i duwāzda tark*, later called *tāj-i ḥaidarī*.

[5] 'God! God! and 'Alī is the friend of God.' On the Shī'ī sense of *walī* see below, pp. 133–5.

Several Turkish Khalwatī orders (Bairāmiyya and Jilwatiyya), claiming to be Sunnī, were linked with the same tradition, whilst among the many political aspects we may mention the rising in A.D. 1416 of Muṣṭafā Bürklüja supported by Shaikh Badr ad-dīn, son of the *qāḍī* of Simaw.[1] Shāh Ismā'īl in his bid for power found strong support in such parts as had been influenced, especially among the population of the Gulf of Adalia, Sanjaq Teke, whose Takhtajī population is said to be descended from immigrant Iranian *qizil-bāsh*,[2] and the Ottoman sultan Bāyazīd II had difficulty in suppressing the rebellion of Bābā Shāh Kulī in support of Shah Ismā'īl. The Sufi organization upon which the dynasty had come to power continued to exist as the servant of the state, with a *khalīfat al-khulafā'* at the head,[3] but steadily declined, until in time Sufis became targets for the enmity and persecution of the Shī'ī *mujtahids*.

The Ni'matullāhī order was founded by Nūr ad-dīn M. Ni'matullāh b. 'Abdallāh, who claimed descent from the fifth Shī'ī Imām, Muḥammad Bāqir. Born in Aleppo in 730/1330 in a family of Iranian origin, he went to Mecca at the age of 24, where he became pupil, then *khalīfa*, of 'Abdallāh al-Yāfi'ī (1298–1367), who traced his mystical ancestry to Abu Madyan (Egyptian branch). After 'Abdallāh's death, he found his way to central Asia, travelling from *khānaqāh* to *khānaqāh*, Samarqand, Herāt, and Yazd; expelled from Transoxiana by Timur he settled eventually at Māhān near Kirmān, until his death at an advanced age in 834/1431.[4]

Ni'matullāh was prolific writer of Sufi ephemeras, both prose and poetry. He enjoyed the favour of kings and this partiality for the great of the world was continued by his descendants. W. Ivanow writes that this *ṭarīqa* 'was always selective in its membership, and occupied the position of an "aristocratic" organization. Later on it became a fashion in the higher strata of the feudal society to be a member of this affiliation . . . A few decades ago almost the

[1] See *E.I.*[2] i. 869. On this aspect of the Qizil-bāsh and their connections with Anatolian dervish orders see F. Babinger, *Schejch Bedr ed-dīn*, Leipzig and Berlin, 1921, pp. 78 ff., *D. Isl.* xi (1921), 1–106; H. J. Kissling, 'Zur Geschichte des Derwischordens der Bajrāmijja', *Südostforschungen*, xv (1956), 237 ff.

[2] Cf. *E.I.*[1] iv. 627.

[3] See R. M. Savory, 'The Office of Khalīfat al-khulafā under the Ṣafawids', *J. Amer. Or. Soc.* lxxxv (1965), 497–502.

[4] On Ni'matullāh see E. G. Browne, *Lit. Hist. Persia*, iii. 463–73, where examples of his apocalyptic and pantheistic poetry are given and translated.

whole of the class of the junior government clerks, petty tradesmen, and other similar working people in Persia belonged to the "Mullā-Sulṭānī" or "Gunābādī" order, an offshoot of the Ni'matu'l-lāhīs (with headquarters in Baydukht, Gunābād), without in any way forfeiting their Shī'ite orthodoxy in the eyes of the people.'[1]

Mahān has remained the centre of the order but it put out other shoots besides the Gunābādī[2]—Dhū 'r-Riyāsatain and Ṣafī-'Alī-Shāhī. In the founder's lifetime it spread into India, where the Bahmanid ruler of Deccan, Aḥmad Shāh Walī (d. 1436), fostered it in his dominions. Persecuted for a period in Iran, it gained ground after the rise of the Qajar dynasty (A.D. 1779), and is the most active order in Iran at the present time.

The Nūrbakhshiyya[3] may be classed among Shī'ī orders. Nūrbakhsh's doctrines were Shī'ī in tendency though he himself claimed the Imāmate by divine election, not by descent, and in consequence he had an adventurous and hazardous career. The members of the group in Kashmir when under persecution claimed to be Sunnī, no doubt exercising the expedient of *taqiyya* (precautionary dissembling).[4]

An Assessment. The difficulty experienced in treating the history of the orders derives from the need for expressing in a reasonably coherent fashion the development and organization of a movement of the spirit which was not orderly; thus one gives the impression of a precision which did not exist. When, therefore, I trace their development through three stages it must be realized that this is no more than a generalization of trends, and that in the final stage the three continued to exist contemporaneously. I have earlier characterized the stages (as affecting the individual) as surrender to God (*khānaqāh* stage), surrender to a rule (*ṭarīqa* stage), and surrender to a person (*ṭā'ifa* stage), but this simply means a narrowing of the means of seeking the primary aim of the Sufi. With

1 W. Ivanow, *Ismaili Literature: a Bibliographical Survey*, Tehran, 1963, p. 184.

2 The split came after Raḥmat 'Alī Shāh, then—Ṭā'ūs al-'Urafā' Isfahānī—Ḥājjī Mulla Sultān of Gūnābād (='Sultān 'Alī Shāh', a pupil of the famous philosopher of Sabzawār, Ḥājji Mulla Hādī, 1798–1878)—Nūr 'Alī Shāh (d. 1917)—Ṣāliḥ 'Alī Shāh.

3 See above, p. 57.

4 See Muḥammad Haidar, *Ta'rīkh-i Rashīdī*, tr. E. D. Ross, London, 1895, pp. 434–5.

this qualification, that any schema implies a distinction more hard and fast than is justified by the facts, the trends may be summarized:

First (*khānaqāh*) Stage. The golden age of mysticism. Master and his circle of pupils, frequently itinerant, having minimum regulations for living a common life, leading in the tenth century to the formation of undifferentiated, unspecialized lodges and convents. Guidance under a master becomes an accepted principle. Intellectually and emotionally an aristocratic movement. Individualistic and communal methods of contemplation and exercises for the inducement of ecstasy.

Second (*ṭarīqa*) Stage. Thirteenth century, Seljuq period. Formative period = A.D. 1100–1400. The transmission of a doctrine, a rule and method. Development of continuative teaching schools of mysticism: *silsila-ṭarīqas*, deriving from an illuminate. Bourgeois movement. Conforming and making docile the mystical spirit within organized Sufism to the standards of tradition and legalism. Development of new types of collectivistic methods for inducing ecstasy.

Third (*ṭā'ifa*) Stage. Fifteenth century, period of founding of the Ottoman Empire. The transmission of an allegiance alongside the doctrine and rule. Sufism becomes a popular movement. New foundations formed in *ṭarīqa* lines, branching into numerous 'corporations' or 'orders', fully incorporated with the saint-cult.

The organization of what cannot properly be organized, personal mystical life, arose naturally through the need for guidance and association with kindred aspirants. But organization carried within itself the seeds of decay. Through the cult-mysticism of the orders the individual creative freedom of the mystic was fettered and subjected to conformity and collective experience. Guidance under the earlier masters had not compromised the spiritual liberty of the seeker, but the final phase involving subjection to the arbitrary will of the shaikh turned him into a spiritual slave, and not to God, but to a human being, even though one of God's elect.

In addition, the mystical content of the orders had been weakened. In the Arab world especially, the conflict between the exoteric and esoteric doctrines of Islam had been won by the legalists. Islam sought to subject the mystical element to its own standards, to make mysticism innocuous by tolerating much of its outer aspects and forms in return for submission. Order shaikhs vied with one another in demonstrating their loyalty and subservience to the *Sharī'a*, and in the process many orders were emptied of their essential elements and left with the empty husks of mystical terminology, disciplines, and exercises.

The orders had now attained their final forms of organization and spiritual exercises. Innovations had become fully integrated and their spirit and aims were stereotyped. No further development was possible and no further work of mystical insight which could mark a new point of departure in either doctrine or practice was to make its appearance. The following are the chief features:

(*a*) Authoritarian principle. Veneration for the shaikh of the *ṭā'ifa*, inheritor of the *baraka* of *wilāya*, and utter subjection to his authority.

(*b*) Developed organization embodying a hierarchical principle, with a general range of uniformity, variations being expressed in secondary aspects.

(*c*) Two main classes of adherents: adepts and lay affiliates.

(*d*) Initiatory principle: esoteric and power *isnād*. For adepts an elaborate initiation ceremony and common dress; a simpler ceremony, but including the oath of allegiance, for affiliates.

(*e*) Disciplinary principles: solitude, *dhikr*-tasks, vigils, fasting, and other austerities for adepts.

(*f*) The collective *dhikr*, with co-ordination of musical rhythm, breath-control, and physical exercises to excite ecstasy, as pivot of the assembly.

(*g*) A cult related to the tombs of holy men. Association of *walīs*, dead or alive, with the qualities and properties embraced by the terms *baraka* and *karāma*. Stress on *baraka* leading to perpetual hiving off into new orders.

IV

Nineteenth-Century Revival Movements

1. THE DIRECTIONS OF REVIVAL

BEFORE the nineteenth century the world of Islam had suffered no major reverses from the expansion of the West. The Maghrib had been menaced, but a state of power equilibrium had been maintained in the Mediterranean. The Portuguese had blocked Sultan Selim's ambitions to dominate the Indian Ocean, but this was offset by Ottoman Turkey's expansion at the expense of Christian Europe. Europe's earlier expansion by-passed the Ottoman Empire, which embraced the heartlands of Islam. Napoleon's conquest of Egypt in 1798 is generally taken as a convenient point from which to date the first realization of the threat presented by European expansion.

Two developments now led to an intensified Islam—the Wahhābī movement and revival in the orders. Neither was in response to the Western menace, for they had their roots in the eighteenth century; rather, they anticipated the need for reform and for countering the lethargy which had overtaken the Arab world under Ottoman rule. The first of these movements rejected the validity of the solidified system validated by *ijmā'* and especially such practices as compromised the unity and transcendence of God. It stressed a return to the simplicity of a mythical, unadulterated Islam, and interpreted the *jihād* against unbelievers as war against those who, like *baraka*-exploiters, had compromised its purity. The Wahhābī rejects any idea of intermediaries between himself and God since with his view of transcendence no relationship is possible. A ruling tenet was systematic opposition to all innovations, and the Wahhābīs shocked the world of Islam when, in the territories they conquered, they destroyed the tombs of saints, including that of Imām Ḥusain ibn 'Alī at Kerbala in 1802. The political action of the movement was restricted, but its stimulative effect was widespread, and its attack on the orders emphasized the need for reform.

All religious organizations flag in their interior life, and the orders were, as we have seen, very decadent. Within them the true Way of Sufi experience had weakened, though individuals and little circles continued to follow the Sufi Path. The revival that took place in an attempt to meet the situation stems from the work of three men, all born in the Maghrib.

The revival took two lines, traditional and reformist. That along traditional lines derives from the inspiration of an illuminate called ad-Darqāwī, who enlivened emotional fervour and stimulated the urge towards the contemplative life among adherents within the Shādhilī tradition. This resulted in a proliferation of branch orders, mainly in North Africa, with offshoots in Syria and Hijaz. The reformist movement derives from Aḥmad at-Tijānī and Aḥmad ibn Idrīs. The action of the first was centred in the Maghrib, and retained this orientation, though it spread into west, central, and eastern Sudan. It maintained its unity, its *khalīfas* being immunized against the virus of prophetical inspiration to proclaim their own separate Ways. The movement inspired by Aḥmad ibn Idrīs had its centre in Mecca and after Ibn Idrīs's death his chief disciples claimed equally both to perpetuate his Way and to have received heavenly directives to found their own distinctive Ways. Aḥmad ibn Idrīs in particular, responding to the challenge presented by the Wahhābī movement, sought to preserve the inner (*bāṭinī*) aspect of Islam, rejected completely by the Wahhābīs, along with full acceptance of the *ẓāhirī* aspect, and vigorously condemned the accretions which had debased the orders. These aims alienated both the *'ulamā'* and the order-shaikhs in the Hijaz. He also had a pan-Islamic vision. He sought to bind believers together through full adherence to the Law along with an emotionalized Islam based on devotion to the Prophet and a personal embodiment of divine power at work in the world. All these new orders were moved by missionary fervour to augment their membership.

The two Aḥmads both stressed that the purpose of *dhikr* was union with the spirit of the Prophet, rather than union with God—a change which affected the basis of the mystical life. Consequently, they called their Way *Aṭ-Ṭarīqat al-Muḥammadiyya* or *Aṭ-Ṭarīqat al-Aḥmadiyya*, the latter term referring, not to their personal names but to that of the Prophet. They laid less stress on the *silsila* of authority—the Tijāniyya rejected it altogether—

because they emphasized the fact that the Prophet himself had given them direct permission to initiate a Way. The new *ṭarīqas* were also marked by their revulsion against asceticism and by their stress on practical activities. Their Ways maintained established liturgical and ethical Sufism, having little in their method and training that the old Sufis would have regarded as mystical. This is shown by their practice, lack of guidance of neophytes, and rejection of esoteric teaching, and by such aspects as the kind of material drawn from classical Sufism, especially the prophetic tradition, which they incorporated into their manuals to justify every statement. They did not believe in personal guidance and progress along the Path, and in this contrasted with the continuing tradition of guidance maintained by Khalwatī and Shādhilī shaikhs. Few devotees of the dervish type were found in their *zāwiyas*, though *zuhd*-practitioners were still prominent in the traditional orders and especially the new Darqawiyya.

2. THE MAGHRIB

(*a*) *Tijāniyya*

The new outlook in the Maghrib is associated with the Tijāniyya. Abu 'l-ʿAbbās Aḥmad b. Muḥammad b. al-Mukhtār at-Tijānī was born in 1150/1737 at ʿAin Mādī in the south of Algeria. He became affiliated to many orders and a *muqaddam* of the Khalwatiyya. The following account, said to be derived directly from Aḥmad, shows how he received the call at Tilimsān in 1196/1782 to found his own independent order: 'The Prophet gave him permission to initiate during a period when he had fled from contact with people in order to devote himself to his personal development, not yet daring to claim shaikhship until given permission, when in a waking and not sleeping state, to train men in general and unrestrictedly, and had had assigned to him the *wird* which he was to transmit.'[1]

[1] *Jawāhir al-maʿānī wa bulūgh al-amānī fi faiḍ ash-Shaikh at-Tijānī*, Cairo, 1348/1929, i. 43. This book, together with the *Rimāḥ* on the margin by al-Ḥājj ʿUmar, the Tokolor *jihādī* of western Sudan, contains the main body of Tijānī doctrine and principles as well as the life of the founder. Popularly known as *al-Kunnāsh*, or 'The Pandects', the *Jawāhir* was compiled by Abu 'l-Ḥasan ʿAlī al-Ḥarāzimī, Aḥmad's chief disciple in Fez, in 1798–1800 with the authorization of Aḥmad himself. On the soundness of this book and other sources for Aḥmad's life see Jamil Abun-Nasr, *The Tijaniyya*, London, 1965, pp. 24–6.

After this event he went into the desert; the exact circumstances are obscure but he seems to have got into trouble with the Turkish authorities, and eventually settled in the oasis of Abī Samghūn. It was there in 1200/1786 that he received his final revelation (*fatḥ*).[1] In 1213/1798 he left his desert retreat, again it seems under pressure, and moved to Morocco to begin his wider mission from the city of Fez, where he was well received by Mūlay Sulaimān and remained until his death in 1815.

Aḥmad developed his rule on strict lines. At first he had adopted the Khalwatī line for his chain of succession, though his teaching owes much to the Shādhiliyya; the distinction between guidance and instruction (*tarbiya* and *ta'līm*) is evident in his teaching, but did not find its way into the subsequent rules of the order. Obligations, as was to be expected in an order designed to expand, were simple. He imposed no penances or retreats and the ritual was not complicated. He emphasized above all the need for an intercessor between God and man, the intercessor of the age being himself and his successors. His followers were strictly forbidden, not merely to pay the *'ahd* of allegiance to any other shaikh, but to make invocations to any *walī* other than himself and those of his order: 'When the Prophet had given him permission to found his apostolic Way and he had received divine power through his mediumship the Prophet told him, "You owe no favour to any of the shaikhs of the Path, for *I* am your medium and provider in very truth. Abandon all that you have taken in anything concerning the Path".'[2] Tijānīs consequently have only one *silsila* going back to the founder. He stressed the quiet *dhikr* even in congregation, and condemned the visitations and holy fairs (*ziyāras* and *mawsims*) so popular in the Maghrib, for they were all associated with the old *baraka*-possessors. He did not, therefore, at first gain a popular following, but he appointed as local organizers (*muqaddams*) anyone who would profess allegiance, without requiring any training other than in the rules and ritual regulations, the main stress being laid on the abandonment of all ties to shaikhs except himself. Thus at his death agents were already widely dispersed and a contribution-system in full force.

[1] *Jawāhir*, i. 44. There seems to have been yet another stage with his assumption of the rank of *Quṭb al-Aqṭāb* in 1214/1799.

[2] *Jawāhir*, i. 43.

Before Aḥmad's death the Wahhābī movement began to influence north Africa directly.[1] In 1226/1811 Sa'ūd ibn 'Abd al-'Azīz, the Wahhābī leader then master of the Hijaz, sent a message to Mūlay Sulaimān of Morocco inviting its people to follow the path of reform. Mūlay Sulaimān put his son, Abu Isḥāq Ibrāhīm, in charge of the annual pilgrimage caravan which was accompanied by *'ulamā'* who, on their return, had a lot to say about Wahhābī condemnation of the cult of saints.[2] They saw affirmation of Wahhābī principles as a means of weakening the influence of the marabouts. Mūlay Sulaimān drew up a long statement, in which he dealt with these questions of infringement of the Sunna. Aḥmad supported all this, although he was disliked by the *'ulamā'*, in accordance with the policy of subservience to established authority which was to characterize his order. The *khuṭba* which was read in all mosques was regarded by the marabOutic element as a declaration of war and set off an insurrection (1818–22) in which the Amhawsh, the head of the Wazzāniyya, and the recent illuminate, ad-Darqāwī, were involved.

Aḥmad at-Tijānī
c. 1815

(2) 'Alī ibn 'Īsā
Tamalhat *zāwiya*
d. 1844

Muḥammad al-Kabīr
b. Aḥmad at-Tijānī
d. 1827

(3) Muḥammad aṣ-Ṣaghīr
b. Aḥmad at-Tijānī
'Ain Mādī *zāwiya*
d. 1853

(4) Muḥammad al-'Īd
b. 'Alī b. 'Īsā
d. 1876

(5) Aḥmad
d. 1897

(6) Al-Bashīr
d. 1911

(5) Muḥammad aṣ-Ṣaghīr
d. 1892

(7) 'Alī

Although Aḥmad was buried in Fez, where his tomb became an object of visitation, the direction of the order moved to two centres in Algeria. Aḥmad had nominated the *muqaddam* of the *zāwiya* at Tamehalt near Tamasīn, 'Alī ibn 'Īsā (d. 1844), as his successor and directed that the succession should alternate between his own family and that of Alī ibn 'Īsā. 'Alī persuaded Aḥmad's sons to make 'Ain Mādī their home, and when he died

[1] See G. Drague, *Esquisse d'histoire religieuse du Maroc*, Paris, 1952, pp. 88–92.
[2] Aḥmad an-Nāṣirī, *Kitāb al-Istiqsā*, 1316/1898, viii. 145 ff. See also al-Jabartī, iv. 151.

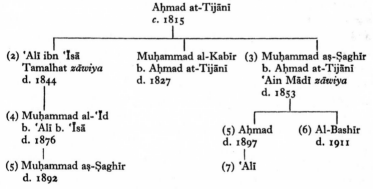

the succession went to Aḥmad's son, Muḥammad aṣ-Ṣaghīr, and then back to the other line.

No serious split in the order occurred until the death of Muḥammad al-ʿĪd in 1876, when the two groups separated following a dispute over the succession. The result is that these two places came to have only a localized direct authority, and groups have made themselves independent all over Africa. But the order's expansion was not thereby weakened, nor did the local leaders claim to found new lines; and by the beginning of the twentieth century it had become one of the most important in Morocco and Algeria.

The order spread south of the Sahara into west Sudan, then Nilotic, and finally central Sudan. It made its first appearance in west Sudan when it was adopted by maraboutic (*zwāya*) groups of the Moorish tribe of Ida-w ʿAlī. But it remained a tribal characteristic and would not have spread among Negroes had it not been taken up by a Tokolor from Futa Toro called al-Ḥājj ʿUmar, who made use of the oath of allegiance to bind followers to himself and propagated the Tijānī Way by force. Since his death in 1864 the order has continued to expand, especially among Fulbe and Tokolor, who regard it as an aristocratic order compared to the more humble Qādiriyya, the only other order that exists in west Africa.

Many Tijānī Maghribīs travelling on pilgrimage settled in Egypt and Nilotic Sudan and introduced their order.[1] We have mentioned how anyone prepared to propagate was made a *muqaddam*. In Nilotic Sudan its followers tend to be mainly the descendants of west Sudan Fulbe and Tokolor who have settled. In central Sudan it spread only this century as a Fulbe characteristic. Outside Africa Tijānī allegiance was negligible. Although it acquired a *zāwiya* in Mecca it was adopted only by some west Sudanese settled there and by migrants.

(*b*) *Traditionalist Revival: The Darqawiyya and Its Offshoots*

Before turning to Aḥmad ibn Idrīs and the movements he inspired which affected eastern Africa and Arabia, we may consider

[1] There were two currents of propagation in Nilotic Sudan during the Egyptian period, one Maghribī, whose chief agent was M. b. al-Mukhtār ash-Shinqīṭī, known as Wad al-ʿĀliya (d. 1882), and the other through movements of western Sudanese, both on pilgrimage and migration. An account of the various agents who worked in Egypt and Nilotic Sudan is given in *Jamāʿat al-waḥdat al-Islāmiyya at-Tijāniyya: ar-Risālat as-Sādisa*, Cairo, 1355/1936.

another Maghribī movement which paralleled that of the Tijānīs and in fact was far more of a popular revival and became the most widespread, numerous, and influential *ṭarīqa* in North Africa. This awakening was set in motion by an ecstatic leader in the Shādhilī-Zarrūqī succession called Abu Ḥāmid (Aḥmad) al-'Arabī ad-Darqāwī (1760–1823) who followed traditional lines. Although ad-Darqāwī was contemporary with at-Tijānī, the two movements do not coincide. Only after ad-Darqāwī's death did his movement become a distinctive Way. Unlike at-Tijānī he received no summons from the Prophet to found a *ṭarīqa*, he wrote little, and he says specifically that his *dhikr* derives from his own teacher, 'Alī al-'Amrān 'al-Jamal' (d. 1779).[1] Throughout his life he seems to have been the victim of circumstances over which he had no control.

Ad-Darqāwī himself stressed non-involvement in the affairs of this world, he was zealous in preaching against the *baraka* exploitation of the established orders, yet his own order became notable, even notorious, as a politico-religious movement. He himself became involved. Mūlay Sulaimān (reg. A.D. 1793–1822) at first sought to make use of the potential power rising from this illuminate to consolidate his position against the Turks in Oran and Tilimsān, but later, as we have seen, condemned the practices of the orders. Ad-Darqāwī had reacted against one of his *muqaddams*, 'Abd al-Qādir ibn Sharīf, for attacking the Turks in Oran (1805–8), yet later he supported the leaders of revolts against the rule of Mūlay Sulaimān. He was no leading spirit in this militant movement, but was used by others. The Sultan became hostile, and ad-Darqāwī was imprisoned. The next sultan, 'Abd ar-Raḥmān (1822–59), released him, and then, as his order diversified, its power weakened and its political activities in Morocco declined.

After ad-Darqāwī's death in his *zāwiya* at Bū-Berīḥ, just north of Fez, among his own tribe, the Banu Zarwāl, there developed around his name what can be regarded as a new *ṭarīqa* in that it is a definite line of ascription. His initiates had already spread widely, forming their own *zāwiyas*, but retaining the ascription. It became the most important order in Morocco, but also spread throughout the Maghrib and even had a few *muqaddams* in Egypt

[1] See Rinn, op. cit., p. 252. His full name was Abu 'l-Ḥasan 'Alī ibn 'Abd ar-Raḥmān al-Jamal al-Fāsī.

and Hijaz. Some long-established *zāwiya* groups attached themselves to the new line; these included the Amhawsh and the Ḥansaliyya, who deserted their Nāṣiriyya attachment and joined the Darqawiyya for political rather than religious reasons. The following are the more important branches:

1. Foundation *zāwiya* at Bū Berīḥ, where ad-Darqāwī and most of his successors are buried. Offshoot *zāwiyas* and agents at Tetwan, Tangier, Ghumara, etc. The headquarters moved to the nearby *zāwiya* of Amajjūṭ (Amjot) after 1863.

2. Badawiyya. This is the south Moroccan Tāfilalt branch, sometimes referred to as the Shurafā' of Madagra. The founder, Aḥmad al-Badawī, disciple of ad-Darqāwī, is buried in Fez, but the branch was organized (*zāwiya* of Gaūz) by his successor, Aḥmad al-Hāshimī ibn al-'Arbī, after whose death (1892) troubles over the succession led to the foundation of rival *zāwiyas*.

3. Bū-Zīdiyya. Founder: Muḥammad ibn Aḥmad al-Būzīdī (d. 1814), pupil of ad-Darqāwī. His pupil, Ibn 'Ajība (Abu 'l-'Abbās Aḥmad, d. 1809), is distinguished for his large literary output.[1]

4. Ghummāriyya. Founder: Aḥmad ibn 'Abd al-Mu'min, tomb at Tushgan.

5. Ḥarrāqiyya. North Morocco. Founder was Abu 'Abdallāh M. b. M. al-Ḥarrāq, d. 1845.

6. Kattāniyya. *Zāwiya* in Fez founded (*c.* 1850) by Muḥammad ibn 'Abd al-Wahhāb al-Kattānī. His grandson bearing the same name developed it from 1890. Imprisoned by the *wazīr* Aḥmad, al-Kattānī was freed on his death and his order grew. Considerable expansion took place during the reign of Mūlay 'Abd al-'Azīz, būt Mūlay Rafid treated him so harshly that he died. All the *zāwiyas* were closed and the order almost disappeared but was reorganized (*c.* 1918) under the direction of 'Abd al-Ḥayy.

7. Bu 'Azzāwiyya or Habriyya. Founded in north-eastern Morocco (*zāwiya* of Driwa) by Muḥammad (al-Habrī) ibn Aḥmad aṭ-Ṭayyib al-Bū-'Azzāwī, d. Marrakish 1914.

[1] See J. L. Michon, art. Ibn 'Adjība in *E.I.*[2] iii. 696–7.

8. Algerian branches:

(*a*) Mehājiyya or Qaddūriyya. Founder: Sidi Bū-ʿAzza al-Mehājī of Mostaganam, who was succeeded by his pupil, Muḥammad b. Sulaimān b. al-ʿAwda al-Qaddūr of Nedroma.

(*b*) ʿAlawiyya. Founded by Aḥmad al-ʿAlawī, who, after serving his apprenticeship in the ʿĪsāwiyya, became a pupil of M. al-Būzīdī (d. 1909), then declared his independence in 1914. He died in 1934 and is buried in the *zāwiya* of Tigzit, Mostaganam.

(*c*) In addition there are *zāwiyas* connected with: Muḥammad al-Misūn b. M. (Sīd al-Misūn), chief of the Algerian branch, d. 1300/1883; ʿAdda ibn Ghulām Allāh, d. 1860, tomb and *zāwiya* near Tiaret; Al-ʿArbī *Ībn ʿAṭiyya* ʿAbdallāh Abu Ṭawīl al-Wansharīshī.

9. Madaniyya: (*a*) Tripolitanian and Hijazian branch formed after ad-Darqāwī's death by Muḥammad Ḥasan ibn Ḥamza al-Madanī. Born in Medina, disciple of Darqāwī in Bū-Berīḥ, he returned to Medina, where he initiated many *khalīfas*. After ad-Darqāwī's death he settled in Tripoli, where he formed his own *ṭarīqa*, and died in Misurata in 1363/1846. Under al-Madanī's son and successor, Muḥammad Ẓāfir, it became a new and distinctive order rather than a branch, and *muqaddams* were widely dispersed in Tunisia, Algeria, Libya, Fezzan, Hijaz, and Turkey where it played a Pan-Islamic role.[1] From it branched:

(*b*) Raḥmāniyya.[2] A Hijazi branch founded by M. ibn M. ibn Masʿūd b. ʿAbd ar-Raḥmān al-Fāsī, who went to Mecca in 1850 where he built a *zāwiya*, and died in 1878.

(*c*) Yashruṭiyya, founded by ʿAlī Nūr ad-dīn al-Yashruṭī, born in Bizerta 1793, died in Acre 1891.

The order drew its membership from a wide range of social groups. Townspeople recited their *dhikrs*, attended local *ḥaḍras*, and occasionally went on visitations, but lived their normal life. Among mountain tribesmen and villagers attachment through the local *muqaddam* was felt as a renewed link with spiritual power and evoked an enthusiasm that often came into conflict with the older

[1] See below, p. 126.

[2] To be distinguished from the Khalwatī-Ḥafnawī-Raḥmāniyya founded by Muḥammad ibn ʿAbd ar-Raḥmān al-Geshtulī al-Jurjurī, d. 1208/1793.

orders and resented the political control of a foreign power.[1] Apart from the parasites who attach themselves to *zāwiyas*, this order had quite an unusal number of adherents who lived recognizably as dervishes, bearing a staff, wearing the ragged, patched *muraqqa'a*, and with a rosary of large wooden beads around the necks (forbidden to Sanūsīs), wandering from place to place, reciting litanies and chanting the Qur'ān. This wandering-dervish aspect goes back to ad-Darqāwī himself. It was also an order which gave scope to women and in 1942 it is reported that there were eight women circle-leaders (*muqaddamāt*) in Morocco.[2]

3. MOVEMENTS DERIVING FROM AḤMAD IBN IDRĪS

(*a*) *Aḥmad ibn Idrīs.*

The other great reformer was Aḥmad ibn Idrīs b. M. b. 'Alī.[3] Born at Maisūr near Fez in 1173/1760 into a pious family, he passed through the usual stages of induction into the religious disciplines, and one of his teachers, Abu 'l-Mawāhib 'Abd al-Wahhāb at-Tāzī, initiated him into his own order.[4] Another teacher in the Sufi Way was Abu 'l-Qāsim al-Wazīr. Brought up in the formal Sufi tradition grafted on to the legal tradition, Aḥmad reacted against the saint-veneration of the Maghrib which went

[1] About 1836 the *muqaddam* 'Abd ar-Raḥmān Tūtī became involved in resistance to the French occupation of Algeria and the resistance of the Darqawiyya continued in some form or another until 1907.

[2] G. Drague, *Esquisse d'histoire religieuse du Maroc*, Paris, 1951, p. 266 n.

[3] Short biographies have been appended to editions of Aḥmad's *Kanz as-sa'ādati wa 'r-rashād*, Khartoum, 1939, pp. 9–18 (by Shams ad-dīn b.'Abd al-Muta'āl b. Aḥmad b. Idrīs), the collection *Majmū'at aḥzāb wa awrād wa rasā'il*, Cairo, 1359/1940, pp. 201–5, by 'Abd ar-Raḥmān b. Sulaimān al-Ahdal, Muftī of Zabīd, pupil of Aḥmad; and a collection of Aḥmad's *risālas* entitled *Majmū'a Sharīfa*, Cairo, n.d., pp. 119–78, mainly concerned with his *aḥzāb*, pupils, eulogizing *qasīdas*, and the like.

[4] This was the Khaḍiriyya, the line initiated by 'Abd al-'Azīz ibn Mas'ūd ad-Dabbāgh in 1125/1713 on direct inspiration from that light of saintship, al-Khaḍir. He was originally Nāṣiriyya and his shaikh was M. b. Zayyān al-Qandūsī. On Ibn ad-Dabbāgh see *Adh-Dhahab al-ibrīz fī manāqib 'Abd al-'Azīz*, by Aḥmad ibn Mubārak al-Lamṭī, his successor and organizer of the order, and M. al-Kattānī, *Salwat al-anfās*, lith. Fez, ii. 197–203. From this Aḥmad ibn Mubārak the direction of the Khaḍiriyya, as the order came to be called from the name of the supernatural initiator, went to 'Abd al-Wahhāb at-Tāzī. Aḥmad ibn Idrīs did not succeed at-Tāzī, nor claim to carry on the Khaḍiriyya, as is often stated.

under the guise of *taṣawwuf*[1]. His biographer says that he based his Sufi practice solidly on the Qur'ān and Sunna, accepting only these as *uṣūl* (foundations) and rejecting *ijmā'* (consensus), except that of the Companions upon which the Prophet's Sunna is based.[2] Clearly this came later in his life, after he had come under Wahhābī influence. 'His concern was not confined to teaching *awrād* and *adhkār*, to urging people to go into retreat and insulate themselves from mankind. Such practices might be of advantage for the personal development of the individual disciple, but they were not suitable for the higher purpose at which he was aiming, that is, the unity of the endeavour of Muslims united in the bond of Islam.'[3]

Aḥmad soon abandoned the Maghrib, never to return. After accomplishing the pilgrimage in 1799 he settled in Cairo for further studies, and then lived obscurely in the village of Zainiyya in Qinā Province. He returned to Mecca a second time in 1818 and settled there. As a reformist cleric, claiming to restore the pure faith as it was before it had been corrupted by the *'ulamā'*, an upstart moreover, not a recognized member of the religious hierarchy of a place which had just experienced the rigours of Wahhābī domination, he was naturally not welcome. The *'ulamā'* 'whose hearts were eaten up with hatred and envy, disputed with him, but his divinely inspired floods of eloquence gushed forth and it was demonstrated that he stood squarely in the orthodox path'.[4] He became one of the most eminent teachers in the holy city and grouped around himself a great number of pupils, and of the many who took the *ṭarīqa* from him simply 'to partake of his power'(*li 't-tabarruk*) was Muḥammad Ḥasan Ẓāfir al-Madanī.[5] The enmity of the *'ulamā'* was never assuaged and a charge of heresy was brought against him. His life was so much endangered that he had to flee in 1827 to Zabīd and then to the town of

[1] It is related that 'once the famous saint of the Maghrib, al-'Arabī ad-Darqāwī, stood naked while he was teaching. He was subject to trances (*ṣāḥib al-ḥal*) and said, pointing to the Sayyid (Aḥmad ibn Idrīs), "Behold a saint unlike other saints, a *ghawth* unlike other *aghwāth*, a *quṭb* unlike other *aqṭāb*." The Sayyid averted his eyes, stripped off his gown and threw it over him. Since then that man was never seen naked' (*Tarjama* appended to Aḥmad's *Kanz as-Sa'ādati wa 'r-rashād*, Khartoum, 1939, pp. 14–15). Obviously an attempt to exalt Aḥmad at the expense of ad-Darqāwī. Censorious writers at all times have condemned *tamziq*, this spontaneous 'rending' and stripping of garments by an ecstatic overcome by a *ḥāl*. These various Arabic terms are explained in subsequent chapters or the glossary may be consulted.

[2] Shams ad-dīn b. 'Abd al-Muta'āl, op. cit., pp. 13–14.

[3] Ibid., p. 16.

[4] Ibid., p. 12.

[5] See below, p. 126.

Ṣabyā in 'Asīr, which at that time still paid allegiance to the Wahhābīs, who left him in peace since he was sympathetic towards their reformist tenets; and he died there in 1837.

Whereas the Tijāniyya remained unified, even later internal troubles not leading to the formation of new lines, the Idrīsiyya split up immediately the master died, and his more influential pupils embarked upon independent courses. The most important of these were Muḥammad ibn 'Alī as-Sanūsī, founder of the Sanūsiyya, and Muḥammad 'Uthmān al-Mirghanī, founder of the Mirghaniyya. These and a number of other offshoots were independent *ṭarīqas*, making only cursory acknowledgement of their debt to Aḥmad ibn Idrīs, and consequently followed different lines in their teaching and exercises. The Sanūsī was the only order which retained Aḥmad's quietist mode of *dhikr* and which banned music, dancing, and extravagant movements. Attainment of ecstasy in the normal crude sense was not the aim of the Sanūsī *dhikr*. The *ikhwān* were expected to work for their living and were withdrawn from the world into self-sufficient *zāwiya*-centres in oases in the Saharan wastes. What was stressed was the *dhikr* of meditation. Through contemplation of the Prophet's essence the *murīd* sought to attain identification with him.[1] The Mirghaniyya, inheriting a particular hereditary Asiatic Sufi tradition, took almost the opposite course. They stressed the value of music and physical exercises in their devotions, though excesses were not allowed. They had no *zāwiyas*, no *fuqarā'* dedicated to a life of service and devotion. They placed no stress upon the way of striving and contemplation, emphasizing rather the holiness of the Mirghanī family, through whom the ordinary man could attain salvation.

These two orders, important in their influence upon history, the Mirghanī in the world from the beginning, an Asiatic order which tempered its modes of expression to Kushitic African life, and the Sanūsī, striving at first successfully to fulfil its destiny within the Saharan wastes only to suffer spiritual eclipse as a post-Second World War kingdom, merit a fuller description.

(*b*) *Mirghaniyya or Khatmiyya.*

Towards the end of the eighteenth century the Mirghanī

[1] See the special invocation series of blessings upon the Prophet in as-Sanūsī's *As-Salsabīl al-mu'īn*, pp. 14 ff.

family, after long residence in central Asia, made their way to Mecca, whose *shurafā'* recognized their claim to descent from the Prophet. Muḥammad 'Uthmān's grandfather, 'Abdallāh al-Maḥjūb (d. 1207/1792), was a well-known Sufi[1] and Muḥammad 'Uthmān followed in his footsteps. Like as-Sanūsī he sought initiation into as many orders as possible, but his real shaikh was Aḥmad ibn Idrīs. Aḥmad sent him as a propagandist of reform to Egypt and the Nilotic Sudan (1817) just before Muḥammad 'Alī's conquest. He was not outstandingly successful, but he took a Sudanese wife, and their son, al-Ḥasan, was eventually to establish the *ṭarīqa* as the most important in eastern Sudan. Muḥammad 'Uthmān returned to Mecca and then accompanied Aḥmad to Ṣabyā, but after his master's death he returned to Mecca, where he pursued a course of rivalry with Aḥmad's other pupils, Muḥammad ibn 'Alī as-Sanūsī and Ibrāhīm ar-Rashīd. Each of these claimed to be Aḥmad's successor and founded his own independent *ṭarīqa.* In Mecca Muḥammad 'Uthmān was at first more successful than the others, since his family was known there. He showed himself to be no reformist shaikh like Aḥmad and won the support of some Meccan *shurafā'*. He makes little acknowledgement in his writings of his debt to Aḥmad, and like the Sanūsī, claims that his *ṭarīqa* is comprehensive, embracing the essentials of the Naqshabandiyya, Shādhiliyya, Qādiriyya, Junaidiyya, and the Mirghaniyya of his grandfather; 'therefore anyone who takes the *ṭarīqa* from him and follows his Path will link himself on to the chains (*asānīd*) of these *ṭarīqas*'.[2]

He sent his sons into different countries: south Arabia, Egypt, Nilotic Sudan, and even India. In each of these countries a nucleus of followers had been formed before his death in 1268/1851 at Ṭā'if, to which he had withdrawn in consequence of the increasing hostility of the *'ulamā'*. The propaganda was most successful in the Egyptian Sudan, where his son, al-Ḥasan (d. 1869), had settled at Kasala and founded the township of Khatmiyya. When Muḥammad Aḥmad proclaimed himself the Mahdī in the Sudan in 1881 the Mirghanī family, which like all other established orders had vested interests in the Turco-Egyptian regime, opposed

[1] His works are given in *G.A.L.* ii. 386; *G.A.L.S.* ii. 523. Popular etymology gives the origin of the family name as a compound of *mīr* (for *amīr*) and *ghanī* (a rich man), but the word is more likely to be a corruption of a place-*nisba* like Marghinān, since the first vowel is short.

[2] Aḥmad ar-Ruṭbī, *Minḥat al-aṣḥāb*, pp. 88–9.

his claims, and during the Mahdiyya the family went into exile. But with the re-occupation in 1898 Mirghanī authority once again reconstituted itself. The Mirghanīs strongly opposed the breaking away of *khalīfas* to found their own branches, but there was one exception whose independence was admitted by Muḥammad ʿUthmān. This was the Ismāʿīliyya founded in 1846 by Ismāʿīl ibn ʿAbdallāh (1793–1863) at El-Obeyd in Kordofan Province of eastern Sudan.[1]

The Islam of eastern Sudan, soundly based on Arabic, had tempered legalism with mysticism. The religious leaders had combined the roles of *faqīh* (jurisconsult), *faqīr* (Sufi), and *muʿallim* (Qurʾān teacher) under the one comprehensive term of *feki*, and their establishment which combined all these functions was known as a *khalwa* (retreat). The new emphases brought a different type of religious rivalry and order loyalty; no stress was placed upon ascetic and mystical practice and teaching, but complete reliance upon the Mirghanīs, loyalty to whom earned assurance of paradise. The old family and tribal orders continued to survive and maintained the old spirit, as against the legalistic fanaticism soon to burst out in the Mahdī's repudiation of his Sufi heritage.

(*c*) *Sanūsiyya.*[2]

Muḥammad ibn ʿAlī as-Sanūsī (1787–1859) had been involved in the disputes over the succession to Aḥmad ibn Idrīs. He founded (1838) his first *zāwiya* at Abu Qubais, a hill overlooking the Kaʿba, but though he won a following he could not maintain himself against both the *ʿulamāʾ* and the Mirghanī family strongly entrenched in Mecca. He was forced to leave Mecca (1840) and settled eventually (1843) in the hills known as Jabal Akhḍar in the interior of Cyrenaica, where he founded Az-Zāwiyat al-Baiḍāʾ. This relatively fertile region in the midst of the bleak desert was centrally situated both for influencing nomadic tribes and for contact with the caravan traffic coming from central Sudan. Though he

[1] See Ismāʿīl's own account in *Al-ʿUhūd al-wāfiya fī kaifiyyat ṣifat aṭ-Ṭarīqat al-Ismāʿīliyya*, Cairo [1937?], pp. 2–12; and for a general account see J. S. Trimingham, *Islam in the Sudan*, 1949, pp. 235–6.

[2] Two studies of the order in English may be mentioned: the first, by E. E. Evans-Pritchard, *The Samusi of Cyrenaica* (Oxford, 1949), is in its main stress that of a social anthropologist, whilst Nicola Ziadeh's *Sanūsīyah* (Leiden, 1958) studies it as a revivalist movement within Islam.

won over many nomadic tribes in Cyrenaica, he awakened little response among cultivators and urban people attached to the old orders, and his missionary outlook caused him to look southwards to the semi-pagan, mutually hostile, tribes of the Sahara, and beyond them to the black peoples of central Sudan. In 1856 he moved his headquarters from al-Baiḍā' to Jaghbūb deep in the Libyan desert, both to avoid Turkish interference and to strengthen his influence in central Sahara. There he founded a multi-function *zāwiya*, which resembled the ancient *ribāṭ* in its frontier-like character but was far more comprehensive in its Islamic and social characteristics.

More closely than any other of Aḥmad's successors Muḥammad ibn 'Alī followed his aims in urging the elimination of the causes of disunity among Muslims. Like Aḥmad he advocated a return to the primitive sources of Qur'ān and Sunna. Since this implied the rejection of *ijmā'* and *qiyās* and consequently the whole edifice of legalistic Islam, a result probably never envisaged by either Aḥmad or Muḥammad ibn 'Alī, the enmity of the *'ulamā'* was assured.[1] Muḥammad ibn 'Alī claimed that all the *silsilas* of existing orders had been brought together and unified in himself, and in his book *As-Salsabīl al-ma'īn fī 'ṭ-ṭarā'iq al-arba'īn* he describes their *dhikr* requirements to show how his Way fulfils them all.[2] His writings cannot be called mystical in any strict sense of the term; his *Al-Masā'il al-'ashar*, for example, deals with 'The Ten Problems' encountered when carrying out ritual *ṣalāt*. He carried on Aḥmad's aim in seeking to purify practical Sufism from extravagant and irregular features. He laid stress on the devotional aspects of *dhikr* recital, censuring the noisy and frenzied exhibitions with which *dhikr* had become associated. At the same time, since he was also a practical missionary, he did not forget the needs of the ordinary people and allowed practices connected with the honouring of saints.

The Sanūsī sought to achieve a simple Islamic theocratic

[1] See Abu 'Abdallāh M. b. A. 'Ullaish (d. 1299/1881), *al-Fatḥ al-'alī*, and extract translated in Depont and Coppolani, *Les Confréries religieuses musulmanes*, Algiers, 1897, pp. 546–51.

[2] The *Salsabīl* (written in 1260/1843) is not original but is based, as M. b. 'Alī acknowledges (Cairo edn., A.H. 1353, p. 4), upon the *Risāla* of Ḥusain b. 'Alī al-'Ujaimī (d. 1113/1702), which gives the *dhikrs* of the 40 *ṭarīqas* which maintain the spiritual equilibrium of Islam. Al-Murtaḍā az-Zabīdī (d. 1205/1791) also imitated 'Ujaimī's work in his *'Iqd al-jumān*.

organization of society by peaceful means. Hence he centred his movement in inaccessible regions of the Sahara, remote from centres of privilege like Mecca, for only in a country without a history was such an aim capable of achievement, though history was in fact to catch up with and overrun this order. His ideal of the unity of thought, worship, and action led to the most comprehensive *zāwiya* organization. Each local *zāwiya*, a cell of Islamic culture set in a nomadic or animistic environment, was the means by which adherents were organized and through which expansion was effected. Each formed a complex of buildings constructed around an inner courtyard with a well. These embraced the residence of the *muqaddam*, representative of the Sanūsī, his family, slaves, and pupils, a mosque, school, rooms for students, cells for keeping vigils, and a guest block for the use of passing travellers and caravans. The whole interrelated construction was surrounded by a wall and could be defended if need arose. Around it were lands cultivated by the *ikhwān*. The *zāwiya* was no alien settlement but regarded as belonging to the tribe in whose region it was situated, from whose members many of the *ikhwān* were drawn. Thus it was a centre of tribal unity and this gave it strength to survive. E. E. Evans-Pritchard writes: 'Unlike the Heads of most Islamic Orders, which have rapidly disintegrated into autonomous segments without contact and common direction, they have been able to maintain this organization intact and keep control of it. This they were able to do by co-ordinating the lodges of the Order to the tribal structure.'[1]

(*d*) *Other Idrīsī Derivations*

Aḥmad ibn Idrīs's own sons did not immediately claim the succession. His son Muḥammad recognized Ibrāhīm ar-Rashīd as his father's successor and the followers in Ṣabyā paid allegiance to him. Another son, 'Abd al-Muta'āl, rallied at first to the Sanūsī, spending some time with him at Jaghbūb, then went to Dongola on the Nubian Nile and constituted himself head of the order. In Arabian 'Asīr, Muḥammad and his descendants maintained their line in unison with the Nilotic one, and it was in 'Asīr that Muḥammad ibn 'Alī (1876–1923), great-grandson of Aḥmad, became a temporal ruler when he founded the Idrīsid dynasty of 'Asīr in 1905.

[1] E. E. Evans-Pritchard, op. cit., p. 11.

Ibrāhīm ar-Rashīd (d. at Mecca in 1874),[1] a Shā'iqī of the Egyptian Sudan, carried on the propagandist traditions of Aḥmad, whose authentic successor he claimed to be. He established *zāwiyas* at Luxor and Dongola as well as Mecca, where he won a popular following, especially after successfully vindicating himself from charges of heresy raised by the *'ulamā'*.[2] A nephew and pupil of his, called Muḥammad ibn Ṣāliḥ, branched out in 1887 into a derivative, the Ṣāliḥiyya,[3] with its seat at Mecca, which became influential in Somalia through the preaching of a Somali, Muḥammad Gūlēd (d. 1918) and the formation of collective settlements. The movement of Muḥammad ibn 'Abdallāh al-Ḥasan ('the Mad Mullah') had its origin among the Ṣāliḥiyya.

Muḥammad al-Majdhūb aṣ-Ṣughayyar (1796–1832), great-grandson of Ḥamad ibn Muḥammad (1693–1776),[4] founder of the Majdhūbiyya, a Shādhilī derivative, in Dāmar district in Nilotic Sudan, after studying under Aḥmad ibn Idrīs in Mecca, returned to the Sudan, revivified his hereditary *ṭarīqa* and propagated it among Ja'liyyīn and Beja tribes.

4. THE ORDERS IN ASIA

The revival which has just been described hardly extended to Asia, yet Mecca in the nineteenth century was the most important order-centre in the Muslim world, almost every order being represented there.[5] The Wahhābīs had abolished the orders along with the saint-cult in those parts of Arabia which they controlled, but after Muḥammad 'Alī's campaigns their political authority became confined to the Najd and the orders flourished in the Hijaz.[6] In 'Asīr, as we have seen, Aḥmad ibn Idrīs actually

[1] To be distinguished from the Moroccan Rashīdiyya (also known as Yūsufiyya), an order in the Shādhilī tradition (but independent of the Jazūlī succession) founded by Aḥmad ibn Yūsuf ar-Rashīdī, d. 931/1524–5.

[2] See A. le Chatelier, *Les Confréries musulmanes du Hedjaz*, Paris, 1887, pp. 94–7.

[3] See J. S. Trimingham, *Islam in Ethiopia*, 1952, pp. 243–4.

[4] See *Ṭabaqāt* of Wad Ḍaif Allāh, ed. Mandīl, 1930, pp. 70–1.

[5] C. Snouck Hurgronje has given us a picture of the life of Mecca at the time of his stay there in 1884–5; English translation *Mecca in the Latter Half of the 19th Century*, 1931, especially pp. 201–9 on the orders in Mecca. The fundamental study of the orders in the Hijaz is A. le Chatelier, op. cit.

[6] Hadramawt remained a closed area to *ṭarīqas* other than the 'Alawī (and its branches) which for centuries had maintained the region as a family preserve, though they had certainly helped in tempering the uncompromising legalism of the Tarīm-trained shaikhs.

found sanctuary under the Wahhābīs from the persecution of the Meccan *'ulamā'*. His pupils found greater responsiveness in Africa than in Arabia, yet all orders derivative from him were represented by *zāwiyas* in Mecca and most of the founders lived there. Although the Sanūsī like Aḥmad himself found Mecca an impossible place in which to pursue his aim of instituting a reformed *ṭarīqa* his *zāwiya* on Abu Qubais continued to flourish; *zāwiyas* were founded in other towns of the Hijaz; and the order even gained the allegiance of some of the bedouin.[1]

In Mecca the orders were in an equivocal position. They exercised so great an influence among pilgrims that Mecca became a great diffusion centre, for many were initiated into one or more lines, while others returned as *khalīfas*, sporting a tubular case around their necks containing their *ijāza* (licence to teach or propagate). For example, the first Indonesian Minangkabau shaikh of the Naqshabandiyya received his initiation in Mecca around 1840; though it also worked the other way, for it was primarily from Mecca that the Indian Naqshabandiyya found varying degrees of foothold in Arab towns. Returned pilgrims (except in Negro Africa) frequently wielded an influence in their homelands which far outweighed that of the official representatives of Islam.[2]

At the same time, the *'ulamā'* and *shurafā'*, the Meccan ruling class in all religious and civil matters under the protection of the Khedival or Ottoman regimes, resented the influence of the order-leaders,[3] since not only was reverence diverted from their presences, but also money from their purses. Persecutions of order-leaders were common. We have seen how an independent like Aḥmad ibn Idrīs was forced to leave the Hijaz. An especially revolting case was the persecution of the Shādhilī, 'Alī ibn Ya'qūb al-Murshidī as-Sa'īdī, who was condemned for heresy by the Majlis of the *'ulamā'* in 1886 and handed over to the secular authority, which tortured him to death.[4] At the same time, measures taken by the secular authority weakened the influence of the leaders of the orders.

[1] See C. Snouck Hurgronje, op. cit., pp. 55–6.

[2] On the influence of such returned pilgrims in Indonesia in the nineteenth century see C. Snouck Hurgronje, op. cit., Book IV: The Jāwah.

[3] On the hostility to the order-shaikhs of 'Awn ar-Rafīq, the Grand Sharif (1882–1905) or political head of Mecca, see C. Snouck Hurgronje, 'Les confréries religieuses, la Mecque et le Panislamisme', in his *Verspreide Geschriften*, 1923, iii. 199.

[4] See A. le Chatelier, op. cit., pp. 97–9.

When Muḥammad ʿAlī conquered the Hijaz in 1813 he instituted the system which had long been in force in many parts of the Ottoman Empire,[1] by placing the orders from the administrative point of view under a *shaikh aṭ-ṭuruq*, one being appointed for each town. A. le Chatelier wrote:

The role of this agent was apparently limited in that his function was to act as intermediary between the local authorities and the orders in his district in regard to such temporal matters as participation in public ceremonies, the practice of their ritual in mosques, the administration of *awqāf*, and the recognition of their dignitaries. These functions do not at first sight seem to be of such a nature as to give him a general authority over the orders . . . but the practice of always choosing as *shaikh aṭ-ṭuruq* a popularly venerated person or the head of a family enjoying great religious influence, produced a situation whereby in fact his authority came to be substituted for that of the chiefs of the orders. Becoming accustomed to address themselves to him in material matters the *muqaddams* came to recognize him as their spiritual master. Charged only with sanctioning their nominations he came to designate them himself and they came to accept him as their hierarchical superior. His *taqrīr* or administrative licence became the equivalent of an *ijāza* or canonical licence.

The first transformation led to a second—the grouping by town of the representatives of each order under the direction of one of them, who, originally personal agent of the *shaikh aṭ-ṭuruq*, came to impose himself as disposer of religious power and to replace, under the title of *shaikh as-sajjāda*, the provincial *nāʾib*.[2]

New movements of the spirit in the Arab Near East found other forms of expression than through mystical orders, few new orders being founded.[3] The family orders were well established

[1] Each city had its *shaikh ash-shuyūkh*. In Damascus the head of the Sumaiṣātiyya *Khānaqāh* held this post automatically; see al-Qalqashandī, *Ṣubḥ*, iv. 193, 221, etc., xii. 412. The actual authority of the *shaikh* varied according to local circumstances. Egypt differed in that the authority of the *shaikh aṭ-ṭuruq* extended over all the orders in the country. At the beginning of the twentieth century thirty-two orders are listed as coming under al-Mashyakhat al-Bakriyya; see M. Tawfīq al-Bakrī, *Bait aṣ-Ṣiddīq*, Cairo, 1323/1905, p. 381. Only the main orders it seems were officially recognized for there were many others not given in this list.

[2] A. le Chatelier, op. cit., pp. 4–5. C. Snouck Hurgronje says (op. cit., p. 177) that 'when two important sheikhs of one tarīqah, or more rarely when two tarīqahs, get into conflict with each other, the authority of such a Sheikh at-Turuq is of no value'.

[3] The main activity in this respect took place in the Khalwatiyya; but is

and family tradition and communal allegiance assured their continuity.[1]

After the Wahhābī incursion into Syria in 1810 when Damascus was threatened, the head of the Naqshabandiyya there, Ḍiyā' ad-dīn Khālid (1192/1778–1242/1826), following a visit to India, was moved to undertake reforms.[2] He succeeded in uniting into a more unified *ṭarīqa*-cluster various branches in Syria, Iraq, and eastern Turkey. His attempt did not succeed, in that after his death his *khalīfas* regarded their groups in Aleppo, Istanbul, and other towns as fully independent organizations.

Shaikh Khālid's propaganda was successful in causing members of important Qādirī families in Kurdistan to change over to the Naqshabandiyya, with considerable effect upon the subsequent history of Kurdish nationalism. 'Abdallāh, son of a prominent Molla Ṣāliḥ, having become Naqshabandī, made Nehrī his centre and the family came to wield temporal power, especially under 'Ubaidallāh (1870–83), who imposed his authority over a wide area. He was at enmity with another family, the Barzānī. One of Khālid's *khalīfas* called Tāj ad-dīn had established himself at Barzān, a Kurdish area in northern Iraq, and his line became an important factor in Kurdish nationalism. Tāj ad-dīn's son, 'Abd as-Salām, and grandson, Muḥammad, gained spiritual ascendancy among villagers in the mountains north of the Zāb river, who abandoned their Qādirī allegiance and came to form a new tribal grouping, the Barzānī, virtually independent of Ottoman authority. In 1927 the order acquired special notoriety when a disciple of the fifth head, Aḥmad, proclaimed his master an

not to be taken as a symptom of new life since fission was an ever-recurring process in this order. New groups included:

Ṣāwiyya: Aḥmad b. M. as-Ṣāwī, d. 1241/1825 in Madina. Pupil of Aḥmad ad-Dardīr.
Ibrāhīmiyya: Qushdali Ibrāhīm, d. 1283/1866 in Skutari.
Khalīliyya: Ḥājjī Khalīl Geredelī, d. 1299/1881 in Gerede.
Faiḍiyya: Faiḍ ad-dīn Ḥusain, d. 1309/1891 in Istanbul.
Ḥālatiyya: Ḥasan Ḥālatī 'Alī A'lā, d. 1329/1911 in Edirne.

[1] A notable figure of the 'Aidarūsiyya of the previous century was 'Abd ar-Raḥmān ibn Muṣṭafā, whose travels took him outside the narrow confines of Ḥaḍramī Islam into India (where the family order had long been established, yet without becoming more than a small holy-lineage *ṭarīqa*), Hijaz, Syria, and Egypt, where he died in 1778. Many people took the *ṭarīqa* from him without this leading to any extension of the order, which remained a family affair.

[2] His first master is said to have been M. b. Aḥmad al-Aḥsā'ī, of a well-known Arab Shī'ī family, d. Baghdad, 1208/1793–4, but he later visited India, where he made contact with 'Abd al-'Azīz, son of Walī Allāh.

incarnation of God and himself as his prophet.[1] The prophet survived a few months only and the new religion died with him.[2] The subsequent history of the Barzānīs has no place in a history of the religious orders.[3]

Although there was no revival in the Near Eastern world the reformist tendencies of the age affected the orders. They came under bitter attack from those influenced by Wahhābī rigorism, from *'ulamā'* resentful of their influence, and from the reformers and new men. They were subjected to pressures of various kinds, often through government agency, as, for example, in the suppression of extravagances such as the *dōsa* ceremony in Cairo. Yet no genuine reform movements took place. This is especially true of Turkey, Syria, and Iraq. The Bektāshīs suffered a severe setback when the Janissary corps was abolished in 1826,[4] yet under the relatively tolerant regime of 'Abd al-Majīd (1839–61) the order re-established itself and regained widespread influence. This shows that the Janissary link was by no means integral to the vitality of the order. The main spread of the order into Albania took place during this century after the suppression of the Janissaries; whole communities reacting against the Sunnī Islam of the Turkish conquerors attached themselves to the order. Its main centres were in Tirana and Āqcē Ḥiṣār.

At the same time, during this century throughout the whole Islamic world, the orders still fulfilled their role of catering for the religious needs and aspirations of vast numbers of ordinary people, and attacks on them had relatively little effect. The

[1] It is not clear whether the idea came from Aḥmad himself, at any rate he did not repudiate it, see *Report by H.B.M.'s Government to the Council of the League of Nations on the Administration of Iraq*, 1927, p. 23.

[2] Aḥmad's aberrations (he became a Christian at one time) are to be understood as those which to his confused mind he thought a *malāmatī* ought to take.

[3] On the history of the leaders in modern times see C. J. Edmonds, 'The Kurds and the Revolution in Iraq', *M.E.J.* xiii (1959), 1–10.

[4] See the contemporary, though hostile, account of the meetings of *'ulamā'* with the heads of the leading orders, and the imperial decrees and *fatwās* issued in Mohammed Assad-Éfendi, *Précis historique de la destruction du corps des Janissaires par le Sultan Mahmoud, en 1826*, ed. and tr. A. P. Caussin de Perceval, Paris, 1833, pp. 298–329. The three leading Bektāshī chiefs were executed, all lodges in Constantinople and its environs were destroyed and those in the provinces were handed over to other orders, their superiors and many dervishes were exiled, their *awqāf*, lands, and villages confiscated, and the wearing of their special dress and other distinctions prohibited.

causes which led to their virtual eclipse during the twentieth century will be discussed in the last chapter.

The orders transcend all boundaries of political loyalties within Islam. Sultan ʿAbd al-Ḥamīd's attention was drawn to this aspect, and its possible value in his pan-Islamic vision, through a work written by the son of the founder of the Madaniyya (-Darqawiyya) order, Shaikh Muḥammad ibn Ḥamẓa Ẓāfir al-Madanī of Misurata in Libya. This work, *An-Nūr as-Sātiʿ* (The Brilliant Light),[1] is primarily an account of the teaching of the order following stereotyped lines, but it has a section dealing with the principles underlying the pan-Islamic movement. These, we have seen, were found earlier in the work of Aḥmad ibn Idrīs, though all his pupils rejected this aspect of his teaching, even the Sanūsī choosing a passivist role in the Sahara. Shaikh Ẓāfir contributed to the propaganda of the movement. The sultan allotted him a house near the palace of Yildiz Kiosk and three Madanī *tekkēs* were established in Istanbul. From these went out propaganda seeking to influence shaikhs of various orders. Emissaries, protected through the imperial power, won recruits among Algerians employed by the French (there were two *zāwiyas* in Algiers), but in Morocco its relationship with the Turkish government discredited it. In Barka it became linked with the Sanūsiyya, which won over many Madanī members. *Muqaddams* were also found in Egypt and the Hijaz.

In Syria the Madanī *ṭarīqa* was represented by a distinctive *ṭāʾifa*, the Yashruṭiyya. Founded by a Tunisian, Nūr ad-dīn ʿAlī al-Yashruṭī (born in Bizerta in 1208/1793), who moved to Acre in Palestine in 1266/1850, where he died in 1310/1892.[2] He initiated lavishly, and *zāwiyas* were founded in Tarshīḥa (A.H. 1279), Jerusalem, Haifa, Damascus, Beirut, and Rhodes.[3]

ʿAbd al-Ḥamīd gathered around himself other order-leaders,

[1] Published in Istanbul in 1301/1884. M. Ẓāfir's association with ʿAbd al-Ḥamīd began before the latter succeeded to the sultanate; see A. le Chatelier, op. cit., pp. 114–15; Walī ad-dīn Yakan, *al-Maʿlūm wa ʾl-majhūl* (Cairo, 1327/1909), i. 169–77, and also, for Abu ʾl-Hudā aṣ-Ṣayyādī, i. 100.

[2] An account of the life, letters, and Sufi principles of Nūr ad-dīn ʿAlī is given in *Riḥlat ilā ʾl-Ḥaqq* (privately printed, Beirut, n.d. but completed in 1954) by his daughter Fāṭima al-Yashruṭiyya, who had to remove the headquarters of the order to Beirut after the Palestine tragedy of 1948.

[3] The propagator of the Shādhiliyya in the Comoro Islands in the Indian Ocean, where it has become the major *ṭarīqa*, Saʿīd ibn Muḥammad al-Maʿrūf (d. Moroni 1904), was initiated in Acre.

the most notorious being, Abu 'l-Hudā M. aṣ-Ṣayyādī (1850–1909) of the Ṣayyādiyya branch of the Rifā'iyya, a long-established family order near Aleppo. Abu 'l-Hudā began his career as a simple *faqīr*, chanting Sufi songs in the streets of Aleppo where he discovered that he possessed unusual powers. He next appears in Istanbul, where his singing and extraordinary powers in the Rifā'ī tradition attracted the attention of the youth who was to become Sultan 'Abd al-Ḥamīd II (1876–1909). In a remarkable way he was able, through his astrological and divinatory powers, to maintain an influence over the sultan which lasted throughout all changes until his final overthrow. He influenced the sultan's religious policy. He was a fanatical believer in the divine right of the Rifā'ī *ṭarīqa*, its saints, and of the Arab role in Sufism.[1] All reformers of the second half of the nineteenth century, such as Jamāl ad-dīn al-Afghānī, al-Kawākibī, and Muḥammad 'Abduh, disliked his influence upon the sultan and his views about lineal and traditional Islam, regarding him as an example of all that they were countering.

In central Asia there is little of significance to record for this century. In Turkistan and in the Caucasus there was a revival of the Naqshabandiyya in the 1850s.[2] This order had penetrated into Daghistan at the end of the eighteenth century and a leader called Shaikh Manṣūr (captured 1791) sought to unite the various Caucasian tribes to oppose the Russians. He won over the princes and nobles of Ubichistan and Daghistan, as well as many Circassians who, after the suppression of the Murīd movement and the imposition of Russian rule (1859), preferred exile to submission. The order is credited with the definitive winning over of these Caucasian groups to Islam, even if only as a factor uniting the various clans.

The Sufi intellectual gnostic tradition, crushed in the Arab

[1] See Abu 'l-Hudā's *Tanwīr al-Abṣār fī ṭabaqāt as-Sādat ar-Rifā'iyya*, Cairo, 1306/1888.

[2] 'The brotherhood of the Vaisis, an offshoot of the great Sufi fraternity of Naqshbandiyya, was founded at Kazan' in 1862 by Bahauddin Vaisov. Its membership consisted mainly of small artisans, and its doctrine was a very curious mixture of Sufi mysticism, puritanism and Russian socialism—somewhat resembling that of the Populists. The Vaisis were considered by other Muslims as heretics. In 1917, the son and successor of the sect's founder, Inan Vaisov, received some arms from the Bolshevik organization of Kazan'. He was killed while fighting for the Reds in Trans-Bulak in February 1918' (A. Bennigsen and C. Lemercier-Quelquejay, *Islam in the Soviet Union*, London, 1967, p. 243).

world and the Maghrib through the Sufis' subjection to legalism and conformity, survived in Shīʿī Iran, where what has been called the Isfahan school of theosophy shone in the prevailing gloom with such lights as Mullā Ṣadrā and Mulla Hādī Sabziwārī (1798–1878). In India in the eighteenth century a Naqshabandī called Quṭb ad-dīn Aḥmad, more generally known as Shāh Walī Allāh of Delhi (1703–62), brought a new intellectual impulse to religious thought within the context of the orders,[1] whilst a somewhat earlier contemporary Chishtī, Shāh Kalīm Allāh Jahānābādī (1650–1729), infused vigour into the sphere of Sufi practice and devotion. Walī Allāh sought to introduce a new spirit into Islamic thought and to reconcile the dichotomy between *sharʿ* and *taṣawwuf*:

He laid the foundation of a new school of scholastic theology; bridged the gulf between the jurists and the mystics; softened the controversy between the exponents and the critics of the doctrine of *waḥdat al-wudjūd* and awakened a new spirit of religious enquiry. He addressed all sections of Muslim society—rulers, nobles, *ʿulamā'*, mystics, soldiers, traders, etc.—and tried to infuse a new spirit of dedication in them. His seminary, Madrasa-i Raḥīmiyya, became the nucleus of a revolutionary movement for the reconstruction of religious thought in Islam and scholars flocked to it from every corner of the country. . . .

Shāh Kalīm Allāh's work was in a different direction. He revived and revitalized the Čishtī order on the lines of the saints of its first cycle, checked the growth of esoteric tendencies, and sent his disciples near and far to propagate the Čishtī mystic ideals. The rise of a number of Čishtī *khānḳāhs* in the Pandjāb, the Deccan, the North West Frontier, and Uttar Pradesh was due to the efforts of his spiritual descendants.[2]

The remarkable thing is that the Naqshabandī revival in India influenced the Arab Near East and few major Arab towns were without a circle of devotees. On the other hand, the Chishtī line did not spread westwards. A Chishtī (Ṣābirī) called Imdād Allāh settled in Mecca in about the middle of the century and gained great influence among Indian pilgrims, but did not confer the *ṭarīqa* on non-Indians. We may, therefore, say that, though there took place this extension and foundation of new *khānaqāhs* in India, the work of these men had no such outcome as that which resulted from the inspiration of Aḥmad ibn Idrīs.

[1] For a study of his doctrine see A. Bausani, 'Note su Shāh Walīullāh di Delhi', *Annali*, N.S. x (1960), 93–147.

[2] K. A. Nizami in *E.I.*[2] iii. 432–3.

Now come the first warnings of a different sort of change which was completely to bypass the orders. So far most significant movements of thought in Muslim India had taken place through and within the orders, but after Shāh Walī Allāh the inspiration for change came from outside them. It is significant that Walī Allāh's son, ʿAbd al-ʿAzīz (1746–1824), and grandson, Ismāʿīl (1781–1831), were important figures in the new outlook which was opening up.

Parallel with the Muḥammad-emphasis of the two Maghribī Aḥmads was that of a third, Aḥmad Barelvī (d. 1831), a disciple of Walī Allāh's son, ʿAbd al-ʿAzīz, who followed fundamentalist and even political lines while maintaining his Sufi heritage. Aziz Ahmad writes:

Sayyid Aḥmad Barelvī continued the Walī-Ullāhī tradition of synthesizing the disciplines of the three major Ṣūfī orders in India, the Qādirī, the Chishtī, and the Naqshbandī, and uniting them with a fourth element of religious experience, the exoteric discipline which he called *Ṭarīqa-i Muḥammadīyah* (the way of Muḥammad). His explanation was that the three Ṣufī orders were linked with the Prophet esoterically, whereas the fourth one being exoteric emphasized strict conformity to religious law. . . . He thus harnessed whatever was left of the inward Ṣūfī experience in the decadent early nineteenth-century Muslim India to the dynamism of a reformist orthodox revival.[1]

Subsequent change in the religious climate of India lies largely outside the scope of this study. Within the orders there was little significant movement, simply sporadic activities such as that of Mawlānā Ashraf ʿAlī of Thana Bhawan (d. 1943). At the same time, the Sufi intellectual background continued to manifest itself in many aspects of Indian life and influenced reformers like Muḥammad Iqbāl.

Discussion of the orders in regions where Islam penetrated after it had attained its definitive form has been excluded from this study, but a brief reference to the orders in south-east Asia in the nineteenth century is necessary in view of the fact that here too their decline in the twentieth century is as marked, so I am told, as in the heartlands of Islam.

The spread of the orders in the Malay peninsula, mainly in the nineteenth century, came about through the medium of the

[1] Aziz Ahmad, *Studies in Islamic Culture in the Indian Environment*, Oxford, 1964, pp. 210–11.

pilgrimage. The main orders which spread were the Qādiriyya, Naqshabandiyya, and the Sammāniyya. The Aḥmadiyya-Idrīsiyya was introduced in 1895 and thrived for a time, though with a restricted range.

Into Indonesia, too, the pilgrimage was the means through which the Sufi Way penetrated. The first documentary evidence appears in the sixteenth century in the form of mystical poetry and other writings. In Sumatra early mystics were Ḥamza Fanṣūrī (d. *c.* 1610) and his disciple, Shams ad-dīn as-Samaṭrānī (Pasai, d. 1630). These men were gnostic-type mystics and consequently left no enduring organization behind them. One ʿAbd ar-Raʾūf ibn ʿAlī of Singkel introduced the Shaṭṭāriyya into Acheh in 1090/1679, not from India as might have been expected, but from Mecca where he was initiated by Aḥmad Qushāshī, and he came to be honoured as the regional saint. Later, contact with Hadramawt which became such a feature of Indonesian life, led to the settlement of Arabs in certain parts who introduced their own orders.

The Islamization of Java is associated with the legend of 'the nine saints', active on the north-east coast in the early sixteenth century, who taught the mystical Way and inaugurated a new era in Indonesian life. The strongest local emphasis seems to have been the quest for *ʿilm*: that is, initiation into esoteric knowledge became the aim of devotees of the religious life. The Shaṭṭāriyya, the earliest known order, was introduced from the Hijaz towards the end of the seventeenth century.

The Naqshabandiyya, too, was introduced from Mecca (and behind that from Turkey) into Minangkabau (Sumatra) about 1845. Disputes arose between its adherents and the established Shaṭṭārī devotees, but largely on legalistic and secondary issues rather than mysticism. The Sammāniyya entered Sumatra through ʿAbd aṣ-Ṣamad ibn ʿAbdallāh (d. *c.* 1800), a Sumatran pupil of as-Sammānī who lived in Mecca and initiated pilgrims from his own country.

The orders spread into all these parts after they had acquired their definitive form. Desire to maintain the organization and liturgical forms of the parent orders, together with the diffusion of their books in Arabic, ensured an over-all uniformity of practice, and the differences are found in omission and response, in minor aspects such as the form festivals take, and in their social and political repercussions. No creative adaptation is apparent. The acquired forms and beliefs were blended into the new human environment, but by juxtaposition rather than fusion, the old and new existing parallel to each other.

In this aspect the similarity with and difference from west African Islam is apparent. The difference between African and Indonesian Muslims in religion derive both from the different pre-existing cultural background and the nature of the early Islamic missionaries. Snouck Hurgronje showed that the Indian merchants who settled in Malaysian and Indonesian ports laid more stress on thinking than upon acting, and this opened the way for the reception of forms of heterodox mysticism. In Africa, on the contrary, the whole stress was laid upon acting, and, in fact, in Negro Africa proper, not only did heterodoxy have no opening, but the mystical Way proper did not gain Africans.[1] There does not seem to be any genuine affinity between Africans' belief in the unity of life and the Sufi doctrine of *al-waḥdat al-wujūdiyya*. Indonesians achieved a far greater degree of genuine religious syncretism than did Africans.

While speculative mysticism, unknown in Negro Islam, was enjoyed by some Indonesians, the orders did not play a greater role among them than in western Sudan Islam. G. H. Bousquet, assessing the studies of Dutch students of Islam in Indonesia, writes:

> On trouve, chez les auteurs, extrêmement peu de choses sur les confréries mystiques, les tariqas, leur organisation, leurs dhikrs, leurs exercices spirituels. Ce silence s'explique au moins en très grande partie par leur peu d'importance en Indonésie. Il n'existe rien rappelant les zaouias.[2]

Whereas Islamic law as affecting social life was largely ignored, the liturgies and practices of the orders were accepted without difficulty. Shaikhs produced some textbooks and large numbers of little pamphlets in Arabic and local languages, but they were devoid of originality. We can sum up by saying that although mysticism as an individual way was enthusiastically followed by

[1] The contrast between African Negroes and Hamites in their response to both the saint-cult and the *dhikr* is brought out in my *The Influence of Islam upon Africa*, London and Beirut, 1968.

[2] G. H. Bousquet, 'Introduction à l'étude de l'Islam indonésien', *R.E.I.* 1938, 201.

the few, the collective aspects of the orders, *ḥaḍras*, and pilgrimages to shrines, assumed a relatively minor importance in Indonesian Muslim life.

The element which stands out from what we have written in this chapter is that nineteenth-century revivalism in the orders was primarily directed towards and effective in missionary activities on fringe areas of the Muslim world. In many parts of Africa, Nilotic Sudan, and Somalia, the association was direct, in west Africa it was more indirect.

V

The Mysticism and Theosophy of the Orders

WITH Muḥammad, *Khātim al-anbiyā'* (Seal of the Prophets), the cycle of prophecy (*dā'irat an-nubuwwa*) was closed, but God did not thenceforth leave His people without guidance on the way to Himself. For the majority, the guide was the revealed Law (*Shar'*) which is for the whole community, and the *'ulamā'* were the inheritors of the prophets as the guardians and interpreters of the Law.

For others, the exoteric Law, though accepted, was not enough. Religion is not only revelation, it is also mystery. For those who became known as Shī'a (men of the Party of 'Alī, Shī'at 'Alī), the guide through this world of divine wisdom (*ḥikma ilāhiyya*) was the infallible Imām. The Imām was also *walī Allāh* and the closing of the prophetical cycle heralded the opening of another—*dā'irat al-walāya.*[1] A Shī'ī Sufi, 'Azīz ad-dīn an-Nasafī, explains the Shī'ī sense of *walī*:

> Des milliers de prophètes, antérieurement venus, ont successivement contribué à l'instauration de la forme théophanique qui est la prophétie, et Mohammed l'a achevée. Maintenant c'est au tour de la *walāyat* (l'Initiation spirituelle) d'être manifestée et de manifester les réalités ésotériques. Or, l'homme de Dieu en la personne de qui se manifeste la *walāyat*, c'est la *Ṣāḥib al-zamān*, l'Imām de ce temps.[2]

For others, those who came to be known as Sufis, direct communion with God was possible. Their mission, though an individual search, was to maintain among men a realization of the inner Reality which made the *Shar'* valid. This Way normally involved a guide, but of these there were many, and their

[1] See H. Corbin, *Histoire de la philosophie islamique*, Paris, 1964, i. 45. For convenience sake we distinguish *walāya* with a *fatḥa* as applying to the Shī'ī conception and *wilāya* that of the Sufis. The term cannot be translated without misleading implications but the meaning will become evident from subsequent discussion.

[2] Translated by H. Corbin, op. cit., i. 102.

whole concept of guidance was different from that of the Shī'īs. Sufis adopted their own conception of *wilāya*, but their *awliyā'* (plural of *walī*) were ordinary men singled out by God. At the same time, the conception of a pre-creation *wilāya* from eternity was incorporated into Sufi thought from eastern gnosticism,[1] though this concept never fitted comfortably into the purer structure of Sufism. They were to ascribe a pre-creation existence and a hierarchical structure to these *awliyā'* and link them with the government of the world by virtue of *an-Nūr al-Muḥammadī* (lit. 'the Muhammadan Light'), immanent in them all. Some Sufis did not hold that any *dā'irat al-wilāya* succeeded *dā'irat an-nubuwwa*, for the latter was only a particular mode, finite and passive, of God's communication with man, whereas *wilāya* is abiding (*istiqrār*) and ever-active and infinite.[2] This does not imply any inferiority of law-transmitting apostles to saints, since every apostle is also a *walī*. Ibn al-'Arabī writes: '*Wilāya* is all-embracing. It is the major cycle (*dā'ira*). . . . Every apostle (*rasūl*) must be a prophet (*nabī*), and since every prophet must be a *walī*, every apostle must be a *walī*.'[3] It is only prophecy as a function and mode of communication that is finite. There are many grades of *walīs* and this is typified by the superiority of al-Khaḍir to Moses in knowledge.[4]

'Sanctity' is not an adequate translation of *wilāya*, nor 'saint' of *walī*, in either Shī'ism or Sufism, though we have generally

[1] See the quotation from al-Junaid, below, p. 141.

[2] Al-Ḥakīm at-Tirmidhī, who was a contemporary in time (third/ninth century), if not in gnostic concepts, with al-Junaid, did however set a term to *wilāya*. He has a book on the subject which has only recently been resurrected and has been admirably edited and provided with supporting material from other authors by 'Uthmān Ismā'īl Yaḥyā, *Kitāb Khatm al-awliyā'*, Beirut, 1965. This edition also contains Tirmidhī's spiritual autobiography, pp. 13–32.

At-Tirmidhī claimed that *wilāya* was limited in time, since, like *nubuwwa*, it also had a Seal who will be manifested at the end of time. He wrote: 'The Seal of Sanctity (*khatm al-wilāya*) will be the mediator for the saints on the Day of Resurrection, for he is their lord, predominant over the saints as Muḥammad was predominant over the prophets' (op. cit., p. 344). Ibn al-'Arabī drew much of his inspiration concerning *nubuwwa* and *wilāya* from Tirmidhī, though he gave everything his own unique stamp and interpretation. With him (as with Sa'd ad-dīn Ḥamūya) 'the absolute Seal who will come at the end of time' is Jesus, or better, *an-Nabi* 'Īsā, to avoid any identification with Christian conceptions; but he also has a category of seals who parallel the prophets. The Muḥammadan seal, he says, 'is actually here at the present time. I made his acquaintance in the year 595 [1199] . . . in Fez'; *Al-Futūḥāt al-Makkiyya*, Cairo, A.H. 1329, ii. 49; other references to 'Īsā as *the* Seal, ii. 3, 9, etc.

[3] *Futūḥāt*, ii. 256.

[4] See below, p. 136, n. 2.

adhered to current usage in this book. In the Sufi sense *walī* is better translated 'protégé' of God; like *mawlā* it can be 'protector' or 'patron' as well as 'client'. With the Shīʿa it signifies the Imām, the Word of God, the everliving Guide.

The Sufi guides, like the Imāms, also possess esoteric knowledge, but, unlike the Imāms, their esoteric knowledge has come to them, not by genealogical, but by spiritual progression.[1] In fact, it came to them by a twofold action of God: by transmission from Muḥammad, through a chain of elect masters, and also by direct inspiration from God, often through the mediation of al-Khaḍir, like Gabriel to Muḥammad.

These three trends of spiritual guidance are fully within the heritage of Islam, though they were never reconciled. Both Sufism and Shīʿism were attempts to solve the perpetual Islamic dilemma of a once-for-all final revelation, but they each fully recognized the once-for-all nature of the final prophetic mode of divine communication. However, they did not think that with the closing of this stage God's direct dealings with men were at an end.

The mission of both Sufis and Shīʿīs[2] was to preserve the spiritual sense of the divine revelation. Both were concerned with the equation $\frac{\textit{Tawḥīd}}{\textit{Sharʿ}} > \textit{Ḥaqīqa}$, but their Ways were quite different. Whilst in many respects Sufis and Shīʿīs come close together, in others, some fundamental, they are poles apart. This hinges upon their different conceptions of the basis of the community. Sufis are within the main stream of Islam, for them the basis is the

[1] There is no sound evidence for linking Shīʿī gnosticism with any of the Twelve Imāms, except perhaps Jaʿfar aṣ-Ṣādiq. Their alleged sayings, now forming a vast corpus beginning with ash-Sharīf ar-Raḍī's (d. 406/1015) *Nahj al-balāgha*, devoted to Imām ʿAlī, being unlikely to go back to them. This does not affect their validity for Shīʿīs; for them it is the Imām who speaks, whoever put it on paper, but others are likely to take a more critical attitude. This is not to say that all the material in such compilations is spurious; see L. Veccia Vaglieri, 'Sul "Nahj al-balāġah" e sul suo compilatore aš-Šarīf ar-Raḍī', *Annali*, Nuova serie, viii. 1–46; G. Oman, 'Uno "specchio per principi" dell' Imām ʿAlī ibn Abī Ṭālib', *Annali*, N.S., x (1960), 1–35.

[2] Writers on Sufism have fought shy of dealing with the question of the relationship of Sufism and Shīʿism. L. Massignon was concerned with the relations of Shīʿīs with al-Ḥallāj; but otherwise the only scholars who have attempted to deal with it have approached it from the Shīʿī viewpoint—we may mention Henri Corbin, W. Ivanow, and Sayyid Husain Nasr. It is not a subject for this book, since I am only dealing cursorily with the mystical foundations of the orders, yet I feel I should at least indicate my own position on the question.

sharīʿa; for the Shīʿa the basis is the Imām, the infallible leader. Sufis lived and thought upon a quite different plane from that of Shīʿīs. They believed in the possibility of direct communion with God, and their aim was the perfection of the soul, the spiritual ascent to God. Sufis are marked off from Shīʿīs by the two techniques of *ṭarīqa* and *dhikr*; the dominant movement is following the Path. Shīʿīs, on the contrary, needed a mediatory Imām, and they plunged into a world of mysteries, hidden meanings, and secret initiatory transmissions. Sufis also came to adopt a gnostic approach, tapping Shīʿī as well as other gnostic sources, especially after the open profession of Shīʿism was banned. But when Sufis adopted elements from the Shīʿī gnostic system the orientation of such elements changed. In this respect the change was similar to the parallel adoption of Neoplatonic and Christian elements into Sufism; once incorporated they are no longer Neoplatonic, Christian gnostic, or Shīʿī.

We have mentioned that ʿAlī followed Muḥammad as the starting-point of Sufi chains and here, too, misconceptions have arisen. Although Sufis trace their esoteric chains back to ʿAlī,[1] and accord his line high honour, it is not as Imām in any Shīʿī sense. When Junaid was asked about ʿAlī's knowledge of *taṣawwuf* he answered the question rather obliquely: 'Had ʿAlī been less engaged in wars he might have contributed greatly to our knowledge of esoteric things (*maʿānī*) for he was one who had been vouchsafed *ʿilm al-ladunnī*.'[2]

Sufis have rarely been Shīʿīs except in Persia;[3] and we give

[1] The esoteric trend began long before the *ṭarīqas* developed the concept of a chain of transmission from ʿAlī in the fifth/eleventh centuries. At one time, as is seen from the *silsilas* of Ṣadr ad-dīn ibn Ḥamūya (Appendix A), there were parallel chains, both having ʿAlī as the starting-point, but one passing through a series of Imāms.

[2] As-Sarrāj, *Lumaʿ*, p. 129. Reference is given to the passage in the Qur'ān concerning the encounter between Moses and God's servant (identified with al-Khaḍir): 'One of our servants . . . whom We had taught knowledge peculiar to Us (*wa ʿallamnāhu min ladunnā ʿilm^{an}*)'. This phrase, important in Sufism, refers to the esoteric truth validating the exoteric Law of Moses (representative of the Law) who asks God's servant, 'May I follow you on the understanding that you teach me, from what you have been taught, a *rushd*?' Qur'ān, xviii. 65–6. Sufis take *rushd* to mean 'right guidance', a *ṭarīqa*, and the *murshid* (a derivative from the same root *r·sh·d*) is the 'guide'. This passage, as-Sarrāj says, has been the source used to support the conception of the superiority of *wilāya* over *nubuwwa*, believed in by many Sufis as well as Shīʿ īs. It is easy to see how Khaḍir becomes for Sufis the prototype of the *murshid*.

[3] R. A. Nicholson wrote, 'Sūfism may join hands with freethought—it has

due allowance for the indulgence provided by the doctrine of *taqiyya* (precautionary dissembling). They have regarded Shīʿī beliefs about the Imām as incompatible with Sufism. Similarly in adopting the Shīʿī *baiʿa*, the oath was given to the initiating *murshid* as representative of the founding *walī*, in whose hands the *murīd* was to be like the corpse in the hands of the washer, and they thought of the chain carrying the founder's doctrine back to ʿAlī and the Prophet in a quite different way from Shīʿī conceptions. Most Sufis were concerned, since Junaid led the way, with maintaining their stand within the main Islamic stream, to which they made compromises and within which they came to be tolerated. Any lack Sufis may have felt in regard to such a gnostic-type concept as *Ṣāḥib az-Zamān*, 'the Master of the Hour' (the Mahdī), was eventually compensated for by the idea of *Quṭb al-ʿĀlam wa 'z-Zamān* (the Axis of the Universe and the Hour).

Although our concern is primarily with the exoteric expression of Sufism, we have to say something about beliefs in relation to practice. Islamic mysticism has proved so attractive to western students of Islam that it is necessary to take a balanced view of what was actually involved in practice.

We have defined mysticism prosaically as the organized cultivation of religious experience aimed at direct perception of the Real. Sufism is a Way before it becomes a theosophy, and this is where self-deception arises. The doctrine is an attempt at rational expression of mystical experience. Mysticism, as the intuitive, spiritual, awareness of God, belongs to the realm of natural and universal, not revealed, religion, and thus at the mystical level there seems no essential difference between religions, since the experience is virtually the same. Direct experience takes precedence over historical revelation, and from this derives the opposition of the guardians of the Law to mysticism. Ibn al-ʿArabī wrote—'God is known only by means of God. The scholastic theologian says: "I know God by that which he created", and takes as his guide something that has no real relation to the object

often done so—but hardly ever with sectarianism. This explains why the vast majority of Sūfīs have been, at least nominally, attached to the catholic body of the Moslem community. ʿAbdallāh Anṣārī declared that of two thousand Sūfī Sheykhs with whom he was acquainted only two were Shīʿites'; *The Mystics of Islam*, London, 1914, pp. 88–9.

sought. He who knows God by means of phenomena, knows as much as these phenomena give to him and no more.'[1]

At the same time, whilst it is true that the essential differences between religions lie elsewhere than on this plane of experience, still mysticism cannot be regarded as one and the same in whatever religious sphere it is manifested, though the distinctions (cultural, content, tendency) are relative and do not infringe the essential unity of mystical experience. The religion professed does far more than merely colour linguistic and other forms of symbolic expression. The nature of mysticism is shown by its manifestations within the whole setting of a particular religious culture, and in Islam it is associated with and conditioned by (even though it counterbalances) recognized ritual and worship. Islamic mysticism, even in its fully developed form, cannot be regarded as a syncretism. It is true that it incorporated and welded together many different spiritual insights, yet through this process of assimilation they have been changed and given a uniquely Islamic orientation. The works of the Islamic mystics cannot be studied, appreciated, and valued apart from their environment (Christian students have too frequently read their own ideas into the expressions of Muslim mystics), nor apart from their practical outcome in the works of the orders.

As well as mysticism we need to define the sense in which we are using the term 'theosophy', for this word too can mean many different things. Whilst mysticism is a responsive movement of the soul towards God which involves a grappling with reality on interior levels, theosophy is that sacred philosophy which springs from such inward illumination; it is the mysticism of the mind as distinguished from the mysticism of the heart.

Mysticism and theosophy are, therefore, the personal experience and expression of the mystery which lies within the religions, the testimony of the realities which lie beyond empirical experience. Muslim mysticism is a valid expression of Muslim truth along lines of insight which could have been reached in no other way. The mystic speaks the imaginative language of vision, symbol, and myth, through which he can express truths beyond the reach of formal theology. 'Gnostics', writes Ibn al-ʿArabī, 'cannot

[1] Ibn al-ʿArabī's commentary on his own *Tarjumān al-Ashwāq*, ed. and tr. by R. A. Nicholson, London, 1911, p. 115; for the text of the commentary see Beirut edition, 1966, p. 136.

explain their feelings (*aḥwāl*) to other men; they can only indicate them symbolically to those who have begun to experience the like.'[1] The tragedy of the higher theosophist in the realm of expression arises from the fact that he has to reduce intense personal experience to the level of abstract thought at which level communication with the non-initiate becomes impossible.[2] One medium of communication open to the Muslim, for whom non-verbal forms of religious symbolism (except calligraphy and abstract art) are banned, is poetry. Poetry in the Arab and Persian world is no solitary art, but receives its expression in the assembly. Poetry has its arts of delivery, chant, and musical accompaniment, and it was around the latter that controversy arose.

Sufism as it developed came to embrace different spheres of experience, and these need bringing out if we are to see the relationship between such aspects as following the Way and receiving divine gifts, or how *ṭarīqa* and *wilāya* come to be associated.

(*a*) We have the mysticism which seeks perfection, the purification of the *nafs* (soul)—the Way of *mujāhada*, the spiritual *jihād*; the Way of ascent through different stages (*maqāmāt*) leading to God. The life of contemplation (*mushāhada*), to which asceticism is an essential preliminary, is based upon recollection (*dhikr*) of God. This must be carried out under direction.

(*b*) In integral association with this Way through personal effort is the way of illumination (*kashf*, 'unveiling'). As they pursued their Way, Sufis were favoured with a mystical endowment (*ḥāl*), which is a free gift from God. The distinction between *maqām* and *ḥāl* brings together these two aspects of the Path:

[1] *Tarjumān*, p. 68; Beirut edn., p. 42. Sufis have a favourite expression concerning the need for discretion in divulging the mysteries, 'he who experiences God, his lips are sealed' (*man 'arafa 'llāh^a kalla lisānuhu*).

[2] And is also liable to be misinterpreted. 'Ain al-Quḍāt al-Hamadānī felt that he had been wrongly convicted through such misunderstanding. In the Defence he composed in prison shortly before his execution he wrote, 'The *'ulamā'* can hardly be unaware that every department of knowledge has its mutually agreed terminology whose meaning is known only to those who have followed a course of training . . . Similarly with the Sufis, they have their own exclusive terms whose meanings they alone know. I mean by Sufis those persons who have directed their aspirations wholly towards God and are dedicated to following the Way to Him'; *Shaqwā 'l-gharīb*, ed. in *J. Asiat.* ccxvi (1930), 40, 41.

'States are gifts whilst stages are acquisitions.'[1] There is presupposed in the reception of a *ḥāl* the carrying out of a definite disciplined rule of life. Illuminism[2] is this faith in the possibility of the sudden flash of divine light.

The association of these two comprises the *sulūk*, the *scala perfectionis* of the orders, whereby the distinction between Creator and created can be transcended. This association of the way of striving and illumination by divine light can be comprehended when we realize that this kind of thing is a fact of everyday experience. We may think of the scientist pursuing his laborious way of experiment to whom the solution comes in a sudden flash of intuition, but there is no flash without the toil. Such insights give the appearance of something given. The next sphere, however, bears the relationship of genius to intuition.

(*c*) The mystical gift just mentioned must be distinguished from the gnostic genius or the mystical gnosis (*ma'rifa*, with Shī'īs *'irfān*) which enables those so favoured to unveil the secrets of the unseen world of reality and contemplate the mysteries of being. This is different from the enlightenment of the mystics, although the same term, *ma'rifa*, may be used, and the theosophy behind the orders draws upon both types with a resultant confusion. With the Sufis the divine mysteries are revealed by degrees, in proportion to a person's spiritual growth and his receptivity, but there are men of special gifts who have been given a mystical understanding of life which has nothing to do with either ascetic discipline or the Sufi technique of the Way, nor with the gift of *wilāya*, though like *wilāya* it is an individual charism. We may

[1] *Fa 'l-aḥwāl mawāhib wa 'l-maqāmāt makāsib*; *Ar-Risālat al-Qushairiyya*, Cairo, 1319, p. 32. Sufis regard these two aspects as being expressed in the Qur'ānic promise, 'Those who endeavour in Us, them We shall direct in Our Ways' (xxix. 69).

This usage of the Qur'ān as a support for an already taken up position is not to be confused with the Sufi interpretation of the Qur'ān (*ta'wīl* or *istinbāṭ* = drawing out the hidden sense), allegorical, hermeneutical, and mystical. The reason why *ta'wīl* is not referred to in this book is simply that it belongs to the eclectic aspect of Sufism; it did not form part of the ordinary Sufi's approach and certainly not that of the orders.

[2] This is a dangerous word to use. I am using it in the widest sense, much wider than *ishrāq*, which has become a term describing a particular metaphysic of illumination associated with Yaḥyā as-Suhrawardī al-Maqtūl. It has little relationship with the orders, but an individual pursuit of men like as-Simnānī. Other illumination terms (*tajalliyāt*, *lawā'iḥ*, *lawāmi'*) are used by Sufis for different expressions of their experiences.

think of as-Suhrawardī al-Maqtūl, Ibn al-ʿArabī, and Ibn Sabʿīn, and of non-Muslim parallels such as Plotinus, Eckhart, and Boehme. In spite of the uniqueness of this genius, men have sought this gnosis and techniques for its attainment have been developed. It is through such techniques, through the marriage of Man and Nature, that have arisen the 'masteries' of magic which hold man in thrall to a naturalistic world.

(*d*) Finally, we have to distinguish *wilāya*. Extrinsically this is within the sphere of Sufism; intrinsically it has little relationship with mysticism. This seems confusing, in that the founders of the orders all came to be regarded as *walīs*, whereas mystics like al-Muḥāsibī were not *walīs*. But the essence of early teaching on *wilāya* is that *walīs* were unknown to their fellow men.

For practical purposes we need to distinguish two types of *walīs*: those chosen to be with God from eternity and those of humanity who were, it seems, picked out by God to receive special favours through the action of grace (*minna*). The first conception was an early development in Sufi thought, since we find al-Junaid affirming: 'God has an élite (*ṣafwa*) among His servants, the purest among His creation. He has chosen them for the *wilāya* and distinguished them by conferring on them unique grace (*karāma*) . . . These are they whom He created for Himself to be with Him from eternity.'[1]

This gift like the gnosis just discussed has nothing to do with merits or traversing a Path. It is possible to be a *walī* and be completely devoid of mystical gifts, and it is equally possible to be a mystic, illuminated with the highest vision of God, without being a *walī*.[2] The divorce of *wilāya* from *taṣawwuf*, and the link of the orders with *wilāya*, signify the weakening of the relationship of the orders with mysticism.[3]

Since it is impossible in a general study such as this to treat at all fully the conceptions of the different orders, we will content ourselves with mentioning certain dominant conceptions and tendencies common to most orders, bearing in mind the distinctions which have just been brought out.

The Muslim mystic begins with the *Tawḥīd* (Unity) and the

[1] *Rasā'il al-Junaid*, ed. A. H. ʿAbd al-Qādir (London, 1962), text, p. 41.

[2] I am well aware that, apart from agnostic *wilāya*, diverse writers from as-Sulamī to Ibn al-ʿArabī and his followers regard gnosis as the distinguishing mark of *wilāya*.

[3] See the account of ash-Shaʿrānī in chap. viii, pp. 220–5.

Shar' (revealed Law), and through his following the Path he seeks to penetrate to their inner significance (*al-ma'nā 'l-bāṭinī*). He believes that *Tawḥīd/Shar'*, experienced as one Reality, is the world's foundation and its subsistence. He is deeply aware of the mystery of being and believes that it is possible to eliminate the element of non-being and attain union with God along lines of Islamic insight. The Unity is central, but the Sufi attached a mystical meaning to it (the doctrine of unification), as he did to the *Shar'*. The Muslim theosophist goes much further. But the doctrine of the theosophists is not our concern, except in so far as aspects become part of the thought of the orders. The great theosophists, those who have gone through crises in which the world of invisible things is revealed, have generally dwelt upon the fringe of Islam, condemned by the orthodox to whom God and the mystery of life are unknowable.

Al-Qushairī prepared the way for Muslims to find a *via media*:

The *Sharī'a* is concerned with the observance of the outward manifestations of religion [i.e. rites and acts of devotion (*'ibādāt*) and duties (*mu'āmalāt*)]; whilst *Ḥaqīqa* (Reality) concerns inward vision of divine power (*mushāhadāt ar-Rubūbiyya*). Every rite not informed by the spirit of Reality is valueless, and every spirit of Reality not restrained by the Law is incomplete. The Law exists to regulate mankind, whilst the Reality makes us to know the dispositions of God. The Law exists for the service of God, whilst the Reality exists for contemplation of Him. The Law exists for obeying what He had ordained, whilst the Reality concerns witnessing and understanding the order He has decreed: the one is outer, the other inner. I heard the learned Abu 'Alī ad-Daqqāq say, 'The phrase *Iyyāka na'budu* (Thee we serve) is for sustaining the Law, whilst *Iyyāka nasta'īn* (Thy help we ask) is for affirming the Reality'. Know that the Law is the Reality because God ordained it, and the Reality is also the Law because it is the knowledge of God likewise ordained by Him.[1]

Those who maintained the teaching of the order-leaders went to the extreme in affirming their orthodoxy. We do not consequently find any *ṭarīqas* avowedly deriving from the teaching of men like Ibn al-'Arabī or Ibn Sab'īn;[2] although the developed

[1] *Ar-Risālat al-Qushairiyya*, Cairo edn., A.H. 1319, p. 43. The two phrases quoted by ad-Daqqāq are from the Fātiḥa, the opening chapter of the Qur'ān.

[2] This is not to deny the existence of consciously maintained *silsilas* claiming to be from such men as al-Ḥallāj. Ibn Taimiyya says that Ibn Sab'īn's *dhikr*

ideas of *taṣawwuf* can hardly be conceived of without taking into account the influence of the first, which ideas seeped in an indirect way into the teaching of the orders. Consequently, and in spite of this apparent accommodation with the *Sharīʿa*, the order-leaders never overcame the suspicion of orthodoxy. The orthodox in general did not hesitate to denounce the dictum of al-Qushairī just quoted that 'the *Sharīʿa* is the *Ḥaqīqa*'. They especially distrusted the claim that Sufism was an esoteric Way, a mystery religion, open only to an elect. This aspect the order-leaders were especially concerned to tone down and succeeded in doing so, turning Sufism eventually into a system of devotion, higher morality, and emotional exercise and release. At the same time, in their notion of *wilāya* they fostered and secured the practical acceptance of their own doctrine of election.

We have shown that Sufism could never be fully accommodated into the Islamic prophetical structure, but was allowed to exist parallel to it, and that orders were the means whereby aspects of the Sufi outlook were mediated to the capacity and needs of the ordinary man. It is far beyond the scope of this study to enlarge upon the Ways of Sufism in its many variations; for this the best guides are the works of the Sufis themselves, provided that one guards against any attempt to reduce Sufism to a single pattern or to systematize it as a philosophical system. We shall not attempt to do more than draw attention to particular aspects which find expression (and in some respects a system) in the orders.

A brief reference to early mysticism is perhaps called for here. Early mysticism had to face the implications of the doctrine of *tanzīh*, that there can be no reciprocal communion between God and man, since there can only be love between like and like, and God is totally unlike anything He has created.[1] The mystics

formula (*khirqa* Sabʿīniyya) was *laisa illāʾllāh* (there is nothing but God) and that its *isnād* relied 'upon the authority of Ḥallāj among other impious men'.

Ibn Sabʿīn, an intellectually illuminated gnostic and not necessarily a Sufi, after being expelled from Ceuta, eventually took refuge in Mecca with his considerable following of novices and adepts. He survived in Mecca for a long while, but was eventually put under house-arrest and died in 669/1270. The poet Shushtarī, who took his place at the head of the devotees (*mutajarridīn*), brought to Egypt before Ibn Sabʿīn's death about 400 adepts, including Abu Yaʿqūb al-Mubashshir, the hermit of Bāb Zuwaila in Cairo; L. Massignon, art. 'Shushtarī', *E.I.*[1] iv. 393.

[1] For the Sufi of the Path theological questions of transcendence and immanence have no meaning. His experience of the mystery of the Godhead and of

broke the barrier set up by the formulators of such a doctrine, since the very foundation of the mystical approach is the belief, in fact the experienced knowledge, that there is an inner kinship or relationship between human and divine, between Creator and created, though the interest of the mystics was always in the God-pole, not the man-pole, in this God–man relationship. The doctrine of love (Qur'ān, v. 59) preached by early mystics like Dhū 'n-Nūn al-Miṣrī, Rābi'a al-'Adawiyya, al-Muḥāsibī, and al-Ḥallāj, was viewed with the gravest suspicion by conformists to the narrow path of legal Islam,[1] and, in the subsequent period, when ways of securing right of asylum for the mystical Way were being sought (it was found, for instance, that the legalists could swallow camels more easily than gnats), mysticism lost its simplicity and direct intensity of communion through its being transformed into an esoteric Way and also a transformation of relationship—was there in fact any distinction at all between God and man?

This early mysticism was unknown to the men of the orders. They did not read the writings of early mystics.[2] It is true that their sayings were quoted in the order literature in the form of mystical *ḥadīth*, but these sayings were not used in order to teach their Way but carefully chosen and quoted with the aim of illustrating and supporting a particular order aim, doctrine, or discipline. The scarcity of *ḥadīth* props, both prophetic and mystical, in the writings of the early Sufis should be compared with their profusion in the order-leaders' writings on Sufi discipline, as, for example, in the *'Awārif* of Shihāb ad-dīn as-Suhrawardī. The first were writing out of direct experience, the second were obsessed with the need to show authority and precedent for every statement.

The orders were the vehicles, not the substance, of the mystic life; imperfect vehicles, it is true, but they were the organized means by which the vast accumulation of Sufi experience was

union fuse as one. The problem exercised men like the elder Ghazālī, who grasped the dangers of *tanzīh* (see, e.g., his *Iljām al-'awām 'an 'ilm al-kalām*, Cairo edn., A.H. 1351, p. 33) though he never transcended this duality in ideated experience. The philosophical Sufis had their own definitions of *tanzīh*.

[1] This was one of the issues in the persecution of Sufis during the reign of al-Mu'tamid (A.D. 870–93), referred to by al-Qushairī, *Risāla*, p. 112.

[2] We can get some idea of the popularity of works through the number of manuscripts which survive; many books have disappeared, whilst some of the most significant works survive in only one copy.

mediated to many different types of aspirants. We are not, therefore, concerned with making direct recourse to the thought of mystics and theosophists, but with the interpreters and utilizers of their works, and more especially with those elements of their theosophical thought which were taken up and adapted by the order-formulators to become an integral part of their liturgies, nativity dramas, and prayer manuals.

One difficulty in understanding and interpretation arises from Sufi terminology. Sufism was not a doctrine, we have said, but an activity, a pilgrimage in depth. Sufis could not keep their experiences to themselves, they had to express them in words. To enable them to do this they had provided themselves with a specialized vocabulary complementary to that of legalistic Islam. For example, *ilhām*, generally translated 'inspiration', is in their usage near in meaning to personal 'revelation', though contrasted with *waḥy*, exoteric impersonal prophetic revelation. Similarly, *karāmāt* applied to the charismata of saints was contrasted with *mu'jizāt*, prophetic evidential miracles. Terms taken from the Qur'ān were given specialized meanings. Dhu 'n-Nūn, on being asked the meaning of *tawba*, replied, 'The "repentance" of the common herd is from sins, whilst the repentance of the elect is from inattention (*ghafla*).'[1] Expressions, however, which are most integral to Sufi thought and expression, keywords like *ma'rifa*, *wajd*, *ma'nā*, and *ḥaqīqa*, are not found in the Qur'ān. Nothing of this provides any difficulty, one can always learn the vocabulary; the difficulty arises from the fact that every mystical writer of insight transforms the meaning of the terms he employs to conform to his own subjective emotional usage, since his meaning is based upon his personal imaged experience (and one must allow too for their disordered or inchoate imaginations), not on some objective concept for which a particular term stands. This is all taken very seriously by many western students of Sufism as well as by apologists for Sufi pantheism. However, the orders have simplified it for us. Within them the meanings of the terms became stereotyped, in the same way as the 'stages' were marked out according to the patterns developed by those leaders who stabilized the insights and practices of the founder. Consequently, self-deception must

[1] *Ar-Risālat al-Qushairiyya*, edn. cit., p. 9; Shihāb ad-dīn, '*Awārif*, p. 338. *Ghafla* in a strict sense (as here) is momentary forgetfulness of God; in a wider sense it is preoccupation with self.

be added to spiritual pride as one of the hazards of the dervish life, since the methods and patterns tended to be followed automatically without necessarily corresponding to any felt inner experience. The meaning of the terminology degenerated from relationship to God to relationship to a dead saint or living shaikh, the medium between God and man. Thus *murāqaba* (lit. awareness, but also contemplation, meditation)[1] by degrees acquires new meanings, until it comes to signify, in the orders, participation in the being of that which is being contemplated—God, Muḥammad, or one's director, living or dead.

Since the orders are, on the one hand, practical Ways, and, on the other, repositories of esoteric beliefs—to some even of divine wisdom (*ḥikma ilāhiyya = theosophia*)—their doctrine is not clearly formulated. Cult more than belief integrated the *ikhwān*. Beliefs have to be abstracted from the accounts of *dhikr* practice to discover what is being aimed at, from the reported sayings, prayers,[2] and songs of founding shaikhs and order formulators, and from books on Sufi conduct or rules (*ādāb* or *ḥuqūq aṭ-ṭarīq*), which embrace both regulations concerning such matters as the inter-relationships between shaikh and novice and the rules for ritual. Especially valuable are the lives of the leaders and collections of their sayings (*ḥikam*). One may claim that in the orders Sufi doctrine and teaching was conveyed through sayings, precepts, and parables. A Sufi artist like Jalāl ad-dīn Rūmī paints his word-pictures, parables, and allegories without conscious application, without attempting to expound, portraying those aspects of Reality he was gifted to see without attempting to build up some theory about the meaning of existence. A popular work like Aḥmad ibn M. al-ʿAbbād's *Al-Mafākhir al-ʿaliyya fī 'l-maʾākhir ash-Shādhiliyya* consists of a collection of the sayings of Abu 'l-Ḥasan ʿAlī, arranged under subject headings, with a long section devoted to his *aḥzāb*, but nothing in the nature of coherent doctrinal formulation, since the *ṭarīqa* does not possess any. All this is apart from the gnostic chain, which claims to transmit and interpret an esoteric doctrine reserved for the fully initiated alone.

[1] In the early systematic study of Sufism by as-Sarrāj this was the first of the mystical states; see *Kitāb al-Lumaʿ*, ed. R. A. Nicholson, pp. 54–5.

[2] A valuable study of the devotional material, much of a high spiritual order, which is given in the prayer manuals of the orders, is Constance Padwick's *Muslim Devotions*, London, 1961.

The Truth which the seeker seeks is existential; it must be apprehended by the whole personality. The cognitive aspect, therefore, is mediated through its integral union with practice. Action, the song, exercise and dance, with the attendant symbolism, is the primary form of communication. Teaching is relatively subordinate, and in any case is inseparable from progressive experience. The master taught the seeker Sufi symbolism by stages, continually testing his progress and allotting increasingly exacting litany tasks. As the seeker practised these, it was believed, he was able to apprehend the unteachable, to seize upon truth intuitively. In practice, the three main spheres of religious apprehension—belief, the ritual through which, and the way of life in which, it is expressed—are brought into harmoniously balanced relationship. Faith is not intellectual apprehension as such. Belief retains its hold because it is a system of life. Ritual is the medium which conveys, re-enacts, teaches intuitively, and binds. So Sufism developed mystical techniques to enable the seeker to arrive at *ma'rifa* (esoteric knowledge). *Ma'rifa*, therefore, is no intellectual gnosis, but direct 'perception' of God.

Masters of the Way realized that the mystical tendency is highly dangerous as an individual experience, since the soul under the influence of a 'state' is wide open to delusion and self-deception. There are mystic Ways to other gods than God. Hence they insisted upon the necessity for guidance under an experienced director. In the next stage they themselves became the medium between God and man. Jalāl ad-dīn Rūmī writes:

> When the Pīr has accepted thee, take heed, surrender thyself (to him): go, like Moses, under the authority of Khizr. . . . God has declared that his (the Pīr's) hand is as His own, since He gave out (the words) *the Hand of God is above their hands*[1] . . . If any one, by rare exception, traversed this Way alone (without a Pīr), he arrived (at his goal) through the help (and favour) of the hearts of the Pīrs. The hand of the Pīr is not withdrawn from the absent (those who are not under his authority): his hand is naught but the grasp of God.[2]

The last phrase shows that Jalāl ad-dīn saw even the lone seekers as being spiritually under guidance.

[1] Qur'ān, xlviii. 10, referring to the oath of allegiance given to the Prophet at Ḥudaibiya.

[2] Jalāl ad-dīn Rūmī, *Masnawi*, tr. R. A. Nicholson, London, 1926, i. 162.

In the final stage they denied the right of the individual, not merely to seek a Path by trial and error, but even under guidance, for the shaikhs were the mediators, and the allotting of spiritual tasks became a mechanical process. The *murīd*'s initiation involved the surrender of his will to that of the shaikh. A Tijānī manual begins, 'Praise is due to God who gave a means to everything and made the mediating shaikh a means to union with God.'[1] Although the orders are the embodiment of the mystical experience, yet their distinctive feature is that 'knowledge' of the divine rests upon *wilāya*, and *wilāya* is transmitted through the shaikh. We have said that changes took place in the meaning of Sufi terms: the word *tawajjuh* (mental concentration), for example, comes to mean in the terminology of eastern orders, the spiritual assistance rendered by the saint to his devotee, or by the *murshid* to his *murīd*. In this exercise the shaikh (in a state of *jadhb*?) concentrates upon the *murīd*, picturing the spinning of a line of linkage between his pineal heart (*al-qalb aṣ-ṣanawbarī*) and the heart of the *murīd* through which power can flow. At the same time, the *murīd* concentrates upon becoming a passive vessel for the inflowing power of the shaikh. With others *tawajjuh* is the attempt to contact the spirit of a dead shaikh.[2]

The masters of the Way were fully conscious of the dangers of incurring the charge of *bid'a* (innovation). Islam was spared the Christian conception of heresy as deviation from norms of belief. Orthodoxy is a matter of practice rather than belief; it is conformity to the Law; the welfare of the community involves surrender to the Law. We have seen that there is nothing surprising in the order-leaders insisting upon observance of the *Sharī'a*, since they believed that this was coexistent with the divine Unity; they simply claimed that there was an outer and an inner knowledge (*al-'ilm aẓ-ẓāhirī* and *al-'ilm al-bāṭinī*). The *ṭā'ifas* tended, therefore, to be in an ambivalent position. They were rarely attacked on the ground of belief, but usually on the ground of deviations in practice.

The first concern of the founder and leaders of a *ṭā'ifa* was to assert their orthodoxy. This was simply obtained by the truly

[1] M. 'Alwān al-Jawsqī, *As-Sirr al-Abhar*, Cairo, n.d., p. 3.
[2] See for different aspects of [*awajjuh*], pp. 58, 213–14.

Islamic expedient of producing an *isnād*.[1] In order to avoid any reproach of *bid'a* all a shaikh needed was to demonstrate that he had followed the course of a well-known Sufi. He could then use the authority of his master and all the transmissory links right back to one of the first four Caliphs as a prop (*sanad*) for his teaching and practice. This is that chain of authority or mystical *isnād* called the *silsila*. As new ideas were fostered on eminent Sufis of past ages in order to make these ideas respectable,[2] so the *silsila* provided a doctrinal as well as a power-line going back to these 'rightly-guided ones'. This claim that these caliphs were Sufis was invented during the period when Sufism was struggling for recognition against the opposition of the legalists. Ibn Khaldūn rejects all such claims. None of the early caliphs, he says, 'was distinguished by the possession of any particular religious practice exclusively peculiar to him'.[3] 'Alī al-Hujwīrī relates[4] each caliph to different aspects of the Sufi Path: Abu Bakr represents the contemplative Way (*mushāhada*), 'Umar the purgative Way (*mujāhada*), 'Uthmān that of friendship (*khulla*) with God, and 'Alī is the guide to the principles and practice of divine Reality (*Ḥaqīqa*). In practice the *silsilas* of the *ṭarīqas* are traced back to only three of these caliphs. 'Alī is the primary source, some have a line to Abu Bakr[5] or 'Umar,[6] but I have not come across a line to 'Uthmān.[7]

The developed *silsila* of the orders embraces two divisions: *silsilat al-baraka* (chain of benediction), connects the present shaikh

[1] It seems unnecessary to follow Ibn Khaldūn (see *Muqaddama*, tr. Rosenthal, iii. 93) in attributing this craving for an *isnād* to Shī'ī practice.

[2] 'Alī al-Hujwīrī gives an illuminating instance of this practice when he writes of al-Khuldī (d. 348/959), 'He is the well-known biographer of the Saints . . . He has many sublime sayings. In order to avoid spiritual conceit, he attributed to different persons the anecdotes which he composed in illustration of each topic' (*Kashf al-mahjūb*, pp. 156–7). The reference is to al-Khuldī's *Ḥikmat al-awliyā'*, a work now lost but drawn upon freely by later biographers.

[3] Ibn Khaldūn, *Muqaddama*, tr. F. Rosenthal, iii. 93.

[4] *Kashf al-Maḥjūb*, pp. 70–4.

[5] For example, Naqshabandiyya, Yasaviyya, and Bektāshiyya; see D'Ohsson, *Tableau*, iv. 2. 626, al-Wāsiṭī, *Tiryāq*, p. 47.

[6] For example, the Rifā'iyya. Of the 'Uqailiyya, a Syrian branch of the Baṭā-'ihiyya which Ibn ar-Rifā'ī made famous, founded by a Kurd called 'Uqail al-Manbajī ibn Shihāb ad-dīn Aḥmad, we read, 'He was the first to introduce *al-Khirqat al-'Umariyya* into Syria' (al-Wāsiṭī, *Tiryāq*, p. 47).

[7] Evliya Chelebi says that the Zainiyya (Suhrawardī line, see Appendix C) trace their line to 'Uthmān; see von Hammer's translation (London, 1845–50), I. ii. 29.

through the founder of the *ṭā'ifa* with the founder of the *ṭarīqa*; whilst *silsilat al-Wird* (chain of initiation) connects the *ṭarīqa*-founder with one of the first khalīfas and the Prophet.[1] Recitation of these chains forms part of the spiritual exercises of members of the orders. Other terminology may be used. The Naqshabandīs call the chain from the founder to the Prophet *silsilat adh-dhahab* (the chain of gold), and that from the founder to the shaikh *silsilat at-tarbiya* (chain of upbringing), the links being called *shuyūkh at-tarbiya*, or, with Suhrawardīs, *shuyūkh al-asātidha*.

Sufism which, in its simple development, we believe to be a natural interiorization of Islam, had come to embrace, not only this theory of election but also a theosophy which was basically alien to Islam. Without overstressing pantheistic tendencies we may point out that the Sufi's relationship to God was unusual. When 'possessed' (*majdhūb*) he was not responsible for his words and actions, he could do and say things which would be blasphemous if said by others.[2] In other words, the phenomenon of temporary loss of personality (*wajd*) provided an opportunity for introducing the inexplicable. Since all order-leaders were professed Sufis, their writings were necessarily full of the Path they laid out for others to follow. The founder's particular bent indicated the general tendency and emphasis. A perusal of the writings giving the principles behind the practice, the teaching to be followed, and especially the prayers, litanies, nativity-recitals, and poems, would give orthodoxy frequent reason for condemnation. Yet such men as the Ḥanbalīs Ibn al-Jawzī and Ibn Taimiya tried and failed. It is very difficult to be convicted of heresy in Islam where judgement on a man's interior motives is reserved to God and man's judgement is based largely on a person's action. Only if a shaikh introduced innovations in religious

[1] But it may happen that the two or more *silsilas* are traced through to companions of the Prophet. Thus of the initiators of ash-Shādhilī (see Maghribī initiatory table) it is claimed that M. ibn Ḥarāzim linked him with Abu Bakr (*silsilat al-baraka*), Ibn Mashīsh with 'Alī (*silsilat al-irāda*), and Abu 'l-Fatḥ al-Wāsiṭī with 'Umar.

[2] 'Ain al-Quḍāt al-Hamadānī explains in his Apologia: 'Sufis have utterances which they call *shaṭḥ*. This term refers to those peculiar expressions which spring to their lips when in a state of intoxication and under the intense ebullition of ecstasy (*wajd*). When in such a state a man is incapable of restraining himself' (*Shaqwā 'l-gharīb*, ed. in *J. Asiat.* ccxvi (1930), 61). All the Sufi manuals deal with this phenomenon, see Abu Naṣr as-Sarrāj, *Kitāb al-Luma' fi'l-taṣawwuf*, ed. R. A. Nicholson, pp. 375–409.

law, or repudiated it, could he be condemned. Consequently, the leaders stressed that their religious practice was fully in line with the *sharī'a* and their writings are choked with *ḥadīths* justifying it.

The orders claim to possess an esoteric system inherited through the links of the chain (*ahl as-silsila*). This is taught only to a few adepts who have persevered through a full course of training and have received manifestations of divine graces. Here again one must reiterate that no abstract doctrines are taught. In order thought Sufism is primarily the Way of Purification (*ṭarīq al-mujāhada*). This is the first path that emerged with the movement from self-denying devotion to mysticism. This was soon paralleled with that of the States (*aḥwāl*), bestowed upon the *sālik* regardless of striving as signs of God's favour, yet at the same time in practice in intimate association with each stage of the Path, which may be summarized as purification/vision (*mujāhada/kashf*). Sufism systematizes the personal striving, but it affirms none the less the role of the divine initiative, the gratuity of the gift of visions and graces, and the passive receptivity of the *nafs* (soul) that, as it empties itself of the contingent, receives.

Out of these unveilings (very strongly influenced from earlier sources) grew up an esoteric system. Some people thought it wrong to express the esoteric doctrine in writing for anyone to read. Thus al-Ghazālī wrote at the beginning of his *Iḥyā'*: 'The concern of this book is with practical knowledge (*'ilm al-mu'āmala*) only, rather than contemplative knowledge (*'ilm al-mukāshafa*) which one is not allowed to set down in books, *though it is the real purpose of the seeker*.'[1] The deepest esoteric teachings did in fact find their expression on paper for all to read, but reading does not mean understanding; it still remains 'secret' and 'hidden' to the uninitiate and unilluminate. Al-Ghazālī himself did not understand, that is why he writes in this way. Anyway this belief in a secret doctrine always persisted within the orders. Many joined hoping to attain this knowledge-with-power, but in practice what was taught was the method of the Way. The teaching is experienced by the *murīd* as he carries out his exercises in the *khalwa*. In the ordinary way the stress is on the allocation of prayer-tasks, the times and modes of recitation, participation in other forms of devotion, pursuance of a course of ascetic discipline, fulfilment of the order's material obligations, and acceptance of the

[1] Al-Ghazālī, *Iḥyā'* (Cairo, 1358/1939), i. 10–11.

جدول السلوك

	١	٢	٣	٤	٥	٦	٧
a	النفس الأمّارة xii. 53	النفس اللوّامه lxxv. 2	النفس المُلْهَمة xci. 7-8	النفس المطمئنّة lxxxix. 27-8	النفس الراضية	النفس المرضيّة	النفس الكاملة
b	السير الى الله	السير بالله	السير على الله	السير مع الله	السير في الله	السير عن الله	السير لله
c	عالم الشهادة	عالم البرزخ	عالم الأرواح	عالم الحقيق	عالم الأركان	عالم الغيب	عالم كثرة ووحدة
d	حالة الميل الى الشهوات	حالة المحبة	حاله العشق	حالة الوصلة	حالة الفناء	حالة الحيرة	حالة البقاء
e	محلة الصدر	محلة القلب	محلة الروح	محلة السرّ	محلة سر السر	محلة الفؤاد	محلة مستوى السر
f	شريعة	طريقة	معرفة	حقيقة	ولاية	ذات الشريعة	ذات الكل
g	نوره أزرق	نوره أصفر	نوره أحمر	نوره أبيض	نوره أخضر	نوره أسود	نور لا لون له

1	2	3	4	5	6	7	
The Carnal Soul	The Soul Admonishing	The Inspired Soul	The Tranquil Soul	The Contented Soul	The Approved Soul	The Perfected Soul	a
The Journey *to* God	The Journey *by* God's [power]	The Journey *upon* God	The Journey *with* God	The Journey *within* God	The Journey *from* God	The Journey *into* God	b
The Evidential World (of the senses)	World of the Isthmus [Purgatorial World]	World of the Spirits	The World of Reality	The World of Principles	The World of the Unseen	The World of Plurality and Oneness	c
State of Inclination to Lusts	State of Love	State of Passion	State of Union	State of Passing Away or Transition	State of Bewilderment	State of Abiding [in God]	d
Abode: the Breast	Abode: the Heart	Abode: the Spirit	Abode: the Mystery [of the Heart]	Abode: the Mystery of the Mystery	Abode: the Inmost	Abode: the Covert ('Ground') of the Mystery	e
Sharīʿa	Ṭarīqa	Maʿrifa	Ḥaqīqa	Wilāya	Dhāt ash-Sharīʿa (Essence of the Revealed Law)	Dhāt al-Kull	f
Light: Blue	Light: Yellow	Light: Red	Light: White	Light: Green	Light: Black	Light: Colourless	g

spiritual experiences, supra-normal exploits, and continuing power of the saints.

The stages of the Path, as mediated through the orders, should be given, since they constituted a very real thing with the dedicated dervishes and are found in the popular manuals. Symbolic schemes were produced. Whilst these were based on the Sufis' versions of their spiritual pilgrimage, the mystical scheme adopted in the orders became stereotyped. We reproduce on pages 152 and 153 the commonest diagrammatization of the Seven Stages, taken from As-Sanūsī's *Salsabīl* from the section dealing with the Khalwatiyya,[1] but it is widespread and found in other order manuals, though with variations.[2]

This schema is related to the fantasy of 70,000 veils of light and darkness (inner side light and outer side dark) intervening between the individual soul and the Reality they obscure. Hence the need for seven series of purifications of the *nafs* or soul, in order that these may be rent aside, 10,000 at a time. Readers who are acquainted with the writings of Sufis will be able to follow the map, others could have no better introduction than 'Aṭṭār's *Manṭiq aṭ-Ṭair*, where the seven valleys traversed by the birds of the quest are: Search, Love, mystic Apprehension, Detachment/Independence, Unity, Bewilderment, and Fulfilment in Annihilation.[3] Here only tbe briefest indication towards the clarification of the schema can be given. What needs to be brought out is that the purpose of the discipline of the *dhikr* (in its comprehensive sense), which will be described in chapter seven, is to achieve this purification. The aspirant has: (d1) to purify his *nafs*, i.e. his

[1] As-Sanūsī, *Salsabil*, p. 105.

[2] The diagram is given, for example, in the popular Qādirī manual, *Al-Fuyūḍāt ar-Rabbāniyya*, compiled by Ismā'īl ibn M. Sa'īd, p. 34. The different versions, if not accompanied by a commentary, help to clear up confusions; thus the just-mentioned Qādirī version shows that c4 is, '*Ālam al-Ḥaqīqat al-Muḥammadiyya* (see p. 163), c5 is '*Ālam al-Lāhūt*, 'World of the Godhead', and c7 *Kathra fi 'l-waḥda wa waḥda fi 'l-kathra*, 'multiplicity in unity and unity in multiplicity'.

[3] The form was first devised by Ibn Sīnā (d. A.D. 1037) with a philosophical aim (*Risālat aṭ-ṭair*, ed. L. Cheikho in *al-Mashriq*, iv (1901), 882–7) and taken up as a Sufi pilgrimage in a little treatise with the same title, which is attributed to Muḥammad al-Ghazālī but is much more likely to be by his brother Aḥmad (d. A.D. 1126), except for the last two *faṣls* which have been added by a later hand. This has also been edited by L. Cheikho in *al-Mashriq*, iv. 918–24. It is presumably from this that 'Aṭṭār (completed his *Manṭiq* in 573/1177–8) adopted the conceit (cf. Qur'ān, xxvii. 16) as a framework for his stories.

personality-self, from its inclination to *shahawāt*, that is, the thoughts and desires of the natural man, and (d2) substitute these with love (*maḥabba*); then (d3) he must be cast into the flames of passion (*ʿishq*), to emerge (d4) in the state of union (*wuṣla*), with (d5) transmutation of self (*fanā'*), through (d6) the gifts of dazzlement and wonder (*ḥaira*), to (d7) everlastingness (*baqā'*).

The stages through which the *nafs* progresses to its annihilation in fulfilment are: I, when the carnal mind is dominant, the soul 'unregenerate'; II, when it is 'accusatory' and is resisted but still unsubmissive; III, when it is 'aspiring'; IV, when the carnal mind is completely subdued and 'the soul at rest' (Qur'ān, xiii. 28); V, when the soul is (God-)satisfied; VI (God-)satisfying, approved; and VII, clarified or sanctified.[1]

Each of the seven stages of purification or apocalypses of the veils is distinguished by the appearance of a different coloured light. The order of the colours and their significance varies, but colourlessness is the sign of the final stage of no individualization (*taʿayyun*) or limitation, but only a realm of pure Being and absolute Unity: *lā ilāha illā Anā.*

The order manuals, especially those of the nineteenth-century orders, tend to treat this process along the lines of an ethical–ascetical, rather than a mystical, pilgrimage. The orders have special *dhikrs* corresponding to the seven spiritual attributes and stages in purification of the *nafs*. As a typical example we give a translation of the relevant section of the Mirghanī treatise, *Minḥat al-aṣḥāb*, by Aḥmad ibn ʿAbd ar-Raḥmān ar-Ruṭbī:[2]

It is your duty, my brother, to struggle with the soul, this being the major *jihād*, to the end that the soul may be delivered from reprehensible attributes through their substitution by praiseworthy ones.

(*a*) The Unregenerate Soul (*an-nafs al-ammāra*) has among its attributes: ignorance, stinginess, covetousness, pride, anger, lust, envy, heedlessness, ill-nature, interfering in things not one's concern, and the like;

[1] This final stage is given in the table as *an-nafs al-kāmila*, 'the Perfected Soul'. In the *Fuyūḍāt* it appears as *an-nafs aṣ-ṣāfiya*, 'the Clarified Soul'; elsewhere as *an-nafs aṣ-ṣafiyya*. *Ṣafā* or *ṣafwa* is defined as 'to be pure from all existing things', and as 'the essence of *fanā'*'; it is 'one of the names of perfection' (Hujwīrī, *Kashf*, tr., p. 58). In the table its meaning is quite unequivocal.

[2] From the collection of treatises entitled *Ar-Rasā'il al-Mirghaniyya*, Cairo, 1358/1939, pp. 93–4. A longer account of the soul's purification is given in as-Sanūsī, *Salsabīl*, pp. 183–92. Since the phraseology is frequently identical they must have their origin in a common source.

together with hatred, mocking and injuring others either physically or verbally, and suchlike bad things. This is the reprobate soul, but struggle with it will promote it to:

(*b*) the Second Stage (*maqām*), which is the Blameworthy Soul (*an-nafs al-lawwāma*), and its attributes are: blame, speculation, vanity, opposition to people, secret hypocrisy, and love of fame and authority. Therefore its attributes are blameworthy too, for they are maladies for which there is no other remedy than persistent *dhikr* and struggle, until they are got rid of, when one attains:

(*c*) the Third Stage, when it becomes the Inspired Soul (*al-mulhama*), all of whose attributes are praiseworthy. Its qualities are generosity, contentment, knowledge, humility, patience, gentleness, forbearance of injury, pardoning everyone and accepting their excuses, witnessing that 'God holds by the forelock every creature' (Qur'ān, xi. 56), hence he would never criticize anything whatsoever in creation. This soul is called 'inspired' because God infused it with both immoral and moral qualities. Therefore, gird up your loins, abandon sleep, praying earnestly and repeating the *dhikr* until daybreak, so that you may attain to:

(*d*) the Fourth Stage, in which the soul becomes Tranquil (*muṭma'inna*). Among its qualities are liberality, trust (*tawakkul*), gentleness, adoration, gratitude, contentment with fate, and patience under calamities. Among the signs which show that the pilgrim has entered the fourth grade in which the soul is named 'tranquil' is steadfastness under any conditions, his only delight being in behaving like the Chosen One (the Prophet) until he is promoted to:

(*e*) the Fifth Stage, in which the soul is called Contented (*rāḍiya*). Among its attributes are renunciation of everything save God, fidelity, godfearingness, contentedness with all that takes place in the world without palpitation of heart and with no remonstrance whatsoever. That is because he is absorbed in contemplation of absolute Beauty. He who is in this grade is immersed in the sea of grace with God. His prayer will not be rejected, it being understood that, out of modesty and courtesy, his tongue will be incapable of making petition unless absolutely impelled to do so, only then may he ask and his request cannot fail.[1] The *dhikr* of this *maqām* is *Ḥayy*. Keep on with it, so that your transitoriness (*fanā'*) may fade and you will attain immortality (*baqā'*) in the *Ḥayy*.[2] Then you enter upon:

[1] Nowhere is the unillumined ethical nature of the Path more obvious than here, since for the mystic in this advanced stage no problem of answer to prayer arises; the problem has been solved by being *re*solved, transcended.

[2] The whole stress within the Junaidī tradition (as contrasted with the Bisṭāmī tradition, where the concept was different) was on the attributes, the

(*f*) the Sixth Stage, in which the soul is called Approved (*marḍiyya*). Among its attributes are subtlety of nature, abandonment of all save God, kindness to all creatures, prompting them to prayer, forgiving their sins, loving them, with compassion towards all, helping them to expel the dark sides of their natures and souls and thereby to bring forth the lights of their spiritual nature. . . . Among the attributes of this soul is union between love of the created and the Creator. This is something amazing, and it is very difficult except for those who have attained this grade. This soul has been called 'approved' because the Real is satisfied with it. Its movement is from God (*sairuhā 'an Allāh*); in other words, it has acquired what it needed of knowledge from the Living and Self-subsisting Itself. The soul has returned from the Unseen World (*'Ālam al-ghaib*) back to the Evidential World (*'Ālam ash-shahāda*) by God's permission, in order to benefit mankind with the graces which God has bestowed upon it.[1] When the soul is promoted to:

(*g*) the Seventh Stage, wherein it is called the Perfect Soul (*an-nafs al-kāmila*), its qualities embrace all the good attributes of the souls which have already been described. Thus he becomes complete. The name with which this perfected one should occupy himself is 'al-Qahhār' (the Subduer), which is the seventh Name. This is the purest of the grades, because the name Qahhār is one of the names of the Quṭb. The shaikhs have said: 'From this name the Quṭb supplies the aspirants with lights, gifts, and glad tidings'; and also, 'the joy that illuminates the hearts of the aspirants, and the delights and trances that overcome one without cause are due to the provision of the Quṭb rather than to their *dhikrs* and turning their faces to their Lord (*tawajjuhātuhum li Rabbihim*).'

Abu Ḥāmid al-Ghazālī's interiorized ethical approach, on the one hand, and that of the orders in their interpretation of the Path on the other, are most important in view of the explicit extrinsic approach of Islamic legalism which judges only the external, a person's responsibility for his actions, but not the motive for the actions; for example, murder but not hatred.

Yet in spite of their stress upon morality (e.g. *tawba* meaning 'repentance' and not some esoteric signification), the orders could never solve the problem of the distinction between the spiritual and the ethical. The ethical virtues (the craving for inward

annihilation of the imperfect (*fanā'*) and their replacement by positive attributes; see al-Qushairī, *Risāla*, ed. 1319, pp. 36–7. It was this which kept the tradition firmly within orthodoxy.

[1] This is the journey back to the world of manifestation, return to consciousness of the plurality of the world, a return in a transformed state as a *murshid* (*Quṭb*) to try to make the world more perfect.

purity is not such) have nothing to do with the spiritual pilgrimage. They offer, say the Sufis, knowledge of the goal, but leave one deficient in the power of reaching it. This was Abu Ḥāmid's tragedy. The *malāmatī* need not bother about the moral law, this is understood even if it scandalizes, but what about the *walī*? This too is a religious and not an ethical term, since the *walī*'s *wilāya* is either gifted or intrinsic, quite independent of his moral qualities. The lives of the saints show that they are above any moral code.

The *murshid* measures the *murīd*'s progress through these stages by interpreting the visions and dreams which the *murīd* experiences whilst carrying out his personal *dhikr* exercises in *khalwa*. Dream interpretation thus forms an important element in the orders. As-Sanūsī writes of the Khalwatiyya, 'The adherents of this order, as well as the Kubrawiyya, cultivate the practice of dream-interpretation (*ta'bīr ar-ru'yā*), so much so that some of the leaders have said that it is the pivot (*madār*) upon which their Path rests.'[1] Ibn 'Aṭā' Allāh, author of the first systematic treatise on the *dhikr*, wrote:

> What first visualizes itself to him from that (supernatural) world are the angelic substances and the spirits of the prophets and saints in an attractive form by means of which certain realities are emanated into him. That is but the beginning, until he reaches the stage when images are transcended and he encounters the manifestation of al-Ḥaqq in everything. Such is the fruit of the quintessence of the *dhikr*.[2]

Vision of that mysterious spirit of Islamic gnosis, al-Khaḍir, is important, especially in respect of saintship and the founding of a new *ṭā'ifa*. Generally identified with Ilyās (Elias) as 'the servant of God', conductor and instructor of Moses, of *sūra* 'The Cave' (xviii. 64–81), al-Khaḍir possesses *ḥikma* (wisdom) (verse 65) and *al-ism al-a'ẓam* (the greatest Name), knowledge of which confers saintship and ability to do supra-normal things. Hypostatized as a person he represents in Sufi thought the inner light of *wilāya*, parallel to, and contrasted with, the apostolic-legalistic aspects of prophesy signified by Moses. His mediatory

[1] As-Sanūsī, *Salsabīl*, p. 99. There is a large literature on the subject of dream-interpretation which involves the coloured lights seen by those engaged in the discipline of the *khalwa*, an aspect stressed by as-Sanūsī in his account just referred to, concerning dream-interpretation among the Khalwatiyya.

[2] Ibn 'Aṭā' Allāh, *Miftāḥ al-falāḥ*, ii. 95.

role was expressed epigrammatically by the Egyptian, 'Alī ibn M. Wafā' (d. A.D. 1398): 'Ilyās is to the saints what Jibrīl (Gabriel) is to the prophets.'[1] Naturally the opponents of mysticism had no use for this concept. Ibn 'Aṭā' Allāh quotes Ibn al-Jawzī as denying the existence of al-Khaḍir.[2] Many stories are told in the *manāqib* and hagiographa about this figure. His great significance is his appearance in visions and dreams (*ru'yā* and *manām*); the first experienced while waking and the other while sleeping. 'Abd al-'Azīz ibn ad-Dabbāgh was given the *wird* and *baraka* of *wilāya* by al-Khaḍir in 1125/1713 at the tomb of 'Alī ibn al-Hirzahim at Fez.[3]

The gnostic's path is different from this process of the Way, but even this needs mentioning here, since in some form it is found in all the manuals. Here the seeker traces the stages of cosmic evolution. The stages of *sharī'a*, *ṭarīqa*, and *ḥaqīqa* are represented as bridging four spheres of existence or natures—human, angelic, dynamic, and divine natures.

All the theist orders claim the Law as the starting-point, a basis for further progress in either the directed or illuminative life. This is expressed in the following quotation from a Mirghanī manual which can be paralleled in all the orders:

> Hold firmly, my brother, to the *sharī'a*, because you cannot approach the Path except through the *sharī'a*; nor can you approach the Reality (*Ḥaqīqa*) except through the *ṭarīqa* . . . *Sharī'a* is the root, *ṭarīqa* is the branch, and *ḥaqīqa* is the fruit. You cannot expect to find fruit except through the existence of root and branch, and the branch could not exist except through the root. He who sticks to the *sharī'a* and does not follow a Path is corrupt. He who follows a Path and does not stick to the *sharī'a* is a heretic (*zindīq*).[4]

[1] Ash-Sha'rānī, *Lawāqiḥ*, ii. 24. This complementary parallelism between the *wirātha Khaḍiriyya* and *wirātha Mūsāwiyya* is brought out in the sayings of 'Alī Wafā' and Abu 'l-Mawāhib M. ash-Shādhilī (1417–77) quoted by Sha'rānī, op. cit. ii. 24 and 63. In these discourses, as also in conversation, whenever al-Khaḍir's name is mentioned the speaker adds *wa 'alaikum as-salām*, as though he were present. Similarly with certain saints.

[2] Ibn 'Aṭā'Allāh, *Laṭā'if al-minan*, i. 87, referring to Ibn al-Jawzī's *'Ujālat al-muntaẓar fī sharḥ ḥāl al-Khaḍir*.

[3] See *Adh-Dhahab al-ibrīz fī manāqib 'Abd al-'Azīz* by Ibn ad-Dabbāgh's disciple, Aḥmad ibn Mubārak al-Lamṭī. Al-Jabartī records (*'Ajā'ib*, Cairo edn., 1959, ii. 43) that Muṣṭafā ibn Kamāl ad-dīn al-Bakrī 'encountered al-Khaḍir on three occasions'.

[4] Aḥmad ibn 'Abd ar-Raḥmān ar-Ruṭbī, *Minḥat al-Aṣḥāb*, Cairo, 1358/1939, p. 96.

The theosophists represent these three stages as bridging four spheres of existence. In the *Ghawthiyya*—or, better, the alternative title, *Mi'rājiyya*—an interesting little questionnaire addressed to God by 'Abd al-Qādir al-Jīlānī (whom God respectfully addresses in every sentence as '*Yā Ghawth al-a'ẓam*'), God says, 'Every phase between *Nāsūt* and *Malakūt* is the *Sharī'a*; and every phase between *Malakūt* and *Jabarūt* is the *Ṭarīqa*; and every phase between *Jabarūt* and *Lahūt* is the *Ḥaqīqa*.'[1]

'*Ālam an-Nāsūt* is 'the world of humanity', perceived through the physical senses; the material phenomenal world, which Abu Ḥāmid al-Ghazālī (who adopts the terminology if not the substance) calls '*Ālam al-mulk wa 'sh-shahāda*.

'*Ālam al-Malakūt*, 'the world of sovereignty', is the invisible, spiritual, angelic world,[2] that which is perceived through insight and the spiritual faculties. According to some it is the uncreated macrocosm.

'*Ālam al-Jabarūt*, 'the world of power', is the celestial world, that which is perceived through entering into and partaking of the divine nature. It is also the world of the divine Names and Qualities.

'*Ālam al-Lāhūt* is 'the world of the Godhead', not perceived, since now the phenomenal is absorbed into timeless unicity.

Although this sort of thing belongs to the realm of speculative mystical theology, these spheres constantly appear in the order manuals in regard to the Sufi Path. In this respect, as in the quotation given above ascribed to 'Abd al-Qādir:

Nāsūt is the natural human state in which one lives following the rules of the *sharī'a*;

[1] Quoted in Ismā'īl b. M. Sa'īd's compilation, *Al-Fuyūḍāt ar-Rabbāniyya*, a manual for the average adherent, Cairo, A.H. 1353, p. 4. This questionnaire is most valuable to show how theosophical ideas were represented for the ordinary adherent. It was not, of course, written by 'Abd al-Qādir, for it is stylistically direct and simple and contains material no Ḥanbalī would have written. 'Abd al-Qādir would have been shocked to read it, but the belief in a secret esoteric doctrine allows one to foist beliefs and sayings upon an early Sufi.

[2] *Bāṭin al-kawn* in Suhrawardī, '*Awārif*, p. 62.

Malakūt is the nature of angels, to reach which one treads the *ṭarīqa*, the path of purification; whilst

Jabarūt is the nature of power, to attain which one follows the way of enlightenment, *ma'rifa*, until one swoons into

Fanā', absorption into Deity, the State of Reality (*Ḥaqīqa*), often called in the order literature *'Ālam al-Ghaib*, 'the (uncreated) world of the mystery'.

We have already shown how mysticism, working within the purely unitarian system of Islam, diverged into two directions—pantheism and saint-veneration—whilst at the same time maintaining a middle path. After centuries of mystical experimentation speculative mysticism came to embrace a Logos doctrine[1] which, without impairing the divine Unity, provided a philosophical basis for the practical devotion to saints and Prophet which had formed in response to people's need. Ibn al-'Arabī, with his doctrine of the Unity [*a priori*] of Being (*waḥdat al-wujūd*), taught that 'all things pre-exist as ideas in the knowledge of God, whence they emanate and whither they ultimately return'.[2]

He developed more fully the doctrine of the pre-existence of Muḥammad before creation. This is the doctrine of *An-Nūr al-Muḥammadī*,[3] the Muhammadan Light, the image of God in its primary entity, the divine consciousness, the pre-creation light from which everything was created. It is also called *al-Ḥaqīqat al-Muḥammadiyya*, that is, cosmic Muḥammad in his absolute reality. The world is a manifestation of that Light; it became incarnate in Adam, the prophets, and the *Aqṭāb* (sing. *Quṭb*, 'Axis'), each of whom is *al-Insān al-Kāmil* (the Perfect Man).

The work of the systematizers of the orders[4] was to apply the philosophy of Sufism to the needs of the ordinary believer. They

[1] Al-Ḥakīm at-Tirmidhī (d. A.D. 898) was the first within an Islamic context to write about the Logos, for which he uses the word *Dhikr*: '*Wa kāna 'llāh*^{u} *wa lā shai'un, fa jarā 'dh-Dhikr*' (*Khatm al-Wilāya*, ed. 'Uthmān Ismā'īl Yaḥyā, p. 337).

[2] R. A. Nicholson in *The Legacy of Islam*, Oxford, 1931, p. 224.

[3] The concept has been frequently discussed; see, for example, 'Afīfī, *The Mystical Philosophy of Ibn al-'Arabī*, Cambridge, 1939.

[4] The orders were more concerned with mediating works such as 'Abd al-Karīm al-Jīlī's *Al-Insān al-Kāmil*, or his commentary on Ibn al-'Arabī's *Al-Asfār 'an risālat al-anwār fīmā yatajallā li ahl adh-dhikr min al-anwār*, published with al-Jīlī's commentary, Damascus, 1348/1929, pp. 293 ff.

had to disavow beliefs which might be labelled pantheistic, for any such profession would give the *'ulamā'* the opportunity to condemn for which they were always waiting. It was easy to exercise pressure upon professional institutional Sufism. In Egypt in the mid-fourteenth century the directive given by Mamluk authority to the *shaikh ash-shuyūkh* affirms that the only way to God is through the Qur'ān and the Sunna as embodied in *Shar'*. The Shaikh 'shall censure anyone who inclines towards belief in *ittiḥād* or *ḥulūl*, or claims that it is possible to attain to God by any way other than that defined by the Prophets'.[1] Naturally many orders maintained their own exclusive secret doctrine and particularly censured members who leaked any of the doctrine; for this reason ash-Shiblī and Ṣafī ad-dīn al-Ardabīlī censured al-Ḥallāj.[2]

Through the popular devotional manuals of the orders these theosophical doctrines percolated into the people's religion. They are more evident in eastern orders. Here is a quotation from the *mawlid* of Muḥammad 'Uthmān al-Mirghanī, whose teaching owes more to inherited family tradition, especially the Naqshabandī, than to his more austere master, Aḥmad ibn Idrīs:

When God wished to project these higher and lower worlds He took a fistful of His Light and it was Muḥammad ibn 'Adnān. He (the Prophet) said to Jābir, 'The first thing God created was the Light of your Prophet as an answer to His problem and I was a prophet when Adam was yet water and clay.' The Prophet said to Gabriel, 'How old are you, O Gabriel?' He said, 'I do not know, except that a planet appears in the Fourth Heaven once every 70,000 years (these are the concealed signs) and I have seen it 72,000 times exactly.' The Prophet said, in order to make known his rank and the secret of his Light, 'By the glory of my Lord, I am that planet which you have seen, O Gabriel, in the

[1] Al-'Umarī, *At-ta'rīf bi 'l-muṣṭalaḥ ash-sharīf*, Cairo, A.H. 1312, p. 128. The distinction between *ḥulūl* and *ittiḥād* is that between the Ḥallājian doctrine of *al-ittiḥād al-mu'īn*, the union of God with the individual (*ḥulūl* must not be confused with the Christian doctrine of incarnation) and *al-ittiḥād al-'āmm al-muṭlaq*, the absolute union of divinity and the universe, professed by Hindu pantheists; on this distinction see Massignon's works on the beliefs of al-Ḥallāj and R. A. Nicholson's article '*Ittiḥād*' in *E.I.*[1], ii. 565. The distinctions between these and *waḥdat al-wujūd*, it need hardly be said, counted for nothing with the *'ulamā'* who condemned them all, as did the orthodox middle-of-the-road Sufis; as-Simnānī, for instance, regarded belief in *ittiḥād* as *kufr*.

[2] Al-'Aṭṭār, *Tadhkirat al-awliyā'*, ii. 26; *Ṣafyat aṣ-Ṣafā*, according to B. Nikitine in *J. Asiat.* 1957, p. 389.

sky of the Benefactor, and other things which pens cannot put on paper and even the two writers of good and evil cannot preserve.'[1]

Crudely expressed though it may be, this conception has more than an academic interest, since it is heard at every *dhikr*-gathering. The same author in another work writes, 'Muḥammad, . . . God's essence (*laṭīf*), the mystery within the Adamic creation, Light of lights, Mystery of mysteries, Spirit of spirits'.[2] Sufi tradition, which needs no *isnād*,[3] ascribes to Muḥammad such sayings as, 'I am the Light of God and all things are from my Light.' The Perfect Man as Logos is the essence of every mystical experience. These conceptions can be held along with full attachment to the doctrine of the Unity.

But we must go further, for this conception comes still nearer to the people in the *Quṭb* (Axis). In this conception *nubuwwa* is absorbed into *wilāya*. The inner Sufi doctrine, like that of the Shī'īs, is that *wilāya* is superior to *nubuwwa* as a function, in that the latter is passive and finite, whilst *wilāya* is ever active, timeless. The need for direct knowledge of the Word of God brings *al-Ḥaqīqat al-Muḥammadiyya*, the Logos, in every epoch to take on the form of one known as *Quṭb zamānihi* (the Axis of his age), who manifests himself only to a few chosen mystics.[4] The conception of the *Quṭb* upon whom the world subsists (Sufi equivalent of the Shī'ī *Imām*) at the head of an invisible hierarchy of *awliyā'* goes back long before the time of Ibn al-'Arabī, and is popularly regarded as having originated with Dhū 'n-Nūn al-Miṣrī, inheritor of Egyptian gnostic tradition. During the course of succeeding ages this conception was vulgarized; it became a degree of mystical attainment, then every holy man became a *quṭb*, and

[1] *Mawlid al-Mirghani*, chapter 2. This conception is found in all *mawālid*.

[2] M. 'Uthmān al-Mirghanī, *Al-Jawāhir al-mustaẓhara*, p. 6, in the collection *al-Majmū'at al-Mirghaniyya*.

[3] The legalists constantly reproach the Sufis for not inventing an *isnād* to accompany their traditions.

[4] Jīlī (d. *c.* 1410) writes of these manifestations in *Al-Insān al-Kāmil* (tr. in part by R. A. Nicholson in *Studies in Islamic Mysticism*, Cambridge, 1921, p. 105), 'The Perfect Man is the *Quṭb* (axis) on which the spheres of existence revolve from first to last, and since things came into being he is one (*wāḥid*) for ever and ever. He hath various guises and appears in diverse bodily tabernacles (*kanā'is*): in respect of some of these his name is given to him, while in respect of others it is not given to him. His own original name is Mohammed. . . . In every age he bears a name suitable to his guise (*libās*) in that age.' See also Jīlī's commentary on Ibn al-'Arabī, *Asfār*, pp. 299 ff.

it became necessary to define the Axis of the Universe by an epithet or complement as *al-Quṭb al-Ghawth*, *Quṭb al-Aqṭāb*, or *Quṭb al-ʿĀlam*, though these terms too lost significance when applied indiscriminately. When Jaʿfar al-Mirghanī sings, 'I am the first who existed',[1] he is identifying himself, not with the *quṭb* of the Sufi hierarchy, but with the Logos *Quṭb*. This idea lies behind the claims to seek absorption in the shaikh as in the following from a Chishtī source: 'In the first stage the disciple is expected to love and look to his Shaikh as his all in all. He acts, talks and prays like the Shaikh; he eats, drinks and walks like the Shaikh and constantly meditates upon him. Having been, by this process, spiritually transformed into the Shaikh, the student (murid) is spiritually introduced to the Prophet.'[2]

It will be readily understood why Sufism, in many circles at least, centred around the personality of the shaikh. He is the symbol of the *Quṭb*, invisible, unlimited. In Shīʿī Sufi orders the assimilation of the *Quṭbī* and *Imāmī* conceptions is peculiar. With Twelver Sufis the *Quṭb* is the representative of the Imām on earth; hence the hatred of the *mujtahids* for Sufis. The first pillar of the Gūnābādī branch of the Niʿmatullāhiyya is *walāya* or 'allegiance' to the *Quṭb*, who is the actual present head of the order, even though through him all things subsist.[3]

The saints (*ahl al-ghaib*) form a hierarchical structure with the *Quṭb* at the head. It is an old conception. ʿAlī al-Hujwīrī writes: 'Of those who have power to loose and bind and are the officers of the Divine court there are three hundred called *Akhyār*, and forty, called *Abdāl*, and seven called *Abrār*, and four called *Awtād*, and three called *Nuqabā'*, and one called *Quṭb* or *Ghawth*.'[4]

The terms and numbers vary and the following quotation gives the general lines of the pyramidal structure as understood in Nilotic Sudan:

Shaikh Ḥasan ibn Ḥasūna (d. 1664) was asked about the rank of Mūsā

[1] From the most popular Mirghanī processional hymn; see songs appended to Jaʿfar's *Qiṣṣat al-miʿrāj*, Cairo, A.H. 1348, p. 124.

[2] Quoted by J. Takle in *The Moslem World*, viii (1918), 252–3, from the book of a Calcutta leader of the Chishtiyya.

[3] There was at one time a close association between the Niʿmatullāhiyya and the 40th Nizārī Imām. This Imām, known as 'Aṭā'-Allāh in Niʿmatullāhī circles, migrated with a group of followers from Khurasan to Kerman and the group subsisted as a sect known as the 'Aṭā'allāhīs.

[4] *Kashf al-maḥjūb*, tr. R. A. Nicholson, p. 214.

ibn Ya'qūb. He replied, 'He holds the rank of *fard* among the Sufis. This is other than the *Quṭb*, the four *awtād* [supports], the seven *nujabā'* [nobles], and the forty *abdāl* [substitutes]. Their number [that is, the *afrād*] is equivalent to that of those who took part in the Battle of Badr [that is, three hundred], and they hold in relation to the *Quṭb* the status of privates [to the general].'[1]

The *awliyā'* were the very embodiment of popular concepts; but in addition, if of lesser importance, most Sufi ideas were vulgarized. *Fanā'*, for example, became a vague pantheism behind the practice of the *dhikr* ecstasy. It might be attained through the mediumship of the shaikh, or by loss of personality in him; at any rate, not through a lifetime of costly progress from one *maqām* to another, but according to an individual's susceptibility. Why bother about discipline when 'one *jadhba* (attraction) from God is equal to all the work of mankind and jinnkind.' The *majdhūb* (enraptured one), a familiar aspect of traditional Islamic society, is regarded as having lost his personal consciousness in the divine Oneness.

[1] *Ṭabaqāt* of Wad Ḍaif Allāh, ed. Mandīl, p. 145; ed. Ṣidaiq, pp. 152–3.

VI

The Organization of the Orders

THE first stage of Sufi organization was the circle of pupils and adepts around a master. In Khurasan the location of such a group was a centre called a *khānaqāh*. This was not a building designed specially for the purpose but simply a dwelling taken over to house a shaikh and his dervishes. Such a centre was still a circle even though it occupied a building in which rooms were set aside for assembly (*jamā'at-* or *samā'at-khāna*) and for prayer (*muṣallā*), and frequently the whole circle went on tour for a year or longer. Many such centres are recorded in the eleventh century in the life of Abu Sa'īd ibn Abī 'l-Khair (A.D. 967–1049),[1] among them Khānaqāh-i Sarāwī, founded in Nishapur by Abu 'Alī ad-Daqqāq (d. A.D. 1016), who was the master of both Abu Sa'īd and al-Qushairī. Another in the same city, that of Abu 'Alī aṭ-Ṭarsūsī (d. 364/974), survived until 548/1154 when it was destroyed by the Ghuzz. Few of these early *khānaqāhs* survived as long as that, but the tombs of these early masters (or the site tradition) were preserved, and during stage two of *ṭarīqa* development their mausoleums were restored or erected, and then there took place the opposite process—the presence of the tomb leading to the association of a *khānaqāh* with it.

These stage-one associations had a minimum of rules to regulate their life in common. An early record of such rules, that of the just-mentioned Abu Sa'īd for members of his *khānaqāh* at Mayhana in Khorasan, is translated by R. A. Nicholson:[2]

[1] Muḥammad ibn al-Munawwar, *Asrār at-tawḥīd fī maqāmāt ash-Shaikh Abī 's-Sa'īd*, written *c.* 1200. This account of Abu Sa'īd is the basis of R. A. Nicholson's study of him in *Studies in Islamic Mysticism*, Cambridge, 1921, pp. 1–76.

[2] R. A. Nicholson, *Studies*, p. 46. The various Sufi manuals of the period deal in a general way with the manners of Sufis in association, see for example, as-Sarrāj, *Luma'*, pp. 174 ff.; al-Hujwīrī, *Kashf*, pp. 341–5 (reception to be accorded a visiting dervish and the rules he must observe), pp. 345–7 (rules to be observed when travelling). An analysis of the rules of the *ḥalqa* of the Tunisian Ibāḍī, Abu 'Abdallāh M. b. Bakr (d. 440/1048), given by R. Rubinacci

i. Let them keep their garments clean and themselves always pure.
ii. Let them not sit in the mosque or in any holy place for the sake of gossiping.
iii. In the first instance let them perform their prayers in common.
iv. Let them pray much at night.
v. At dawn let them ask forgiveness of God and call unto Him.
vi. In the morning let them read as much of the Koran as they can and let them not talk until the sun has risen.
vii. Between evening prayers and bedtime prayers let them occupy themselves with repeating some litany (*wirdí ú dhikrí*).
viii. Let them welcome the poor and needy and all who join their company, and let them bear patiently the trouble of (waiting upon) them.
ix. Let them not eat anything save in participation with one another.
x. Let them not absent themselves without receiving permission from one another.

Furthermore, let them spend their hours of leisure in one of three things: either in the study of theology or in some devotional exercise (*wirdí*) or in bringing comfort to some one. Whosoever loves this community and helps them as much as he can is a sharer in their merit and future recompense.

Respect for the spiritual freedom of each member necessitated their having regulations for their common life, but it will be seen that the shaikh is not mentioned; he remained essentially a guide in spiritual matters, he is no autocrat of a convent, and they did not even have to seek his permission if they wished to be absent but sought it from their companions. The idea of a spiritual *futuwwa* was formed in such groups as a basis for their common life as well as relationships in their wandering life.

In Arab-controlled regions some of the frontier-posts known as *ribāṭs*[1] had become centres of devotees but are not to be equated

in *Annali*, Nuova serie, x, 1960, 37–78, is of interest to all concerned with early monastic communities.

[1] *Ribāṭs* were founded in frontier regions as Muslim cells in a non-Muslim environment. They were watch-stations and frontier-posts, whose guards were often effective propagators of Islam. Two early *ribāṭs* in north Africa were those of Monastīr (Tunisia) founded in 180/796 (Al-Bakrī, p. 26, tr. pp. 78–9) and Sūs founded in 206/821. Al-Yaʿqūbī in his *K. al-Buldān*, composed in A.D. 891, writes: 'From Sfax to a place called Bizirta is an eight-days' journey. At every stage there is a strong point, each close to the other, garrisoned by pious men and *murābiṭūn*' (B.G.A. vii. 350; tr. Wiet, p. 213). The teaching centre established by Wajjāj ibn Zalwī al-Lamṭī, where ʿAbdallāh ibn Yāsīn (d. 1059), instigator of the Murābiṭ movement, received his training, was known as

with the Iranian *khānaqāhs* in that the master–pupil relationship did not figure in them. However, in stage two of organizational development, the centre of a teaching and guiding master was frequently designated by the same term, *ribāṭ*, such as that of the uncle and nephew Suhrawardīs on the banks of the Tigris, whilst the Iranian term *khānaqāh* was adopted in Iraq, Syria, and Egypt, but not the Maghrib, for an association of Sufis founded and sponsored by non-Arab political rulers and their officials, Ayyūbid and Seljuqid. Both types of institutions were specially designed for Sufi groupings and to serve their aims, but were quite different in construction in that the *ribāṭ* was centred upon a master, whilst in the *khānaqāh* the congregational outlook dominated and the officially appointed head was an administrator rather than a shepherd of souls. At the same time, *ribāṭ* was a non-committal term since there continued to exist the frontier-mentality *ribāṭs* and there were also others, as in Mecca, which were little more than endowed hostels for Sufi travellers and pilgrims.

In the development of organized Sufism *zāwiyas* were more important than most of those just described, but here the institution was a man. They were small modest establishments, centred around one shaikh; at first impermanent, especially since such men were frequently migrants themselves. It was through these men, migrant or settled, that self-perpetuating *ṭarīqas* came into being. They were not endowed like *khānaqāhs* and *ribāṭs*, though in

Dār al-Murābiṭīn (*Rawḍ al-Qirṭās*, ed. Tornberg, 1839, p. 46). Al-Maqdisī in his *Aḥsan at-taqāsīm* (completed A.H. 375) mentions the *ribāṭs* found in the various Islamic countries. Many of those in Khurasan (see pp. 333–4) were associated with the tombs of *ṣaḥāba* who had fallen in battle. Some were well endowed with *awqāf*. Ribāṭ an-Nūr near Bukhara was associated with an annual *mawsim*. At the same time, a place where an ascetic withdrew to wage the spiritual *jihād* was also known as a *ribāṭ* and in time the latter became the dominant usage. The frontier *ribāṭs* changed their character from centres of defence and proselytism to centres of Sufi devotion and teaching. Ibn Marzūq (14th century) writes, 'Dans la terminologie des *fuqarā*, *ribāṭ* est une expression qui désigne le fait de retenir son âme en luttant contre les passions (*ǧihād*) et en faisant preuve de circonspection à l'égard du mal (*ḥirāsa*). Chez les théosophes, ce mot désigne les endroits où l'on demeure en permanence pour se livrer à la dévotion' (Ibn Marzūq, *Musnad*, ed. and tr. E. Lévi-Provençal, *Hespéris*, v, 1925, 35–6). Al-'Umarī, in the middle of the 14th century, refers to 'the pious men who are called *murābiṭs*' (*Masālik*, tr. Gaudefroy-Demombynes, 1927, p. 204). On Maghribī *ribāṭs* see G. Marçais, 'Note sur les Ribāṭs en Berbérie', *Mél. R. Basset*, ii (1925); J. Oliver Asin, 'Origen arabe de rebato', *Boletin de la Real Academia Española*, Madrid, 1928; and 'Alī ibn 'Abd ar-Raḥmān ibn Hudhail, *L'Ornement des âmes*, tr. L. Mercier, Paris, 1939, pp. 115–21, and cf. pp. 71–4; *E.I.*[1] iii. 1150–3.

time when they became family residences they tended to accumulate *awqāf*.

A *khānaqāh* normally consisted of a central courtyard (*qā'a* or *sahn*), having cloisters (*riwāqs*) along two sides, within which were situated the cells (*khalwas* or *ṭibāq*, s. *ṭabaqa*) of the Sufis. On one side was the main hall, the focus of their communal life, where their common devotional exercises took place. This was generally simple in construction. In front of the *miḥrāb* was the sheepskin of the shaikh upon which he reclined during ceremonies and receptions. Over the niche was engraved the name of the founder and religious phrases such as the *shahāda*. Frequently there was a separate mosque, whilst kitchens and other offices, and sometimes a bath-house, were attached. Both resident and migrant Sufis were provided with food and lodging, and the residents with clothing and other perquisites.[1]

Here is a description of al-Khānaqāh al-Qadīm in Aleppo, founded by Nūr ad-dīn ibn Zengī in 543/1148, and 'constituted a *waqf* for Sufi devotees':

It is striking in size and spaciousness. It has a reception-room for the shaikh, a domed chamber for the *fuqarā'*, a large hall (*īwān*), and an oratory (*qibliyya*). On the eastern side of the courtyard of the convent is a door which leads one down to a reservoir fed by a conduit from Ḥailān. Its gateway, which dates from the time of its bequeathing, is large. The door which opens on to the street has two platforms (*dakka*) and was erected by Ḥusām ad-dīn al-Burghālī when he was its shaikh before the invasion of Timur [A.D. 1400]. This convent formerly had a kitchen which provided the Sufis' meals but is now closed and ruined. At one time Shaikh Shihāb ad-dīn as-Suhrawardī had his *sajjāda* in it.[2]

[1] Many *khānaqāhs* were not built specially for the purpose but existing houses were bequeathed by their owners as pious foundations. Thus Amīr 'Alā' ad-dīn Ṭaibōghā of Aleppo constituted his house a *waqf* for Arabized Sufis (*aṣ-Ṣūfiyyatu 'l-must'ariba*) in 631/1234; Abu Dharr Sibṭ ibn al-'Ajamī (d. 1479), *Kunūz adh-dhahab fī ta'rīkh Ḥalab*, quoted by M. Rāghib aṭ-Ṭabbākh, *I'lām*, Aleppo, 1923, iv. 435. Although adapted and added to in the course of time there were very considerable architectural differences, but functionally they followed the same lines.

[2] Abu Dharr quoted by M. Rāghib aṭ-Ṭabbākh, *I'lām*, iv. 240. The decline of these establishments in Aleppo was not so much due to its sacking by Timur in A.D. 1400 as to the shift in Sufi emphasis from the *khānaqāh* to a tomb-*zāwiya*.

The reference to as-Suhrawardī does not mean that he was shaikh of the *khānaqāh*, but simply that he stayed there. He was assigned a place for his prayer-mat as shown in Ibn Baṭṭūṭa's account of the conditions of admission given below on p. 171.

The best-preserved *khānaqāh* in Aleppo today is the Farāfrā, built in A.D.

Many descriptions of this kind are found in local topographies, but they provide little information about their methods of administration, functions, and ceremonies. More can be gleaned from this description by Ibn Baṭṭūṭa of *khānaqāhs* in Cairo in 1326:

Each *khānaqāh*[1] has a shaikh and superintendent (*ḥāris*) who organizes their affairs admirably. . . . These men are celibate, there being separate *khānaqāhs* for the married.[2] Their duties include attendance at the five ritual prayers, passing the night in the *khānaqāh*, and attendance at their *dhikr* gatherings held in its hall (*qubba*). It is also customary for each one to occupy his own special prayer-mat. When they pray the Daybreak Prayer they recite Sūrat al-Fatḥ (48), Sūrat al-Mulk (67), and Sūrat 'Amma (78); then sections of the Qur'ān are brought in and distributed among the *faqīrs*, who recite the whole Qur'ān,[3] and perform a *dhikr*. Following this the Qur'ān-reciters chant in the eastern fashion. They do the same after the 'Aṣr Prayer.[4]

The *khānaqāhs* were not strictly guidance-centres[5] but associations of people prepared to live a common life under discipline. They had their rules regarding the admission of Sufis into their companionship, whether for a shorter or longer length of time.

1237 by an-Nāṣir Yūsuf II, 'Portail à alvéoles, iwân, sanctuaire avec coupole sur alvéoles, mihrâb avec mosaïque de marbre, et linteau de bois sculpté (décor à défoncement linéaire); cellules de soufis. Restes d'un étage. Au Sud-Est, annexe avec d'autre cellules' (J. Sauvaget. 'Inventaire des monuments musulmans de la ville d'Alep', *R.E.I.* v (1931), 84–6).

[1] Ibn Baṭṭūṭa writes *zāwiya* but I have changed this to *khānaqāh* to avoid confusion, since he has just said that what he is describing are *khawāniq*. He is simply using the term with which he is most familiar.

[2] The celibate Sufi was exceptional. Wives were not allowed to live in the *khānaqāh*, though the families of Sufis might be found in associated compounds or villages. In a different type of institution, more especially those associated with tombs, Ibn Baṭṭūṭa found Sufis living with their families. The shrine (*rābiṭa*) at 'Abbādān had 'associated with it a *zāwiya* inhabited by four dervishes *with their families* dedicated to the service of the *rābiṭa* and the *zāwiya*' (*Riḥla*, 1928 edn., i. 118). But in general, Sufis at this stage, though few were celibate in the strict sense, found that a normal family life was incompatible with the dedicated pursuit of the Path.

[3] *Khatmat al-Qur'ān* (sealing the Qur'ān).

[4] Ibn Baṭṭūṭa, 1928 edn., i. 20.

[5] Many *khānaqāhs* gave courses in the Islamic sciences. Maqrīzī says (*Khiṭaṭ*, 1326 edn., iv. 283) that Khānaqāh Shaikhū (founded by Amīr Saif ad-dīn Shaikhū in Cairo in 756/1355) offered courses in all four schools of *fiqh*, *ḥadīth*, and the seven readings of the Qur'ān. This particular *khānaqāh* seems to have been more like a *madrasa*. From his description the Jamāliyya (founded in the same city in 730/1330) was a combined Ḥanafī *madrasa* and *khānaqāh* (*Khiṭaṭ*, iv. 237–40, 279), but this was unusual, and normally the Sufi aspect was the dominant one.

They had to assure themselves that those seeking admission were genuine, and had been trained and initiated by a qualified shaikh. Ibn Baṭṭūṭa continues:

When a new arrival makes his appearance he has to take up his stand at the gateway of the *khānaqāh*, girded around the middle,[1] with the prayer-mat slung over his back, his staff in his right hand and his ablution-jug in his left. The gatekeeper informs the steward[2] who goes out and ascertains from what country he has come, what *khānaqāhs* he has resided in during his journey (or training), and who was his initiator. If he is satisfied as to the truth of his replies, he brings him into the *khānaqāh*, arranges a suitable place for him to spread out his prayer-mat, and shows him the washroom. He then restores himself to a state of ritual cleanliness, goes to his mat, ungirds himself, and prays two prostrations. After this he clasps the hand of the shaikh[3] and of those who are present, and takes his seat among them.[4]

The *khānaqāh* and mausoleum of Sultan Baibars al-Gāshankīr in Cairo (built 706/1307–709/1310) provided for 400 Sufis,[5] whilst that of Siryāqūs had 100 cells for individual Sufis.[6] Tombs became a normal feature of these various types of establishment, but whilst the *ribāṭs* and *zāwiyas* housed the remains of the founder and his successors, the *khānaqāhs*, like that of Baibars II just mentioned, had only the tomb of the secular founder. A few possessed relics; Ribāṭ al-Āthār situated outside Cairo had a piece of iron and wood said to have belonged to the Prophet.[7]

The decline of the *khānaqāh*-type of Sufi centre is associated with the *ṭā'ifa* stage, manifested institutionally in the form of tomb-*zāwiyas*. In non-Arab Asia they continued to be called *khānaqāhs*, but the focal point, the justification for their existence, was the tomb. In central Asia these tomb-*khānaqāhs* varied from

[1] *Mashdūd al-wasṭ*, to indicate that he had been properly initiated with the *shadd*; see below, p. 185.

[2] The steward (*khadim*, diákonos,) who Ibn Baṭṭūṭa has shown was in charge of the domestic arrangements, must have been an important official, like the cook of the Bektāshī *tekkés*.

[3] This *muṣāfaḥa* is described below (pp. 186–7). Here its significance is that he pledges obedience to the shaikh and promises to obey the rules of the *khānaqāh* so long as he remains there.

[4] Ibn Baṭṭūṭa, *Riḥla*, Cairo, 1928, i. 20.

[5] Maqrīzī, *Khiṭaṭ*, A.H. 1326 edn., iv. 276. In the same enclosure was a *ribāṭ* (here = barracks) for 100 soldiers and a *qubba* to receive Baibars' remains, where *ḥadīth* was also taught. The *khānaqāh* is described by K. A. C. Creswell. *The Muslim Architecture of Egypt*, Oxford, 1959, ii. 249–53.

[6] Maqrīzī, *Khiṭaṭ*, iv. 285.

[7] Ibid. iv. 295.

the elaborate mausoleums built by Turkish and Mongol rulers to moderate structures where one *īshān*, the local term for 'shaikh', lived with his family and followers. All these *khānaqāhs*, great and small alike, dispensed hospitality to travellers as well as wandering Sufis. Community living tended to be a winter custom and with the approach of spring the dervishes set off again on their travels. Most *īshāns* made periodic visitations into the steppes to collect contributions from the Kirgiz and other nomadic tribes.

Though related to a particular Way these institutions were independent expressions of divine blessing upon mankind through a man whose holiness was perpetuated through his tomb and his successors, whether or not these were hereditary. The tomb-*zāwiya* of the founder-saint was the centre of the complex, branch *zāwiyas* deriving their validity from the saint in the same way as the mother *zāwiya*, though they too soon had their tombs. The consequence of this change in religious orientation was that anonymous associations like the old-type *khānaqāhs*, urban, turned inwards, and with little outreach into society, decayed and died. They expressed nothing sufficiently vital to keep them going, except free accommodation and meals, and they survived as long as their endowments continued to yield. In the account of al-Khānaqāh al-Qadīm in Aleppo just quoted, Abu Dharr says that in his time the kitchen had ceased to function.

Tomb-*khānaqāhs* and *zāwiyas* which, from their inception, were associated with a shaikh, survived as long as their founder's *baraka* continued to manifest itself. These had their phases of prosperity and decline, it is true, but there were thousands of them and new ones were continually being formed. They began in the house of anyone thought to have *baraka*, and in association with tombs, became the focuses of spiritual life over much of the Islamic world. If the *baraka* kept on functioning, whether in association with a living or dead *walī*, pilgrims and offerings flowed in. Their importance in the social life of Islamic countries can be seen from travellers' narratives such as those of Ibn Jubair and Ibn Baṭṭūṭa. In Asia the latter finds hospitality everywhere with groups of *fuqarā'* who are generally associated with a tomb, as at the convent ascribed to Abu Isḥāq al-Kāzerūnī (d. A.D. 1034) at Kazerun, west of Shiraz, under the aegis of whose name and *baraka* a powerful insurance corporation came into being.[1]

[1] See below, p. 236.

These institutions were not conspicuous for their poverty, yet at the same time their revenues were not expended in rich living for their inmates. D'Ohsson confirms this for eighteenth-century Turkey:

Mais quelque considérables que puissent être les ressources d'un monastère quelconque, jamais les chefs ne se permettent rien qui se ressente du luxe et de l'ostentation. L'excédent de leurs revenus est distribué aux pauvres, ou employé à des établissements pieux et charitables. Les *Scheïkhs* et les *Derwischs* sont scrupuleusement attachés à ce principe inviolable de leur état: habitués dès leur enfance à toutes les privations, ils n'en sont que plus fidèles à l'observation de leurs statuts.[1]

The framework of order organization in their final *ṭā'ifa* stage will be described in general terms since the differences between the main Sunnī orders in this respect relate to secondary aspects.

Throughout the Arab world we find at the head of each *ṭā'ifa* the shaikh. He is the spiritual heir of the founder, whose qualities and powers become inherent in him upon his succession. He is called *shaikh as-sajjāda* (master of the prayer-mat, or skin) (Pers. *sajjāda-nishīn*), since he inherits that of the founder as symbol of his authority. 'In Sonusa', writes Ibn Baṭṭūṭa, 'live descendants of Aḥmad ar-Rifā'ī, among them Shaikh 'Izz ad-dīn who is now *shaikh ar-riwāq* and holder of the *sajjāda* of ar-Rifā'ī.'[2] *Sajjāda* (or *bisāṭ*, *pōstakī*) signifies the 'throne' of the order, in that on it the shaikh is enthroned when engaging in ceremonies of initiation and investiture.

Succession to the *sajjāda* is spiritual and the shaikh was not necessarily a descendant of the founder though in time lineal succession tended to become the rule. The head nominated as his successor a member of his own family, and if he failed to do this before he died various divinatory methods for ascertaining his wishes from his incorporeal existence were employed. The hereditary principle, although it frequently led to the succession of incompetent or worldly men, was an important factor in holding the order together. In Syria hereditary succession did not become universal. In some orders, notably Khalwatī and Shādhilī, the shaikh was elected. At the Qalandarī establishment in Aleppo,

[1] D'Ohsson, *Tableau*, IV. 2, 665–6.
[2] Ibn Baṭṭūṭa, *Riḥla*, Cairo, 1939, i. 238; tr. Gibb, ii. 436.

where celibacy was practised, the dervishes elected their shaikh.[1] In other Syrian orders, as with the Rifāʿiyya, hereditary succession was the rule from the beginning.

Under the shaikh are a number of *khalīfas* or *muqaddams* appointed by him directly to take charge of districts or town sections. Each is given a licence (*ijāza*) stating what he is authorized to undertake. Heads of small local orders will retain the power of initiation in their own hands, but when an order expands *khalīfas* are authorized to confer it. *Khalīfas* are given special functions concerned with organization and ritual. One may be nominated the *wakīl* of the *ṭā'ifa*. In Syria and Egypt this was generally a distinct office and an important one since the *wakīl* was responsible for administration and finance. He sent out delegations to collect dues and levy contributions and also organized *mawlid* and other celebrations. Immediately under the shaikh there was a *nā'ib* or deputy. In Syria orders often had a *naqīb* or guardian of the liturgy, who directed the music.

A large order had sectional leaders under each regional *khalīfa*, whose titles do not necessarily make clear their actual positions. *Muqaddam* as used in the Maghrib was equivalent to *khalīfa* elsewhere, but the title was given to any local shaikh in the East; *murshid* and especially *pīr* were common in Iranian and Indian spheres; in Egypt *shaikh* was the usual term, with *ʿammnā* (our uncle) as a more familiar expression. Subordinate leaders often trained aspirants and organized local *dhikr* gatherings, and a city would have many sectional groups. The charge of many *muqaddams* or *khalīfas* was often maintained in the same family. In these cases it was customary for the shaikh to authorize or confirm the investiture. Many of these, more especially in towns, did not have *zāwiyas* and then the charge was not necessarily hereditary within one social group, and communal functions would take place in the street or in houses or encampments of members as well as that of the local leader.

Other language areas had their own terminology. Turkish orders, including the Bektāshiyya, called their superior *pīr-evi* or simply *dede*, and the superior of each convent was a *pōstnişīn* (he who sits on a sheepskin), or just *bābā*, equivalent of shaikh. The Mawlawī head, generally known as *Čelebi Mulla*, had other titles,

[1] F. J. Bliss, *The Religions of Modern Syria and Palestine*, New York, 1912, p. 253.

including *Mewlānā hunk'ār*, a form of Persian *Khudāwandg'ar*. Arabic terms were frequently employed. One who was linked to a Bektāshī lodge through family or village relationship, though uninitiated, was called an *aşik* (Ar. *'āshiq*), the initiated one was called a *muhip* (Ar. *muḥibb*), a 'professed' was a *talip* (*ṭālib*), a dervish was a *murīd*, and a lay 'affiliate' who had been through the initiation rite (*nasip*) was a *muntesip* (*muntasib*).

Order organization could only be made clear by describing particular groups, which is not practicable here. The main difference is the contrast between eastern and western orders in regard to these titles and the functions they carry. In the Ottoman Empire the head of each Khalwatī branch was himself the *khalīfa* of the branch-founder. He was represented by *nā'ibs*, who had under them *muqaddams*. In the East, therefore, as we have already pointed out, the *muqaddam* was an inferior agent, whereas in the Maghrib he was the deputy of the order-head. Further, the *khānaqāhs* and *tekkēs* of the Iranian and Turkish traditions were quite different from the multi-function *zāwiyas* of the Maghrib. The *khānaqāhs* of Arab regions did not normally house a true community, but were collections of individuals, though living under discipline. The binding force of Turkish *tekkēs* varied according to the order, but they generally housed true communities. As the members lived a life of discipline their families lived outside the building.

Membership embraced two main grades: the 'professed' and lay affiliates. The first were the dervishes,[1] commonly called *fuqarā'*,[2] who formed only a small section of the fraternity. The term *darwīsh* was used more especially for the classical dervish of the Arab Near East, Persia, central Asia, and Turkey; *faqīr* was used everywhere in Arab regions and elsewhere, but was imprecise in meaning. *Ikhwān* was also in wide usage, especially in the Maghrib. In Syrian Arabic the *ṭā'ifa* was often called the

[1] *Darwīsh*, pl. *darāwīsh*, is frequently derived from a Persian phrase 'seeking doors', i.e. 'mendicant', but is probably connected with a root meaning 'poor': Avestan *drigu*, Middle Persian *drgwš*, Parzand *daryōš*.

[2] Singular *faqīr*, 'a poor one', in the sense of 'one in need of God's mercy'. In spite of the general association of dervishes with begging, many orders, indeed the majority, disapproved of begging in public. The institution to which they were attached which subsisted on endowments and gifts, catered for their material needs. Even itinerant friars, especially those of the *malāmatī* tendency, often made it a rule to live by voluntary offerings and the labour of their own hands.

akhawiyya (fraternity). In addition to these professed brethren any individual could be invested as an associate.[1] He was admitted at a form of service which included the oath of allegiance to the founder and his living *khalīfa*. He received little Sufi training but was trained to take part in the ritual. Such members carried on their normal occupations and mode of life, but were subject to the guidance and authority of the shaikh and his *khalīfa*, and took part in the collective assemblies (*majālis adh-dhikr*). Some orders admitted women as affiliated members, though relatively few had dervishes, *faqīrāt* or *khawātāt*. As will be shown in chapter eight, certain classes, occupational guilds, districts, towns, or lineages were linked with particular orders.

The orders found their fullest social development in the Maghrib. Everything was concentrated upon the *zāwiya*, a unique institution formed under special social and physical environmental conditions. Its full development took place in the fourteenth century during the Marīnid and ʿAbd al-Wādid period. We have mentioned earlier[2] that these two dynasties founded *madrasas* at the same time, perhaps in recognition of the way the *zāwiyas* were becoming centres for teaching Islamic as well as mystical sciences.

The *zāwiya* is a complex of buildings surrounded by a wall. Central is the domed tomb of the founder, and his successors might be buried there or in separate tombs. There is a small mosque or *muṣallā*, a Qur'ān school, and a room for indoor recitals, though *ḥaḍras* were normally held in the courtyard. One or more teachers teach the children to recite the Qur'ān, and a disciple who is a *faqīh* may teach legal sciences or *ḥadīth*, as well as the principles of mysticism, to disciples in the *zāwiya*. Then there are the rooms where live the present shaikh and other members of his line with their wives, children, and servants, together with housing for affiliates, pilgrims, and travellers. The whole is a self-sufficient institution having cultivation and animals, and receives gifts of all kinds. In towns a *zāwiya* was on a much more limited scale. This institution became a characteristic of Moorish Saharan life but did not spread south of that waste, not even into Nilotic Sudan where the orders were strong,

[1] There were no special terms for affiliates, though they might be referred to as *awlād aṭ-ṭarīqa*, *khuddām*, *ḥairān*, or *ikhwān*. In central Asia tertiaries were called *muḥibbān* or *ʿazīzān*, whilst Bektashīs and other Turkish orders had their *ʿāshiqān*.

[2] See above, pp. 8 n., 50.

but where the equivalent of *zāwiyas* were village communities founded on the holiness of an immigrant (generally Nubian) shaikh.

In the East the term *zāwiya* is given to more humble places of prayer and dervish cells. Corresponding terms for the convent and the tomb-centred institution, we have shown, are *khānaqāh* in central Asia and India, and *tekkē*[1] or *dargāh*[2] in the Ottoman Turkish sphere. In India *jamā'at khānah* and *dāerah* were also used. Whilst *khānaqāhs* in Egypt and Syria were unspecialized institutions, those in India from their inception and in central Asia from the fourteenth century were the equivalent of the Arab world's *zāwiyas*, in that they tended to be specialized to a particular shaikh and his line. K. A. Nizami explains the difference between the terms used in India:

Though broadly used in the sense of hospices these terms differ in their connotation. The *khanqah* was a spacious building which provided separate accommodation for each visitor and inmate. The *jama'at khanah* was a large room where all the disciples slept, prayed and studied on the floor. The Chishti saints built *jama'at khanahs*; the Suhrawardis constructed *khanqahs*. Common people, unable to appreciate the distinction, used the word *khanqah* even for the Chishti *jama'at khanahs*, and now the term is used for all places of spiritual activity without distinction. The *zawiyahs* were smaller places where mystics lived and prayed, but unlike inmates of *khanqahs* and *jama'at khanahs*, did not aim at establishing any vital contact with the world outside. In the 17th and 18th centuries another type of *khanqahs*, the *daerahs*, came into existence. The primary aim of these *daerahs* was to provide place for men of one affiliation to devote their time to religious meditation. They were smaller than the *zawiyahs*.[3]

The Indian form, displaying distinctive regional characteristics, may also be a comprehensive institution, though the whole establishment is not necessarily situated on the same ground. A. W. Sadler gives an account[4] of his visit in 1961 to the shrine of the nineteenth-century founder of a hereditary Chishtī association at

[1] *Tekkē*, *tekyē*, or *tekiyē*, a derivative from Arabic *ittikā'*, was perhaps first employed in the sense of 'refectory'.

[2] *Dargāh* (Persian 'a court') used in India for a shrine or tomb.

[3] K. A. Nizami, *Religion and Politics in India during the Thirteenth Century*, 1961, p. 175 n. On the organization of *khānaqāhs* see the same author's 'Khanqah Life in Medieval India', *Studia Islamica*, viii (1957), 51–69.

[4] A. W. Sadler, 'Visit to a Chishtī Qawwālī', *Muslim World*, liii (1963), 287–92.

Hyderabad (Andhra Pradesh, Deccan) called Ghulām Muʿīn ad-dīn Khāmosh (d. 1872) and the associated *khānaqāh.*

The shrine . . . is a large building, done in the Moghul style, with a marble onion-dome on top. Inside, in the centre, is of course the tomb of Khāmosh. The saint's body was buried in plain ground, in accordance with Qur'ānic law; but over this burial plot stands a large marble canopy, somewhat similar in construction to the baldachin sometimes found over a Roman Catholic altar. Over this canopy, and extending up to the ceiling of the dome, were what appeared to be paper streamers, in bright colours, and big red-glass lamps. Inside this 'baldachin' was a tomb sculpture, presumably of the saint reclining in death, and covered with a cloth, so that only the outline of the figure could be seen. On top of the figure was a tray filled with flower petals, and leaning against it a broom of long peacock feathers, for dusting off the cloth. Also inside the shrine building were a number of other tombs, these being open (without canopy), but with the same tomb sculpture, cloth cover, flower tray, and peacock broom. These marked the graves of certain chosen disciples and relatives of the saint.[1]

Associated with the shrine in the same compound is a mosque and the residence of the *pīr*, the great-grandson of the founder, whilst 'beside the shrine is a walk which leads through a grape arbor to a large meeting hall where the annual ceremony on the anniversary of the saint's death (*ʿurs*) takes place'. The *khānaqāh* is situated in another part of the city adjacent to the central *jāmiʿ*. This was occupied by twenty Chishtīs with their families who 'constitute a specially disciplined élite within the wider dervish community'. The *qawwālī* (recital), more formally *samāʿ*, is held there on the thirteenth of each lunar month.

D'Ohsson provides information about the Turkish *tekkēs* in the eighteenth century. Each *tekkē* normally housed some twenty to forty dervishes. They had benefactions for their support and to provide the dervishes with food and lodging. Each one normally ate in his cell, but three or four were allowed to eat together. Those who were married had the right to have their own habitation, but were obliged to sleep in the *tekkē* once or twice a week, and especially on the night preceding their dances. An exception was the convent of the Mawlawīs, where no married dervishes were allowed to pass the night.[2]

[1] A. W. Sadler, 'Visit to a Chishtī Qawwālī', *Muslim World*, liii (1963), p. 289.
[2] D'Ohsson, op. cit., iv. 2, 662–3.

We have said that an order or *ṭā'ifa* begins as a local *zāwiya* whose shaikh appoints regional *khalīfas*, whose houses frequently become daughter *zāwiyas*. *Ṭā'ifas* undergo cycles of expansion, stagnation, decay, and even death. In the time of Ibn Baṭṭūṭa Rifā'ī *zāwiyas* were widespread in Anatolia among Turks. Then they disappeared almost completely, so it seems, to be replaced in that region by Turkish orders. But, although reduced, the Rifā'ī has continued to be a universal *ṭarīqa* as widespread as the Qādiriyya right up to the present day. The Suhrawardiyya has never been a unified order, but always a *ṭarīqa*, a line of ascription from which derived hundreds of *ṭā'ifas*. Similarly with the Qādiriyya; the descendant of 'Abd al-Qādir in Baghdad is not recognized as their superior by any Arab Qādirī *ṭā'ifa*. Even the nineteenth-century Tijāniyya, as it expanded, has tended to lose its centralized authority. The shaikh of the central Darqāwī *zāwiya* has no control over the many offshoots. But more concentrated, limited, or parochial orders, like the Nāṣiriyya, Wazzāniyya, 'Īsāwiyya, and Kattāniyya in the Maghrib, and the numerous family orders in Nilotic Sudan, Egypt, and Syria, are fairly coherent. Liaison between the central house and derivative or affiliated groups is maintained through tours undertaken by the shaikh or his emissaries, even where no actual control is exercised, during which they collect offerings, and may settle disputes and conduct rallies to stimulate zeal.

An exception to the general rule was the Mawlawiyya. Essentially an urban and sophisticated order, it always maintained a centralized organization. Even though localized in Turkey its convents were widely dispersed, but these, together with the few in Arab regions (Damascus, Aleppo, Tripoli, and Homs), all acknowledged the authority of the Chelebi of Qonya, who maintained his right to confirm the accession of the local heads.

The *qubba* (domed tomb) of the founder is the focal point of the organization, a centre of veneration to which visitations (*ziyārāt*) are made. Offerings in money and kind are made regularly and are associated with requests for the intercession of the *walī* or a thanksgiving for benefits received. The sanctuary and its territory are sacred (*ḥaram* or *ḥurm*) where refugees from vengeance or justice can seek sanctuary.

The ritual of approach to a tomb (*ādāb az-ziyāra*) has its place in the order manuals and should not be completely ignored here.

We have mentioned that many people seek initiation from a shaikh simply for his *baraka* (*li 't-tabarruk*), in other words, to establish a relationship with a source of power, and so it is with pilgrimage to a shrine. The simplest form is to stand in front of the tomb and recite the Fātiḥa, which is caught by the symbolic act of raising the hands, palms upwards, during the recitation and then transferred by passing them down upon the face. There are many procedures for intercession to God through the saint. Muḥammad al-Kattānī gives an account of some of these in the preface to his book on the notables of Fez, *Salwat al-anfās*, for example: 'Among the peculiar properties of the *Ṣaḥīḥ* of al-Bukhārī, so some say, is that he who opens it or a section of it before the tomb of a saint and reads whatever single *ḥadīth* his eyes fall upon, commending himself to God through the mediumship of the masters of his chain right back to the Prophet, at the same time expressing his need, may, if God will, find his wish fulfilled.'[1]

The anniversary of a saint's birth (*mawlid*, popularly pronounced *mūlid*, in the Maghrib *mulūd*, in Turkish *mevlid*, *mevlūd*) or his death (*ḥawliyya*) is a great celebration, the central point of the popular liturgical year. The celebrations attract pilgrims from neighbouring villages and tribes, or, depending upon their fame, from a still wider area. Special concerts of *mawlids* are held, animals sacrificed, and offerings made. They are generally associated with a fair attended by traders and pedlars, mountebanks, and storytellers.

An essential distinction between eastern and western orders is shown by comparing the stress laid by each upon training, apprenticeship in the discipline of the mystical Path, and in the ceremony of investiture. In the East the orders were stricter and more rigid in discipline and organization, and had many more dervish-type disciples than in the Maghrib. But whereas in Asia the orders were related to certain sections of the population, in the Maghrib they came at one period to embrace from half to three-quarters of the people, and there could be few who did not have some relationship through the local marabout. This is accounted for by the stress the Berbers placed upon *baraka*, strong though this belief also was in the East. The concept of *baraka*, originally a gift from God, not vouchsafed through a rigorous following of

[1] M. b. Jaʿfar al-Kattānī, *Salwat al-anfās*, lith. Fez, 1316/1898, i. 65–6.

the Path, was further diluted by its association with hereditary holiness.

Initiation and Investiture. Sufi dress was an important outward sign of the Sufi way of life as the very name, derived from *ṣūf* (wool), worn by the early ascetics (*zuhhād*), bears witness. Like other material symbols it came to have an inner significance and investiture with such a garment soon became a sign of initiation. The use of wool went out of fashion during the eleventh century A.D. in favour of the patched garment called *muraqqaʿa* or *khirqa*.[1] ʿAlī al-Hujwīrī (d. 465/1072) wrote:

The Ṣūfī shaykhs observe the following rule. When a novice joins them, with the purpose of renouncing the world, they subject him to spiritual discipline for the space of three years. If he fulfil the requirements of this discipline, well and good; otherwise, they declare that he cannot be admitted to the Path (*Ṭarīqat*). The first year is devoted to service of the people, the second year to service of God, and the third year to watching over his own heart. . . . The adept, then, who has attained the perfection of saintship takes the right course when he invests the novice with the *muraqqaʿa* after a period of three years during which he has educated him in the necessary discipline. In respect of the qualifications which it demands, the *muraqqaʿa* is comparable to a winding-sheet (*kafan*): the wearer must resign all his hopes of the pleasures of life, and purge his heart of all sensual delights and devote his life entirely to the service of God.[2]

Evidence for the donning of a *khirqa*, the double attribution this conveys, and the importance of credentials is shown in the following account of dervish life by Muḥammad ibn al-Munawwar, writing between A.D. 1180 and 1203:

The Pīr, by laying his hand on the disciple's head and clothing him in the *khirqa*, indicates to all and sundry that he knows and has verified the fitness of that person for companionship with the Ṣūfīs . . . It is for this reason that the Ṣūfīs, when a dervish whom they do not know comes into the convent or desires to associate with a party of dervishes,

[1] I have found no evidence which substantiates the statement of Massignon that there was an essential distinction, signifying a conflict of ideals, between *ṣūf* and *muraqqaʿa*, 'le froc blanc étant le signe de ralliement de tous les sunnites stricts et disciplinés, tandis que l'étoffe rapiécée de loques bigarrées deviendra la marque de tous les moines errants, indisciplinés et gyrovagues, les "*calenders*" hindous des Milles et Une Nuits', L. Massignon, *La passion d'al-Hallāj*, Paris, 1922, ii. 51.

[2] ʿAlī al-Hujwīrī, *Kashf*, tr. R. A. Nicholson, pp. 54–5.

enquire of him: 'Who was thy "Pīr of companionship"?' (*Pīr-i ṣuḥbat*),[1] and 'From whose hand didst thou receive the *khirqa*?' The Ṣūfīs hold these two *nasabs* in very high regard: indeed, there is no *nasab* in the Path (*Ṭarīqat*) except these two. If anyone should fail to establish these two relationships to a Pīr who is exemplary (*muqtadā*), they drive him forth and will not admit him to their society.[2]

Three essential elements make up initiation or companionship, to use the older term: *talqīn adh-dhikr*, *akhdh al-'ahd*, and *libs al-khirqa*.[3]

Talqīn, verbal noun of *laqqana*, has the meaning 'to prompt, inculcate, teach by repetition', but in respect of Sufi initiation it means 'to give (secret) instruction'. Mystery was associated with the giving (*laqqana*) of the Seven Words[4] associated with the seven stages of the mystic Path.

Akhdh al-'ahd means literally 'taking the compact' and involves a *bai'a*, homage, oath, or covenant of allegiance. It is used in such phrases as: *'ahd al-yad*, swearing obedience to the shaikh with the handclasp (*muṣāfaḥa*), which may be extended to *akhdh al-yad wa 'l-iqtidā'* (taking the shaikh as exemplary). *'Ahd* (or *akhdh*) *al-khirqa* is the compact involved in investiture with the habit. The justification for investing with the habit is the Qur'ānic (vii. 26), '*Libās at-takwā dhālika khair*', a phrase frequently introduced into the ceremony. The particular type of *khirqa* may be indicated: *akhdh khirqat al-irāda*, means 'assuming the habit of the novitiate'. This was frequent in the East, but not in the Maghrib, where the *khirqa* did not become common.[5] In the Arab world too it tended to become a formal act, like 'capping' in

[1] The *Pīr-i ṣuḥbat* is the master who gives the training and is not necessarily the same as the *pīr-i khirqat*. The *pīr-i ṣuḥbat* of Abu Sa'īd ibn Abī 'l-Khair (A.D. 967–1049) was Abū 'l-Faḍl as-Sarakhsī, yet he sent him to Abu 'Abd ar-Raḥmān as-Sulamī (d. 1021), author of *Ṭabaqāt aṣ-Ṣūfiyya*, to be invested with the *khirqa* in Nishapur.

[2] Muḥammad ibn al-Munawwar, *Asrār at-tawḥīd fī maqāmāt ash-Shaikh Abī Sa'īd*, ed. V. A. Zhukovski, St. Petersburg, 1899, p. 55, tr. R. A. Nicholson, *J.R.A.S.* 1907, 167.

[3] See as-Sanūsī, *Salsabīl*, p. 3.

[4] See below, pp. 190, 206.

[5] The *khirqa* was apparently used by early western Sufis, many of whom had been trained in the East, but later became merely a sign of *faqīr*-dom. The patched garment was more generally called *muraqqa'a*, but it represented only one aspect of the tradition and was not equivalent to the graduating *khirqa*. In the nineteenth century the *muraqqa'a* was worn expecially by Darqāwīs and Haddāwīs (whose special term was *handāsa* or *derbāla*), and by Khalwatīs and so by the followers of Muḥammad Aḥmad, the *mahdī* of Nilotic Sudan, a heritage from his repudiated Sufi past.

a European university, for the habit disappeared and only the headgear remained. Thus the ceremony tended to become divested of its esoteric significance. The *khirqa* as a dual-frock consisted of *khirqat at-tabarruk*, corresponding to *silsilat al-baraka* (chain of heads of the *ṭā'ifa* from the shaikh to the *ṭarīqa*-founder), and *khirqat* (= *silsilat*) *al-Wird*, chain of heads of the *ṭarīqa* from the founder to the Prophet.[1] These two in association comprised, in stricter orders, *khirqat aṣ-ṣuḥba* (the vestment of companionship), which term with earlier masters had the significance of 'discipleship'.[2] There were many different types of *khirqa*: *khirqat al-khidma* (service = a first stage), or *at-ta'līm* (teaching), or *at-tarbiya* (guidance). Obviously Ibn Baṭṭūṭa's investment with the *khirqa* of the Suhrawardiyya[3] would mean nothing to genuine initiates. The founder of the order wrote about the purpose of the *khirqa*:

Investment with the *khirqa* establishes a bond between the shaikh and the aspirant and makes the aspirant subject himself to the discipline (*taḥkīm*) of the shaikh; this *taḥkīm* being permissible in law[4] . . . This *khirqa* is the symbol of the oath of investiture (*mubāya'a*). It is the first step towards *ṣuḥba*, the ultimate goal [of the aspirant] being *ṣuḥba*, the basis of all the aspirant's expectations. It is related that Abu Yazīd [al-Bisṭāmī] said, 'He who has no master then Satan is his

[1] This is to be distinguished from the wearing of two *khirqas*, indicating at one period investiture by two shaikhs (as in as-Sarrāj, *Luma'*, pp. 191 and 194, and in Ibn Khallikān, ed. de Slane (1842), i. 256, 4, and tr. de Slane, i. 502, n. 5); and also from its double aspect in respect of clothing, since investment included the head-gear as well as the frock. Shaikh Abu Bakr ibn Hawār al-Hawāzanī al-Baṭā'iḥī, a former highway robber, when repenting out in the desert, was invested with the *khirqa* consisting of a *thawb* (gown) and *tāqiya* (headgear) by Abu Bakr aṣ-Ṣiddīq in a dream, finding them on him when he woke up; see al-Wāsiṭī, *Tiryāq al-muḥibbīn*, Cairo, A.H. 1305, pp. 6, 42–3, and cf. ash-Sha'rānī, *Lawāqiḥ*, ii. 125. The head-gear was important in eastern orders in that it served as a distinguishing mark. Ibn Baṭṭūṭa refers to these distinctive aspects of dress as when he writes of the tattered gown and felt hat (*libāsuhu muraqqa'a wa qalansuwa libd*) of a devotee at Ḥalī in 'Asīr al-Yaman; *Riḥla*, Cairo edn., 1928, i. 155.

[2] *Ṣuḥba* is another of those terms whose actual significance needs to be ascertained, unless specified as in the following quotation from al-Wāsiṭī (writing *c.* 1320): ''Izz ad-dīn Aḥmad al-Fārūthī said, "I associated with Shihāb ad-dīn 'Umar as-Suhrawardī *ṣuḥbat at-tabarruk* and attended his courses. One day he suggested investing me with their *khirqa*, but when it was conveyed to him that my *khirqa* was Aḥmadiyya he said, 'Please excuse me, my boy, all of us are embraced within the *khirqa* of Aḥmad ar-Rifā'ī'." ' (*Tiryāq*, p. 60.)

[3] See above, p. 36.

[4] Shihāb ad-dīn as-Suhrawardī, *'Awārif*, p. 69.

leader.' Abu 'l-Qāsim al-Qushairī related about his own shaikh, [Abu] 'Alī ad-Daqqāq,[1] that he said, 'A tree that grows by itself without anyone planting it produces leaves but no fruit', which is true, yet it may happen that it bears fruit like trees that grow in *wādīs* and on hills, though the fruit will not have the taste of garden fruit.[2]

The word *wird* in other senses will be discussed in the next chapter. Here we simply affirm that *Wird* (distinguishing it with a capital) is the equivalent of *ṭarīqa*, the spiritual Path the order exists to maintain, and so *akhdh al-Wird*, 'to take the *Wird* (of Shaikh X)' is 'to take the *ṭarīqa*, that is, the rule of Shaikh X'.

Ceremonies were more elaborate in the Iranian and Turkish spheres than in the western Islamic world and candidates were invested with other garments in addition to the *khirqa*. In certain Turkish and eastern orders these included the *sirwāl* (trousers), *ḥizām* (girdle), *pishtimāl* (waistband), and the *tāj* (headgear).[3] These systems of initiation derived from Shī'ī and *futuwwa* orders. Ibn Jubair, when in Syria in the late sixth/twelfth century, refers to 'a *ṭā'ifa* known as the Nabawiyya who are Sunnīs believing in *futuwwa* and all pertaining to manliness. Whosoever they admit into their order because they perceive he possesses these qualities, they gird him with the trousers.'[4] Similarly, Ibn Baṭṭūṭa says in regard to *al-akhiyyat al-fityān* of a *zāwiya* in Qonya: 'Their characteristic costume is the trousers as that of the Sufis is the *khirqa*.'[5] Initiation also involved imbibing the *futuwwa* drink of

[1] Al-Hujwīrī, *Kashf*, pp. 162–3. For the quotation see Qushairī's *Risāla*, 1901 edn., p. 134.

[2] Shihāb ad-dīn, *'Awārif*, p. 70.

[3] Dervishes of the different orders were distinguished by the colour, material, and shape of their headgear or habit. D'Ohsson describes the dress of the principal Turkish orders; see *Tableau*, IV. ii. 629–33. In the East the headgear was generally called *tāj*, usually turbans given different shapes by the manner in which they were folded. The Bektashī turban had 12 folds, the Gulshenī 8, Qādirī 6, and Jilwatī 18. Mawlawīs wore a tall conical *kulāh* made of felt. Colour was not necessarily an indication of the order, for whereas Qādirīs in Turkey affected black, those in Egypt had white or green banners and turbans. The majority of dervishes let their facial hair grow and some their head hair. Accessories, apart from the prayer-mat, ablution jug, etc., varied. In the East some dervishes carried around a meditation stick, a small crooked stick of wood or an iron rod which they placed under the armpit or forehead as an aid to meditation, others used the meditation *ḥizām* for this purpose.

[4] Ibn Jubair, *Travels*, ed. W. Wright and M. J. de Goeje, 2nd edn., 1907, p. 280.

[5] Ibn Baṭṭūṭa, Cairo edn., 1928, i. 187. Ibn al-Jawzī had earlier used the same parallel when writing of the *fityān*: 'Entrance into their order is effected through investiture with trousers as the Sufis invest the *murīd* with the *muraqqa'a*' (*Talbīs Iblīs*, Cairo, A.H. 1340, p. 421).

salted water, and the orders adopted this practice though they changed to sweetened water. In these orders the *shadd* (girding) meant 'initiation', and was the culminating point of the ritual. Similarly with *rabṭ al-maḥzam*, binding of the girdle or shawl. In both terms the stress is on binding with the turban-cloth or girdle, or both, with a specific number of knots, but the term may refer to the whole ritual. The *ḥizām* was worn mainly by Persian and Turkish, not Arab, Sufis.[1]

We will describe first the affiliation ceremony, which bound the non-dervish adherent to a particular shaikh and his line. Such a form of affiliation was found as early as the time of Shihāb ad-dīn as-Suhrawardī, who distinguishes between two types of *khirqa*—that with which the novice was invested and that given to a *mutashabbih* (imitator):

Know that the *khirqa* is of two types—that of the novitiate (*irāda*) and that of the benediction (*tabarruk*). The primal one which the masters intend for aspirants is that of the novitiate, whilst that of benediction is similar to the other except that the first is for the genuine *murīd*, whilst that of benediction is for the *mutashabbih*, in other words, he who imitates the Sufis. The essence of the *khirqa* is that the genuine candidate who enters into discipleship (*ṣuḥba*) with the shaikh, surrendering himself and becoming like a small child with his father, is reared up by the shaikh in his God-given wisdom.[2]

Ibn Baṭṭūṭa shows the way in which *khirqa* investiture had degenerated in his time. He writes: 'I met in this city [Hurmuz] the holy peregrinating shaikh, Abu 'l-Ḥasan al-Aqṣārānī, a Rūmī [Greek] in origin, who entertained me and returned my visit, when he garbed me with a garment (*thawb* = *khirqa*) and gave me the girdle of companionship[3]—this acts as a support when squatting [to carry out religious exercises]. Most of the Persian dervishes gird themselves with it.'[4]

The initiation ceremony for the ordinary adherent, as modified in stage three and as it has come down to the present time, differed

[1] It is specifically pointed out that the Egyptian Wafā'iyya 'had a distinctive Sufi *khirqa* of special design consisting of a *tāj* and a *shadd* first adopted by [Muhibb ad-dīn] Abu 'l-Faḍl' (d. 888/1483), perhaps through Turkish influence; Tawfīq al-Bakrī, *Bait as-Sādāt al-Wafā'iyya*, p. 58. The *shadd* was, however, maintained by many Egyptian artisan corporations; see E. W. Lane, *Modern Egyptians*, Everyman edn., pp. 515–16.

[2] *'Awārif*, p. 73.

[3] Ibn Baṭṭūṭa uses the Persian *kamar-i ṣuḥbat*.

[4] Ibn Baṭṭūṭa, *Riḥla*, Cairo edn., 1928, i. 173.

only in details between the different orders. It was called the *'ahd* and the essential aspect was the *bai'a* (vow of allegiance), given sacramentally to the shaikh, associated with assent to a formula of promises, and the granting of permission to recite a special *dhikr* and one or more *aḥzāb*. The following gives the general requirements of the Qādiriyya.[1]

The *murīd*, in a state of ritual cleanliness and after praying two *rak'as*, sits facing the shaikh, their thighs pressed together and their right hands clasped (*muṣāfaḥa*), and recites the Fātiḥa and other formulae in the intention of the Prophet and the shaikhs of the different *silsilas*, especially those of the Qādirī line. The shaikh then dictates to him, to be repeated sentence by sentence, a prayer asking for God's forgiveness, testifying that the *'ahd* he is taking is the *'ahd* of God and His Apostle and that the hand of the shaikh is that of 'Abd al-Qādir, and promising that he will recite the *dhikr* in obedience to the dictates of the shaikh. Then the shaikh, after praying silently three times, 'O Unique, O Sublime, breathe on me', recites *āyat al-mubāya'a* (Qur'ān, xlviii. 10) and other relevant verses (e.g. xvi. 93), and *kalimat at-tawḥīd*, three times. The *murīd* affirms his acceptance of all the conditions and the shaikh addresses him: 'I also have accepted you as a son to me.' After a prayer of consecration the shaikh gives him to drink from a cup of water (pure or sweetened) or oil, and concludes the ceremony with the giving of the *murīd*'s personal *dhikr* and closing prayers.

This initiation is necessary, not only for those who hold office, but for all who wish to participate in the collective *dhikr*,[2] though the attachment of affiliated members tended to be rather loose, often simply a matter of attachment to the family shaikh. The formula of a simple *bai'a* given to me by the shaikh of a small Shādhilī *ṭā'ifa* runs:

O God, I have repented before Thee, and accept as my teacher Shaikh X as my shaikh in this world and in the next, as guide and leader to

[1] See Ismā'īl ibn M. Sa'īd, *Al-Fuyūḍāt ar-Rabbāniyya*, Cairo, A.H. 1353, pp. 27–31. The Khalwatī *'ahd* ceremony is in all essentials the same. Al-Jabartī gives two descriptions of it in his biography of Muḥammad al-Ḥafnawī (*'Ajā'ib*, Cairo, 1959, ii. 268–70); one is that transmitted by al-Bakrī aṣ-Ṣiddīqī (d. 1749) and the other is a quotation from *al-Futūḥāt al-ilāhiyya* of Zakariyā al-Anṣārī (d. 916/1510). E. W. Lane describes the initiation into the Khalwatī-Demerdāshiyya in *Modern Egyptians*, Everyman edn., p. 250.

[2] In the East only these took part in the collective *dhikr*, but in Africa (excluding Egypt) many uninitiated joined in.

Thy Presence, and as director (*murshid*) in Thy Path. I will disobey him neither in word nor in deed, neither overtly nor covertly. Confirm me, O God, in obedience to him and his *ṭarīqa* in this world and the next, and in the *ṭarīqa* of the shaikh of shaikhs and imām of imāms, the Quṭb of the community, my Lord Abu 'l-Ḥasan ash-Shādhilī, God be pleased with him!

After this the shaikh and *murīd* repeat together the Fātiḥa and *tahlīl*.

The life of a *ṭarīqa* rests upon Sufi tradition and succession. It is through initiation in the full sense taken by a dervish that a man enters into this spiritual world in such a way that succession is assured. Initiation may be 'spiritual'—the Uwaisī-Khaḍir tradition—but normally it comes through guidance under a this-world master. The initiation of a dervish was naturally more complicated than that of an affiliate. Admitted first at a simple ceremony he underwent a period of service[1] to the community in the convent. During the same period or later he was given a course of progressive training until ready to take the full *bai'a*. At the *'ahd* he receives instructions which include the famous, 'Be with your shaikh like the corpse in the hands of the washer; he turns it over as he wishes and it is obedient', and with the *muṣāfaḥa* he vows his submission. He is baptized with water or milk, vested with a *khirqa*, and given a rosary (*tasbiḥa*) and a book of prayers (*awrād*) from which he promises to recite as given permission. He is then attached to a convent to lead a life according to rule, to pray, fast, keep silence and vigils, and so forth.[2]

[1] The necessity for a working novitiate is stressed in the manuals; see as-Suhrawardī, *'Awārif*, pp. 79–80.

[2] It may be asked why fasting has hardly been mentioned. The reason is that fasting is not a task in itself but an aspect of the technique of the retreat which is itself an aspect of the pursuit of the Way and an essential part of convent life. The allocation of fasting-tasks parallels guidance in *dhikr*-tasks. We need only outline the general nature of the Forty-day Retreat (*arba'īniyya*) which involves fasting. This is kept in a special cell within the fraternity-house. This cell is quite dark and so small that it is impossible to lie down and the inmate has to sleep in his squatting meditation-pose, hunched over his knees. As instructed by his guide he performs the *dhikr* incessantly and only comes out (if at all, depending upon his guide's instructions) to perform the *wuḍū'* (ablution), to take part in communal recitals, and to commune with his guide. Otherwise, speaking is totally prohibited. Abstention from food follows a graduated scale and only during the last three days does he abstain completely. On the Qādirī conditions for the Forty-day Retreat see Ismā'īl b. M. Sa'īd, *Fuyūḍāt*, A.H. 1353, pp. 64–5.

The austerities required of Khalwatīs were more stringent than in other orders

The Bektāshīs, we have shown, fall into two main categories: the village communities (*qizil-bāsh*) and the dedicated dervishes attached to a lodge. The natural communities had something like an age-grade system involving initiation by the hereditary village priest, whereas the dervish association was voluntary. The initiation ceremony was called *ikrār ayīnī*,[1] ceremony of confession of faith (*iqrār*), or *aynicem* (the name for the central ritual, directed according to occasion) by which one becomes a *muhip* (*muḥibb*) and is qualified to take part in the ceremonies of the order. When he had progressed sufficiently to make his profession the dervish goes through a further oath ceremony (*vakfi vucut*) and becomes entitled to wear the *tāj* or headgear of the order. The celibate dervish went through still another ceremony, *mujerret ayīnī*. Evliya Chelebi visited the famous Bektāshī convent at 'Uthmānjiq built by Bāyazīd II in consequence of a dream on the site of the grave of Qoyun Bābā, alleged successor of Ḥājjī Bektāsh. There, after his cure from an eye infection, he was admitted into the Bektāshiyya (presumably a nominal associate membership) and wrote: 'I have ever since kept the symbols of Dervishship which I received at the Convent, viz. the habit (*khirka*); the carpet (*Sejáde*), the standard (*A'alem*); the drum (*Tabl Kúdúmi*); the halter (*Pálehenk*),[2] the stick (*Assa*), and the head-dress or crown (*Táj*).'[3]

A Shādhilī manual describes four grades of affiliation:

Know that affiliation[4] to the Shādhilī and other lines is effected through training under a master (*bi 'l-akhdhi 'anhum*). My master, Ibrāhīm al-Mawāhibī, said,

'Know that there are four grades to such training. The first is by the handclasp (*muṣāfaḥa*), the allocation of graduated *dhikr* tasks (*at-talqīn li 'dh-dhikr*), investment with the frock (*khirqa*) and with the

and were expected to be maintained. Al-Muḥibbī quotes a description of these (as well as of the categories of saints and forms of *dhikr*) in a notice on a Damascene Khalwatī of Kurdish origin called Aḥmad ibn 'Alī al-Ḥarīrī al-'Usālī (d. 1048/1638), from whom stemmed a definite Syrian Khalwatī line; see *Khulāṣat al-athar*, i. 248–51, and cf. i. 253–6, 257–9, 389, 428–33.

[1] A description of *ikrār ayīnī* is given in J. K. Birge, *The Bektashi Order of Dervishes*, 1937, pp. 175–201.

[2] *Pālāheng* (Persian) is a 'cord' or 'halter' with an emblem (*teslīm tash*) worn around the neck, with which the *murīd* of certain Turkish orders was invested at the end of his novitiate.

[3] Evliya Chelebi, tr. von Hammer, ii. 96.

[4] *Intisāb*, lit. tracing one's spiritual lineage.

turban-tassel (*'adhaba*);[1] purely as a means of meriting benediction and affiliation (*nisba*).

'The second concerns training in the tradition (*riwāya*)[2] and consists of reading the writings of the order without receiving any explanation of the meaning; and this similarly is solely for the purpose of meriting the benediction and the affiliation.

'The third is training in *dirāya* (understanding), and consists of an exposition of the books in order to grasp their meaning. This likewise does not involve any practice in them (the methods).

'These three sections as a rule are the only ones normally involved, and there is no objection to the trainee having a number of shaikhs to guide him to the best of their ability.

'The fourth is the undertaking of the actual training (*tadrīb*), receiving instruction (*tahdhīb*), and undergoing progressive development through service, by the ways of self-mortification (*mujāhada*), leading to enlightenment (*mushāhada*) and absorption of self into the Unity (*al-fanā' fī 't-tawḥīd*) and subsistence in it (*al-baqā' bihi*). This process the aspirant must not undertake except with his exemplar's permission.'[3]

A novitiate was required of all who aspired to become full dervishes, but the requirements varied greatly. Mawlawīs imposed a novitiate of 1,001 unbroken days' service to the community, of which the last period was spent in the kitchen. Before admission to this there was a ceremony of presentation at an assembly of the dervishes.[4] The chief cook acted as sponsor, the *chelebi* administered the oath, capped the novice, and counselled him regarding his duties.

Khalwatī shaikhs, in particular, enforced a strict novitiate.[5] The aspirant entered upon this at a *talqīn* ceremony. The shaikh, after prayers, took the novice by the hand and whispered in his ear the first 'word', *lā ilāha illā 'llāh* (no god but God), telling him to repeat it 101, 151, or 301 times a day. The novice must then go into retreat. He is expected to report to his shaikh the

[1] *'Adhaba* (also called *dhu'āba*) is the loose end of the turban left hanging behind the head (or over the left ear by some Sufis, Qalqashandī, *Ṣubḥ*, iv. 43), and one supposes refers to the completion of the winding.

[2] *Riwāya* and *dirāya* are *ḥadīth* terms; *riwāya* being the chain of transmission by reliable reporters, and *dirāya*, scrutiny and internal evidence.

[3] Aḥmad b. M. b. 'Abbād, *Al-Mafākhir al-'aliyya fī ma'ākhir ash-Shādhiliyya*, Cairo, A.H. 1327, p. 116.

[4] The ceremony is described by D'Ohsson, *Tableau*, IV. ii (1791), 635–7, and H. Guys, *Un derviche algérien en Syrie*, Paris, 1854, pp. 225–7.

[5] The particular form given here is taken from D'Ohsson, *Tableau*, IV. ii. 633–4.

visions and dreams he experiences, and it is by means of these that the shaikh gauges his progress and is able to decide when the novice has passed stage one and he can breathe into his ear the second 'word', *Yā Allāh*. There are seven 'words' in all,[1] the other five being: *Yā Huwa* (O He), *Yā Ḥaqq* (O Truth), *Yā Ḥayy* (O Living), *Yā Qayyūm* (O Eternal), and *Yā Qahhār* (O Subduer), and they are associated with the seven spheres (*aflāk*) and the seven lights whence emanate the seven principal colours.[2] This whole novitiate, called *chillā* (retreat), takes some six to twelve months, and when he has completed the course (*takmīl as-sulūk*) the novice is admitted as a full brother. This type of novitiate distinguishes the Khalwatiyya from most other orders.

The importance of dreams and visions in the whole scheme of the Sufi Path can hardly be overstressed; the literature of Sufism and the hagiographa in particular are full of them, and their significance in the life of individuals and society. Ibn al-ʿArabī's *Al-Futūḥāt al-Makkiyya* derives directly from such an experience and he shows how the decisive stages of his life were marked by dreams. Visions of the Prophet and al-Khaḍir were the decisive point in the authorization of an illuminate to strike out along his own way. They were a convenient way of obtaining permission from long-dead Sufis to teach their doctrines and *awrād*, thus leading some people to assume the continuity of line from al-Junaid or another early Sufi.

A visualization of God even was possible. We read in a Qādirī manual in the section describing the conditions governing the Forty-day Retreat (the *Arbaʿīniyya*): 'And if, during the course of his retreat, a form reveal itself to him and say, "I am God", he should reply, "Praise is due to God (alone)! nay rather thou art by God"; and if it be for testing it will vanish; but if it remain it will be a genuine theophany (*at-tajallī al-ilāhī*) in an outward form which does not contradict *tanzīh bi laisa*', that is, the doctrine of 'exemption', the wholly other, that God 'is not' in any way like His creatures.[3] Abu Ḥāmid al-Ghazālī's account of his encounter

[1] Al-Jabartī mentions (*ʿAjā'ib*, 1959 edn., ii. 270) this association of the seven words with the seven soul-states (see above, p. 153) in connection with the initiatory instructions given to the *murīd* by al-Bakrī aṣ-Ṣiddīqī. As-Sanūsī (*Salsabīl*, p. 98) gives *ten* words for the Khalwatiyya.

[2] The schema of the Path given in the previous chapter (p. 155) shows the relationship of colours to other Sufi phenomena.

[3] Ismāʿīl ibn M. Saʿīd, *Al-Fuyūḍāt ar-Rabbāniyya*, A.H. 1353, p. 64.

with God in a dream at a significant stage in his spiritual pilgrimage is interesting.[1]

The following extract from a manual in common use among *muqaddams* gives the conditions of admission to the nineteenth-century Tijānī *ṭarīqa*, which has no dervishes or adepts:

You must be an adult Muslim in order that it may be correct for you to take the *awrād*, for they are the work of the Lord of men. You should ask permission from your parents of your own free will before you take the *ṭarīqa*, for this is one of the means of union (*wuṣūl*) with God. You must seek for one who has a genuine permission to initiate you into the *awrād*, so that you will be well-connected with God.

You should absolutely abstain from any other *awrād* than those of your shaikh, since God did not create two hearts within you. Do not visit any *walī*, living or dead, for no man can serve two masters. You must be strict about performing the five prayers in congregation and in observing the legal obligations, for they were prescribed by the best of creation [the Prophet]. You must love the shaikh and his *khalīfa* throughout your life since for the generality of created beings such love is the main means of Union; and think not that you can safeguard yourself from the craft of the Lord of the Universe, for this is one of the characteristics of failures. You must not malign, nor bear enmity against your shaikh, otherwise you will bring destruction upon yourself. You must not desist from reciting the *awrād* as long as you live, because they contain the mysteries of the Creator. You must believe and trust in all that the shaikh says to you about the virtues, because they are amongst the sayings of the Lord of the first and last. You must not criticize any good thing that seems strange to you in this *ṭarīqa*, or you will be deprived of their virtue by the Just Ruler.

Do not recite the *wird* of the shaikh except after permission and proper initiation (*talqīn*), because that came in plain speech. Gather together for the office (*waẓīfa*)[2] and the Friday *dhikr* with the brethren because that is a safeguard against the wiles of the devil. You shall not read *Jawharat al-Kamāl* except in a state of ritual cleanliness, because the Prophet will come at the seventh reading. Do not interrupt (the recitation of) anyone, especially one of the brethren, for such interruption is one of the methods of the devil. Do not be slack about your *wird*, nor postpone it on some pretext or other, because on him who takes the *wird* and then either abandons it altogether or neglects it punishment will fall and he will be destroyed. Do not go and confer

[1] Muḥammad al-Murtaḍā, *Itḥāf*, i. 9.

[2] The *waẓīfa* consists of *al-istighfār* (once), *ṣalāt al-fātiḥ* (50 times), *ash-shahāda* (100 times), and *Jawharat al-Kamāl* (11 times or more).

the *awrād* without being properly allowed to give them, because he who does that and does not repent will come to an evil end and disaster will fall on him. You must not tell your *wird* to anyone except your brother in the *ṭarīqa*, because that is one of the essentials of the etiquette of the spiritual science.[1]

There are three types of *ijāza* (licence). The first is that given to a dervish or adept giving his qualifications and permitting him to practise in the name of his master; the second is given to a *khalīfa* or *muqaddam* authorizing him to confer the *wird*, that is, admit others into the *ṭarīqa*; whilst the third type simply affirms that the holder has followed a particular course of Sufi instruction. A clear distinction is made between one's true guide—*shaikh at-tarbiya* (upbringing), or *shaikh aṣ-ṣuḥba* (discipleship)[2]—and the various *shuyūkh at-taʿlīm* (instructors) whose courses one has followed. The fact that Sufis claimed several initiations and possessed a number of *ijāzas* has caused confusion and misunderstanding, for many *ijāzas* were only concerned with announcing that the recipient had followed a course, perhaps absorption of a Sufi book, and been given a licence to teach it,[3] or to recite a word of power, such as ash-Shādhilī's *Ḥizb al-Baḥr*, with power. In India even choirmen (*qawwāls*) were given a singing licence (*ijāzat-nāma-samāʿ*).

An *ijāza* at its simplest takes a recognized form: 'This is to certify that Muḥammad, son of (full genealogy), who took the *ṭarīqa* from the Khalīfa Muṣṭafā (then follows the *silsila* of *khalīfas* back to the founder) has found his adept Ṭāhā, son of (full genealogy), worthy to be admitted to the Order. He is, accordingly, given authority to act according to the rules of the order (then follows a statement of the things he is permitted to carry out) since its secrets have been revealed to him.' The *khalīfa* affixes his seal to the document,[4] and it is frequently worn rolled in a tubular case (a full *ijāza* might well be two yards long) on the

[1] M. ʿAlwān al-Jawsqī, *As-Sirr al-abhar fī awrād Aḥmad at-Tijānī*, Cairo, n.d., p. 3.

[2] He is generally, though not necessarily, the initiator into the *silsila* covering both *ijāza irāda*, that of the *murīd*, and *ijāza 't-tabarruk*, the permission which links with the shaikh's *baraka*.

[3] Thus Abu ʿAmr al-ʿAzafī was given an *ijāza* by al-Bādisī to teach his *Maqṣad*; tr. G. S. Colin in *Archiv. Maroc.* xxvi (1926), 163.

[4] Other attestations may be given and must be given if the recipient is the shaikh's own son.

flank.[1] A complete *ijāza* often contained the *wird* and recommendations such, for example, as the *waṣiyya* or testament said to have been given by ʿAbd al-Qādir al-Jīlānī to his son ʿAbd ar-Razzāq.[2] The Nilotic Sudan hagiographer, Wad Ḍaif Allāh (d. A.D. 1809), reproduces part of an *ijāza* given by Ibn Jābir to a disciple in A.D. 1574:

Praise be to God, the Lord of the Universe, and peace be upon the Apostles. Verily, the brother of Faqīh Ibrāhīm, the pious, learned and humble one, the son of Umm Rābʿa, I believe to be worthy of mastership and leadership. I, therefore, appoint him a *quṭb* in rank, an interpreter to his own age and time, a tutor to aspirants, an example to those who guide, a refuge for the poor and destitute, a revivifier of the sun of knowledge after its setting.

I authorize him to pass on and teach to the people all that he has truly received and heard from me. I also authorize him to propagate and broadcast the knowledge we have referred to. Let anyone to whom such knowledge is communicated be exceeding careful lest he be spiritually destroyed.[3]

In the past *ijāzas* frequently dealt with the question of *rukhaṣ* (sing. *rukhṣa*), an aspect of Sufi life we have hardly referred to. These are 'dispensations' or 'indulgencies'. They include such everyday necessities as the holding of private and public assemblies (*ḥaḍras*) at which they hold concerts (*samāʿāt*), and indulge in jesting (*mizāḥ*), dancing (*raqṣ*), and the rending (*tamzīq*) and divesting of garments. They embrace 'contemplation of youth' (*naẓar ilā 'l-murd*), soliciting of alms (normally reprehensible), and taking up arms in a holy cause. They may cover the use of the rosary, neglect of mosque attendance, and non-observance of ritual *ṣalāt* during a period of ʿ*uzla* (retirement).

[1] Sir Richard Burton gives a translation (Appendix III of his *Pilgrimage*) of an *ijāza*, which he says, gave him authority, as Darwīsh ʿAbdallāh, to act as a *murshid* in the Qādirī order, but in fact it simply says that he has been given instruction in the Saying of Unity with authority to recite it 165 times after each *farīḍa* (obligatory ritual prayer) and on any other occasion according to his ability. This *ijāza* was four feet five inches long and about six and a half inches broad.

[2] See *al-Fuyūḍāt ar-Rabbāniyya*, pp. 35–8.

[3] *Ṭabaqāt* of Wad Ḍaif Allāh, ed. Ṣidaiq (1930), p. 33; ed. Mandīl (1930), pp. 31–2.

VII

Ritual and Ceremonial

LITURGICAL development within the main stream of Islam was completed early in its history, never to be renewed within legal religion. Subsequent growth came through the Sufis. Their organized seances were entirely separate from ritual *ṣalāt*, but in the course of time, when Sufism was brought to the level of the average man, the very *dhikr* of the divine names was so vulgarized and associated with *ṣalāt* as an extra personal appendage, as to become despiritualized. The Sufis' deeper devotions, however, were maintained in other ways as a separate expression.

The ritual of an order constitutes a Way, a rule of life, by following which the *murīd* may hope so to purify his *nafs* as to attain union with God. *Ṭarīqa* materializes itself in the *dhikr* (recollection), whose regular practice leads the predestined *'ārif* to the state of *istighrāq* (immersion) in God. *Dhikr*, therefore, forms the framework of the *ṭarīqa*. Although Syriac Christian usage of the allied term *dukhrānā* in the same technical sense is significant, *dhikr* is solidly based on the Qur'ānic injunction, 'Remember God with frequent remembrance and glorify Him morning and evening.'[1] The early Sufis found in *dhikr* a means of excluding distractions and of drawing near to God, and it has come to mean a particular method of glorifying God by the constant repetition of His name, by rhythmic breathing either mentally (*dhikr khafī*) or aloud (*dhikr jahrī* or *jalī*). *Dhikr*, the manuals tell us, is the 'pivot' of mysticism. Supreme importance is given to the Names and Words (= phrases), for by means of their recital divine energy transfuses the reciter's being and changes him.

Control of the breath was an early characteristic, both a natural outcome of the attempt to practise *dhikr* and an absorption from the ascetic heritage of eastern Christianity. Abu Yazīd al-Bisṭāmī

[1] Qur'ān, xxxiii. 41, fortified by many other verses: ii. 153, iv. 104, vii. 206, xiii. 28, xviii. 24, xxiv. 36–7, xxix. 44, lxxvi. 25.

(d. A.D. 874) is reported as saying, 'For gnostics, worship is observance of the breaths', and Abu Bakr ash-Shiblī (d. A.D. 945) as observing that '*Taṣawwuf* is control of the faculties and observance of the breaths'.[1]

Music, other than the chanting of the *ādhān* and Qur'ān, has no real place in the ritual of Islam, but played a great role in the worship of Sufis. Sufis soon found, or perhaps absorbed the fact from older religious practice, that music, with its vagueness and lack of precise images, not only has mystical power to draw out the deepest emotions, but also, when co-ordinated with symbolic words and rhythmical movements, has power over man's will. The *samā'* (spiritual concert) became a feature of early Sufi practice, but of what it consisted, apart from the singing of mystical poems to induce ecstasy, it is difficult to tell, since most writers spend their time either attacking or justifying, rather than describing, these 'excesses'. The lawfulness of music as an aid to Sufi devotions was under discussion in legal and Sufi circles long before the formation of definite orders.[2]

The form taken by the Sufi *samā'* at the turn of the eleventh century is described by Aḥmad al-Ghazālī in his *Bawāriq al-ilmā'*[3] in somewhat vague terms, when writing a spirited defence of these practices. The earlier form of seeking ecstasy was through music and the dance, of which genus the only survival is the Mawlawī form. Aḥmad showed that it embraced three physical techniques: dance, whirl, and jump, and that every movement is symbolic of a spiritual reality.

> The dancing is a reference to the circling of the spirit round the cycle of existing things on account of receiving the effects of the unveilings and revelations; and this is the state of the gnostic. The whirling is a reference to the spirit's standing with Allāh in its inner nature (*sirr*) and being (*wujūd*), the circling of its look and thought, and its penetrating the ranks of existing things; and this is the state of the assured one. And his leaping up is a reference to his being drawn from the human station to the unitive station.[4]

[1] 'Aṭṭār, *Tadhkirat al-awliyā'*, text and tr. given by R. A. Nicholson, 'The Origin and Development of Sufiism', *J.R.A.S.* 1906, 344.

[2] See the summary of this discussion given by Professor J. Robson in the introduction to his edition of two *Tracts on Listening to Music* (London, 1938), one of which condemns and the other approves of *samā'*.

[3] Edited and translated by J. Robson in ibid.

[4] Ibid., pp. 99–100.

A *samā'* session involves teaching, since Aḥmad writes that the group

gather together in the early morning after finishing the dawn prayer, or after the evening [prayer], after finishing their office (*wird*), be it recitation [of the Qur'ān], *dhikr*, or any act of worship whatsoever. When they sit down, he of their number who has the most sensitive voice recites such a passage as . . . Then the *shaikh* speaks about the meaning of these verses in a manner suited to the station of mystical practices (*sulūk*).[1]

After this teaching session the *qawwāl* or singer begins singing Sufi poems to move them to ecstasy:

When they experience within them a stirring which affects them like the commotion of one who is called to the service of a mighty king and to appear before Allāh (Exalted is He!), he who falls into ecstasy does not rise till he is overpowered, and the people do as he does. The dance is not to be affected or feigned, nay, their movements must be in accordance with the state, like one who is overcome by terror or unavoidable trepidation. Then when their spirits receive a mystical apprehension (*ḥaẓẓ*) of the unseen states, and their hearts are softened by the lights of the divine Essence and are established in purity and the spiritual lights, they sit down, and he who chants (*muzamzim*) chants a light chant to bring them forth by degrees from the internal to the external. Then when he stops, someone other than the first reciter recites such [a passage] as 'This is our gift, so be lavish, or withhold without account' . . . and such like. Then if there is among them anyone in whom remains the residue of a state or of absorption, the *qawwāl* repeats [what he uttered] in a lighter voice than the first; and if they remain seated, he does it a third time in a voice intermediate between the heavy and the light, since the complete ranks are three, the rank of men, the rank of the angel, and the rank of Lordship (*rubūbiyya*) at which there is absolute quiescence. Then they get up from the place of audition and go to their dwellings and sit watching for the revelation of what appeared to them in the state of their absorption in ecstasy. After audition some of them dispense with food for days on account of the nourishment of their spirits and hearts with unseen mystical experiences (*wāridāt*).[2]

What needs bringing out is the way in which this form of Sufi practice contrasts with the standard form of later *dhikr* gatherings. Some changes were already taking place connected with enlarging

[1] J. Robson in *Tracts on Listening to Music*, 1938, p. 105. It will be noticed that the recitation of *awrād* and *adhkār* was part of the personal practice of the Sufi.

[2] Ibid., pp. 112–13.

their scope, for Aḥmad writes: 'Things went on like that till the common people imitated them, and the good was mingled with the corrupt, and the system was disordered.'[1] New methods certainly were being adopted at this time: Aḥmad himself worked out special nuances involved in the recitation of the divine names,[2] and the different Ways now beginning to be specified were each characterized by specific invocation series. Aḥmad al-Yasavī is said to have introduced the 'rasping saw' *dhikr*, a tradition which no doubt attests to its central Asian origin. For this the *hā* is expired very deeply, then *hī* aspired as low as possible;[3] and it sounds much like sawing. All this is based on the technique of control of the breath[4] and enunciation, given fuller development through contact with *yoga*-practising circles. Hence, parallel to the breath-control aspect of the *samā'*, were the practices of individual *dhikr* techniques. Arabic and Persian translations of the *Amṛta-kuṇḍa*, which deals with the principles of Yoga, were known in Sufi circles at this time.[5] Later, definite Yoga practices were adopted by Indian orders, such as the Ghawthiyya, an offshoot of the Shaṭṭāriyya, founded by Shāh Muḥammad Ghawth of Gwalior

[1] Ibid., p. 113/177.

[2] Aḥmad has a book on the subject, *Kitāb at-tajrīd fī kalimat at-tawḥīd*.

[3] A description of the Ghawthiyya form of *adh-dhikr al-minshārī* is given by Sanūsī, *Salsabīl*, pp. 127–8.

[4] The question of soul and spirit, *nafs* and *rūḥ*, which Sufis constantly contrast, is involved. 'He who hears with his heart is genuine, he who hears with his soul is a fraud' (Aḥmad ar-Ruṭbī, *Minḥat al-aṣḥāb*, 1939, p. 92). So far as the *dhikr* is concerned it is necessary to ensure that the methods are *spirit*ual and not *psycho*logical, and to distinguish between carnal (*nafsiyya*) and spiritual (*rūḥiyya*) breathing. *Nafs* is the breath that, coming from the bowels, passes through the glottis; it is carnal and sensual. *Rūḥ* comes from the brain and passes through the nostrils. Through *rūḥ* one discerns spiritual qualities. The Sufis distinguished different kinds (or shades) of *rūḥ*, but we are only concerned to indicate that the practice of the *dhikr* in the more esoteric circles was very elaborate.

[5] The Arabic text has been edited and analysed by Yūsuf Ḥusain, 'Ḥawḍ al-Ḥayāt: la version arabe de l'Amratkund', *J. Asiat.* ccxiii (1928), 291–344. The preface says that it was originally translated into Persian, then Arabic, by Qāḍī Rukn ad-dīn Samarqandī who lived at Lakhnauti in Bengal during the reign of Sultan 'Alā' ad-dīn Mardān I (1207–12), though the actual texts which survive are not his translations.

The system of Patanjali was known to the Indian Sufis and al-Bīrūnī made an Arabic translation of the *Yōga-Sutrā* entitled *Kitāb Pātanjal al-Hindī fī 'l-Khalāṣ min al-amthāl*; see Louis Massignon, *Le Lexique technique de la mystique Musulmane*, 2nd edn., 1954, pp. 81–98. H. Ritter has provided an edition of the text, 'Al-Bīrūnī's Übersetzung des Yoga-Sutra des Patañjali', *Oriens*, ix (1956), 165–200.

(d. 1562–3).[1] As-Sanūsī describes the more important of the eighty-four poses (*jalsa*) of the Jūjiyya, as he calls it, and seems to accept them as legitimate methods.[2]

By the time of Ibn 'Aṭā' Allāh (d. 709/1309), second Alexandrian successor of Abū 'l-Ḥasan ash-Shādhilī, the new Yoga-type methods had reached Egypt, though not the Maghrib,[3] and he is the first to write a systematic treatise on the *dhikr*. He opens his book, *Miftāḥ al-Falāḥ*:[4] 'Recollection of God . . . is the very prop upon which the Way rests . . . I have not come across anyone who has composed a comprehensive and satisfactory book on the subject . . . and this gap a friend suggested I should fill.'[5]

An early collection of the *dhikrs* associated with distinctive orders is the *Risāla* of Ḥusain ibn 'Alī al-'Ujaimī (d. 1113/1702), which contains the *dhikrs* or *wirds*, with *isnād* of transmission, of the forty orders which maintain the spiritual equilibrium of Islam. His work found imitators, or rather cribbers, the best known being the *'Iqd al-jumān* of M. ibn al-Ḥusain al-Murtaḍā az-Zabīdī (d. 1205/1791) and *As-Salsabīl al-ma'īn fī 'ṭ-ṭarā'iq al-arba'īn* of

[1] The practices are dealt with in Muḥammad Ghawth's *Baḥr al-Ḥayāt*, a translation of *Amṛta-kuṇḍa* (Delhi, 1311) and his *Jawāhir-i Khamsa*, *G.A.L.* ii. 418, *G.A.L.S.* ii. 616.

[2] See As-Sanūsī, *as-Salsabīl al-ma'īn*, Cairo 1353/1935, pp. 131 ff. Ibn Baṭṭūṭa writes *jōkī*, pl. *jōkiyya*.

[3] The new methods did not apparently reach the Maghrib before the middle of the 14th century. Rulings on the legality of Sufi practices were frequently sought from *fuqahā'*, and some like Ibn al-Jawzī and Ibn Taimiyya took special interest in the question. These requests for *fatwās* sometimes throw light on the forms taken by *dhikr*-gatherings:

> Shaikh aṣ-Ṣāliḥ Abu Fāris 'Abd al-'Azīz b. M. al-Qairawānī [d. 750/1349] . . . was asked about a group known as *fuqarā'* who gathered together for dancing and singing. When they had finished they partook of the agape which had been previously prepared, as their last repast. Then they followed that by reciting a 'tenth' of the Qur'ān and offering a *dhikr*, and afterwards began again singing, dancing and weeping. They claim that this is all part of the process of drawing near to God and obedience to Him. They invite others to join with them in this, castigating those of the *'ulamā'* who do not take part (al-Wansharīsī, *Al-Mi'yār*, lith. Fez, A.H. 1314, xi. 23).

The protests, it seems from this account, were against the traditional form of gathering.

[4] Doubts that have been thrown upon the authenticity of the attribution of this book to Ibn 'Aṭā' Allāh appear to have little foundation; none of those closest in touch with him appears to have had any misgivings about the attribution.

[5] Printed on the margin of ash-Sha'rānī's *Laṭā'if al-minan*, Cairo, A.H. 1357, ii. 89.

Muḥammad ibn 'Alī as-Sanūsī (d. 1859), who acknowledges his indebtedness.[1]

The initiation of the novice into the first stage of the Sufi Path means his deliberate choice to redirect his life from self to God by following a proved path; and a proved path implies his pursuing a course which leads to the surrender of will, the transformation of desire from self-centredness to God-centredness, a seeking not so much to escape from self as to transcend or transmute self, and thus enter into timeless experience. This is the aim of the mystic; the achievement of ecstasy, which later came to be an end in itself, is not his aim. The mystical experience was something other and rarer than this type of psychic experience. The directors of souls knew that ecstasy can be induced with comparative ease through a variety of ways. At the same time, they were aware that the ecstatic experience was an unavoidable accompaniment of the way along which they were guiding their aspirants. The extent to which they should permit the use of psychological techniques was one of their problems.

The change that came about from the twelfth century onwards was the completion of the mechanization (if one may so put it) of mystical experience; the realization that this experience can be induced for the ordinary man in a relatively short space of time by rhythmical exercises involving posture, control of breath, co-ordinated movements, and oral repetitions. By this century the dervishes had acquired a complete technique. They employed all sorts of methods to condition the person, open up his consciousness to the attractions of the supra-sensible world: sacred numbers and symbols; colours and smells, perfumes and incense; ritual actions and purifications; words of power, charm-like prayers and incantations, with music and chant; invocations of angels and other spirit beings; even the use of alcohol and drugs.[2]

[1] *Salsabīl*, p. 4.

[2] The Ḥaidariyya, a qalandarī group founded by the Nishapuri, Quṭb ad-dīn Ḥaidar (d. 618/1221), discovered the qualities and permitted his dervishes the use of hemp (*kunnab*); see Maqrīzī (*Khiṭaṭ*, ed. A.H. 1325, iii. 205–9), who says that it was widely used by *fuqarā'*.

Later, coffee became an essential aspect of all *dhikr* gatherings. Its introduction is associated with a Shādhilī called Abu 'l-Ḥasan 'Alī ibn 'Umar (d. at Mukhā in Yemen in A.D. 1418), who became acquainted with the beverage when he resided at the court of Sa'd ad-dīn II, sultan of Ifāt-Zaila' in southern Ethiopia. It was taken up by Yemeni and Hadrami Sufis and its subsequent diffusion throughout the Arab world under Sufi auspices was rapid. On its value for Sufis (including

The practical goal of Sufism for the majority came to be the attainment of ecstasy (*wajd* = *faqd al-iḥsās*, 'loss of consciousness'). This is not the *wajd* (encounter with God) of the Sufis;[1] it was in fact a degeneration which the early masters of Sufism had perceived and warned against when dealing with the question of *samā'*. The Sufi Way, whose reaches depend so much upon the individual's temperament and innate gifts, is for an élite only. Sufis recognized that the majority of mankind are 'born deaf', devoid of the faculty for mystical sensitivity. The devotional techniques of the orders were a crude attempt to mediate the same effects, give an illusion of a glimpse into Reality, to the ordinary man. So Sufis came to equate the ecstatic trance with loss of consciousness in the divine unity, and this development is one of the signs of what has been called the degeneration of Sufism, but may be regarded as its adaptation to the needs and capacity of the ordinary man.

Ecstasy is attained through the repeated enunciation of short invocations, with control of the breath, co-ordinated with body exercises, balancing, and inclinations. This is done to the accompaniment of both vocal and instrumental music, for music helps to free the physical effort from conscious thought, since both mind and will must be suspended if ecstasy is to be attained. All this is so ordered that it induces a special experience whereby loss of consciousness is regarded as 'union', an emotional identification of seeker and sought. To some this experience became a drug for which soul and body craved. For the ordinary lay member, participation in the ritual of the *dhikr*, which for him only occasionally leads to the trance-ecstasy, provides at lowest a release from the hardships of everyday existence, and, at a higher level, some measure of freedom from the limitations of human life and a glimpse at transcendental experience. In the Sufism of the orders this ecstasy or trance-like 'state' is called a *ḥāl*, though in Sufism proper *ḥāl* more strictly refers to the succession of illuminations, through experiencing which the Sufi progresses a further 'stage' (*maqām*) towards the goal of spiritual perfection.[2]

the *dhikr* invocation *yā qawī*, repeated 116 times) as given in *Ṣafwat aṣ-ṣafwa fī bayān ḥukm al-qahwa*, by 'Abd al-Qādir ibn al-'Aidarūs, see art. 'Ḳahwa' by C. van Arendonk, in *E.I.*[1] ii. 632.

[1] See, for example, al-Kalābadhī, *Kitāb at-ta'arruf*, ed. A. J. Arberry, Cairo, 1934, pp. 82–3.

[2] There are considerable differences between authors in the definition of

Three main types of practice are distinguished: *dhikr al-awqāt*, the daily office, *dhikr al-khafī* (and *bi 'l-jalāla*) is one's personal recollection, whilst *dhikr al-ḥaḍra* is the communal exercise. *Dhikr al-awqāt* for the average adherent consists of the repetition of short formulae after two or more of the regular canonical prayers. This is an obligatory exercise for which there is strong Qur'ānic support, 'When your prayers are ended, remember God, standing, sitting or lying down' (iv. 104). Permission to recite is given by the shaikh. The simplest form among Qādiriyya consists of the repetition of *subḥān Allāh*, *al-ḥamdu li'llāh*, and *Allāhu akbar*, each repeated thirty-three times. As a common form of supererogatory prayer following ritual *ṣalāt* it must be distinguished from the secret-conferring of *dhikr* phrases by the *murshid*.

This repetition is generally carried out with the aid of a rosary (*tasbiḥa*, *tasbīḥ*, or *sibḥa*) and the orders affect particular forms. The Qādirī has 99 beads divided into three sections of 33 each; that of the Tijānīs consists of 100 beads divided 12, 18, 20, 20, 18, 12. There are other rarer combinations: Khalwatīs have a 301-bead rosary, and there are 1,000-bead rosaries, used for special individual tasks, and even on communal occasions as on the first, third, seventh, and fortieth nights succeeding a funeral. The rosary acquired symbolical importance through its use in ceremonies of initiation, institution, and other cult practices. It was a symbol of authority and the rosary of the *ṭā'ifa* founder was inherited by his successors, being especially reverenced since it was impregnated with the *baraka* of a lifetime's recital of the divine names. It was kept in a special box and provided with a guardian (*shaikh as-sibḥa*) and an attendant (*khādim as-sibḥa*).[1]

The proper *dhikr khafī* (occult recollection), with which the descriptions in the manuals are mainly concerned, is based upon the rhythm of breathing: exhalation–inhalation. With closed eyes and lips, using the basic *tahlīl* formula,[2] the recollector (*dhākir*) exhales, concentrating on *lā ilāha*, to expel all external distrac- ... en in inhaling he concentrates on *illā 'llāh*, affirming that

... *ḥāl* and *maqām*, but I am following al-Qushairī's distinction, *fa* ... *wāhib wa 'l-maqāmāt makāsib*, that a *ḥāl* is a divine gift, whilst a ... ained by human effort (*Risāla*, Cairo, 1901, p. 32). It is a reciprocal p... awing near to God through veil-stripping.

... -'Abdarī (d. 737/1336), *al-Mudkhal ash-Shar'*, Cairo, ii. 83.

... *illā 'llāh* (there is no god but God) is the negation–affirmation (*na*... formula, the first part of the *shahāda* (testimony).

all is God. The whole process or techniques are set out elaborately in the manuals, frequently so complicated that they are untranslatable without a commentary. Here is a Naqshabandī *dhikr khafī* expressed simply:

He must keep the tongue pressed against the roof of his mouth, his lips and teeth firmly shut, and hold his breath. Then starting with the word *lā*, he makes it ascend from the navel to the brain. When it has arrived at the brain he says *ilāha* to the right shoulder and *illā 'llāh* to the left side, driving it forcefully into the pineal heart[1] through which it circulates to all the rest of the body. The phrase *Muḥammad rasūl Allāh* is made to incline from the left to the right side, and then one says, 'My God, Thou art my goal and satisfying Thee is my aim.'[2]

As-Sanūsī's *Salsabīl* is full of these descriptions, incorporated piecemeal, some of which seem to be incomplete. The following is his description of a Qādirī *dhikr*, presumably an Indian group:

Sitting cross-legged, he seizes with the big toe of the right foot and (the toe that) adjoins it the vein called *kaimās*, which is the great vein situated in the hollow of the knee joint, and puts his hands on his knees, opening his fingers in the form of the word 'Allāh'. He begins with the *lām*, sustaining it until his heart is opened and the divine lights disclosed. Then he sets himself to perform with the *dhikr* '*Āward burdāyay*',[3] which is the *dhikr* of the *fanā'* and *baqā'*, attributed to the shaikh of shaikhs, 'Abd al-Qādir. For this he sits in the just-mentioned position, turning his face inwards towards his right shoulder, saying *hā*; turning his face left saying *hū*; lowering his head, uttering within himself the word *ḥayy*; and carrying on repeating without respite.[4]

Naqshabandīs follow the Malāmatī tradition in respect of the *dhikr*, ruling out public seances and recitals (*samā'āt*)[5] and con-

[1] *Al-qalb aṣ-ṣanawbarī*. The heart, shaped like a pine-cone, contains the whole truth of man.

[2] Quoted from Tāj ad-dīn ibn [Zakariya] Mahdī Zamān ar-Rūmī, *Risālat fī sunan aṭ-Ṭā'ifat an-Naqshabandiyya*, Cambridge, Add. MS. 1073, pp. 4–5. The same exercise is described by as-Sanūsī (*Salsabil*, pp. 116–17) in different terms and in more detail.

[3] Persian *Āward burd* (contesting) is the term used for a particular form of the discipline of breath-control.

[4] As-Sanūsī, *Salsabīl*, pp. 58–9.

[5] Some congregations allowed themselves a dispensation (*rukhṣa*) from this rule. D'Ohsson describes how those in Turkey met once a week after *ṣalāt al-'ishā'* on Thursday night to recite the obligatory prayer-sequence called *Khatm-i Khawājagān*: 'This is done seated on a long sopha. The leader chants the prayers which constitute the confraternity, and the assembly responds in chorus, sometimes *Hu*, and sometimes *Allah*. In some towns these Naqshabandīs have special halls for their *dhikrs*' (D'Ohsson, *Tableau*, IV. 2, 628–9).

centrating on the *dhikr khafī*. Their eleven principles show the exercise-aims of the *ṭarīqa*. The first eight were formulated by ʿAbd al-Khāliq al-Ghujdawānī and the last three were added by Bahā' ad-dīn an-Naqshabandī.[1]

1. *Yād kard* (remembrance, or 'making mention'), both oral and mental. Be always repeating the *dhikr* imparted to you so that you may attain the beatific vision. Bahā' ad-dīn said; 'The aim in *dhikr* is that the heart be always aware of *al-Ḥaqq*, for its practice banishes inattention.'
2. *Bāz gasht* (restraint). The *dhākir*, when engaging in the heart-repetition of the 'blessed phrase',[2] should intersperse it with such phrases as, 'My God, Thou art my Goal and Thy satisfaction is my aim', to help to keep one's thoughts from straying. Other masters say it means 'return', 'repent', that is, return to *al-Ḥaqq* by way of contrition (*inkisār*).
3. *Nigāh dāsht* (watchfulness) over wandering, passing, thoughts when repeating the 'blessed phrase'.
4. *Yād dāsht* (recollection), concentration upon the divine presence in a condition of *dhawq*, foretaste, intuitive anticipation or perceptiveness, not using external aids.[3]
5. *Hōsh dar dam* (awareness while breathing). The technique of breath-control. Said Bahā' ad-dīn; 'The external basis of this *ṭarīqa* is the breath.' One must not exhale in forgetfulness or inhale in forgetfulness.
6. *Safar dar waṭan* (journeying in one's homeland). This is an interior journey, the movement from blameworthy to praiseworthy qualities. Others refer to it as the vision or revelation of the hidden side of the *shahāda*.
7. *Naẓar bar qadam* (watching one's steps). Let the *sālik* (pilgrim) ever be watchful during his journey, whatever the type of country through which he is passing, that he does not let his gaze be distracted from the goal of his journey.
8. *Khalwat dar anjuman* (solitude in a crowd). The journey of the *sālik*, though outwardly it is in the world, inwardly it is with God. 'Leaders of the *ṭarīqa* have said, "In this *ṭarīqa* association is in the crowd (assembly) and dissociation in the *khalwa*".' A common weekly practice was to perform their *dhikr* in the assembly.
9. *Wuqūf-i zamānī* (temporal pause). Keeping account of how one is spending one's time, whether rightly—and if so give thanks, or

[1] The following list is adapted from that given by the above-mentioned *Risāla* of Tāj ad-dīn ibn Mahdī Zamān ar-Rūmī.

[2] *Al-kalimat aṭ-ṭayyiba* (Qur'ān, xxxv. 10), i.e. the *shahāda* formulae.

[3] The meaning of *dhawq* varies according to author or context.

wrongly—and if so asking for forgiveness, according to the ranking (of the deeds), for 'verily the good deeds of the righteous are the iniquities of those who are near (to God)'.

10. *Wuqūf-i 'adadī* (numerical pause). Checking that the heart-*dhikr* has been repeated the requisite number of times, taking into account one's wandering thoughts.
11. *Wuqūf-i qalbī* (heart pause). Forming a mental picture of one's heart with the name of God engraved thereon, to emphasize that the heart has no consciousness or goal other than God.[1]

Most orders have regular *dhikr* recitals in congregation,[2] known as the *ḥaḍra*, and as such forms part of a more or less elaborate liturgical recital. The word *ḥaḍra* which has taken the place of the term *samā'* of older usage, means 'presence'. This is not taken to refer to the presence of God (like *al-Ḥaḍrat ar-Rubūbiyya* (the Divine Presence) of the Sufis), since God is omnipresent, but to the presence of the Prophet. The shift of emphasis is characteristic especially of the orders deriving from the two Aḥmad's of the nineteenth-century reform movements.[3] Muḥammad 'Uthmān, founder of the Mirghaniyya, at the beginning of his nativity poem describes how the Prophet appeared to him in a dream and 'ordered me to write a *mūlid* rhyming in *hā* and *mīm*, which I did, and he gave me the good tidings that he will be present when it is read. So I have written this that people may be honoured by his coming when it is read.'

The *ḥaḍra* at its simplest consists of two parts: (*a*) the reading

[1] These eleven 'words' have deeper meanings not found in the ordinary manuals. In 9 and 10 we may picture the *wāqif* who has ceased to seek, through having transcended time and space, and passed away (*waqfa qalbiyya*) in the Sought.

[2] E. W. Lane's *Modern Egyptians*, chap. 24, gives accounts of *dhikr* performances; also in his *Arabian Society in the Middle Ages*, 1883, pp. 73–8. D'Ohsson (*Tableau Général*, IV. 2, 1791), has accounts of the *ḥaḍras* of the Rifā'īs (pp. 641–8), Sa'dīs (pp. 648–9), and Mawlawīs (pp. 649–55). The Mawlawī *samā'* has been frequently described, see for example H. Guys, *Un derviche Algérien en Syrie*, 1854, pp. 227–31. The *ḥaḍra* of the 'Īsāwiyya is described by É. Dermenghem, *Le culte des saints dans l'Islam maghrébin* (Paris, 1954), pp. 303–18. A great merit of the orders is that their exercises were all open, an aspect which helped to disarm the orthodox; the only exception was the Bektāshiyya; see D'Ohsson, op. cit. IV. 2, 657. *Dhikrs* were frequently held in mosques, even in Syria. We read that Aḥmad b. Sulaimān al-Qādirī ad-Dimishqī (A.D. 1517–96) 'presided over a *ḥalqat adh-dhikr* in the Umawī mosque on Fridays immediately after the prayer'; al-Muḥibbī, *Khulāṣat al-athar*, i. 208.

[3] See above, pp. 106–7.

of the office (*ḥizb*, *waẓīfa*, etc.) of the order and other prayers, perhaps interspersed with music and songs (*anāshīd*); and (*b*) the *dhikr* proper, accompanied throughout by music with songs, and generally introduced with a special prayer called 'The Opener' (*Fātiḥat adh-dhikr* or *Istiftāḥ adh-dhikr*). The *ḥaḍra* takes place every Friday (our Thursday night) and on special occasions during the Islamic year or the calendar of the *ṭā'ifa*, or the life of a member such as a birth or circumcision. It is celebrated in the house of the order or that of a member or the *zāwiya* of the local shaikh.

The general Shādhilī *dhikr* pattern begins with *Fātiḥat adh-dhikr*,[1] which can be as simple as 'Yā Wāḥid, yā Allāh', then they sit down in a circle (*dā'ira*) in the position assumed by the worshipper after a prostration. The leader is in the centre, around him is grouped the choir (*munshidūn*), and around them the devotees. They recite together the *waẓīfa* (office) of the order which takes some thirty minutes and which all, literate or illiterate alike, know by heart. After that they begin the *dhikr*, first chanting the *tahlīl* (the formula *lā ilāha illā'llāh*) slowly, then faster, the leader indicating the change of tempo by an ejaculation or clapping his hands or other means.[2] Then the leader rises and all stand, the outer circle linking hands and usually shutting their eyes as an aid to concentration. Movements become faster, backwards and forwards, swaying right–left right–left, then change to jumping. All the time the singing is going on and on. After a period the leader breaks off, movement ceases, but the tireless *munshidūn* go on singing, the group chanting the while the word Allāh, or reciting the song, verse by verse after the choir. Then the physical *dhikr* begins anew.

Great flexibility is allowed within the over-all norm of the *ḥaḍra*. Here is another example of a Shādhilī *dhikr* I have attended. The participants sit either in a circle, or in two lines facing each other, the singers and shaikh in the centre or at one end. The *dhikr* commences with the recitation of the *tahlīl* in a loud voice (the stages are called *marātib adh-dhikr*) for about two hours (no count being made), but with variations. Then, at a sign from the

[1] In the Qādiriyya the *naqīb* calls for Fātiḥat al-Qur'ān with the formula: *Awwal qawlī sharaf li 'llāh al-Fātiḥa*, 'I open my mouth by honouring God with the Fātiḥa.'

[2] Rarely have I been able to tell how the shaikh rings the changes, but one has to take into account the fact that even a non-participant cannot help being affected by the *dhikr* and, whilst certain faculties are stimulated, others are dulled.

shaikh, they subside to the ground cross-legged and continue silently (though the rhythmic breathing in unison is very audible), swaying from side to side or backwards–forwards. Next, on their feet again, the word Allāh is repeated for half an hour aloud, followed by *huwa*, *ḥaqq*, *ḥayy*, *qayyūm*, and *qahhār*, in that order, the five taking half an hour (these 'Seven Words' are related to the sevenfold scheme). The *ḥaḍra* is closed with one or more long prayers from the collection *al-Ma'āthir al-'aliyya*, by which time everyone has returned to a more normal state of consciousness.

The Qādirī *ḥaḍra*, often called a *lailiyya*, falls into three phases: a recital of al-Barzanjī's *Mawlid an-Nabī*; then the 'office' of the order which is the *dhikr* proper with hymns; and the third consists of *madā'iḥ*, which in this case means hymns or sacred songs, and one long prayer from the manual. The 'office' of the Qādirī order varies according to the individual *khalīfas*, both in the litanies, methods, and number of times recited, but they fall within a narrow range.[1]

The *dhikr*, it will be seen, follows a graduated scale of effort, and follows a sequence of divine names. To begin with they pronounce the name with slow, clear enunciation, accompanied by slow rhythmical movements, swaying from side to side, or up and down on the toes, or backward–forward inclinations.[2] Then,

[1] One shaikh told me that the 'office' of the order in congregation consists of any or all of the litanies of *al-wird aṣ-ṣaghīr*, carried out by the individual initiate after one or more of the five ritual prayers, which he gave me as follows:

FORMULAE		عدد
at-tasbīḥ	سبحان الله	١٠٠
al-ḥamdu or *taḥmīd*	الحمد لله	١٠٠
al-ḥawqala	ولاحول ولا قوّة الا بالله العلى العظيم	١٠٠
al-basmala	البسملة	١٠٠
al-istighfār	استغفر الله العظيم	١٠٠
at-tawba	تُبتُ لله	١٠٠
aṣ-ṣalāt	الصلاة على النبي صلى الله عليه وسلم	١٠٠
at-tahlīl or *hailala*	لا إله الا الله	١٠٠

Al-wird al-kabīr, according to this shaikh, consists of the repetition of the *tahlīl* 70,000 times.

[2] Mirghanī congregational *dhikr* movements: 'When uttering the *dhikr* he should incline his head towards the right side while saying *lā*; and should incline it towards his chest while saying *ilāha*; and towards the heart while saying *illā'llāh*, that is, the left side, and should aspirate it from his navel up to his heart so that the glorious name Allāh will settle in the heart and burn out all

concentrating on one attribute, the pace is quickened, the ejaculations become more and more staccato and change to grating, barking, or growling. At some point the leader will call an abrupt halt, but the *munshidūn* continue singing; the recollectors (*dhākirs*) relax vacantly, in another world, and then the *dhikr* begins anew. The regulation is entirely in the hands of the presiding shaikh.[1]

The recitation of *mawlid an-nabī* is a very important aspect of many *ḥaḍra* gatherings. The celebration of the Prophet's birthday with *samā'āt* was an old Sufi, though not popular, practice, but this special form of *opera* for performance on this occasion developed late. Surprisingly, the first real *mawlid*, so far as I am aware, was composed in Turkish. The author, the first strictly Ottoman poet, was a Khalwatī, known as Sulaimān Chelebi (d. 825/1421), court chaplain to the Bāyazīd captured by Timur.[2] The poem was recited within Sufi circles, and official celebrations on the actual birthday, 12 Rabī' I, seem to have only been inaugurated in 996/1588 by Murād III.[3] There was always a great contrast between official celebrations surrounded with great pomp and those of the people filled with simple piety and popular fervour and enjoyment.

Mawlid recitations in the Arab world had taken their characteristic form in the time of as-Suyūṭī (1445–1503) and the first, Arabic *mawlid* (apart from the earlier type of memorial to the Prophet like al-Būṣīrī's *Burda* and *Hamziyya*) was *Mawlid Sharaf an-Anām* by 'Abd ar-Raḥmān Ibn ad-Daiba' az-Zabīdī (1461–1537). The popularization of these recitals is comparatively late, not becoming universal until the end of the eighteenth century, and is especially characteristic of the nineteenth-century orders with their stress upon the presence of the Prophet. Many

wicked notions. He should also accentuate the *hamza* and lengthen the *alif* (ā) moderately or a little more. The *hā* in the word *ilāh*^{a} should be followed by *fatḥa* and the *hā* in the word Allāh by *sukūn*' (Ar-Ruṭbī, *Minḥat al-aṣḥāb*, p. 87.)

[1] Qādirī practice is guided by *Sirr al-asrār wa naẓhar al-anwār* attributed to 'Abd al-Qādir and Ismā'īl b. M. Sa'īd's *Al-Fuyūḍāt ar-Rabbāniyya fī 'l-ma'āthir wa 'l-awrād al-Qādiriyya*.

[2] On Sulaimān Chelebi see E. J. W. Gibb, *A History of Ottoman Poetry* (London, 1900, i. 232–48), who translates extracts from his *mevlid*. A full translation is that of F. Lyman MacCallum, *The Mevlidi Sherif*, London, 1943. Many other Turkish poets, such as Āq Shams ad-dīn Zāde Ḥamdi, wrote *mevlids*, though none attained the popularity of that of Sulaimān Chelebi.

[3] According to D'Ohsson, *Tableau général*, ii. 358, who gives an account of the official ceremony celebrated with great pomp in the mosque of Sultan Aḥmad in the eighteenth century.

of these order-founders wrote a *mawlid*, but the first to achieve renown was that of al-Barzanjī (d. 1766). It was adopted by the older orders, the Qādirī in particular, and was a feature in their renewed popularity at the end of the eighteenth century. This has ever since been the most universally performed *mawlid*, most of the others being practised only within a particular order circle.[1] Nativity recitals of this kind never became universal in the Muslim world or even the Arabic-speaking world. In the Maghrib *mawlid* celebrations rather take the form of *qaṣīda* recitals sung in honour of the Prophet by a special class of *qaṣā'idīn*.[2]

On the occasion of the Prophet's nocturnal ascension (on the eve of 27 Rajab) and sometimes on other occasions the *mi'rāj* story is recited in place of the *mawlid*. This is the legend according to which the Prophet on the night of his miraculous flight to Jerusalem (which has for its point of departure sūra xvii. 1) on a celestial steed called Burāq, ascended through the seven heavens within 'a two-bows'-length distance' from the divine throne. The legend plays an important part in the symbolism by which Sufis describe the ascent of the soul, as, for example, in Ibn al-'Arabī's *Kitāb al-Isrā' ilā 'l-maqām al-asrā*. Some *mawlid* poems, like that of Sulaimān Chelebi, also include the *mi'rāj*. The most popular recitals are one composed by al-Barzanjī and *Qiṣṣat al-mi'rāj al-kubrā* by Najm ad-dīn al-Ghaiṭī (d. 1576),[3] with the *ḥāshiya* (marginalia) of ad-Dardīr (d. 1786).[4]

The *mawlid* follows a standard form. After introductory praises to God and an invocation, the poem begins with a description

[1] For example, *Simṭ ad-durar* (String of Pearls) generally known as *Mawlid al-Ḥabshī* after its author 'Alī ibn M. al-Ḥabshī of the 'Alawī (Ḥaḍramī) *ṭariqa*. The Tijānī founder did not compose a *mawlid*, so naturally in such a self-centred *ṭariqa* his followers do not recite one. However, they have an equivalent in that they hold that the Prophet comes (provided the ritual has been properly observed) during the seventh reading of *Jawharat al-kamāl*; see M. 'Alwān al-Jawsqī, *As-Sirr al-abhar*, p. 3, quoted above, p. 191. M. ibn al-Mukhtār (Wad al-'Āliya, d. 1882), who introduced the Tijāniyya into the Egyptian Sudan (see my *Islam in the Sudan*, pp. 237–8), did in fact write a *Mawlid Insān al-Kāmil* which has been published, but I do not know if it is recited.

[2] See E. Dermenghan, *Le Culte des saints dans l'Islam maghrébin*, Paris, 1954, p. 186. Mālikī doctors condemned the celebration of the festival (cf. Ibn al-Ḥājj, *Al-Madkhal*, 1320, i. 153 ff.), but that would have made no difference had it really caught on with the people.

[3] See Ibn al-'Imād, *Shadharāt adh-dhahab* (Cairo, A.H. 1351), viii. 406–7.

[4] Authors of *Mi'rāj* poems in Turkish include Ghanī Zāde Nādirī, Nāyī 'Uthmān Dede, and Naḥīfī.

of an-Nūr al-Muḥammadī, the eternal principle of creation and prophetical succession, in which the Light manifested itself from Adam, through the Prophets, to the birth of Muḥammad. The point in the recital when the Prophet descends is the most solemn part of the recital. At the words 'Our Prophet was born' (*wulida nabiyyunā*) or equivalent phrase,[1] all stand to welcome him with the words, *Marḥaban, yā Muṣṭafā* (Hail to thee, thou Chosen One), or *Yā Nabī sallim ʿalaik* (O Prophet, God's blessings be on thee). The poem then goes on to trace certain aspects of the Prophet's life, with the stress on the miraculous and his virtues (*manāqib*). The songs which are interspersed between the various sections follow a liturgical pattern, invocation and response. An account of the *lailiyya* of the Mirghanī order will show the pattern.[2]

The *lailiyya* begins with a procession (*zaffa*) from the *khalīfa*'s house, where the company have assembled, to the house where the *mawlid* is to be held. Green flags are carried on special occasions. During the procession the *munshids* chant the following *shaṭḥ* (the author claims to be the Logos *Quṭb*) by Jaʿfar ibn Muḥammad ʿUthmān al-Mirghanī, which they call the *safīna* (ship):

> By the power of my design did I quaff the cup of knowledge;
> By the welcome of every gift was I called.
> My Beloved refreshed me with a draught of knowledge;
> You see, my friend, my judgement is above all creatures,
> I am a pillar of the universe—a gift from my Lord.
> I am the treasure of lights in the midst of creation;
> I am the chosen of the chosen, above the heavens;
> I am the door, my authority is over east and west.
> I am the flash of light above creation;
> I am the first who existed.[3]

[1] In Sulaimān Chelebi's *mevlid* the solemn moment occurs at this point in Amīna's recital:

> 'Came a White Bird borne upon his wings straightway,
> And with virtue stroked my back as there I lay.
> Then was born the Sultan of the Faith that stound,
> Earth and heaven shone in radious glory drowned.

Translated by E. J. W. Gibb (op. cit. i. 246), who remarks, 'It is when this couplet has been reached at the Mevlid meetings that the sherbet and sweets are brought in and handed round; these are presented first to the chanter, then to the assembled guests.'

[2] This is adapted from the writer's *Islam in the Sudan*, pp. 215–16.

[3] The few lines quoted above are taken from the version given at the end of Jaʿfar b. M. ʿUthmān al-Mirghanī's *Quṣṣat al-Miʿrāj*, Cairo, A.H. 1348, pp. 123–4.

Upon arrival at the compound the performers squat in a circle with a lamp, an incense burner, and all their footwear in the centre. At one side are the four *munshids*. First, the *khalīfa* calls for 'Al-Fātiḥa', and all recite it in concert. Then they chant the *tahlīl* a hundred times and the *munshids* sing a *madḥa* called *al-munbahya*, in which the help of God is sought.

The second stage is the chanting of the *Mawlid an-Nabī* composed by the founder of the *ṭarīqa*. This is divided into fourteen chapters called *alwāḥ* (sing. *lawḥ*, 'tablet'). It opens with a chapter on the uniqueness of Islam, followed by an account of the founder's dream in which he saw the Prophet, of how God created that luminous substance, the Light of the Prophet, first of all before Adam, of his physical birth and an account of his ancestry, the story of the angels removing his heart and cleansing it, the *mi'rāj* story, the prophetic call, and a description of his physical appearance and character.

The *khalīfa* chants the first chapter and afterwards he indicates those of the company whom he wishes to continue. Many, though illiterate, know some section by heart. The *khalīfa* also reads the chapter on the Prophet's birth and when he gets to the words, 'he was born . . .', all rise and chant a *madḥa*. When this *lawḥ* is completed a hymn of welcome to the Prophet (*taḥiyyatu qudūmihi*) is chanted while still standing; all the rest is done sitting. After the chapter on the *mi'rāj* a special *qaṣīda* is sung of which the first hemistich of each verse is by Ibn al-'Arabī and the second by M. Sirr al-Khatm (d. 1915). The *mawlid* lasts about two hours.

There now follows an interlude during which the *munshids* chant *qaṣīdas* in honour of the Prophet and the company is refreshed with tea or coffee. The final stage is the *dhikr*. Here the real attempt to produce effects begins. It commences very slowly, the *dhākirīn* standing in a circle, with the *tahlīl* formula, accompanied by rhythmical bowing of the head and body, first to the right then to the left, the hands hanging loosely. Then the measure is quickened, more stress being laid upon the last syllable, and the movements change to backward–forward jerking. With each change the voice is made more raucous until, at the final stage of jumping up and down, the words have degenerated to a pectoral barking noise or that of a rough saw. Such a section of one formula is called a *ḍarb*, and is followed by others, each new word or formula constitutes a new time for the *dhikr*. A *qaṣīda* is usually sung between each *ḍarb*, but the singing is going on throughout the whole *dhikr*, the *munshids* and frequently the *khalīfa* walking round and round within and without the circle to excite the performers, sometimes crying out '*madad, madad, yā* Mirghanī'. The *dhikr* is closed with the *ḥizb* called the Prayer of the Khatmiyya *Ṭarīqa*, a prayer for mankind (*du'ā' li 'l-insān*), and the Fātiḥa. After that they all relax and the names of persons for whom prayer is requested are mentioned when they say the Fātiḥa, and finally the food is brought in. No attempt is made in this *ṭarīqa* to produce any ecstatic phenomena.

These *mawlid* recitals are confined to Sunnī communities for among Shī'īs the Passion Plays had the effect of inhibiting the need for indulgence in the collective *dhikr*, since they offered the outlet which the *dhikr* and the *mawlids* provided in Sunnī communities. In the sphere of mediumship the *rābiṭa* and *tawajjuh* which will be described shortly helped to bridge the gap between Sunnīs and Shī'īs with their belief in the relationship to the supernatural through 'Alī and the Imām of the Age.

As-Sanūsī describes[1] the chief methods of the Naqshabandiyya as *adh-dhikr al-khafī, adh-dhikr al-khafī bi 'l-jalāla, ar-rābiṭa bi 'sh-shaikh*, two techniques of *murāqaba*, and *tawajjuh*. The last three are techniques which have so far been only briefly referred to. They are all based on concentration. The difficulty is that the three terms do not mean the same thing at different periods and in different orders.[2] There are two main eastern types: that whereby the devotee concentrates his whole being upon the spirit of the saint or of his present director with the aim of achieving communion or even union with him, and possession by the spirit of the saint or shaikh.

Murāqaba, spiritual communion, is to be distinguished from the *rābiṭa* method. The word 'contemplation' may translate the method (to gaze upon as upon a picture) but not the process. What is being attempted is to unveil the mystery of life (*sirr* = μυστήριον

[1] As-Sanūsī, *Salsabil*, pp. 116–17.

[2] Vambéry refers to a Naqshabandī form of *tawajjuh* in common: 'How often was I forced to witness one of the khálka [*ḥalqa*] (circle) which devotees form by squatting down close to each other in a ring, to devote themselves to tevedjüh [*tawajjuh*] (contemplation), or as the Western Mohammedans call it, the murakebe [*murāqaba*] of the greatness of God, the glory of the Prophet, and the futility of our mortal existence!' (A. Vambéry, *Travels in Central Asia*, New York, 1865, p. 222).

rather than 'secret') by losing oneself in it.[1] The Sufi used the method of picturing the Prophet or a saint or his *murshid*, the last tending to become the commonest. In addition, there are other forms of *murāqaba* as on a verse of the Qur'ān.

The normal relationship of novice and director has often been described as spiritual sonship (*al-wilādat al-ma'nawiyya*), but the relationship described by these terms is entirely different. *Murāqaba* is a technique, participation in that which is being contemplated. One method seeks to attain 'union' with the shaikh as Jalāl ad-dīn Rūmī was mystically one with Shams ad-dīn at-Tabrīzī and after his death with Ḥusām ad-dīn. When the shaikh was dead it was frequently done at the tomb. The Sufi, of course, does not suppose that the spirit of the saint is in the tomb but finds this course an aid to contemplation.[2]

The term *rābiṭa* does not in itself express the true aim of the process; even to translate it 'the Bond or Link' with the shaikh is quite inadequate. As-Sanūsī writes:

This is hardly practicable except to one whose soul is so refined by nature (*or* in whom the tendency is innate). In order to attain this he must visualize interiorly the image of his shaikh. He imagines his image as though on his right shoulder. Then picturing from the right shoulder to his heart a line which can act as a passage whereby the spirit of the shaikh can take possession of that organ. This process maintained

[1] These methods have relationship with the platonic regard (*'udhrī*-love), 'the contemplation of adolescents' (*naẓar ilā 'l-murd*) or a beautiful face or form (*al-wajh al-ḥasan*) of an earlier age of Sufism. The aim was to attain perceptivity (*wujūd*) through absorption in beauty, perceiving the reality within phenomena. A notable exponent of this method was Aḥmad al-Ghazālī, about whom Ibn al-Jawzī tells the following anecdote: 'A group of Sufis went to see Aḥmad al-Ghazālī and found him alone with a young boy with flowers in between them, and he was gazing at the flowers then at the boy alternately. When they had seated themselves one of them said, "Maybe we have disturbed you?" and he replied, "You certainly have!" And the company argued with one another concerning the method employed to induce ecstasy (*tawājud*)' (*Talbīs Iblīs*, Cairo, 1928, p. 267). The coming of the Sufis had broken Aḥmad's contemplation. Sufis found or invented a *ḥadīth* upon which to hang this practice, 'I saw my Lord in the form of a youth (*amrad*)', but there were obvious dangers, there were many scandals, and masters permitted the practice only to the most advanced adepts. In the third stage it was prohibited altogether in the Arab world, the occasional reference, as in 'Abd al-Ghanī an-Nabulsī's works, does not mean anything. On the subject see *Ar-Risālat al-Qushairiyya*, Cairo, 1319, p. 184; and the whole section on *ṣuḥbat al-aḥdāth*, in *Talbīs Iblīs*, pp. 264–77.

[2] The reformist Muslim has completely misunderstood this, as so many other Sufi practices, through equating it with popular deformations.

continuously will ensure his attaining absorption in the shaikh (*al-fanā' fī 'sh-shaikh*).[1]

Elsewhere as-Sanūsī shows that *rābiṭa* is a general custom in eastern orders, and refers to this form of meditation as a guard against random thoughts: 'He has an additional support who props himself on "the bond with the shaikh", that is, conjuring up the image of the shaikh in a vision, seeking protection in him from the attacks of the wild beasts of the valleys of destruction.'[2] We read in a Qādirī book:

Ar-Rābiṭa is superior to the *dhikr*. It involves keeping to the forefront of one's mind a mental image of the shaikh.[3] This for the *murīd* is more beneficial and suitable than the *dhikr* because the shaikh is the medium (*wāsiṭa*) by which the *murīd* attains the supreme Reality. The more the strands connecting him with the shaikh increase the more do the emanations[4] from his inner being increase, and he soon attains his goal. The *murīd* must, therefore, first lose himself (*yufnā*) in the shaikh and then he may attain *fanā'* in God.[5]

Tawajjuh, a formation from *wajh* (face), and meaning 'facing', 'confrontation', is employed in relation to the act of facing the *qibla* during ritual prayer. The word was frequently used by Sufis in relation to God,[6] but with the development of the system of direction the *qibla* became the *murshid* who was the gateway to God, and there are injunctions in the manuals: 'Make thy shaikh thy *qibla*.' There was also *tawajjuh* to the Prophet. As a Sufi technique it is a development of the third stage, for it is not described in the earlier manuals.[7] Even then it is a relatively rare technique in the Arab world and so many references are vague, as in the following by 'Alī ibn Muḥammad Wafā': '*Murāqaba* means concentrating your whole being upon the face of your Beloved (*Maḥbūb*), whilst *tawajjuh* involves the worshipper in

[1] As-Sanūsī, *Salsabīl*, p. 117.

[2] Ibid., p. 48. Yet in his account of the Junaidiyya (a late order no doubt deriving from a vision of al-Junaid) he distinguishes ordinary visualization of the shaikh (p. 56) as part of the normal *khalwa* exercises from *rabṭ al-qalb bi 'sh-shaikh* (p. 57).

[3] *Taṣawwur ash-shaikh* (visualization [adoration] of the guide), in other orders.

[4] *Fuyūḍāt*, here translated 'emanations': *faiḍ* = '(divine) grace'.

[5] Ismā'īl ibn M. Sa'īd, *Al-Fuyūḍāt ar-Rabbāniyya*, p. 26.

[6] The Qur'ānic basis is Abraham's assertion, 'I have turned my face towards Him who created the heavens and the earth' (vi. 79).

[7] See above, pp. 58, 148.

so readying the mirror of his heart in unclouded purity that his Beloved is reflected in it.'[1] The term is more common in relation to concentration upon a Qur'ānic word, for example, the Shādhilī manual *al-Mafākhir al-ʿaliyya* has a 'Section concerning confrontation with the phrase "no god but God" '.[2]

An account of 'initiation by *tawajjuh*' according to seventeenth-century Hindu Sufism is given by Tawakkul Beg,[3] a layman who passed two sessions in the *khānaqāh* of the Qādirī, Mullā Shāh Badakhshī (d. 1661), but was eventually dismissed as a serious student. 'Your vocation', Mullā Shāh told him, 'is that of arms.' The method he describes involves no training (he spent much of his time making a collection of the shaikh's poems), but was a process in which the subject is worked upon with the aim of inducing temporary ecstatic phenomena, such as visions of 'lights ineffable'. But spiritual 'awareness' is not something that can be attained overnight by such methods (nor through so many 'instant' types of *dhikr*), but by the costly way of training and discipline.

Certain terms associated with the cult should be defined more clearly. Apart from *dhikr*, which has already been studied, the, word *wird* is most important. It is difficult to define on its own, but when used in the context of ritual there is usually no difficulty. The three main usages are: (*a*) the *ṭarīqa*, (*b*) a special prayer or litany, and (*c*) the 'office' of the *ṭarīqa*.

As we have seen[4] *wird* may mean the *ṭarīqa*, the spiritual Path the order exists to maintain, so 'to take the *wird* of Shaikh Abu 'l-Ḥasan' is to be initiated into the Shādhilī *ṭarīqa*. The *wird* is the substance of the *ṭarīqa* defined in one or more prayers or cycles of prayers.

Wird (access) was at first used in relation to the particular times which the Sufi devoted to God (cf. the 'Hours') and so came to designate the particular *dhikr* or *ḥizb* which he recited on these occasions. Such a *wird* has no precise form but is compounded of

[1] Shaʿrānī, *Ṭabaqāt*, ii. 37.
[2] Aḥmad ibn ʿAbbād, *Mafākhir*, Cairo, A.H. 1327, pp. 137–8.
[3] The translation by A. de Kremer, 'Mollâ-Shâh et le spiritualisme oriental', *J. Asiat.* VI *sér.* xiii. 105–59, has become well known since it has been frequently quoted in part; see T. P. Hughes, *Dictionary of Islam*, London, 1885, pp. 121–2, E. Sell, *The Faith of Islam*, Madras, 1920, pp. 167–70; D. B. Macdonald, *Religious Life and Attitude in Islam*, Chicago, 1909, pp. 197 ff. It should not be assumed that this method was a common practice like *dhikr*.
[4] See above, p. 184.

adhkār (remembrance formulae) and *aḥzāb* (sing. *ḥizb*), prayers in which the essential elements are interspersed sections and phrases from the Qur'ān, and the ninety-nine divine names, especially those with significance in the order. Each *ṭarīqa* and each order-derivative has its own *awrād* composed by its leaders. These form the 'theme' of the order. The prayer-manuals are full of *aḥzāb* for particular times of the day or year or for special occasions.

It is open to any believer to make use of these *awrād*, but in addition there is the personal *wird*, whose cumulation marks the *murīd*'s full initiation. At the beginning of his novitiate the novice is allocated his first secret *wird*. This is the custom of *talqīn* (to teach by word of mouth), and, as we have seen, the ceremony was also called 'taking the wird' (*akhdh al-wird*). As he progressed in the Path his guide gave him permission to recite additional, longer, and more exacting *awrād*.

We have shown that mystery is attached to the recital of the *Wird* proper, the succession of *aḥzāb* which have been described, but we should make clear that when *awrād*, plural of *wird*, is used it usually means much the same as *aḥzāb* for such prayer-sections, complete in themselves, but partial in reference to the *Wird* proper of the order. When the *murīd* is initiated he is allotted initially only one of these litany 'tasks', whose blessing he seeks to infuse throughout his whole being through repetition; and then, as he progresses, he is assigned more difficult and significant tasks, until at last he has been given the complete *Wird* as a full initiate. The instructions which Muḥammad ibn 'Alī as-Sanūsī gives in the following extract are followed by most shaikhs:

When the adept is an ordinary man he should be but gradually initiated in the precepts; thus only easy prayers should be laid upon him until his soul is gradually fortified and strengthened. Then instruction should be increased by the addition of invocations on the Prophet . . .When the results produced by the practice of the *dhikr* and by profound faith have wiped out the impurities of the soul, when with the eyes of the heart one sees nothing in this world and the next except the Only Being, then one can begin the full prayer.[1]

Ḥizb in some orders (especially in Egypt) embraces the same usages as *wird*: a form of prayer drawn up by the founder or a successor to be recited at set times, hence it is also used of the

[1] Quoted from L. Rinn, *Marabouts et Khouan*, Algiers, 1884, pp. 89–90.

office of the order recited at the communal *ḥaḍra* in which the prayer is used, and consequently is sometimes applied to the fraternity itself.

Apart from these usages associated with orders the prayer-manuals are full of *aḥzāb* and *awrād* which any Muslim may learn for his personal use. Order-heads disapproved of their *murīds* doing this without authority because they were following a course, but did not object to their general use. Some *aḥzāb* became particularly famous like ash-Shādhilī's *Ḥizb al-Baḥr* (Incantation of the Sea), said to have been communicated to him by the Prophet himself.[1] Such a *ḥizb* is no simple prayer (it is not very profound devotionally); it is rather a magical incantation which, the author affirmed, contained the Greatest Name (*Ism Allāh al-Aʿẓam*) and, if recited rightly, gets moving currents of grace and ensures supernatural response.

Still another word, though with stricter application, is *rātib* (pl. *rawātib*), which means something fixed, and therefore the fixed office of a *ṭarīqa*. It was frequently applied to certain non-obligatory *ṣalāts* or litanies. The *rātib* of ʿAbdallāh ibn ʿAlawī al-Ḥaddād (d. 1720), founder of the Ḥaddādiyya (–ʿAlawiyya–ʿAidarūsiyya), is famous and widely recited in Hijaz, Hadramawt, and the east African coast. In certain orders (Shādhilī and Tijānī) *waẓīfa* is the term used for the office of the order, and also it may signify a litany assignment.

Most orders have one special prayer of power, generally recited during the first part of the congregational *dhikr*. With the ʿĪsāwiyya it is *Subḥān ad-Dā'im* (Praise to the Eternal),[2] an amplification of a *ḥizb* bearing the same title composed by al-Jazūlī, with additions by as-Suhailī and Aḥmad ibn ʿUmar al-Ḥārithī, pupil of al-Jazūlī and master of Ibn ʿĪsā. This must be recited daily by the adept after the morning (*Ṣubḥ*) prayer and forms a regular part of the congregational *ḥaḍra*. Whereas this is long, the Qādirī

[1] *Ḥizb al-Baḥr* is found in all collections. It is quoted by Ibn Baṭṭūṭa (i. 40), and an abridged translation is given by Richard Burton in his *Pilgrimage*, chap. 11. It contains many Qur'ānic quotations or reminiscent phrases, and quotes repeatedly the mysterious letters at the beginning of certain *sūras*. This has given it magical qualities and ensured its popularity. On the powers ascribed to its recitation see Ḥājjī Khalīfa, iii. 58.

[2] Translated by É. Dermenghem, *Le Culte des saints dans l'Islam maghrébin*, Paris, 1954, pp. 305–11. Partial translations will be found in L. Rinn, *Marabouts et Khouan*, pp. 311 ff. and R. Brunel, *Essai sur la confrérie religieuse des ʿAïssaoua au Maroc*, Paris, 1926, pp. 73–5.

equivalent, *al-Qunūt*, entirely composed of Qur'ānic phrases, is very short. Similar prayers of power are *Wird as-Sattār* with Khalwatīs, *Awrād al-fatḥiyya* of the Hamadāniyya,[1] *Jawharat al-kamāl* of the Tijāniyya, *Unmūdhaj* of the Kittāniyya, *Ṣalāt Mashīshiyya* of the Darqawiyya, and *ad-Dimyāṭiyya* (poem of the Ninety-nine Names of Perfection, *al-Asmā' al-ḥusnā*) of the Hanṣaliyya.

[1] Sanūsī, *Salsabīl*, p. 107.

VIII

Role of the Orders in the Life of Islamic Society

So important were the orders in traditional society that an attempt should be made to bring out aspects of their social and religious significance during stage three, until the present-century process of secularization brought about their rapid decline. This brief excursion into the field of religious sociology is confined in the main to Arabic-speaking peoples, since these are the only peoples of whom the writer has had the personal experience that is necessary if one is to gauge the significance of religious institutions upon society in the past, since it is expressed in the outlook and attitudes of the shaikhs and adherents of the orders as they survive today.

The Islamic world was by no means homogeneous, but it was culturally unified and diversified at the same time. Within the culture were different civilizations (distinguishing 'civilization' as the outward and material form of culture): the civilization of the nomads of desert and steppe, the people of the river valleys whose cultivation was based on irrigation; rainland regions, mountain ranges and their valleys, and the many-faceted life of cities. These differences moulded in many ways the expression of Islam in these societies. Islamic legalistic culture received its fullest expression within town and city, and was found at its weakest among nomads, whether Arab, Berber, or Turkish. And similarly with the religious orders; their popularity and the hold they exercised varied in different environments.

The Islamic world also embraced many different regional cultures. Regional diversity derives from both internal and external factors of differentiation: geographical and ethnic factors and the pre-Islamic religio-social substratum, and external influences, the nature and differences in the historical penetration of Islam. It will be obvious that Iranian Islamic culture differed profoundly from that of Negro Islam.[1] Iran had behind it millennia of advanced culture, and Iranians, receiving the impact of primitive Arab Islam, contributed significantly towards the formation of Islamic culture proper. On the other hand, Islam came to Negro Africa fully developed and was a strong factor in unifying culture.

One thing should be made quite clear, that although the regional differences are distinctive, the dynamic tension between Islam and the regional culture found expression in a remarkable unity of culture. These various culture areas had a common Islamic heritage. Islamic institutions spanned their various strata, both the horizontal and the vertical; the key institution being the *sharīʿa*, the ideal Law which constituted the binding force of the community. The Sufi heritage in none of its aspects, including the institutional, ever truly amalgamated with the *sharīʿa*-bound structure, yet such was its fusion with popular religion in its expression through the orders that it spread almost everywhere. The link with the saint-cult was most important since spirit-veneration became a universal aspect of Islamic expression (Negro Africa is the main exception), although relationship to the orders was not so universal.

The response of regional groups to Sufism in its different manifestations varied considerably, but no summary would be sound, since few local investigations have been carried out, and, given the differences within each Islamic sub-culture, no generalization would suffice. It would be easy to contrast an Iranian world as primarily manifesting an intellectual and poetical response to Sufism with an Arab world whose reaction has been anti-intellectual and conformist. But the reaction of the peoples of the Indian subcontinent could offer no one the opportunity for precise definition, since their heterogeneous range covers every variety of Sufi expression in a way inconceivable elsewhere. Sufism could take root in India, since in a sense it was already there, whereas the Semitic legalistic mentality remained alien to the Hindu ethos. Then again we might depict a Negro Africa as offering virtually no response to the mystical Way, either intellectually or emotionally, adopting form without content and spirit. But this last type of response was certainly not confined to Negro

[1] I distinguish two broad responses of Africans to Islam, the Hamitic and the Negro, in my *Influence of Islam upon Africa*, London–Beirut, 1968.

Africa; and similarly with other responses we might attempt to regionalize.

Furthermore, these cultural differences in response and adaptation exist within the Arabic-speaking world with which this chapter is primarily concerned: the Maghribi and Egyptian Islamic regional cultures, for example, are anything but uniform. These differences condition the responses of the various peoples and occupational groups to Sufism. The same *ṭarīqa* could take on quite different forms in different countries in both doctrines and rites. There is a great difference between the Qādiriyya in the Maghrib and in India. The thought of Indian Qādirīs like Mīyān Mīr is inconceivable to the Moroccan, let alone the discipline of Yoga practices. Similarly, the Moroccans in their turn had their own distinctive practices.

The most, therefore, that will be attempted here without the benefit of regional surveys is to give a series of piecemeal references to the men of the orders in a sociological context in relation to Arabic-speaking peoples, though there are aspects relating to other regions which need presenting even in such a context.

1. *Ash-Shaʿrānī: An Egyptian Shaikh aṭ-Ṭarīqa.* In view of the fact that most books describing Sufism are concerned with Sufi thought, especially theoretical and poetical, during stages one and two, when Sufism had not become a universal aspect of Islamic society, it seems well to stress that this chapter is concerned with Sufism as stabilized in stage three, when the men of the *sharīʿa* in the Arab world had subjected it to their own standards. At the same time, Sufistic expression had allied with popular religion in such a way that it influenced the lives of many ordinary Muslims.

We have ascribed the weakening of the mystical expression in Islam to its diversion in the direction of devotion to saints and concentration upon collective cult 'recollection of God'. With exceptions, such as the Khalwatiyya which provided for the *zāhid*, those who wished to follow the Way did this as solitaries outside the regular Sufi institutions, in which the term *murshid* as applied to the shaikh had become meaningless. Holiness, not spirituality, was the criterion.

In saying this we are not decrying the importance of the orders and their *walīs* as a spiritual force. The orders had become special focuses of Islam, in that they combined this cult of saints with authentic Islamic sentiment and loyalty to the *sharīʿa*. To demonstrate this we will sketch the outlook and way of life of the Egyptian, ʿAbd al-Wahhāb ibn Aḥmad ash-Shaʿrānī (897/1492–973/1565), as a relatively sympathetic figure to typify this stage for Egyptian Sufism in general and of the conformist tendency everywhere, including India which had its orthodox trend, even though Indian Sufism in its comprehensiveness was syncretistic and eclectic.

Ash-Shaʿrānī reveals something of himself in his *Laṭāʾif al-minan*. This is not a true spiritual autobiography but a kind of personal *manāqib* book, a listing of the virtues and spiritual gifts with which he had been endowed, each example accompanied by parallels drawn from the experiences of Sufis of all ages. In other words, he writes his own hagiography, but this is by no means as distasteful as it may seem, for he is disarmingly naïve, he makes no claims for himself, his virtues are examples of the overflowings of God's grace (*al-fuyūḍāt ar-Rabbāniyya*).[1]

Ash-Shaʿrānī was trained within the Shādhilī tradition. He submitted to a true spiritual director, ʿAlī al-Khawwāṣ (d. 1532), an illuminated illiterate,[2] but in relation to whom Shaʿrānī calls himself the *ummī* (untrained) and ʿAlī the *ʿālim* (master). After describing his course in the way of *mujāhada* (purification) he writes:

My introduction [to gifted knowledge][3] took place on the banks of the Nile beside the houses of the Nubians and the sail-driven waterwheels. Whilst I was standing there, behold the gates of divine wisdom[4] opened upon my heart, each gate wider than the distance between the heavens and the earth. I began babbling about the mysteries of the Qur'ān and Ḥadīth, and of deriving from them the principles behind

[1] Other autobiographical material is found in his accounts of his masters in his *Ṭabaqāt*, in *al-Baḥr al-mawrūd*, *Kashf al-ghumma ʿan jamīʿ al-umma*, and other works. My bibliography on ash-Shaʿrānī is too extensive to be given here, but two studies in Arabic may be mentioned: Tawfīq aṭ-Ṭawīl, *Ash-Shaʿrānī imām at-taṣawwuf fī ʿaṣrihi*, Cairo, 1945, and Ṭāhā ʿAbd al-Bāqī Surūr, *At-Taṣawwuf al-Islāmī wa 'l-Imām ash-Shaʿrānī*, Cairo, 1953.

[2] The term *ummī* frequently means untrained in the Islamic sciences, but Shaʿrānī says explicitly that ʿAlī could not read or write (*Ṭabaqāt*, ii. 135; *Laṭāʾif*, ii. 86). In this respect ʿAlī recalls directors like al-Bisṭāmī and al-Kharaqānī. Shaʿrānī's long notice on ʿAlī al-Khawwāṣ in his Sufi lives (*Ṭabaqāt*, ii. 135–53) is composed mainly of his sayings.

[3] *Al-ʿulūm al-wahabiyya* as opposed to *al-ʿulūm al-kasbiyya*, 'acquired knowledge'.

[4] *Al-ʿulūm al-ladunniyya*, knowledge direct from God.

the various Islamic sciences to such a point that I believed myself able to dispense with study of the works of the scholars of the past. I filled some hundred quires with these matters. But when I showed them to my master ʿAlī al-Khawwāṣ he told me to get rid of the lot. 'This knowledge', he declared, 'is contaminated with speculative matter and human acquisitions. Gifted knowledge (*ʿulūm al-wahb*) is far removed from the likeness of such.' So I destroyed them and he set me on a course for purifying the heart (*taṣfiyat al-qalb*) from the blemishes of speculation. He said, 'Between you and unblemished gratuitous knowledge are a thousand stages.' I began to submit to him every inspiration that came to me and he would tell me to avoid such a course or to seek what is higher. So it went on until there came to be what came to be. This is the description of my enlightenment after undergoing the previously-mentioned discipline of *mujāhada.*[1]

Subsequently he describes the way by which he came to know the mysteries of the Sharīʿa.

Ash-Shaʿrānī had a wide knowledge, even some originality, if little critical faculty. He was a prolific compiler of treatises which won great popularity and influence in order circles and have maintained them until the present day. He commends the 'primitive' Way of al-Junaid 'because it fulfils the requirements of the Law'; in fact, because it is accepted. He took a middle course and combined to his own satisfaction *fiqh* with *taṣawwuf*, but was by no means legalistically rigid, witness his attempt to unify the four legal schools,[2] which naturally infuriated the *ʿulamā*'. He displayed considerable courage in his fight for what he thought to be right, not hesitating to criticize jurisconsults (*fuqahā*') and Sufis (*fuqarā*') alike, and naturally incurred the enmity of extremists on both sides.[3] He criticized the obtuseness of the *ʿulamā*' to the spirit of the Law. He likens them to donkeys carrying books they could not comprehend, aptly quoting the Qur'ānic verse: 'The likeness of those who are burdened with the

[1] *Laṭā'if al-minan*, Cairo, 1357, i. 52–3. Two earlier masters on the way of *mujāhada* had been Nūr ad-dīn ʿAlī al-Marṣafī (d. 933/1527, *Ṭabaqāt*, ii. 116–17), and Muḥammad ash-Shinnāwī (d. 932, *Ṭabaqāt*, ii. 120–1).

[2] *Al-Mīzān al-kubrā ash-Shaʿrāniyya* (Cairo, A.H. 1321), which he summarized in *al-Mīzān al-Khiḍriyya* (on the margin of Ṣadr ad-dīn M. b. ʿAR, *Raḥmat al-umma fī 'khtilāf al-a'imma*, Cairo, 1304), and see Perron, 'Balance de la loi musulmane ou esprit de la législation islamique et divergences de ses quatre rites jurisprudentiels par le Cheikh El-Charani', *Revue Africaine*, xiv (1870), 209–52, 331–48.

[3] For his own account of the campaign of the Azharites against him see *Laṭā'if*, ii. 190 ff.

Mosaic Law but would not bear it is that of a donkey loaded with books' (lxii. 5). On the other hand, he expressed opinions concerning corruption within the orders, mentioning especially the Badawiyya, Rifāʿiyya, Bisṭāmiyya, Adhamiyya, Masallamiyya, and Dasūqiyya as contravening the Sharīʿa. Consequently he incurred the penalty of one who takes a middle course. The Khalwatī chief, Muḥammad Karīm (1491–1578),[1] did not regard him as a Sufi at all, whilst Shaʿrānī regarded Muḥammad Karīm as a lax Muslim, legalistically speaking.

Shaʿrānī's theology falls within the Ashʿarite sphere. His mystical thought was quite unsystematic. He had no pantheistic leanings, not even any thought of God as immanent in His creation; upholding the doctrine of 'exemption' (*tanzīh*), in the general sense of the difference (*mukhālafa*) between God and His creation, though it must be admitted that the use of these terms was imprecise and relative. Yet surprisingly he defends Ibn al-ʿArabī, claiming that what is of dubious orthodoxy in his works had been interpolated by others. 'I epitomized *al-Futūḥāt al-Makkiyya*', he writes, 'expurgating from it all that was inconsistent with the letter of the Sharīʿa'.[2]

Shaʿrānī's *zāwiya*, built for him by Qāḍī Muḥyiddīn ʿAbd al-Qādir al-Ūzbeki, was situated in the midst of the teeming life of Cairo. It comprised a mosque, a *madrasa* for *ṭullāb* (law students, at one time there were some 200, of whom twenty-nine were blind), a retreat-centre for Sufis, with a hostel for migrants, and rooms for himself, his wives, and relatives. This was his *ṭā'ifa* and there were no branches. It was no centre for asceticism (and should be balanced by description of a Khalwatī establishment) but a whole Islamic institution in itself, well supported and endowed. Shaʿrānī describes as among God's graces to him the material prosperity by which he was able to support such a place, and gives details, for example, of the vast quantities of food consumed during the nights of the fast and on festivals.

Shaʿrānī clearly regards the orders and their leaders as fulfilling a vital role in Egyptian society. He drew attention to the economic and social disabilities under which the *fallāḥīn* and city

[1] On M. b. Aḥmad b. Karīm ad-dīn see *Khiṭaṭ Jadida*, iv. 109–10. He was a pupil of Shaikh Demerdāsh.

[2] *Laṭā'if al-minan*, ii. 29; see also his *al-Yawāqit wa 'l-jawāhir* (Cairo, 1321), i. 6–15.

poor lived. In this respect he criticized the detachment of the *'ulamā'* from the life of the people, their subservience to Ottoman authority after the conquest of 1517, and their self-seeking and venality. These were the men who begrudged the people their spiritual pleasures. He himself remained detached from the snare of wealth, yet one might quote the remark of Ibn al-'Imād, to illustrate the problem involved in the hereditary transmission of *baraka*, that his son 'Abd ar-Raḥmān (d. 1011/1603) succeeded to his *sajjāda* but 'devoted himself to the accumulation of riches'.[1]

His ethical Sufism and ability to hold the most incompatible views is typical of the men of the orders, for they drew upon the incomparable riches of centuries of Sufi exploration and insight, yet in regard to it they display the same mentality as *fuqahā'*, believing that exercise of the critical faculties is *kufr* or infidelity. So he can state that Reality is revealed through the successive unveilings to free the *nafs* until direct vision is attained, whilst in his development of the doctrine of *wilāya*, extremely important in his scheme of things, he shows that although *walīs* possess illumination (*ilhām* being shafts of light that illuminate the soul), this is a one-way process, and the *walī* can never reach a position when he can cease to be concerned with the requirements of revealed Law. Although a 'favourite' of God, not even a *walī* can attain nearness to God, consequently we translate *walī* as God's 'protégé' rather than 'friend', for friendship would naturally imply some degree of reciprocity in the relationship of the man and his God. The inner belief of many of these men is that communion with God is impossible, though at the same time they are using the conventional terminology of 'union' and *fanā'*. Sha'rānī is more concerned about communion with *awliyā'*, upon whom the Light has shone and from whom it is reflected upon men.

He has all the *walī* material in profusion, a hierarchy of saints, a wonder-world of visions and miracles, a spirit-world inhabited by *jinn* (who, he tells us, attended his lectures with open ears)[2] as well as the spirits of saints and their archetype, al-Khaḍir; all these intensely real in their relationship with mankind. He was an assiduous tomb-visitor, the Qarāfa must have seen him every

[1] Ibn al-'Imād, *Shadharāt adh-dhahab*, viii. 374. The longer account about 'Abd ar-Raḥmān in Muḥibbī's *Khulāṣat al-Athar* (ii. 364) confirms his neglect of his father's *zāwiya*.

[2] *Laṭā'if*, ii. 68. This privilege he shared with the Prophet, see Qur'ān, lxii. 1.

week, and he records his conversations with their inhabitants. 'If one visits a *walī* at his grave', he was asked, 'how is one to know whether he is present or absent?' 'Most *walīs*', he replied, 'are roamers, and not restricted to their graves, they come and go.' Then he gives information as to when one can find certain *walīs* at their tombs. That of Abu 'l-'Abbās al-Mursī, for instance, has to be visited on a Saturday before sunrise to be sure of finding him in residence.[1]

This controversy concerning *wilāya* has not been discussed at all fully, mainly because it belongs largely to theoretical Sufism. The *fuqahā'* in general (excluding the later Ḥanbalīs) came to recognize the possibility of the existence of God's chosen ones, though, since they were in disagreement, they never worked out any official *ijmā'* formula for canonization. Recognition of a *walī* was essentially a practical matter. It might be accorded during his lifetime or after his death. The criteria was popular experience of his thaumaturgic gifts, his clairvoyance, the efficacy of his intercession, guidance received during encounters with him in visions and dreams, and so forth. The orders virtually subsisted upon the exploitation of their own saints. *Wilāya* cannot be transferred by heredity, but the saint's *baraka* can be so transferred. The possession of *baraka* does not make a *walī* and is manifested by many people other than *walīs* and by things too. When *wilāya* is attributed, as it frequently is, to the shaikh of an order it merely means 'spiritual jurisdiction' and would be better vowelled *walāya* in order to distinguish it.

But what about the ordinary man, how does he get attached to an order?

2. *Relationship to an Order*. The main cause of a person's attachment to a *ṭā'ifa* was the family link, and what kept him there were the spiritual, social, and economic benefits derived from that relationship. The *ṭā'ifa* ministered to a religious need; that was primary: its social and other functions derived from this. In a similar, but contrary, sense the purpose of the guild was primarily occupational and economic, but had religious functions.

You were, as it were, born a Shādhilī or a Khalwatī. You were associated with the local shaikh, his initiates and affiliates from infancy when an amulet made by him was hung around your

[1] Ibid. i. 154.

neck and your mother first took you to the tomb of the *ṭā'ifa*-founder where you were offered for his blessing and intercession.[1] If your father were of any note, on the night of your naming-ceremony a *mūlid*-recital was given in your honour; and similar recitals took place at your circumcision and on special occasions such as thanksgiving after illness or safe return from a journey. You learnt to recite the Qur'ān within the precincts of the *zāwiya*. You grew up to the sound of its songs, drum rhythms, and dances, and within the atmosphere of the protection and intercessions of its saints, on the anniversary of whose death you could let yourself go in the saturnalia of the *mūlid*.

At the same time, men and families could choose their *ṭā'ifa*, and changes of allegiance took place for many reasons—in gratitude for a cure, in fulfilment of a vow, as the result of a quarrel, or in response to the rising fame of a new illuminate or a new *ṭā'ifa*. Such changes and fluctuations in popularity account for the rise and decline of *ṭā'ifas*, for these belong to the natural order as human associations, whereas the *ṭarīqa*, belonging to the spiritual order, goes on as long as derivative lines survive. The *ṭā'ifas* were dependent upon the *baraka* (virtue) of their saints (note the English phrase 'the virtue has gone out of it'), and this may fade in both the dead and the living.

Shaikhs of stage three were full members of society, living with their family, maintaining lodgings for dervishes and migrants, whether in a compound embracing a complex of buildings or a Cairene tenement, the whole household being known as a *zāwiya*. But Sufis attached to a convent, even though they had a family in town, lived a life of relative detachment from natural ties, their primary ties being with their spiritual family.

The call to the Sufi life as an individual Way, an aspiration to transcend society, was never lost. It was true that the practice of the mystical Way could lead to indifference to social morality, but the dedicated Sufis or dervishes, whether they lived in a *zāwiya* or wandered about, were not regarded by ordinary people

[1] Evliya Chelebi describes his own *'aqīqa* (eighth-day naming ceremony): 'The Sheikh of the convent of the Mevlevís at Kassempáshá, named Abdí Dedeh, took a bit of bread out of his venerable mouth, and put it in mine, saying, "May he be fostered with the morsels of the poor (fakírs)". The Sheikh of the convent of Mevlevís at the new gate, Tugháné-dedeh, took me upon his arm, threw me into the air, and catching me again, said, "May this boy be exalted in life" ' (*Narrative*, tr. von Hammer, I. ii. 16).

as rebels against society. They were felt to belong to society and to fulfil a social function. The dedicated life is incompatible with the limitations of the family, and most had little or no family life—their relationships with the extended families of their homeland and the interrelated life of the village was lost. Without kinship and social ties they moved about freely. Frequently they settled, living a hermit life, a source of benefit to the nearest village or the local graziers, and after their death their *baraka* was not lost but remained associated with the tomb as a permanent endowment.

Many were the reasons, apart from the call to the life of absolute devotion, that could lead a person to embrace the dervish life. The Sufi Way attracted people of a certain kind of temperament through the fascination of the numinous and mysterious, the call to explore unknown realms open only to those prepared to follow a dedicated life. Again, if you had an enquiring mind your easiest way of exercising it safely in an intolerant society was to assume the cloak of a dervish.[1] We have shown that initiation did not make a Sufi. Many besides Ibn Baṭṭūṭa, whom no one is likely to claim to have been a Sufi, enjoyed collecting *ijāzas*. Most Persian poets were initiated as a matter of course, but many did not follow the Way, being more interested in courts with their patrons and taverns with their wine, conversation, and music, than in *khānaqāhs* and submission to the discipline of an exacting shaikh. Their innate gifts were all that was necessary to enable them to write inspired Sufi poetry, for the mystical experience is not necessarily religious; it may be a purely aesthetic experience. Controversy over whether Ḥāfiẓ, for example, was a Sufi is not a subject for discussion in a book concerned with the phenomena of mysticism. Ḥāfiẓ wrote different types of poetry, including the mystical; through his imagery he may well open a channel to the light. We have mystics like the Arab 'Umar ibn al-Fāriḍ and the Persian Jāmī, who naturally expressed themselves through poetry, and poets like 'Aṭṭār, who were moved by mystical experiences or fancies; both types according to our criteria were Sufis. Or again, we make no distinction between the shaikh who lived a life of worldly indulgence and one who followed a rule of poverty and

[1] Should the sceptic not concern himself with subterfuges, it was done for him. So it has been claimed that 'Umar Khayyām was a Sufi. No one would have been more amused than 'Umar himself to read the latest venture of this kind, *The Original Rubaiyyat of Omar Khayyam*, by Robert Graves and Omar Ali-Shah, London, 1968.

withdrawal since moral distinctions have no relaticn to the concept of *wilāya* in any of its forms. The criterion of his society was the degree to which the shaikh was able to experience the favour of God.

In this third stage there were the seekers who followed the way of guided discipleship, perhaps in a *zāwiya*, perhaps while carrying on their normal occupation like ʿAlī al-Khawwāṣ, chief guide of ash-Shaʿrānī, who maintained no *zāwiya* and made no attempt to exploit his *baraka*, but was first a trader in oils and then, as his *laqab* shows, 'a palm-leaf plaiter'.[1] It was not necessary to withdraw from the society of men in order to live the dedicated life, though temporary withdrawal during the period of training and at intervals afterwards to carry out special exercises was an essential part of following the Way.

It is a step towards understanding to remind ourselves that the world in which the order-shaikhs and their devotees lived is incomprehensible to modern man. As Wilhelm von Humboldt has said in connection with the language problem: 'Each language draws a magic circle round the people to which it belongs, a circle from which there is no escape save by stepping out of it into another.'[2] We, however, are trapped within a circle from which there is no genuine escape. No attempt will be made in this fact-centred book even to enter into that world imaginatively, for this can be done only within the context of a study of Muslim life as a whole, but we should at least draw attention to the fact that the people about whom we are writing were living in an entirely different dimension from that likely to be experienced by readers of this book. They believed, not merely in the reality of the supernatural world, but in it as an ever-present reality. Should we hear someone say that he had found himself in the actual presence of the Prophet, who had called him to a mission, we might feel embarrassed and take him to be suffering from visual and auditory hallucinations. It is the same when we read the lives of the Sufis. Accounts of 'states', moments of epiphany, and evidences of *karāmāt* will be meaningless unless one projects oneself into their atmosphere. We have to remember that each one of us is enveloped in a world of unconscious assumptions which

[1] Shaʿrānī, *Ṭabaqāt*, ii. 136; Ibn al-ʿImād, *Shadharāt*, viii. 233–4.

[2] Quoted from E. Cassirer, *Language and Myth*, tr. S. K. Langer, New York, 1946, p. 9.

give structure and meaning to our experience, shaping our way of expressing that experience in words. We, today, living in an entirely different atmosphere from that of Sufis, falsify our historical view when we question their experience in that vision (the ultimate question is the reality of the source of that experience), the honesty of their accounts, or their mental stability. We are questioning a view of the world of which we have no experience, as well as showing our lack of historical imagination. Our view of life is just as much conditioned as theirs. But to pursue this subject would be to carry us into realms which would be incompatible with the aims of this book. We will, therefore, consider the social significance of the orders along empirical lines.

3. *Religious Role.* The social significance of the orders was many-sided but the religious significance was primary (it will be noted how we are thinking in secular terms). We have seen how their development transformed the spiritual nature of Islam between the twelfth and fourteenth centuries. The grudging recognition accorded to Sufism alongside the Islamic sciences had neutralized mystical intellectual expression in the Arab world. But it was different with practical and institutional Sufism. The *ṭawā'if*, fully blended with the saint-cult: exploiting it, in fact, represented the religion of the ordinary people, since most people's religion is realized in behaviour. Participation in their ritual ministered to the individual's need to oppose or transcend society, raising him temporarily into timeless supernatural experience. Legalistic religion, not concerned with the exercise of a pastoral office and having neither means nor agencies for emotional outlet and few for free intercession, had little to offer men's deeper needs. The legal religion fulfilled a social far more than a spiritual function, and it was the function of the orders to mediate to the ordinary man the inner aspect of Islam. In their concern for men they played in many respects a role similar to that of the local church in Europe. They embodied in themselves the whole *mysterium fascinans* of the age, revealed, esoteric, mystical, and emotional religion. Sufis were of all kinds, differing considerably in type and direction; some lived lives of sobriety, others lived in a dream world, subject to states of ecstatic intoxication; some were ascetics, living in retreat, subjecting themselves to great austerities; others savoured to the full the power they exercised over the lives and souls of men.

All this remained parallel to the orthodox institution. In their spiritual life affiliates could in fact do without the orthodox world.

At the same time, although they arose outside legalistic religion and ministered to deep-seated spiritual urges, the orders were truly Islamic. They responded to the social media in which they found themselves. In their association with formal Islam they always held open the way for illumining the inner aspect of the *sharīʿa*. The shaikhs participated with their *ikhwān* in ritual prayer before reciting their personal *dhikrs*; their *awrād* move with the force of their incorporated Qur'ānic passages; whilst *mūlids* concentrated ecstatic ritual on the Prophet. The humblest *qubba* (domed tomb), *zāwiya*, or *khalwa* served to remind the rudest villager of spiritual realities and social obligations. Sufism under this form embraced a wide range of religious experience, from the primitive nature-mysticism, spirit-raising, and power-cults of folk religion to the refined, desiccated reaches of philosophical monism. Old sacred places were Islamized as saints' tombs,[1] legends from earlier religious strata were incorporated and adapted, whilst *yoga* exercises and ritual dances were assimilated to the forms of the *dhikr*. Though the orders were not in themselves responsible for the remarkable unity of popular religion in Islamic culture they contributed greatly towards its achievement.

We have pointed out that the orders filled the place of an order of clergy lacking in official Islam. In contrast with the *'ulamā'* there were no class distinctions among Sufis. Their shaikhs, it is true, formed a hereditary religious class, but they and their associates were generally close to the people; their institutions, whether Kirghiz *khānaqāh*, Turkish *tekke*, or Maghribī *zāwiya*, in addition to keeping open house, welcoming the poor and voyagers, were providers of spiritual solace, and formed channels of power with the supernatural world. The dervish, recruited from the people and vowed to abstinence and poverty, was one of the people. In this respect both dignified shaikh and ragged dervish contrasted

[1] Certain tombs of visitation (*ziyāra, mazārāt*) in central Asia are sited on the ruins of Buddhist stupas; see M. Aurel Stein, *Innermost Asia*, 1928, ii. 866. In Kashmir both mosques and shrines are frequently built on Hindu or Buddhist sites. The great mosque and the Khānqāh-i Muʿalla of ʿAlī al-Hamadānī in Srinagar are on former Buddhist and Hindu temple sites; and W. R. Lawrence writes, 'when one sees the Musulman shrine with its shady chenars and lofty poplars and elms, a little search will discover some old Hindu *Asthan*' (*The Valley of Kashmir*, London, 1895, p. 286).

with the *'ulamā'* class, who, whatever their social origins, tended to become alienated by their legalistic training and outlook from the real spiritual and social needs of the people. In Syria it was difficult for one born in a village to progress far in the process of legal training and join the *'ulamā'* class, whilst all higher positions were reserved for privileged clerical families. Al-Murādī records[1] how a certain shaikh of Damascus was despised because of his rustic origin; *qarawī fallāḥ* they labelled him. It was much easier to join the legal élite on grounds of training and ability in Egypt than in Syria. The relationship of this class with the people was often strained by the fact that although many had links with respectable orders, they attacked the people's *ṭā'ifas* and their *mūlid* gatherings, the very means that ministered to their needs. The decline of the orders in the modern world has left a void, since the regular clerical class could not take their place.

The methods of devotion practised by the orders were a means of psychic release for the individual, placating him within the community. Their prayers and their occult and thaumaturgic techniques tranquilized mind and emotions, appeasing or curing psychological as well as bodily ills, and this contributed towards both personal integration and social stability. On the occasion of a plague of locusts in Damascus in 1747, 'the head of the Jebawi fraternity then went out with his followers with drums and standards and prayed at the shrine of Sitt Zainab east of Damascus. On coming back in the evening, they all went round the city and made a *Doseh* in front of the Seray. They prayed and invoked God to destroy the locusts.'[2] The very presence of shrines and of those whose personality has been taken by God, whether *majānīn* (possessed) or *majdhūbīn* (attracted), contributed to the welfare of the people. Jean Aubin writes in a study of two texts on the lives of two sayyids in fifteenth-century eastern Iran:

Dans l'Iran du XVe siècle, couvert de ḫānaqāhs, on vit dans un monde de rêves, de présages, de prémonitions, de symboles. En 939/1532–33 Miḥrābī, exprimant une opinion que bien d'autres partagent avec lui, écrit que la présence de déments et de simples d'esprit (maǧānīn va maǧāḏīb) est une condition de prospérité et de bonheur pour une ville, 'car la surface de leur esprit est pure et les événements qui doivent

[1] Al-Murādī, *Silk ad-durar*, Cairo, 1874–83, iii. 276.

[2] From the chronicle of Aḥmad al-Budairī, a master-barber, quoted by G. M. Haddad in *D. Isl.* xxxviii (1963), 269–70.

se produire s'y reflètent; tout ce qui vient d'eux, en parole et en acte, il faut en attendre un résultat, car ce n'est pas sans signification'.[1]

Many orders offered a religious sphere to women, little-recognized in the legal religious set-up. Women could be enrolled as associates, they could be appointed as leaders (*muqaddamāt*) to organize women's circles,[2] and some even became dervishes. But most women found their religious focus in the local *walī*, that is, the saint localized in his tomb, and visitations on Fridays and festival days were the highlights of their religious life. The dualism between male and female religion was brought out on Fridays when the men went off to the Jāmiʿ to display their communal solidarity by participation in ritual prayer, whilst the women were at the saint's tomb or graveyard making their offerings, petitionings, or communings with the spirit of the tomb.

The missionary role of the shaikhs and *faqīrs* is another aspect, both in commending Islam to non-Muslims and in helping the newly-converted to take it to their hearts. The community-free wandering dervishes were one of the agencies whereby Berbers, Indians, Greek Anatolians, Turks, Tatars, and Malays were brought within the orbit of the legal institutions of Islam.[3] Ibn Baṭṭūṭa came across some of these, like Jalāl ad-dīn at-Tabrīzī in the Kāmrūp hills of Assam, who converted many to Islam.[4] Dervishes in the Yasavī tradition constituted the most important factor in the Islamization of the nomads living to the north of the Seyhūn. In Anatolia the *bābās*, through whose agency the conquered Anatolians assimilated Islam,[5] became the great saints whose tombs embodied the spiritual aspirations of the peasantry—a bridge with their inherited underworld of religion and folklore. In India, where ideas were more important than in other missionary

[1] J. Aubin, *Deux sayyids de Bam au XVe siècle: contribution à l'histoire de l'Iran timouride*, Wiesbaden, 1956, pp. 97–8. The reference is to Miḥrābī's book on shrines in Kirman, *Mazārāt-i Kirmān*, Tehran, A.H. 1330, p. 189.

[2] For Morocco see E. Westermarck, *Ritual and Belief in Morocco*, 1926, i. 184.

[3] The *manāqib* of the saints have many accounts of conversions to Islam effected through their agency. On one occasion Jalāl ad-dīn Rūmī saved a young Greek from a lynching and he subsequently joined Islam; Aflākī, *Manāqib al-ʿārifīn*, i. 244.

[4] Ibn Baṭṭūṭa, Paris edn., iv. 216–22.

[5] O. L. Barkan, 'Les derviches colonisateures turcs de l'époque de la conquête et la zaviye', *Vakiflar Dergisi* (*Revue des Wakfs*, Ankara), ii (1942), 279–386.

areas such as Africa, they went to great lengths to accommodate both beliefs and practices to their environment. This does not imply that they consciously compromised with their conception of Islamic belief, since a pantheistic-tinged interpretation of life came as natural to them as to Hindus.

4. *The Social Role of the Orders*, though secondary to the religious, was so important that no study of Islamic society ought to ignore them. In traditional life religion was the synthesis of human activity, all society was religious society. The orders, binding together individuals under a supernatural bond, were themselves a social power. Orders came to be associated in various ways with different strata of society. They frequently had a special relationship with social classes, regions, clans, or occupational groups. Some were aristocratic, favoured by the court and *'ulamā'*, like the Suhrawardiyya in the Sultanate of Delhi in the thirteenth century and the Mawlawiyya in relation to the authorities of Seljuq and Ottoman states. Others had a popular following, as with the contrasting types of Bektāshiyya and Khalwatiyya in Turkey. They might be urban (Mawlawiyya) or rural (Bektāshiyya), or occupational (according to local circumstances like the association of fishermen in Egypt with the Qādiriyya),[1] linked with trade-guilds or the military class, like the relationship of the Janissary corps and the Bektāshiyya. Even the distinctions between orthodox and heterodox or antinomian (in India contrasted as *Ba-Shar'* and *Bī-Shar'* orders) had social significance.

Expansion of the orders depended upon the chances of individual proselytism and their appeal to particular groups. Many later orders tended to be in varying degrees regional. We have shown how, from unpromising beginnings, the Qādiriyya spread so that localized unrelated groups came to be found in most countries, yet it is the image of the *walī* 'Abd al-Qādir, not the Qādirī Way, which has really become universal. Other *ṭarīqas* were purely regional, like the Bektāshiyya confined to Anatolia and European Turkey; the Badawiyya and its branches were mainly Egyptian, the Chishtiyya was Indian, and the Khatmiyya–Mirghaniyya was confined to eastern Sudan and Eritrea. Most

[1] E. W. Lane, *The Manners and Customs of the Modern Egyptians*, Everyman edition, p. 249. This book, first published in 1836, is far the best introduction to traditional Egyptian society and the role of the orders therein.

orders were parochial or tribal; for example, in south Morocco members of the Nāṣiriyya were drawn almost wholly from the population of Wādī Darʿa, where it enjoyed a considerable historical role. Ethnic groups venerated their own saints and associated *ṭā'ifas*. Tribal groups frequently derived themselves from a saint ancestor as in the Maghrib, Nilotic Sudan, and north Somalia. There were no universal shrines as there were universal saints, the latter being commemorated by local shrines (*maqāms*). This regionalism contrasts with the Shīʿite places of pilgrimage, which are universal in their attraction of pilgrims.

The order linkage, and its ceremonial, fulfilled not merely a fraternal, but also a communal function. Each village, town-section or district, each urban craft-guild, each tribe or section, had its tomb-centre, which influenced not merely the lives of affiliated and initiated members, but all who belonged to that particular community or locality. The bond was essentially one of personal attachment to the saint-founder and living *ṭā'ifa* head, expressed on the material plane by relationship to a tomb and associated *zāwiya* or *tekke*. The men of these institutions were in close touch with the people, large numbers of whom were affiliates. They were deeply concerned and implicated in their whole life, reinforcing their sense of identity. They were organizations for mutual help, and a venerated shaikh could voice the people's grievances and condemn tyranny and oppression. They assisted the poor, and ministered to the sick and travellers. The degree to which the *tekkes* did this in Turkey can be seen from Evliya Chelebi's account of his travels. As the *baraka* of their saints protected villagers and tribesmen against harm or calamity, so the power of their protective amulets, by giving the individual confidence, helped to maintain social stability.

The orders and their *walīs*, we might say, consecrated 'secular' institutions. As we have seen they were closely associated with craft and commercial guilds, each of which was under the protection of a saint. In Fez[1] ʿAbd as-Salām ibn Mashīsh is the patron of the scribes (*ḥabīb aṭ-ṭulba*); in Egypt the dancing girls (*ʿawālim* and *ghazāwī*) were devoted to Aḥmad al-Badawī. The Bayyūmiyya in Cairo was linked with the butcher's guild, and a champion of the rights of the poor, Aḥmad Sālim al-Jazzār, towards the end of

[1] For patron saints in Morocco see E. Westermarck, *Ritual and Belief in Morocco*, London, 1926, i. 179–82.

the eighteenth century, seems to have been both guild-master and *khalīfa* of a Bayyūmī group at the same time.[1] This does not imply any identification between the two types of organization. In Ottoman Turkey, too, the orders played a considerable role in their association with these corporations, reception into the corporation involving a special relationship with the order. By virtue of his initiation the affiliate could claim the hospitality, counsel, and help of his brothers in town and country. Merchants found membership of great help when travelling by providing links with brothers in foreign parts. Ibn Baṭṭūṭa found them closely allied to Muslim commerce. At Khansā in China, he wrote, 'We put up at the settlement of the descendants of ʿUthmān ibn ʿAffān, the Egyptian. He was one of the chief merchants who found this town to his liking and settled there . . . His descendants maintained their father's concern for dervishes and relief for the needy. They had a finely-built and well-endowed *zāwiya* known as al-ʿUthmāniyya inhabited by a *ṭā'ifa* of the Ṣūfiyya.'[2] Fairs sprang up at the anniversaries (common term *mūlid*, sometimes *ḥōliyya*) of the orders which affected the whole region.[3] Their centres served as social clubs for different male age-grades. Clerical tribes in the Sahara (*zwāyā* or *ṭulba*) played a vicarious role as practising Muslims on behalf of warrior tribes.

Frequently the orders created new social groupings, new communities, holy clans and tribes. The *baraka* of the saint was exploited by his descendants. In the Maghrib tribes and clans often acquired new beginnings. Sometimes this came about through association with a *zāwiya*; sometimes when a saint was adopted as patron of a tribe it took his name as implying a religious and non-lineal descent. Some, like the Somali Isḥāq and Darūd clans, cling to a belief in an actual descent from an Arab saint—the myth in no wise detracting from the sociological significance of

[1] See al-Jabartī, *ʿAjā'ib*, Cairo edn., A.H. 1322, ii. 110, 201.

[2] Ibn Baṭṭūṭa, 1879 edn., iv. 285–6.

[3] Such fairs are called *mawāsim*, sing. *mawsim*, literally 'season' for some celebration, therefore a gathering of buyers and sellers at a fixed season.

Mujīr ad-dīn (d. 927/1521) describes *mawsims* held on the anniversaries of saints at their tomb-sites in Palestine, when *mawlids* were chanted; see for example his accounts of those of Rubīl ibn Yaʿqūb outside Ramleh and of Abu 'l-Ḥasan ʿAlī ibn ʿAlīl (d. 474/1081) overlooking the sea in the plain of Arsūf, which in Mujīr's time was under the supervision of the local (Ramleh) head of the Qādiriyya, Abu 'l-ʿAwn M. al-Ghazzī (d. 910/1504); *Uns al-Jalīl*, tr. H. Sauvaire, 1876, pp. 211–12.

such beliefs. On the other hand, there are clans actually formed from a saint-ancestor like the Āl 'Aidarūs in Hadramawt. In the Sennar state of Nilotic Sudan holy village communities came into existence through the migration and settlement of a Nubian from the north. In central Asia villages grew up around a tomb or *khānaqāh*. In Kurdistan new Kurdish clans formed or integrated around the descendants of a holy migrant.

In connection with *baraka*-exploitation the Kāzerūniyya provides a notable example. This order came into being through association with the tomb of Abu Isḥāq Ibrāhīm ibn Shahriyār (A.D. 963–1035), a pupil of Muḥammad ibn Khafīf (d. A.D. 982), who died at Kāzerūn, situated between Shiraz and the sea, around whose tomb a convent arose.[1] The order which developed, through 'Umar ibn Abī 'l-Faraj al-Kāzerūnī (d. A.D. 1304), called the Isḥāqiyya or Kāzerūniyya, cannot be regarded as a true *ṭarīqa*, since it does not seem to have been distinguished by any special teaching or method of *dhikr* recital, but rather this order is an example of the exploitation of Abu Isḥāq's *baraka* for which he is in no way responsible. His *baraka* was especially effective as a safeguard against the perils of sea-travel to India and China, whence *baraka*-selling agents were found at sea-ports such as Calicut, the famous port of Malabar, and Zaitūn in China. The order was found in Anatolia in the fourteenth century.[2] Ibn Baṭṭūṭa, who frequently came across their activities,[3] describes the whole insurance system. The intending traveller makes a vow, in fact, signing a promissory-note, stating how much he will pay the holy company if he reaches his destination safely, and more if he survives an especially hazardous situation. The association had an elaborate follow-up organization to exact the amount of the vow, and the proceeds were employed to finance the wide-spread charitable activities of the company. In the course of time the power of the *baraka* must have weakened, since the whole organization faded away in the seventeenth century.[4]

Practical Sufism was a means of social change and reintegration.

[1] On Abu Isḥāq see F. Meier (ed.), *Firdōs al-Murshidiyya: Die Vita des Scheich Abū Isḥāq al-Kāzerūnī*, Leipzig, 1948.

[2] W. Caskel in *D. Isl.* xix. 284 ff.

[3] See Ibn Baṭṭūṭa, Paris edn., ii. 64, 88–92, iii. 244–8, iv. 89, 103, 271.

[4] According to Massignon the Anatolian Isḥāqiyya was absorbed into another group, *Passion*, i. 410 ff.; Köprülüzade Mehmed Fu'ad, 'Abu Isḥāq Kāserūnī und die Isḥāqī-Derwische in Anatolien', *D. Isl.* xix (1931), 18–26.

Life was limited for the ordinary individual who was not a member of a privileged class, and the *ṭā'ifas* were a means whereby a few could cross the bounds of hereditary limitations. The son of a peasant, by attaching himself to a shaikh, could exchange the confines of village life for the vast spaces of the Islamic world, sure of finding everywhere friends and the means to live and train.

Another social aspect is to be found in their role in family life. The most binding units of society were the family (in the wider sense) and the order. Whilst the basis of the family was kinship, the bond of the *ṭā'ifa* was religious. Its members, bound by sacred obligations, formed a holy family. We have shown that complete dedication to the Way meant forsaking the family, but in the *ṭā'ifa* stage the holy family reinforced the natural family for both shaikhs and affiliates, as it consecrated other forms of co-operation such as trade guilds. The women were drawn into this, since the saints and the festal gatherings were theirs too. Visits were paid to the local sanctuary on all crucial family occasions: the mother and child on the fortieth day after child-birth, at marriages and deaths. As well as corporations the saints were patrons of towns, villages, markets, districts, and tribes. The supernatural linkages of order-heads enabled them to exercise roles in conciliation and arbitration. The mediatory role played by the Naqshabandī shaikh, al-Aḥrār, between three warring Timurid sultans witnesses to his immense influence.[1] In sixteenth-century Morocco Abu 'Abdallāh M. b. al-Mubārak resolved tribal quarrels by threats of divine chastisement.[2] The fixing of *diya* after a murder was frequently referred to the shaikhs. A recent example is that arranged by the shaikh of the *zāwiya* of Sidi-Ben-Amar (Nédroma) in Algeria in 1958: 'Dans la région des Bani Ouarsous, il a eu à connaître au cours de l'été d'une grave affaire d'homicide par imprudence et a fixé la *dia* (prix du sang). La réconciliation des deux parties a donné lieu à une imposante cérémonie.'[3] In times of troubles they provided a stable authority. They maintained the right of asylum. Al-Jabartī recounts[4] how in 1768 a Mamluk amīr,

[1] See Muḥammad Ḥaidar, *Ta'rikh-i Rashīdī*, tr. E. D. Ross, London, 1895, p. 113, cf. p. 97, and H. Beveridge, 'The Rashaḥāt-i 'Ain al-Ḥayāt', *J.R.A.S.* 1916, 59–75.

[2] Ibn 'Askar, *Dawhat an-Nāshir*, *Archiv. Maroc.* xix (1913), 194.

[3] L. P. Fauque, 'Où en est l'Islam traditionnel en Algérie?', *L'Afrique et l'Asie*, no. lv (1961), 21.

[4] Al-Jabartī, *'Ajā'ib*, Cairo edn., 1959, ii. 285, 305.

Khalīl Bey, 'took refuge at the tomb of Aḥmad al-Badawī, and they did not kill him out of respect for the saint of the sanctuary'.

5. *Cultural and Educational Role.* The importance of *taṣawwuf* in the culture of Muslim lands is well recognized. The loss to Islamic thought and poetry without Sufism can hardly be contemplated. It was the inspirer of a vast and rich tradition of poetry and music, not merely in educated and sophisticated circles in Persia or among the patrons of the Mawlawiyya in Anatolia, but in simpler spheres and in vernacular expression in Arabic, Persian, Turkish, and Urdu. The orders acted as a bridge between the intellectualism of the high mystical reaches and the poetry of popular devotion. Sufi poets created the vast store of devotional songs which fill a large part of their manuals, and which in non-Arab spheres, especially Turkish, Persian, and Urdu, were an important factor of literary development on popular levels, as with Yūnus Emré and the Bektāshīs, as well as more classical levels like the poetry of Nesīmī.

In Turkey the Mawlawī *tekkes* taught elaborate forms of music, and those of the Bektāshīs fostered both popular music and Turkish poetry. The whole vast range of Arabic and Persian poetry was open to adepts. In regions like Nilotic Sudan, too, special musical modes for singing Sufi poetry to the rhythm of the *dhikr* were evolved.

Many north African *zāwiyas* maintained Qur'ān schools, whilst a few became considerable educational establishments, incorporating *madrasas* where the regular Islamic disciplines were taught. This role of the *zāwiyas* was not confined to north Africa. In Syria, it is true, this aspect was not much in evidence, for there the power and jealousy of the *'ulamā'* was too great to allow Sufi centres much scope in this respect, but the tomb-*khānaqāhs* of central Asia were frequently multi-functional.

6. *Political Role.* The political role of the orders has made its appearance from time to time in preceding chapters. Such consequences, it is unnecessary to stress, were directly contrary to their inner spirit. The factor which enabled them to influence in this respect was the way they bound men in allegiance to a leader, as well as the hold they exercised over men's emotions, and therefore it was those orders which had the greater cohesion, local, tribal,

and nineteenth-century orders, which at times acted in the political sphere.

We find order-leaders aspiring to political power, revolting against established authority, and sometimes actually successful in founding a dynasty. Normally, shaikhs of *ṭā'ifas* were pillars of society and the established order, but *zāwiyas* and *khānaqāhs* were local hagiocracies, and it has sometimes been the fate of the leaders of these institutions to aspire to rule in this world. A *zāwiya* leader might react against established authority out of personal or factional interest or ambition, or he might be a channel for the expression of social discontent, especially where connected with a guild organization. The blind obedience accorded a shaikh assured him of a nucleus of potentially fanatical followers. The most remarkable example of such a movement was that which led to the foundation of the Ṣafawī dynasty in Persia. An unsuccessful revolt fomented by a dervish was that of Bābā Isḥāq ('Rasūl Allāh') against the Seljuq state of Qonya in 638/1240. The same movement of Turkish self-assertion led to the foundation of the dynasty of the Qaramānoghlus in Qonya, which traced its origins back to a dervish named Nūra Ṣūfi. Many examples can be given from the early Ottoman period of the political activities of order-leaders. Consequently, the Ottoman government sought to control them, especially in view of their Shī'ī sympathies (after the suppression of the Bektāshī order the Naqshabandiyya as a strongly Sunnī order benefited from official patronage). The Ottoman policy was one of respect and tolerance, provided the orders remained religio-social congregations. Outside Turkish territories control was difficult and it was easy for such movements to get going even if finally to be crushed. Ottoman authority could support the local Baghdad Qādirī order but could exercise little control over orders in the Kurdish mountains.

Apart from the dangers of order-leaders revolting against established authority, which could only be successful under special conditions, there was always the possibility of their direct intervention in affairs of the state. Consequently the political authorities, well aware of their potentialities, rooted as they were in the lives of the masses, sought to control, regulate, and conciliate them rather than to suppress. The legal recognition of orders goes back to the Ayyūbid and Seljuqid period and derives from the regulations relating to craft and trade guilds. In Egypt, contrary to Turkish and Maghribi regions, the orders' action in the political sphere was almost absent. Their legal existence was recognized and regulated under the *shaikh ash-shuyūkh* and they tacitly supported whatever authority was in power. The Ottoman government had many more problems, in view of the range of their empire and the different types of peoples under their control, but within its own sphere of direct rule it dealt with them carefully through the use of favour and playing off the more influential against each other.

Then there is the contribution which the orders have made towards the militant advance of Islam. The role of the *bābās* in inspiring *ghāzī* warriors in Anatolia is significant, and Evliya Chelebi writes of hundreds of dervishes (including even normally quietist Naqshabandīs) who took part in the final siege of Constantinople.[1]

With this is associated their role in the defence of Islam against external threats. During the Crusading period we have the action of such men as 'Abdallāh al-Yūnīnī (d. 617/1220), nicknamed Asad ash-Shām, who periodically left his *zāwiya* at Yūnīn near Baalbak, where his tomb still exists, to join in Saladin's campaigns;[2] or Aḥmad al-Badawī, an active propagandist at the time of the Crusade of Louis IX; and there was the reaction of al-Jazūlī and his followers against the Portuguese threat to the Islamic integrity of the Maghrib.

They were also used to draw upon supernatural support in wars between Muslims. When Qanṣawh al-Ghawrī inspected his army before he engaged in the battle (1516) which delivered over Syria and soon afterwards Egypt to Ottoman control for the succeeding four hundred years, he had around him dervishes grouped under their respective banners, including the heads of the Badawiyya, Qādiriyya, and Rifā'iyya.[3]

It was especially in the nineteenth century that the orders were in the forefront of Muslim reaction against the expansion of colonialist powers. This manifested itself in Russian Asia (the movement of the dervish Manṣūr in Daghistān) and especially in Africa, where among hundreds of such figures the following are the more important: the Tijānī Tokolor, al-ḥājj 'Umar, in west

[1] Evliya Chelebi, op. cit. I. i. 34.
[2] See Ibn Kathīr, *Al-Bidāya wa'n-Nihāya*, Cairo, A.H. 1358, xiii. 93–4.
[3] Ibn Iyās, *The Ottoman Conquest of Egypt*, tr. W. N. Salmon, 1921, p. 41.

Sudan, the Sammānī Muḥammad Aḥmad, the Mahdī of Nilotic Sudan, the end-of-the-century Sanūsī in Libya, the Ṣāliḥī-Idrīsī Muḥammad ibn ʿAbdallāh Ḥasan in Somalia, and the Fāḍilī-Bakkā'ī-Qādirī Mā' al-ʿAinain and his son, Aḥmad al-Hiba, in Morocco.

7. *The Relationship of the Orders with the Orthodox Institution.* The distrust of the *ʿulamā'* towards the various forms of Sufi expression is easy to comprehend. Islam, expressed in the *Sharīʿa*, is the organizing principle in the life of society, *Ummat an-Nabī*, the community of the Prophet. The *ʿulamā'* regarded the *Sharīʿa* as a sacred trust committed to them. The *Sharīʿa* is the revealed God-guaranteed Way,[1] whereas the *Ṭarīqa* is the Way of the pilgrim towards Truth. The *ʿulamā'*, having triumphed over the Muʿtazilites, had to find a way to muzzle the Sufis, with their pretensions to being a spiritual aristocracy, rebellious to the power of the Law over life and thought.[2] This muzzling had to be achieved in both the intellectual and organizational aspects, and in both the legal institution was only partially successful. In the first aspect the Sufis' conformity to the legal establishment began from the moment they felt the need to support their statements with prophetical *ḥadīths*, and when *ṭarīqa* leaders felt it necessary to express conformity with the *Sharīʿa.* Although Sufism was never included within the Islamic sciences a compromise was reached by the recognition of *taṣawwuf* as the 'science of the mystical life'. In the sphere of practice the *ʿulamā'* were forced to allow non-Sunnī ways of worship to counterbalance the ritual of the mosque. Although organized Sufism brought into existence a religious organization parallel with that of the consensus, yet organization offered a means of control and the *ʿulamā'* in this

[1] The original meaning of *sharīʿa* was 'the path to be followed'; see Qur'ān, v. 52, xlii. 11, xlv. 17.

[2] Recognized by political authority Sufi institutions were never formally recognized by legal authority as teaching institutions. Abu Dharr 'Sibṭ ibn al-ʿAjamī' wrote, 'Les docteurs de la Loi ne font aucune distinction entre la *khānaqāh* et la *zaouïa* et le *ribāṭ*, qui est un local constitué *wakf* pour l'accomplissement des actes de dévotion et des exercices pieux. Les docteurs de la Loi peuvent habiter un *ribāṭ* et percevoir le traitement servi par son *wakf*, mais il n'est point permis à un soufi d'habiter une *madrasa* et d'y percevoir un traitement: la raison en est que l'essentiel (*maʿnā*) du soufisme est compris dans le *fiqh*, tandis que l'inverse n'est pas vrai' (*Les Trésors d'or*, transl. J. Sauvaget, Beirut, 1950, pp. 106–7).

respect could frequently invoke the support of the secular authorities. The *khānaqāhs* and many of the *ribāṭs* of the Arab world were semi-official institutions, whose endowments (*awqāf*) were the key to governmental control. Other measures taken included the appointment of one of the shaikhs, or even someone like a *muftī* from outside the *ṭawā'if*, as *shaikh ash-shuyūkh* to act as liaison agent between them and the government. D'Ohsson writes that in Turkey the shaikhs 'are subordinated to the Muftī of the capital who exercises an absolute jurisdiction over them. This supreme chief has the right of investiture in respect of all the generals of orders, even those like the Qādirīs, Mawlawīs and Bektāshīs in which this office is hereditary. . . . The Muftī has also the right of confirming the shaikhs whom these generals nominate.'[1]

The muzzling of the orders in both aspects was never completed; far from it, for their submission to Islamic standards was one of expediency. As a people's movement popular Sufism could not be suppressed, whilst Islamic life was never without some free souls following the way of illumination to ensure the deeper spiritual life did not atrophy.

Opposition to the orders, to their shaikhs, beliefs, and practices, was continual and vigorous. Official religious authority never reconciled itself, whatever compromises were made, to the existence of centres of religious authority outside their control. Ḥanbalī hostility goes back to the attitude of the founder of the *madhhab* to al-Muḥāsibī, Sarī as-Saqaṭī, and their fellows. The Baghdadī Ḥanbalī, Ibn al-Jawzī (d. 597/1200), devoted something like half his book, *Talbīs Iblīs*, to Sufis,[2] attacking their divergencies from the Law. The Syrian jurist, Ibn Taimiyya (d. 728/1328), was especially prominent in voicing his opposition, issuing many *fatwās* and writing pamphlets condemning eminent Sufis, their practices in seeking ecstasy through music and dancing as well as the people's faith, shrine-visiting with offerings, vows and invocations, as all contrary to the Law. These men do not go so far as to condemn Sufism outright but to denouncing what they regarded as illegalities.

[1] D'Ohsson, *Tableau*, IV. ii. 667–8.

[2] *Talbīs Iblīs*, Cairo edn., 1921 and 1928. There is a partial English translation by D. S. Margoliouth, 'The Devil's Delusion', in *Islamic Culture*, scattered through vols. 9 to 22, Hyderabad, 1935–48; also an article by Sirajul Haq, 'Samā and Raqs of the Dervishes', *Islamic Culture*, 1944, 111–30.

Similar opposition came from institutional Shīʿism. Under Sunnī dynasties like the Seljuqs and Ottomans, Shīʿites opposed Sufism and the orders primarily on religious grounds, since at a critical period in the development of doctrine the Sufis showed that *wilāya* was not a privilege exclusive to a particular lineage but a divine grace freely bestowed. Shīʿī hostility to Sufism is brought out, for example, in the controversy surrounding the condemnation of al-Ḥallāj.[1] The relationship of Shīʿīs with the spiritual world was different from that of Sufis, and Sufi forms of devotion were not so necessary to them since they had their own forms of compensation for the spiritual deficiencies of legalistic religion. When Shīʿism once again became the established orthodox religion of Iran the *mujtahids* proved very hostile to Sufism, and through its support of these *mujtahids* the Ṣafawid dynasty, which had its origin in a Sufi order, became the persecutor of Sufis. One *mujtahid*, Āqā Muḥammad ʿAlī, even earned the title of *Ṣūfi-kush* (the Sufi-slayer), on account of the number of *ʿurafā'* (gnostics) and *darwīshes* whom he condemned to death.[2] Well-known Shīʿī theologians who opposed the orders were Muḥammad Bahā' ad-dīn al-ʿĀmilī (d. 1030/1621), commonly known as Shaikh-i Bahā'ī, and Muḥammad Bāqir al-Majlisī (d. 1110/1699),[3] author of a treatise, *al-Iʿtiqādāt*, against Sufism.

As the power of the orders as a social movement gained ground through their integration with saint-veneration, and as the worldliness of *ṭā'ifa* leaders grew, so opposition between them and the *ʿulamā'* came to be based largely on mundane considerations. In time the *ʿulamā'* linked themselves with respectable orders, since they were no longer mystical, and toyed with Sufi classics or the *Iḥyā'*. As-Sanūsī quotes Shaikh az-Zarrūq as saying that 'the works of [Abu Ḥāmid] al-Ghazālī are the mysticism of the legalists'—*Inna kutuba 'l-Ghazālī taṣawwufu 'l-fuqahā'*.[4] But one

[1] On the hostility of Abu Sahl an-Nawbakhtī (d. 311/923) see L. Massignon, *Passion*, 1922, i. 151–9, 349–51.

[2] E. G. Browne, *Lit. Hist. Persia*, iv. 368, with reference to *Qiṣaṣ al-ʿulamā'* by Muḥammad ibn Sulaimān.

[3] Ibid. iv. 403–4, 409–10, 427–8. 'Attacks on the Ṣūfīs, especially on their Pantheism (*Waḥdatu 'l-Wujūd*), are also often met with in general manuals of Shīʿa doctrine, but several independent denunciations of their doctrines exist, such as Āqā Muḥammad ʿAlī Bihbihānī's *Risāla-i-Khayrātiyya*, which led to a violent persecution of the Ṣūfīs and the death of several of their leaders' (ibid. iv. 420).

[4] As-Sanūsī, *Salsabīl*, p. 9.

must not imagine these sober beings, for whom intellectual conviction (which is no more than admiration for their own orthodoxy) and legalistic moral integrity constituted the greater part of religion, taking part in a *dhikr*, though they sometimes lent the proceedings the dignity of their presence. Al-Ghazālī disapproved of dancing by those in authority, as not being consonant with their dignity and prestige among the people.[1] Yet never to the very end could the men of this class accept the mystical Way in theory and practice as a true guide to Muslim spirituality. Consequently, as will be shown in the next chapter, they made no attempt to save the real things for which the orders stood, however inadequately during their decadence, when a new and more formidable opponent began undermining this range of Islamic spirituality.

[1] See al-Ghazālī, *Iḥyā'*, ii. 267.

IX

The Orders in the Contemporary Islamic World

NINETEENTH-CENTURY religious movements fall into three groups:

Salvation through Return to Origins (the Law):	Wahhābism
Salvation through the divinely-sent Leader (Guide):	Mahdism
Salvation through Ecstasy and Loss of Self-volition in the Sufi shaikh (charismatic leader):	*Ṭarīqa* Revival

These movements, emanating from the more backward parts of the Arab world, had in fact less influence upon Arabs than upon Africans. Each offered a different response by traditional Islam to the challenges of the age, and they undoubtedly met many men's needs. Yet established Islamic institutions, in the persons of the *'ulamā'*, attacked all three, whilst the new men who made their appearance towards the end of the century attacked the *ṭarīqas* in particular.

There was, however, little sign of weakening in the hold the orders exercised over people even at the beginning of this century. *Dhikrs* were still performed in many mosques, even in the Ḥaram ash-Sharīf (until 1917), from which the *'ulamā'* were especially concerned to eliminate them. Both dervishes and lay affiliates were still numerous in Syria, judging by the large numbers who took part in public *dhikrs* on special occasions, to which numerous accounts in travel books bear witness. These occasions provided a marvellous opportunity to see the various types of *dhikrs*. The *Mawlid an-Nabī* festival, still held in Omdurman in the square where the Khalīfa 'Abdullāhi formerly assembled his thousands for Friday prayer (though he prohibited the *dhikr*), was a fascinating occasion in my days in that city. I have travelled with villagers and dervishes from Jerusalem in happier days to take part in the celebrations at the shrine of Nabī Mūsā in the desert hills south of the Jericho road overlooking the Dead Sea.[1]

The late nineteenth and early twentieth centuries saw the orders attacked on all sides, but it was not this which made the difference from past ages. Attackers had never been wanting; their beliefs had been refuted, their practices condemned, their dervishes ridiculed and occasionally executed, and their shaikhs castigated. None of this abated one whit of their popularity. What we have seen in our time has been a process of erosion set in motion through the twentieth-century spread of the process of secularization, with consequent changes in the social order and infiltration of secularist ideas. This process of change has so undermined the orders that in many parts of the Arab world they have declined into almost complete eclipse.

Reform took the form of struggle against *bida'* (innovations, sing. *bid'a*) and reinforcement of the Sunna. So it had been with Muḥammad ibn 'Abd al-Wahhāb, though this type of reform aroused the opposition of the *'ulamā'*, and then towards the end of the century the Salafī movement ascribed the stagnation of Muslim lands to the corruption of life through *bida'*, and stressed that reformation could only come through the elimination of aberrations and a revivification of the Sunna.[2] The Salafī movement, associated with Muḥammad 'Abduh and Rashīd Riḍā, opposed nearly every aspect of the orders as degenerate and *taṣawwuf* proper as unIslamic, whilst tolerating the type of thought signified by the ethical teachings of al-Ghazālī.[3]

[1] The celebration lasted from the eastern Good Friday to the following Thursday. Similarly the Syrian *dōsa* used to take place on Khamīs al-Mashā'ikh to coincide with Maundy Thursday at Homs and other places where there were Sa'dīs.

[2] See, for example, Rashīd Riḍā, *Iḥyā' as-sunna wa imātat al-bid'a*.

[3] A distinction must be made between those castigating the orders as enemies of progress and the opinion of orthodox circles following old lines. The Moroccan historian, Aḥmad ibn Khālid an-Nāṣirī (d. 1897), wrote, 'For many centuries and especially from the 10th [16th] there has appeared in the Maghrib a detestable heresy. This is the formation of an organization of the vulgar people around a living or dead shaikh noted for his sanctity and peculiar gifts. They accord him excessive love and veneration . . . such as they accord no other shaikh.' Then he goes on to describe the way the orders have perverted Sufi terminology and practices; Aḥmad an-Nāṣirī, *Kitāb al-istiqṣā li akhbār duwal al-Maghrib al-aqṣā*, Cairo, 1312/1894, i. 63.

Yet the writer of this condemnation, though a member of the world of the *makhzan*, also belonged to the world of Moroccan saintism, being a member of the Nāṣirī family, which had a vested interest in the *zāwiya* Nāṣiriyya of Tame-

In Turkey misgivings about the orders, as likely to form centres of resistance to progress, began to be expressed in the middle of the century. Ubicini wrote in 1850: 'An Osmanli, who holds a high post in the state, said to me one day, "Depend upon it, our ministers are labouring in vain, and civilization will never penetrate into Turkey so long as the tekiehs and the turbehs (tombs) remain standing".'[1] Concern about the more extravagant practices of the orders in Egypt led to the prohibition of the *dōsa* ceremony of the Sa'diyya in 1881 under a *fatwā* of the Grand Mufti as a 'repulsive innovation' (*bid'a qabīḥa*).[2] They were also forbidden the use of their kettle-drums, called *bāz*. Similarly, the notorious Rifā'ī ceremonies were prohibited by the Ottoman authorities in Turkey and Syria.

Attacks from the *'ulamā'* body and secular authority have been persistent, if intermittent, throughout the whole history of Sufism, though in practice a parallelism of religious authority was admitted; but in the past these attacks had never done more than lead to the condemnation of individual Sufis and the suppression of particular orders. They never affected their position in the life of Muslim communities, since they ministered to a religious need and filled a gap in the expression of the deeper meaning of Islam. We have already stated that the virtual disappearance of the orders in many lands by the middle of the twentieth century has not come through attack, either external or internal. It was the changing outlook that made the attacks of the critics, *'ulamā'*, modernists, and new men, more effective and enabled them to enlist the aid of authority. In Egypt and Turkey governmental action, we have shown, had already suppressed the more spectacular aspects.[3]

grut in the Dar'a. He does not extend his condemnation to all orders, only to such as the Jilāliyyīn, Haddawiyyīn, 'Īsāwiya, Ḥamādisha, Awlād Sīdī Bunu, and Rahāliyyīn, but not orders he held to be more orthodox and holding to the true Sufi principles, such as his own family Nāṣiriyya, and the Tijāniyya, Wazzāniyya, and Darqawiyya. He thus belongs to the reforming tradition of Aḥmad ibn Idrīs and Aḥmad at-Tijānī, rather than to the Salafī movement. Such distinctions are frequently subjective and the lines of demarcation difficult to establish.

[1] M. A. Ubicini, *Letters on Turkey*, tr. Lady Easthope, 1856, i. 108.

[2] See A. le Chatelier, *Confréries musulmanes du Hedjaz*, 1887, pp. 222–5; *E.I.*[1] i. art. '*Dawsa*'. This ceremony continued to be performed in Homs until well into this century, when a token ceremony was adopted.

[3] J. W. McPherson's account of *The Moulids of Egypt* (Cairo, 1941) is almost a lament on their decline and of the effect of governmental restrictions upon *mūlid* festivals.

Turkey, where the secularizing movement of Mustafa Kamal brought about their prohibition in 1925, is an example of what has been taking place less spectacularly in other countries through the process of secularization; changes in the outlook and in the social order undermining confidence in former religious ways.

To begin with there was the spread of ideas of Islamic reform; return to the purity of primitive Islam, condemnation of innovations, and the struggle against superstitions became watchwords. The orders were particularly susceptible to this form of attack, for they had paid the penalty of institutionalization and especially of the adoption of the principle of heredity in holiness. The motive moving many shaikhs (to be qualified by reference to individuals) was not so much communion with God in any pure sense, as to win the favour of God and thereby obtain the this-world enjoyment of the fruits of such recognition. Formerly, legal treatises had been taught together with Sufism in their establishments, but during the last hundred years those seeking Islamic learning had turned almost exclusively to centres such as the Azhar or Qarawiyyīn. This broke the alliance between orthodoxy and Sufism, and meant that the content of studies became formal and unilluminated and that the orders lost the support of many of the *fuqahā'* class.[1]

[1] W. Cantwell Smith has pointed out (*Islam in Modern History*, Princeton, 1957, p. 56) that many nineteenth-century reformers had experienced Sufi influence in their early years—such contrasting persons as the pan-Islamic Afghānī, the Egyptian *'ālim* Muḥammad 'Abduh, the Nubian Mahdī Muḥammad Aḥmad, the philosopher of the Ataturk revolution Ziya Gökalp, and the Pak-Indian Muḥammad Iqbāl.

A well-known Muslim writer said: 'I have a strong leaning towards Sufism; so have many of our educated men. When I was a child of five to nine years old, I used to see the dervishes who came to our village, and I would try to copy their movements, and I came to join in the *dhikr*. Of course, I could not grow up uninfluenced by these early Sufi contacts.'

Light is thrown upon this aspect of the lives of Afghānī and 'Abduh in Elie Kedourie's *Afghani and 'Abduh* (London, 1966). 'Abduh's scepticism went beyond intellectual bounds, since his relationship to Afghānī was that of some form of *tawajjuh* or *rābiṭa* (see pp. 8–14 and letter of 'Abduh to Afghānī on pp. 66–9), a technique Afghānī may have acquired in India. Afghānī also maintained the Sufi distinction between exoteric and esoteric teaching, between what one professes openly and what one divulges to the adept.

So pervasive was Sufi influence in Islamic life that contact was involuntary and unavoidable. But these same men reacted against their shaikhs and mode of worship, and discarded the whole system, even though their thought was coloured

Others, influenced by new conceptions, who felt that Islam must be ready to relate itself to the new world into which they were being drawn, were even more opposed to the orders. Few objected outright to Sufism as an individual spiritual discipline on Ghazālian lines, even though they may have thought it a waste of time, but the form it had taken, its extravagant popular manifestations, was a different matter, and they held the orders responsible for the stagnation that had overtaken life in Muslim countries. They sought to discredit the shaikhs, not merely on this account, but also because they were particularist, limited, unenthusiastic about burning issues like nationalism, and were too attached to clan, family, and local traditions. Especially, they resented the power the *baraka*-exploiters wielded over their adherents and their interference in what these new men regarded as secular matters.[1]

But most important of all was the general process of secularization, meaning by this term the process of change from a social and cultural system informed throughout by religion, to an order in which each sphere of life, science and art, political and economic activities, society and culture, and also morality and religion itself, became autonomous spheres. This movement of change was largely unconscious, unnoticed, and continuous. Only a few generations ago all Muslims were conscious of living *sub specie aeternitatis*. Now the same revolution which has transformed the former Christian world is taking place in the Islamic world. Other-worldly reference is fading. Islam is clung to because of its social and cultural implications, but its spiritual power has weakened. It must be remembered that mysticism as a system of thought was marginal to Islam, as is shown by the fact that the *'ulamā'* feel no sense of loss at its disappearance. The orders, we have shown, were the vehicles, not the substance, of the mystic life, and as the urge to the mystic life weakened so did the orders. In the context of the popularization of mystic insights in the orders

in some respects by their early experiences. Today, in the modern Arab world, children grow up without even that unconscious experience.

[1] In the 1930s it could still happen that an intellectual rejection of religion might be consonant with actual participation in religious rites. A friend wrote: 'The most "modern" effendi who, in conversation, expresses a contempt for religion and who, to all appearance, is engrossed in contemporary politics, may spend his evenings with a dervish group, treating the Shaikh aṭ-Ṭarīqa with medieval deference.' It would be hard to find any parallel today in the Near Eastern Arab world.

one has to translate 'mystic life' in this last phrase by '(supererogatory) devotional life', and, in fact, the devotional loss has been disastrous.[1] The tragedy of the compromise effected between the doctors of the Law and the masters of the interior life is that no true equilibrium was achieved, only an uneasy coexistence. It is noteworthy that there is practically no devotional material in Arabic other than that which has come from the orders, and though these books continue to be sold they are bought mainly by those sections of the population least modified by modern change.

The word *taṣawwuf* conjures up to the mind of the average modern Arab thoughts of speculative abstractions and obscure or erotic poems, on the one hand, and of gross superstition, filthy ragged dervishes, orgiastic dances, and venal charlatan shaikhs caricatured in current literature and magazines, on the other. Opposed by the *'ulamā'*, by the *salafī*-type of fundamentalist reformers, and by the secularized new men, and primarily undermined by changes taking place in the whole social and religious climate, it is hardly to be wondered that the orders are in decline everywhere. This has come about, less by defection, than because the young have not been joining. *Ṭā'ifas* disappear when shaikhs die since there is no one to succeed; their sons, in their intellectual outlook and dominant interests, no longer belong to their fathers' world.

Far more than social stability, the traditional harmony of the life of the spirit has been disrupted. A changing situation requires religion to show that it can still remain relevant to human needs and can confront challenges and opportunities flexibly and constructively, but the clerical classes have not been able to adapt their religious outlook, and consequently their authoritarian system, to men in their actual situation, nor to find new ways of serving the community. Secular ideas are affecting every section of society, though of course in different degrees. What has added to their decline is that many functions of the *ṭā'ifas* have been taken over by secular organizations: new educational facilities, clubs, and societies. Account must also be taken of the way in which economic changes weakened and finally eliminated trade and craft guilds, formerly closely associated with Sufi *ṭawā'if*. The traditional master (patron)–client (protégé) relationship in these guilds has been

[1] I have myself witnessed this complete reaction against the Sufi *ṣuḥba* and *dhikr* since I held my first conversation with a dervish in Jāmi' al-Umawī in Damascus in what he told me was al-Ghazālī's *khalwa* in July 1931.

superseded. It has been shown[1] that in a cotton town in Egypt only the old inhabitants belong to the local *ṭā'ifa*. It has become a conservative association, helping to preserve the identity of the locals and maintain their distinction from the influx of cotton-mill operatives.

In Egypt the Muslim Brotherhood, Ikhwān al-Muslimīn, served as a substitute for the orders, both as a system of guidance for the individual and of service to the community, through its grouping in local associations. In a sense it came out of a *ṭā'ifa*. Ḥasan al-Bannā' (1906–49), founder of the Ikhwān movement, was initiated into the Ḥaṣafiyya *ṭā'ifa* in 1923 by the son of its founder, Ḥasanain al-Ḥaṣafī, and the first benevolent society he founded took the name of the order and was called al-Jam'iyyat al-Ḥaṣafiyyat al-Khairiyya.[2] But the movement, which at one time had within it, in spite of reactionary tendencies, great possibilities, suffered the fate of so many Islamic religious movements when it became involved in politics. In different countries the Muslim Brotherhood has appealed to different classes of the population, but in general the Ikhwān have been opposed to the orders and have contributed towards their decline.

Account must also be taken of the fact that other changes in the social and political order have affected the life and prestige of the order shaikhs. They are no longer sought after to arbitrate in communal and inter-tribal disputes and their wealth has diminished with the decrease in numbers of affiliates and their offerings. The local community is no longer so closely integrated as in the past, but is more and more coming to see itself as part of the life of a larger political entity.

We cannot generalize about the dates when the recession began, or its extent, since this varies in different countries and among different classes of society within them. Social custom does not change uniformly. In the Arab Near East the decline of the orders is so marked since they were strongest in towns, and towns have been most affected by modern change. The Arab is only in exceptional cases mystically minded: he is generally content with the literal, and the way to God along extrinsic lines has been enough for him. The cultivation of *taṣawwuf* has been strongest in

[1] W. M. Carson, 'The Social History of an Egyptian Factory', *M.E.J.* xi (1957), 368.

[2] See Ishaq Musa Husaini, *The Moslem Brethren*, Beirut, 1956, p. 9.

non-Arab lands, with the notable exception of Arabized Hamitic (Berber and Kushitic) communities, and it is within these that it still retains some hold, whereas in the purely Arab Near East both the orders and interest in *taṣawwuf* has almost vanished. In consequence attacks have ceased and there have since appeared a number of sympathetic studies in Arabic of this movement of the Muslim spirit.[1] In the Arabized Hamitic regions (Maghrib and Nilotic Sudan), where the orders were very strong among cultivators and even nomads as well as other classes, their decline has become marked only since 1945.

We have called attention to the importance of Mecca during the eighteenth and nineteenth centuries as a diffusion centre. Its decline in this respect begins with the 1914–18 war period, but the Wahhābī take-over in 1924 spelled the death-blow of the orders there; not that they were suppressed, but authority, regarding them as an unsuitable aspect of the holy city to present to pilgrims, simply showed that it was advisable for them to keep out of sight, 'though nobody will object to your repeating the name of God silently to yourself in the sacred enclosure'.

Relatively few of the new men even attempted to make a genuine appraisement of Sufism. Muḥammad Iqbāl's *The Reconstruction of Religious Thought in Islam* (1930) is notable. This has been called an attempt to reinterpret in a humanist spirit the spiritual experience of the Sufis, especially the Persian Sufi heritage. There is no evidence that Iqbāl followed a Path other than the intellectual and poetical, and his thought proved too speculative and humanistic to awaken response among Muslims outside his own cultural milieu, especially among Arabs. The Azharites derided or condemned the preoccupation which many western orientalists have displayed towards this aspect of Islam.[2] In Iran, on the contrary,

[1] Among understanding Egyptian students of Sufism we should mention especially Abu 'l-'Alā' 'Afīfī, whose last work, *At-Taṣawwuf: ath-Thawra 'r-rūḥiyya fī 'l-Islām* (Cairo, 1963), was limited in scope to stage-one Sufism.

[2] An article in *Majallat al-Azhar* (1372/1952, pp. 892–3) refers to the way certain orientalists, in particular Louis Massignon and Louis Gardet, have been seduced by extreme pantheistic mystics such as Ibn al-'Arabī and states categorically that 'the greater part of what orientalists call Muslim mysticism has no common ground with Islam'; see S. de Beaurecueil, *M.I.D.E.O.* i (1954), 189.

Not only the Azharites but the Moroccan philosopher of Personalism, Mohamed Aziz Lahbabi, also takes the same view. After mentioning *taṣawwuf* as one of the causes of the Muslim decadence, he writes (*Le personnalisme*

modern response to Sufism has been quite different from that of Arabs, but this derives from the fact that intellectual and poetical Sufism, so associated with the reawakening of the spirit of Persian culture after the attempt of Arab Islam to submit it to its own standards, was regarded as a national heritage.

Turkey is the apparent exception to this gradual process of erosion. There the process was accelerated since the orders became a direct object of attack by the secularizing movement, being regarded as something not merely decadent, but politically reactionary and dangerous.

We have mentioned earlier that the orders in many parts of the Turkish empire had been attacked on religious and moral as well as political and partisan grounds, yet they were not thereby stimulated either to undertake real reform or to manifest new life. Reform movements took place in fringe areas and in Africa. All the same, the influence of the orders remained strong right up to the time of their suppression. S. Anderson gives a list[1] of seventeen officially recognized *ṭarīqas* in Constantinople in July 1921. This city had 258 *tekkes*, as well as many unsubsidized small centres or groups which met in private houses. The orders were a natural focus of the reforming zeal of the Atatürk revolution and were abolished in 1925.[2] After that Albania became the stronghold of

musulman, Paris, 1964, pp. 94–5): 'D'origine non islamique, le soufisme a modifié l'esprit originel de l'Islam et en a envahi toutes les structures: c'est avec lui que les musulmans commencent à s'adonner aux diverses variantes du fatalisme (tawakkul, maraboutisme, croyance à la précarité du temps, à l'irréalité du monde, etc., et par conséquent, au renoncement au monde). La retraite des Soufis (sorte de vie monacale particulière) et le maraboutisme vont à l'encontre de toute évolution culturelle, de tout progrès, et aussi des directives que donnent le Coran et la Sunna. On ne doit pas oublier, comme nous le rappelle M. Louis Gardet, que la mystique n'a de l'Islam qu'une "position marginale par rapport aux sciences religieuses officielles" et pour cause! Car l'origine de la mystique n'est pas musulmane; presque toutes les pratiques des Soufis sont amusulmanes, quand elles ne sont pas antimusulmanes.'

With this question we are not concerned, since we have been looking at Sufism, and indeed Islam as a culture, from the historical or sociological point of view. To us Sufism in all its manifestations is manifestly Islamic, but both the Azharites and Mohamed Lahbabi limit themselves to the Qur'ān and Sunna (see Lahbabi, op. cit., p. 1).

[1] *The Moslem World*, xii (1922), 53.

[2] On the suppression of the *tekkes* see H. E. Allen, *The Turkish Transformation*, Chicago, 1935, chapter x. The reformers' attacks were particularly directed against the orders on account of the political role they had frequently played. The blind devotion accorded their heads made them formidable opponents. The immediate occasion for their suppression was the Kurdish revolt of February

the Bektāshiyya, even surviving for a time under Communist rule.[1] The abolition of the orders in Turkey proved decisive and they are not likely to play a major religious and social role again. It is true that there have been reports of *ṭarīqa* activities,[2] sometimes surprising manifestations of saint-veneration,[3] but it is only too easy to misinterpret these things. Veneration for saints had not suddenly disappeared by government decree and therefore did not have to be revived. The older sections in a changing society

1925, led by the Naqshabandī leader, Shaikh Sa'īd; see A. J. Toynbee and K. P. Kirkwood, *Turkey*, London, 1926, pp. 265–70. In June all the *tekkes* of the eastern provinces were closed and in September the decree was extended to the whole of Turkey and embraced the titles and special costumes by which members of the different orders were distinguished.

[1] A Bektāshī *tekke* (tomb of 'Abdallāh al-Maghāwirī) on the western slopes of the Muqaṭṭam hills with a wonderful view over Cairo survived until very recently. There are recent accounts in J. Leroy, *Monks and Monasteries of the Near East*, English tr. London, 1963, chap. 3 (first published in 1958) and Dorothea Russell, *Medieval Cairo*, London, 1962, pp. 137–8. This *tekke* has since been confiscated by the government, but the dervishes, all Albanians, were given a house in Ma'ādī in compensation where their traditions continued to be maintained until the death of the last shaikh, Aḥmad Sirrī Bābāb in 1965; see *M.I.D.E.O.* viii (1964–6), 572–3.

[2] Tijānī activities hit the headlines at one period. This order had gained only a small group of followers in Turkey, but its propaganda was at work during the period of the 1939–45 war, the leader, Kemal Pilavoglu, being openly active in Ankara in 1942. After the triumph of the Democratic Party in the May 1950 elections secularist pressure was relaxed and the new government allowed the reopening of saints' tombs and pilgrimage to them. This provoked a popular reaction. Kemal Pilavoglu organized the destruction of statues of Atatürk and in consequence he and his lieutenants received prison sentences (see H. A. Reed, 'Revival of Islam in Secular Turkey', *M.E.J.*, viii (1954), 274–6). The Bektāshīs also began public activity in Istanbul and the Naqshabandīs in the eastern vilayets, and this led to police intervention in 1953 and 1954.

A recent Naqshabandī group in eastern Turkey is that of the 'Followers of Light', the Nurcus or Nurculars, founded by a Kurd, Sa'īd Nūrsī (1870–1960); see *M.W.* 1960, 232–3, 338–41; 1961, 71–4.

The whirling *dhikr* of the Mawlawīs is enacted yearly in Qonya; for a description of a recent recital see H. Ritter, 'Die Mevlânafeier in Konya vom 11–17 Dezember 1960', *Oriens*, xv (1962), 249–70. It may also be witnessed occasionally as a tourist attraction in Cairo and Lebanese Tripoli.

[3] On pilgrimage to the tomb of Yunus Emre see Sofi Huri, 'Yunus Emre: In Memoriam', *M.W.* xlix (1959), 111–23. Lyman MacCallum writes in the introduction to his translation of *The Mevlidi Sherif* (1943, p. 15): 'In Republican Turkey the Mevlid continues to be chanted in mosques and in homes, and the recital takes place either on some religious festival, such as the Night of Power, or at a time of rejoicing, such as a house-warming or a victory of the Turkish arms, or at a time of mourning. Perhaps its commonest occurrence is on the fortieth day after a death; invitations to such memorial recitals are a common feature of the Istanbul press.' See the account of a mevlid ceremony in Bisbee, *The New Turks*, Philadelphia, 1951, p. 138.

feel a nostalgic longing for elements of the past. The poetry and humanism of a Rūmī influence many new men too. But these things must be placed within the whole setting of the secularization of society. These are 'survivals' from an old way of life; they are no longer ruling forces in men's lives.

It is difficult to convey any balanced assessment of the situation in the Arab world, when, in fact, the orders still exist, *dhikrs* are performed, and *mūlids* observed. In Egypt, after the revolution of 1952, the principle of inevitable hereditary succession was abolished in favour of the elected shaikh and there has followed some stabilization in what are regarded as respectable orders. An Egyptian friend tells me that university students may be found attending and even taking part in *dhikrs*, but he admitted that this illustrates rather the restless search of youth for inner stability than any rebirth in order vitality. Such a course is temporary, whereas the aim of the orders, for the affiliate as well as for the dervish, was that it was a Way to be pursued throughout life, not a temporary course of spiritual uplift. The real deficiency (demonstrated through many disappointed young men) is the lack of qualified guides, spelling the virtual disappearance of the *ṭarīqa* as a Way of spiritual discipline.

The decline in the orders has been less marked in the Maghrib and Nilotic Sudan than elsewhere in the Arabic-speaking world. The French had encouraged the orders in Morocco, recognizing their leaders and festivals, as part of their attempt to maintain a balance between the different forces in the country, especially opposing them to the orthodox, reformist, and progressive. Muḥammad V (reg. 1927–61) supported the Salafīs and prohibited the processions and *mawāsim* of the 'Īsāwiyya and Ḥamdūshiyya, as well as sacrifices (*naḥā'ir*) offered to saints and other prohibited practices.[1] He was successful in promulgating a decree (1946) prohibiting the establishment of new orders and the building of new *zāwiyas* without authorization from the king.[2] In Morocco it is estimated that practising adepts and affiliates number about four per cent of the population, though the number of people actually linked with a *ṭā'ifa*, or rather to its marabouts, is much higher.[3]

[1] See 'Allāl al-Fāsī's lecture, 'Al-Ḥarakat as-Salafiyya fī'l-Maghrib', in his *Ḥadīth al-Maghrib fi 'l-Mashriq*, Cairo, 1956, p. 13.

[2] 'Allāl al-Fāsī, op. cit., p. 21.

[3] Variations between social classes and occupational groups may be illustrated from Morocco. The percentage of practising adepts and affiliates is weaker

In Algeria in 1950 the number of adherents of the three main orders represented there (Khalwatiyya, Shādhiliyya, and Qādiriyya) embraced some half a million members, the Raḥmāniyya (= Khalwatiyya) being the strongest with 230,000 adherents.[1] M. Fauque, after showing that the orders are displaying a little activity, writes; 'Il ne faut pas croire toutefois que l'Islam des *marabout* et des confrèries soit en marche vers des lendemains pleins de promesses. En effet le déclin paraît irréversible, et va semble-t-il de pair avec le progrès de la modernisation du style de vie des populations.'[2]

Here and there an odd order has gained a following in modern times, and even wider fame. The 'Alawiyya, a Darqāwī derivative, founded at Mostaganam (Oran) in 1918 by Aḥmad ibn al-'Alawī (Ibn 'Alīwa: 1872–1934) on his return from travels in India where he learnt new (i.e. non-Maghribī) Sufi doctrines and techniques (methods for *dhikr* and retreat). This order has excited the interest of a number of Europeans,[3] many of whom have written on the founder's life and teachings.[4] The mere existence of such an order witnesses to eternal realities, but its outlook is limited in that its teaching shows no new trend or adaptation for life in a changing world. The *iḥtifāl*, or festival of the order, is highly organized and brings together a motley throng, from Rifian mountaineers to European converts. Even in this order secession has taken place and there are dissident groups in Oran and Relizane.

among the tribes of the plain and the riverains of the Atlantic coast (three per cent), but higher in the Atlas mountains with a maximum of ten per cent in the Territory of Tafilelt, the region adjoining Algeria.

[1] These are the figures given by L. P. Fauque, 'Où en est l'Islam traditionnel en Algérie?', *L'Afrique et l'Asie*, no. lv (1961), 19.

[2] L. P. Fauque, loc. cit., p. 22.

[3] Its attraction for Europeans is related to that search, or rather longing, for enlightenment which provides the various esoteric and theosophical movements with adherents.

Here it may be well to mention the societies in the western world which go under the name of Sufi, in case anyone wonders whether they have anything to do with the subject of this book. But no reader will fail to realize that they are inauthentic, simply because, unlike the 'Alawiyya, they represent no continuous Sufi tradition, but are rootless, invented, superficial theosophies, even if put together by an easterner and however much use they make of quotations from Sufi classics. Sufism is a Way, and though the corruption of the orders has given its outward manifestations a debased significance, the Way itself cannot be corrupted.

[4] The most recent is M. Lings, *A Moslem Saint of the Twentieth Century: Shaikh Aḥmad al-'Alawī*, London, 1961.

The most remarkable *ṭarīqa* event in the last century was certainly the Sanūsiyya. But this century has witnessed the evolution of its shaikh from a *zāwiya*-head to a king, with corresponding decline in its spiritual influence. The phases of the change begin with the order's part in the struggle against the Italians, followed by the 1914–18 war; then its period of suffering and exile during Italian rule, when its leaders had to take refuge in Egypt and elsewhere; next followed the association of the leader with the British during their operations in Libya, subsequently placing the Shaikh, Sayyid Idrīs, at the head of the Emirate of Cyrenaica and then of the Kingdom of Libya. Finally, the discovery and exploitation of oil resources encompassed the ruin of the Order.

Though the orders can never regain their former influence in Islamic life they will continue to exist, for there are always some peasants, artisans, and intellectuals who need the type of spiritual solace they offer, or are ready to seek in them a way of escape or refuge from the anxieties of life in the modern world, as their ancestors found in them a counterbalance to the ordinary man's political, economic, and religious impotence. Modern secular institutions and outlook do not satisfy a minority, who feel the need to maintain spiritual values. In less sophisticated regions the orders retain some authority through their identification with the saint-cult, and villagers continue to believe in the efficacy of the *baraka* associated with the spirit within the tomb. It has been pointed out that a few famous *mūlids* can still draw their thousands, but then the whole western world keeps the festival of Christmas, and how much does this mean spiritually! Even in the Soviet Asiatic Republics, the *ṭarīqas* manage to survive.[1]

The decline in the orders is symptomatic of the failure of Muslims to adapt their traditional interpretation of Islam for life

[1] So little do they count that the Soviet authorities are ready to allow open *dhikr* gatherings. 'During the past few years the Soviet press has revealed that . . . "unofficial" Islam is also represented by Sufi fraternities (*tarika*) which, although forbidden by Soviet law, seem recently to have had an unexpected comeback. It is in Dagestan and the Chechen country that these Sufi fraternities are the most numerous and influential. Most of them are offshoots of the old Naqshbandiyeh *tarika*: Kunta Khoja, Bammat Khoja and Battal Khoja. It appears from a recent article [Sept. 1965] that members of these fraternities hold public seances (*zikr*), accompanied by religious singing and dancing, without any intervention on the part of the authorities' (Bennigsen and Lemercier-Quelquejay, *Islam in the Soviet Union*, London, 1967, p. 181).

in a new dimension. Islam as exoteric religion addresses itself to the whole of humanity, conveying the truth in a form that can be lived by anybody, whereas mysticism is a way open to but few. Yet religion is not only revelation. Mysticism is an essential corollary to exoteric religion, even though it is a spiritual discipline pursued by the few and its social manifestations are subject to corruption. True as the criticisms of the reformers may have been, there is no question that the orders inherited, embodied, and diffused throughout the Islamic world a vast store of spiritual experience and energy, and that without them Islam's spiritual influence is greatly impoverished. They fulfilled an important psychological function in their penetration of society as well as the individual life by spiritual values. Now that has gone. Such things as contemporary concern in Turkey with the spiritual values of Yunus Emre, his love for humanity and human values, are not revivals of the mystical spirit, but expressions of the spirit of humanism, linked with the past and made universal in the spirit of the present.[1]

We need not suppose that change has put to sleep for good the forces which formerly found expression in the orders, for the needs which the orders once served are still there, and means for ministering to them may reappear in new forms and under other aspects in modern life. Sociologically speaking, we have seen religion displaced, or contract from being the regulative principle behind life, sustaining and moulding society, to becoming one among many aspects of social life, though receiving special recognition as a factor of differentiation within the universalism of secular culture. At the same time, Islam continues to be the guiding principle in the personal lives of vast numbers of people, and within Islam the Sufi tradition will continue to fulfil its mission of maintaining the deeper spiritual values through the special linkage and relationship with the spiritual world that the *ṭarīqas* represent. Our concern has been primarily with historical movement and organization, but we will never forget that the *ṭarīqa* is spiritual, whereas the *ṭā'ifa* is authentic only in so far as it embodies the *ṭarīqa*. Although so many *ṭawā'if* are disappearing, yet the genuine Sufi tradition of initiation and guidance is being maintained, along with the teaching of an authentic Sufi theosophy,

[1] See K. H. Karpat, 'Social Themes in Contemporary Turkish Literature', *M.E.J.* 1960, p. 31.

and this will never be lost. The Path, in our age as in past ages, is for the few who are prepared to pay the price, but the vision of the few who, following the way of personal encounter and commitment, escape from Time to know re-creation, remains vital for the spiritual welfare of mankind.

APPENDIX A

Relating to Early *Silsilas*

THE earliest preserved *silsila* is that of Jaʿfar al-Khuldī (d. 348/959). According to Ibn an-Nadīm (d. A.D. 995),[1] al-Khuldī took the *ṭarīqa* from al-Junaid (d. A.D. 910), he from Sarī as-Saqaṭī (d. A.D. 867), from Maʿrūf al-Karkhī (d. A.D. 813), from Farqad as-Sabakhī (d. A.D. 748), from Ḥasan al-Baṣrī (d. A.D. 728), from Anas ibn Mālik (d. A.D. 709), the traditionist, and he from the Prophet.

Al-Qushairī gives the ascription (using the phrase *akhdh aṭ-ṭarīq*) of his own shaikh, Abu ʿAlī ad-Daqqāq (d. A.D. 1016), from whom the links are Abu ʾl-Qāsim Ibrāhīm an-Naṣrābādī (d. A.D. 979)—ash-Shiblī (d. A.D. 945)—al-Junaid—Sarī as-Saqaṭī—Maʿrūf al-Karkhī—Daʾūd aṭ-Ṭāʾī—the Tābiʿūn.[2]

The Imām ʿAlī is not mentioned in these *silsilas* until the fifth/eleventh century. Ibn Abī Uṣaibiʿa (d. A.D. 1270) gives the *khirqa* of Ṣadr ad-dīn Muḥammad ibn Ḥamūya (d. A.D. 1220)[3] which is especially interesting in that it embraces three *silsilas*—through al-Khaḍir, certain ʿAlid Imāms, and a version of the classical ascription. It is therefore in the fullest sense more of an esoteric than a mystical line. The *khirqa* Khaḍiriyya, that is, the spiritual initiation, came directly from al-Khaḍir to his grandfather, Abu ʿAbdallāh Muḥammad, one of the tutors of ʿAin al-Quḍāt al-Hamadānī.

The two lines, quasi-Shīʿī and Sunnī, converge with Maʿrūf al-Karkhī, who is said to have been a Mandaean *mawlā* (client)

[1] Ibn an-Nadīm, *Fihrist*, p. 183.

[2] Al-Qushairī, *Risāla*, 1901 edn., p. 134.

[3] Ṣadr ad-dīn, who was born in Khurasan and was taken to Syria to escape the Mongols, invested with the *khirqa* Ibn Abī Uṣaibiʿa's physician uncle, Rashīd ad-dīn ʿAlī ibn Khalīfa, in 615/1218; see Ibn Abī Uṣaibiʿa, *ʿUyūn al-anbāʾ fī ṭabaqāt al-aṭibbāʾ*, Cairo, 1299/1882, ii. 250–1.

This Damascus branch (whose *nisba* does not refer to Ḥamā and is pronounced Ḥamawaih) were subservient to the Sunnī Ayyūbid rulers and dissembled their Shīʿism, though they maintained the ʿAlid *silsila*. ʿImād ad-dīn was the officially appointed inspector of all the Syrian *khānaqāhs*. His grand-nephew on the Persian side, Saʿd ad-dīn al-Ḥamūya (595/1198–650/1252), was a famous Shīʿī Sufi, *khalīfa* of Najm ad-dīn Kubrā. His numerous works were epitomized by his pupil, ʿAzīz ad-dīn ibn M. an-Nasafī (d. 661/1263) in his *Kashf al-ḥaqāʾiq*.

of 'Alī ar-Riḍā and to have adopted Islam at his hands. At a later stage Sufis were frequently initiated into a *futuwwa* grade, a third line going back to 'Alī.

Ṣadr ad-dīn Abu 'l-Ḥasan Muḥammad ibn Ḥamūya, d. 1220
|
'Imād ad-dīn 'Umar b. Ḥamūya, d. 1181
|
Mu'īn ad-dīn Abu 'Abdallāh Muḥammad ibn Ḥamūya, d. 1135

Abu 'Alī al-Faḍl al-Fārmadhī, d. 1084	Al-Khaḍir
Abu 'l-Qāsim al-Gurgānī, d. 1076	The Prophet
Abu 'Uthmān Sa'īd al-Maghribī, d. 984	
Abu 'Amr M. b. Ibrāhīm az-Zajjājī, d. 310/922 (or 348/959)	
Al-Junaid ibn Muḥammad, d. 910	
Sarī as-Saqaṭī, d. 867	
Ma'rūf al-Karkhī, d. 815	

Alī ibn Mūsā ar-Riḍā (8th Imām), d. 818	Da'ūd aṭ-Ṭā'ī, d. 781
Mūsā ibn Ja'far al-Kāẓim, d. 799	Ḥabīb al-'Ajamī, d. 737
Ja'far ibn Muḥammad aṣ-Ṣādiq, d. 763	Ḥasan al-Baṣrī, 643–728[1]
Muḥammad ibn 'Alī al-Bāqir, d. 731	
'Alī b. al-Ḥusain Zain al-'Ābidīn, d. 712	
Ḥusain ibn 'Alī, d. 680	

'Alī ibn Abī Ṭālib, d. 661
|
Muḥammad the Prophet

[1] Writers who sought to discredit the Sufis, such as Ibn al-Jawzī, had no difficulty in showing that these last four ('Alī to Da'ūd aṭ-Ṭā'ī) had never met each other in this world (cf. *Talbīs Iblīs*, 1928, p. 191). Sufis were well aware of this, but they were not so bound by time and space. The Naqshabandīs have still further *silsilas* whose early links were not related in this life. One comes from Abu Bakr through Salmān al-Fārisī, and in the other it is claimed expressly that Abu Yazīd al-Bisṭāmī received his mantle from Ja'far aṣ-Ṣādiq, 'Lord of the Gnostics', after his death.

The lines of Aḥmad ibn ar-Rifāʿī are given in detail by Taqī ad-dīn al-Wāsiṭī, writing about A.D. 1320, in his *Tiryāq al-Muḥibbīn* (pp. 5–7). His first initiator, ʿAlī Abī ʾl-Faḍl al-Qārīʾ al-Wāsiṭī, is linked to al-Junaid along recognized lines. In addition, he inherited three *silsilas* through his initiation by his maternal uncle, Manṣūr. The first was hereditary, father to son, as far as Junaid, then along regular lines. The second went to Maʿruf al-Karkhī and then the ʿAlid line. The third (pp. 6–7, 42) was unusual. It went to Abu Bakr al-Hawāzanī al-Baṭāʾiḥī who, apart from being given the *khirqa* in his sleep by Abu Bakr aṣ-Ṣiddīq, also joins on to a line of secret gnostic teaching through:

'Sayyid aṣ-Ṣūfiyya' Sahl at-Tustarī, d. 886 or 896
Dhū ʾn-Nūn al-Miṣrī, d. 859
Isrāfīl al-Maghribī (see Sarrāj, *Lumaʿ*, pp. 228, 288)
Abu ʿAbdallāh M. Ḥubaisha at-Tābiʿī
Jābir al-Anṣārī aṣ-Ṣaḥḥābī
ʿAlī ibn Abī Ṭālib, d. 661

Taqī ad-dīn includes other spiritual genealogies than those of Aḥmad ibn ar-Rifāʿī in his work, including the Khurasanian one of Yūsuf al-Hamadānī (p. 47).

APPENDIX B

Ṣūfīs, Malāmatīs, and Qalandarīs

THE distinction between *ṣūfī* and *darwīsh* (or *faqīr*) is the difference between theory and practice. The *ṣūfī* follows a mystical theory or doctrine, the *darwīsh* practises the mystical Way. Of course, one is a *darwīsh* and a *ṣūfī* at the same time and there is no essential distinction in theory. The *ṣūfī* is a *darwīsh* and the *darwīsh* is a *sūfī* since neither can be in isolation from the other, but in practice there is a disproportion of emphasis, some *ṣūfīs* being predominantly intellect or creative imagination, like Ibn al-ʿArabī, and others mainly dervishes, all feeling, emotion, and action. In both instances we find *ṣūfīs* and dervishes dispensing with a guide and relying solely upon themselves (though frequently allowing for a spiritual guide), passively or actively, to achieve the annihilation of self and direct absorption into divine Reality, one by intellectual exercises, the other by psycho-physical practices. Ibn ʿAbbād of Ronda (1333–90) belonged to the Shādhilī tradition, but in a letter to Abu Isḥāq ash-Shāṭibī, who had sought an opinion as to whether a shaikh was indispensable, he wrote that he himself was more guided in his spiritual path by *ṣūfī* writings than by shaikhs.[1] Most of these men who dispense with a this-world guide acknowledge a spiritual guide.

Also involved is the distinction between the *ṣūfī* and the *malāmatī*. This question has been somewhat confused. Abu ʿAbd ar-Raḥmān as-Sulamī (d. 412/1021) regarded the *malāmatīs* (blameworthy ones) as the highest grade of God's slaves, above both the legalists (*fuqahā'* class) and the theosophists, *Ahl al-maʿrifa*.[2] Now these latter, the second category, the *khawāṣṣ*, he

[1] See P. Nwyia, *Ibn ʿAbbād*: *Lettres*, Beirut, 1958, p. 126. Various *fatwās* on the question are quoted from Aḥmad al-Wansharīshī's *Miʿyār* by Muḥammad ibn Tāwīt aṭ-Ṭanjī in his edition of Ibn Khaldūn's *Shifā' as-sā'il* (Istanbul, 1958, pp. 110–34), including one from Ibn Khaldūn himself who was no Sufi and clearly in his writings betrays little except surface comprehension of Sufism.

[2] See his *Risālat al-Malāmatiyya*, edited by Abu 'l-ʿAlā' ʿAfīfī in his *Al-Malāmatiyya wa 'ṣ-Ṣūfiyya wa ahl al-futuwwa*, Cairo, 1364/1945, pp. 86–7. The terminology attached to 'the three ways to God', and the distinctions, vary with the writers: with Najm ad-dīn Kubrā = *akhyār, abrār,* and *shuṭṭār* (see

calls the *Ṣūfiyya*; but these are the 'elect' or 'privileged' rather than simple *ṣūfīs*, those upon whom God has bestowed special knowledge of Himself, who can perform *karāmāt* and penetrate hidden mysteries. The Malāmatīs are *ṣūfīs*: 'Among their principles is disciplined guidance under a *ṣūfī* leader (*imām min a'immat al-qawm*) to whom recourse should be had in all matters pertaining to mystical knowledge and experiences.'[1]

Although the Nubian, Dhū 'n-Nūn, and the Mervian, Bishr ibn al-Ḥārith (d. 277/841), tend to be looked upon as originators of the *malāmatī* tendency, its true origins are to be sought in Nishapur.[2] It is not to be regarded as distinct from *taṣawwuf*, but simply as the Nishapuri school of mysticism. As-Sulamī includes among *malāmatīs*: Sahl at-Tustarī, Yaḥyā ibn Ma'ādh ar-Rāzī, and above all Abu Yazīd al-Bisṭāmī, to whom is ascribed the formulation of the specific doctrines of the school.[3]

The *ṣūfī* is concerned with *tawakkul* ('trust'; Qur'ān, lxv. 3) and that to him involves *inkār al-kasb* (severing the bonds of acquisition and personal action), with training, guidance, and even subjection to his shaikh, affirmed with oath and investment with a *khirqa*, regulated exercises (*dhikr*) and *samā'*. All these the *malāmatī* rejects, at least theoretically. At the foundation of the *malāmatī* tendency is the absolute nothingness of man before God. Contrary to the *ṣūfī*, the true *malāmatī* conceals his progress in the spiritual life. He aspires to free himself from the world and its passions whilst living in the world. Shihāb ad-dīn as-Suhrawardī writes: 'It has been said that the *malāmatī* is one who neither makes a show of doing good or harbours thoughts of evil.' He explained this as follows: 'The *malāmatī* is one whose veins are saturated with the nourishment of pure virtue, who is really sincere, who does not want anyone to be acquainted with his ecstatic states and experiences.'[4] The *malāmatī* is ready to be

his *al-Uṣūl al-'ashara*, ed. M. Molé in *Annales Islamologiques*, Cairo, iv. 1963, 15–22), and with Ibn al-'Arabī = *'ubbād*, *Ṣūfiyya*, and *Malāmatiyya*; *Al-Futūḥāt al-Makkiyya*, A.H. 1326 edn., iii. 34 ff., and see 'Afīfī, op. cit., p. 20.

[1] Sulamī in 'Afīfī, op. cit., p. 108.

[2] Sulamī specifies the three founding fathers of the movement, all Nishapūrīs, as: Abu Ḥafṣ 'Amr ibn Salma al-Ḥaddād (d. 270/883), Ḥamdūn al-Qaṣṣār (d. 271/884), and Sa'īd ibn Ismā'īl al-Ḥairī, known as al-Wā'iẓ (d. 298/910); op. cit., pp. 88, 90. Al-Hujwīrī has a whole chapter in his *Kashf* on *malāma*.

[3] See 'Afīfī, op. cit., pp. 33–4.

[4] Suhrawardī, *'Awārif*, 1358/1939 edn., p. 53.

despised by men that he may lose himself in God. Whereas the *ṣūfī* lives *'alā 't-tawakkul*, relying upon God to provide for him, the *malāmatī* works for his living ('lawful' food for him is earned food), absorbed in God whilst engaged in the affairs of the world. He does not parade his inward way, nor indulge in public *dhikr* gatherings. Confusion has been caused by the fact that many mystical writers tend to regard *malāmatīs* as quietists (*mutawakkilūn*) among the *ṣūfīs*, even as people who lack the will and discipline necessary to struggle along the mystical Path, whereas it is the *ṣūfīs* who are *mutawakkilūn*; and they also confuse him with the *qalandarī*. How wrong they are is soon demonstrated.

The *malāmatī* rejects all outward show, all *ṣalāt* and *tarāwīḥ*, the latter especially since it is only too often a form of piety intended to be seen of men.[1] Contrary to what is generally supposed the *malāmatī* performs duties that are *farā'iḍ*, like ritual *ṣalāt*, even though he rejects them, to avoid attracting attention to himself. Similarly he does not wear the special dress which characterizes the *ṣūfī*. He has no initiating shaikh in the later *ṣūfī* sense of submission though he is ready to seek guidance. As-Suhrawardī writes: 'There is at the present time in Khurasan an association (*ṭā'ifa*) of *malāmatīs* possessing shaikhs who ground them in the fundamentals and keep themselves informed of their spiritual progress. We have ourselves seen in Iraq those who follow this course [of incurring censure] but are not known under this name, for the term is little current on the tongues of the people of Iraq.'[2] The *malāmatī* professes no speculative mysticism about the unicity of being, but is concerned with the elimination of self-consciousness. Of the later orders the Naqshabandiyya is especially associated with the *malāmatī* tradition within *taṣawwuf*. Naqshabandīs practise the personal recollection (*dhikr khafī*), the strict have no public *dhikrs*, and we may recall their injunction about 'solitude in a crowd'.[3]

Whereas as-Sulamī, and even, though with reservations, a characteristic *ṣūfī* guide like as-Suhrawardī, can look reasonably

[1] The *dhikr* repetitions should not be identified with the supererogatory prayers of legal Islam, that is, such things as the *nawāfil* added to the obligatory prayers or the *tarāwīḥ* especially associated with Ramaḍān piety, since these are the same as ritual prayer in form and therefore in spirit, though it is quite true that the *dhikr* recited after ritual prayer has often tended for the average affiliate to have little deeper significance than *tarāwīḥ*.

[2] *'Awārif*, p. 55, l. 13.

[3] See above, p. 203.

at *malāmatīs*, or at least at their theory, since it is simply a particular *ṣūfī* tendency, they regard the *qalandarīs* as reprehensible. Theoretically there is not really all that difference. The danger of Malāmism is the possibility of its becoming antisocial. The rude and unlettered wandering dervishes and *bābās* of the Turkish movements were such *qalandarī* types; then, as Ways were formed, latent antinomian tendencies were accentuated.

The distinction between the *malāmatī* and the *qalandarī* is that the former hides his devotion and the latter externalizes and even exploits it, going out of his way to incur blame. Confusion has been caused because of the derivation of the name *malāma* (blame). The term *qalandarī*, to which the Arabian Nights has given wide currency, covers in its historical usage a wide range of dervish types. It was loosely applied in the East (it was unknown in western Islam) to any wandering *faqīr*, but it was also adopted by certain groups and even distinctive orders were formed, hence the problems of defining the term. To begin with the time of the formation of *silsilas*, Shihāb ad-dīn as-Suhrawardī writes:

The term *qalandariyya* is applied to people so possessed by the intoxication of 'tranquility of heart' that they respect no custom or usage and reject the regular observances of society and mutual relationship. Traversing the arenas of 'tranquility of heart' they concern themselves little with ritual prayer and fasting except such as are obligatory (*farā'iḍ*). Neither do they concern themselves with those earthly pleasures which are allowed by the indulgence of divine law. . . . The difference between the *qalandarī* and the *malāmatī* is that the *malāmatī* strives to conceal his mode of life whilst the *qalandarī* seeks to destroy accepted custom.[1]

Maqrīzī records that about 610/1213 *qalandarīs* first made their appearance in Damascus.[2] According to Najm ad-din M. ibn Isrā'īl of the Rifā'iyya–Ḥarīriyya (d. 1278), their introduction took place in 616/1219, the introducer being Muḥammad ibn Yūnus as-Sāwajī (d. 630/1232), a refugee from Sāwa (destroyed by the Mongols in 617/1220): 'When, under the reign of al-Ashraf, al-Ḥarīrī was condemned, they also disapproved of the *qalandarīs* and exiled them to the castle of Ḥusainiyya.' The Qalandariyya was reintroduced with the Ḥaidarī group, a *zāwiya* being built in 655/1257.[3] A pupil of Muḥammad ibn Yūnus

[1] '*Awārif*, pp. 56–7.
[2] Maqrīzī, *Khiṭaṭ*, ii. 433.
[3] See H. Sauvaire, 'Description de Damas', *J. Asiat.* IX. v. 397, 409–10.

known as Khiḍr Rūmī is credited with the introduction of the tendency into north-west India in the time of Īltutmish which developed into a definite line of ascription as a *qalandarī* order.[1] A Persian *faqīr* called Ḥasan al-Jawāliqī came to Egypt in the time of al-Malik al-ʿĀdil Ketbogha (1294–6) and founded a *zāwiya* of *qalandarīs*, then went to Damascus, where he died in 722/1322.[2] Maqrīzī remarks that they were quietists seeking inward peace, but their means of attaining this involved discarding normal social restraints.

Qalandarī characteristics included the wearing of a distinctive garment,[3] the shaving of the head and facial hair with the exception of the moustache, the perforation of hands and ears for the insertion of iron rings as symbol of penitence, as well as *tathqīb al-iḥlīl* as sign of chastity,[4] all of which are forbidden.

The position was different in the time of Jāmī (d. 1521). This Sufi poet, after quoting the passage from Shihāb ad-dīn, goes on, 'With regard to the kind of men whom we call *qalandarī* today, who have pulled from their necks the bridle of Islam, these qualities of which we have just spoken are foreign to them, and one should rather name them *hashawiyya*.'[5] Both Suhrawardī and Jāmī point out that those in their time who took the dress of *qalandarīs* in order to indulge in debaucheries are not to be confused with true *qalandarīs*.

The Turkish *qalandarīs* eventually became a distinctive order. One group claimed to derive from a Spanish Arab immigrant called Yūsuf al-Andalusī. Expelled from the Bektāshī order because of his arrogant nature, he tried in vain to enter that of the Mawlawīs, and ended by forming a distinct order under the name of Qalandar. He imposed upon his dervishes the obligation of perpetual travel,[6] yet in the reign of Muḥammad II (1451–81)

1 The *dhikr* formulae instituted by the fourth successor of Khiḍr Rūmī, Quṭb ad-dīn b. Sarāndāz Jawnpūrī (d. 1518), is Shīʿī: 'Yā Ḥasan is forced between the two thighs, Yā Ḥusain on the navel, Yā Fāṭima on the right shoulder, Yā ʿAlī on the left shoulder, and Yā Muḥammad in his soul' (Sanūsī, *Salsabīl*, p. 155; pp. 154–64 are concerned with the practices of this Indian order).

2 Maqrīzī, *Khiṭaṭ*, 1326 edn., iv. 301.

3 *Dalaq*, see H. Sauvaire, *J. Asiat.* IX. v. 397.

4 Ibn Baṭṭūṭa, iii. 79–80.

5 Hashawiyya, a sect called also Ṣaqātiyya and Karamiyya, whose members recognize, in God, attributes distinct from His essence. ʿAbd al-Qādir al-Jīlānī uses the word in condemnation in his *ʿaqīda* (see *al-Fuyūḍāt ar-Rabbāniyya*, p. 37). But in this passage Jāmī is using it as a general derogatory term.

6 D'Ohsson, *Tableau*, IV. 2. 684.

a *qalandarī* convent with mosque and *madrasa* made its appearance in Istanbul.[1] Evliya Chelebi refers to an Indian *qalandarī* convent at Kaghid-Khānah (suburb of Scutari) whose *faqīrs* Sultan Muḥammad used to provide with dinners.[2] There was a *qalandarī* order in Aleppo at the beginning of the present century. Mujīr ad-dīn describes a *qalandarī zāwiya* in Jerusalem in the middle of Mamilla cemetery. Formerly a church called ad-Dair al-Aḥmar, it was taken over by one Ibrāhīm al-Qalandarī as a *zāwiya* for his *fuqarā'*, but the *zāwiya* fell into ruins shortly before 893/1488.[3]

[1] J. v. Hammer, *Hist. de l'Empire Ottoman*, tr. Hellert, Paris, 1835–43, xviii. 110, 131.

[2] Evliya Chelebi, *Narrative*, tr. J. v. Hammer, I. ii. 87.

[3] Mujīr ad-dīn, *Al-Uns al-jalīl*, tr. H. Sauvaire, 1876, pp. 198–9.

APPENDIX C

Suhrawardī *Silsilas*

Shihāb ad-dīn Abu Ḥafṣ 'Umar as-Suhrawardī (d. 1234)

- Najīb ad-dīn 'Alī b. Buzghush d. 678/1279
  - Nūr ad-dīn 'Abd aṣ-Ṣamad an-Naṭanzī
    - Kamāl ad-dīn 'Abd ar-Razzāq al-Kāshānī d. 730/1329
    - 'Izz ad-dīn Maḥmūd b. 'Alī al-Kāshānī d. 735/1334
    - Najm ad-dīn M. al-Isfahānī
      - Ḥusain Ḥusām ad-dīn ash-Shamshirī
        - Jamāl ad-dīn Yūsuf al-Ghūrānī
          - Nūr ad-dīn 'Abd ar-Raḥmān al-Miṣrī
            - Zain ad-dīn Abu Bakr Kh^{w}āfī of Tabriz 757/1356–838/1435 **Zainiyya** (Turkish)
  - Ẓahīr ad-dīn 'Abd ar-Raḥmān b. Najīb-Buzghush d. 716/1316
- Nūr ad-dīn Mubārak Ghaznawī d. 1249, Delhi
- Ḥamīd ad-dīn Nājūrī[1] d. 1274
  - Ḥusain (b. 'Ālim) Ḥusain-i Sādāt d. 730/1330

Mīrān M. Shāh (a descendant of Surkh-posh) d. Lahore, 1604 **Mīrān Shāhī**

[1] To be distinguished from the Chishtī Ḥamīd ad-dīn Nājūrī (d. 642/1244); see *Ā'īn-i Akbarī*, 1948, iii. 408

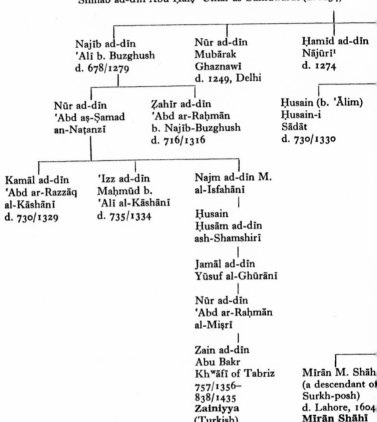

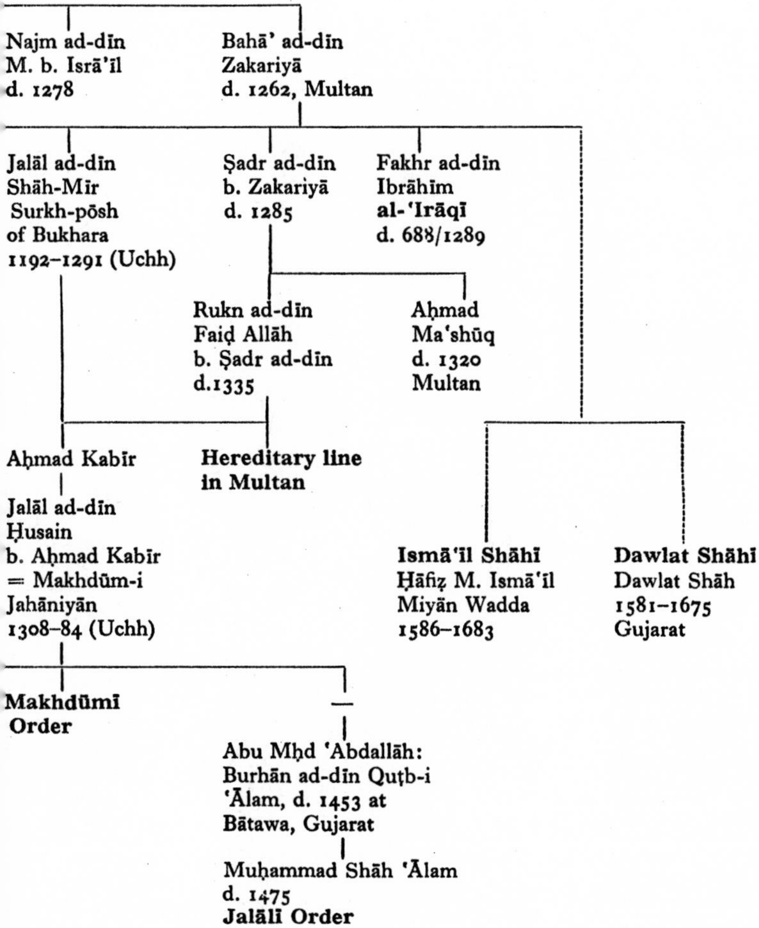
Najm ad-dīn
M. b. Isrā'īl
d. 1278
Bahā' ad-dīn
Zakariyā
d. 1262, Multan
Jalāl ad-dīn
Shāh-Mīr
Surkh-pōsh
of Bukhara
1192–1291 (Uchh)
Ṣadr ad-dīn
b. Zakariyā
d. 1285
Fakhr ad-dīn
Ibrāhīm
al-'Irāqī
d. 688/1289
Rukn ad-dīn
Faiḍ Allāh
b. Ṣadr ad-dīn
d.1335
Aḥmad
Ma'shūq
d. 1320
Multan
Aḥmad Kabīr
Hereditary line
in Multan
Jalāl ad-dīn
Ḥusain
b. Aḥmad Kabīr
= Makhdūm-i
Jahāniyān
1308–84 (Uchh)
Ismā'īl Shāhī
Ḥāfiẓ M. Ismā'īl
Miyān Wadda
1586–1683
Dawlat Shāhī
Dawlat Shāh
1581–1675
Gujarat
Makhdūmī
Order
Abu Mḥd 'Abdallāh:
Burhān ad-dīn Quṭb-i
'Ālam, d. 1453 at
Bātawa, Gujarat
Muḥammad Shāh 'Ālam
d. 1475
Jalālī Order

APPENDIX D

Qādirī Groups

Ahdaliyya: Abu 'l-Ḥasan ʿAlī b. ʿUmar al-Ahdal, buried in Yemen.

ʿAmmāriyya: Example of many ephemeral *baraka*-exploiting movements. A Negro from Morocco called al-Ḥājj Mubārak al-Bukhārī (the *nisba* referring to a connection with the sultan's black guard) attached himself in 1815 to the tomb at Bū Ḥammām in Algeria of ʿAmmār Bū Sena (d. 1780), manifested wonder-working powers, attracted to himself a following, and installed *khalīfas* in many centres in Algeria and Tunisia. Completely illiterate he was instituted a *muqaddam* of the ʿĪsāwī and Hanṣalī orders, but was regarded as a Qādirī, the order of ʿAmmār, by courtesy through Sīdī al-Māzūnī of Kef. See Depont and Coppolani, *Les Confréries religieuses musulmanes*, Algiers, 1897, pp. 356–8; and for recent activity *L'Afrique et l'Asie*, no. lv (1961), 20.

Asadiyya: Turkey, ʿAfīf ad-dīn ʿAbdallāh ibn ʿAlī al-Asadī, buried in Yemen.

Bakkā'iyya: Aḥmad al-Bakkā'i al-Kuntī, d. A.D. 1504. Diffusion among Moors of western Sahara and Sudan, thence to west African Negroes (see my *Islam in West Africa*, 1959, pp. 94–6). Reawakened by al-Mukhtār ibn Aḥmad (1729–1811). Distinct orders from this *silsila* include Fāḍiliyya (M. al-Fāḍil, 1780–1869), Āl-Sīdiyya, Murīdiyya (Senegal: Aḥmad Bamba, d. 1927).

Banāwa: Dekkan in India. Nineteenth century.

Bū ʿAliyya: Algeria, Tunisia, and Egypt. Centre at Nefta where Bū ʿAlī's tomb is situated.

Da'ūdiyya: Damascus, Abū Bakr ibn Da'ūd, d. 806/1403.

Fāriḍiyya: Egypt, sixteenth century, claiming to originate from ʿUmar ibn al-Fāriḍ (d. A.D. 1234); see al-Bakrī, *Bait aṣ-Ṣiddīq*, Cairo, A.H. 1323, p. 381.

Ghawthiyya: Muḥammad Ghawth = M. ibn Shāh Mīr ibn ʿAlī, d. 923/1517. Claimed descent from ʿAbd al-Qādir's son, ʿAbd al-Wahhāb (d. A.H. 1196).

Ḥayāt al-Mīr = founder, *ziyāra* is NE. of Mānshara at Bālākot on the bank of Kunhar Nāla.

(*a*) *Bahlūl-Shāhi*: Bahlūl (Bahāwal) Shāh Daryā'ī, disciple of Shāh-i Laṭīf, disciple of Ḥayāt al-Mīr. Fifteenth century.

(*b*) *Muqīm Shāhi*: Muqīm Muḥkam ad-dīn, *khalīfa* of Ḥayāt al-Mīr.

(*c*) *Ḥusain Shāhi*: Shāh Lāl Ḥusain of Lahore (d. 1599), a disciple of Bahlūl Shāh Daryā'ī, a *malāmatī* who took literally the Qur'ānic verse, 'The life of this world is nothing but a game and a sport' (vi. 32).

Hindiyya: Turkey, Muḥammad Gharīb Allāh al-Hindī.

Jilāla: a common Moroccan name for the *cult* of 'Abd al-Qādir as distinguished from the order which is not important. Introduced from Spain shortly before the fall of Granada (A.D. 1492) by alleged descendants of 'Abd al-Qādir. First reference to a *khalwa* in Fez in 1104/1693; see *Archiv. Maroc.* xi. 319–20.

Junaidiyya: Bahā' ad-dīn al-Junaidī, d. 921/1515 in India. Took the *ṭarīqa* from Abu 'l-'Abbās Aḥmad b. al-Ḥasan, who claimed descent from 'Abd al-Qādir.

Kamāliyya: Kamāl ad-dīn al-Kīt'halī, d. 971/1563–4. India.

Khulūṣiyya: Turkey. Independent *ṭarīqa*?

Manzaliyya: Group in Algeria and Tunisia: lines derive from 'Alī ibn 'Ammār al-Manzalī ash-Shaib (Shu'aib), eighteenth century. Three main centres (see Depont and Coppolani, *Confréries*, pp. 305–7):

(*a*) *Zāwiya* of Manzal Bu Zelfa, affecting north-eastern Tunisia. This is the 'Alī al-Manzalī line. Branches in Jerba, Sfax, and Gabes.

(*b*) *Zāwiya* of Kef: Founder: Shaikh Muḥammad al-Māzūnī of Kef, nineteenth century. Spiritual descent = 'Alī al-Manzalī —Abu 'Abdallāh M. al-Imām—Sīdī al-Ḥājj—M. al-Māzūnī.

(*c*) *Zāwiya* of Nefta: Abu Bakr ibn Aḥmad Sharīf, pupil of Imām al-Manzalī. Southern Tunisia and Algeria.

Mīyān Khel: Mīr Muḥammad, commonly called Mīyān Mīr, born in Siwastān (Sind) in 1550, trained under a solitary called Khiḍr and died at Lahore in 1635. Dāra Shikōh wrote a biography of him called *Sakīnat al-Awliyā'*. Famous *'Urs* on 7 Rabī' II.

Line descended through his cousin M. Sharīf as-Siwastānī. His most famous *khalīfa* was Mulla Shāh Badakhshī, d. 1072/1661.

Mushāri'iyya: Yemen, sixteenth century. As-Sanūsī, *Salsabīl*, p. 147.

Nabulsiyya: Turkish.

Nawshāhī: derives spiritually from Ma'rūf Chishtī Qādirī, but the order and title of *nawshāh*, 'bridegroom', come from Ḥājjī Muḥammad (d. 1604–5), a disciple of Shāh Ma'rūf's *khalīfa*, Sulaimān Shāh. From him derive a number of famous saints and consequently subdivisions, among them:

(*a*) *Pāk-Raḥmānīs*: Pāk 'Abd ar-Raḥmān.
(*b*) *Sachyārīs*: Pāk Muḥammad Sachyār.

Qāsimiyya: Egyptian, nineteenth century; Tawfīq al-Bakrī, p. 381.

Qumaiṣiyya: India. Abu 'l-Ḥayāt ibn Maḥmūd (d. 992/1584), who claimed descent from 'Abd al-Qādir's son, 'Abd ar-Raḥmān (d. A.H. 623). Named after Abu 'l-Ḥayāt's son, Shāh Qumaiṣ of Bengal.

Rūmiyya: Turkish branch. Founder = Ismā'īl ar-Rūmī, Pīr Sānī, 'the second master'. Born in Bansa (Vilayet of Qasṭamūnī), he is said to have founded more than forty Qādirī-*khānahs* in Turkey (see above, p. 44). He introduced a standing *dhikr* in which the participants, with their arms extended over each other's shoulders, recite the formulae, swaying from right to left. Pīr Ismā'īl died in Istanbul in 1041/1631 (?1643) and was buried in the convent of Top Khāne.

Ṣamādiyya: Syria. Muḥammad aṣ-Ṣamādī, d. 997/1589; al-Muḥibbī, *Khulāṣat al-Athar*, iv. 363.

'Urābiyya: Yemen. 'Umar ibn Muḥammad al-'Urābī, sixteenth century. See as-Sanūsī, *Salsabīl*, pp. 65–70.

Waṣlatiyya: Turkey.

Yāfi'iyya: Yemen, 'Afīf ad-dīn 'Abdallāh b. As'ad al-Yāfi'ī, 718/1318–768/1367. *G.A.L.* ii. 176–7, *G.A.L.S.* ii. 227–8.

Zaila'iyya: Yemen. Ṣafiyyaddīn Aḥmad b. 'Umar az-Zaila'ī.

Zinjiriyya: Albanian branch founded by 'Alī Bābā of Crete.

APPENDIX E

Independent Orders of the Badawiyya and Burhāniyya

Aḥmadiyya-Badawiyya

Anbābiyya or *Imbābiyya*: Ismā'īl al-Anbābī, a disciple of Aḥmad al-Badawī, buried in the village of Imbāba. *Mūlid* follows Coptic calendar on 10th Ba'ūna.

Awlād Nūḥ: E. W. Lane, *Mod. Egy.*, p. 249.

Bandāriyya.

**Bayyūmiyya*: 'Alī b. al-Ḥijāzī al-Bayyūmī (1696–1769), pupil of 'Abd ar-Raḥmān al-Ḥalabī.

**Ḥalabiyya*: Abu 'l-'Abbās Aḥmad al-Ḥalabī. Egyptian.

**Ḥammūdiyya*: Muḥammad al-Ḥammūda, pupil of Ḥabīb al-Ḥalabī.

Ḥandūshiyya: Egyptian, Tawfīq al-Bakrī, *B.Ṣ.*, p. 385.

**Kannāsiyya*: Muḥammad al-Kannās.

**Manā'ifiyya* or *Manūfiyya.*

**Marāziqa*: this order traces itself back to Abu 'Amr 'Uthmān Marzūq al-Qurashī (d. 615/1218), who is earlier than Aḥmad al-Badawī, but is classed with the Badawiyya; Sha'rānī, *Lawāqiḥ*, i. 130–1, T. al-Bakrī, *B.Ṣ.*, pp. 392–3. It is also referred to as *Shamsiyya* after a nineteenth-century shaikh, Muḥammad Shams ad-dīn; see le Chatelier, *Confréries*, pp. 178–9.

Shurunbulāliyya.

**Salāmiyya*: al-Bakrī, *B.Ṣ.*, p. 388.

**Shinnāwiyya*: Muḥammad b. 'Abdallāh ash-Shinnāwī, d. at his *zāwiya* at Maḥallat Rūḥ in Gharbiyya in 932/1526.

Shu'aibiyya: Shams ad-din M. b. Shu'aib ash-Shu'aibī, d. *c.* 1040/1630.

Suṭūḥiyya: Jamāl ad-dīn 'Umar as-Suṭūḥī.

* Surviving in 1940.

**Tasqayātiyya*: Muḥammad b. Zahrān at-Tasqayātī or Taskayānī.

Zāhidiyya.

Burhāniyya-Dasūqiyya-Ibrāhīmiyya

**Dasūqiyya*: Ibrāhīm ad-Dasūqī, d. 687/1288. *Silsila* in Tawfīq al-Bakrī, *B.Ṣ.*, p. 383 = Suhrawardī and Shādhilī.

**Shahāwiyya*: al-Bakrī, *B.Ṣ.*, p. 389.

Sharāniba, Sharāniyya, or *Sharnūbiyya*: Aḥmad ibn ʿUthmān ash-Sharnūbī, d. 994/1586.

Tihāmiyya: According to al-Bakrī, *B.Ṣ.*, p. 384, branch of Shādhiliyya.

* Surviving in 1940.

APPENDIX F

Shādhilī Groups in the Maghrib deriving from al-Jazūlī

'Isāwiyya: Muḥammad ibn 'Īsā al-Mukhtār (1465–1524), patron saint of Meknes, where he is buried.

Zāwiya of Dilā' (Tadla district in central Morocco): founded at end of sixteenth century by Abu Bakr b. M. al-Majatī aṣ-Ṣanhājī, 1526–1612. His grandson, M. al-Ḥājj (d. 1671), aspiring to temporal power, was proclaimed sultan at Fez in 1651. When the 'Alawī, Mūlay ar-Rashīd, took Fez (1668) the *zāwiya* was destroyed, but the family re-established itself as a maraboutic clan in Fez.

Wazzāniyya, or *Ṭayyibiyya*, or *Tihāmiyya*: *Zāwiya* of Wazzān founded about 1670 by Mūlay 'Abdallāh b. Ibrāhīm ash-Sharīf (1596–1678). It receives its second name from the fourth shaikh, Mūlay aṭ-Ṭayyib (d. 1767), whilst at-Tihāmī was another grandson of the founder. Many *zāwiyas* in Morocco, Algeria, and Tunisia.

Sharqāwa: Muḥammad ibn Abī 'l-Qāsim ash-Sharqī, d. 1010/1601. Centred at Boujad (Abu 'l-Ja'd). Revived by M. al-Mu'ta, d. 1766.

Ḥamādisha: 'Alī ibn Ḥamdūsh, branched out from the Sharqāwa, end of seventeenth century. Tomb at Jabal Zerhun, near Meknes. Sub-orders, whose adherents belong chiefly to the urban artisan class, include: *Daghūghiyya*, *Ṣaddāqiyya*, *Riyāḥiyya*, and *Qāsimiyya*.

Hanṣaliyya: Sa'īd ibn Yūsuf al-Ahanṣalī (d. 1702) of an old maraboutic family, founded a *zāwiya* at Ait Metrif, which rose to prominence under his son, Abu 'Imrān Yūsuf ibn Sa'īd (d. 1727), who formed the *ṭā'ifa*. A *muqaddam*, Sīdī Sa'dūn, introduced it into Algeria, where it experienced difficulties with the Turks, but with the third *muqaddam*, Aḥmad az-Zawāyā, it became attached to a hereditary Algerian holy line. Main *zāwiya* at Shettaba near Constantine. In Morocco it was suppressed by

Sultan Ismāʿīl, but two *zāwiyas* survived, Ait Metrif and the ancestral centre of Dades.

Khaḍiriyya: ʿAbd al-ʿAzīz ibn Masʿūd ad-Dabbāgh received his *wird* from the supreme initiator, al-Khaḍir, and after spending four years completing the stipulations, declared himself at Bāb al-Futūḥ of Fez in 1125/1713.

Amhawsh: Abu Bakr Amhawsh, disciple of Aḥmad b. M. an-Nāṣir (d. 1717). Both the Hanṣaliyya and the Amhawsh later attached themselves to the Darqawiyya, which is not in the Jazūlī tradition.

Ḥabībiyya: Aḥmad ibn al-Ḥabīb b. Muḥammad al-Lamṭī, d. 1752.

Tabbāʿiyya: original Jazūlī line founded by his *khalīfa* ʿAbd al-ʿAzīz at-Tabbāʿ, known as al-Ḥarrār, d. 1508 in Fez.

APPENDIX G

Madyanī and Shādhilī Groups in Egypt and Syria

*ʿ*Afīfiyya.*

*ʿ*Arūsiyya*: Abu 'l-ʿAbbās Aḥmad b. M. b. al-ʿArūs, d. 1463 in Tunis. Branches in Egypt. Double *silsila* linking with both Shādhilī and Qādirī lines.

*ʿ*Azmiyya*: Muḥammad Māḍī Abu 'l-ʿAzā'im, 1870–1936. Egypt and Sudan.

Bakriyya: Syro-Egyptian. Abu Bakr al-Wafā'ī, d. Aleppo in 902/1496 (D'Ohsson, IV. ii. 622), or 909/1503–4.

**Ḥāmidiyya*: Egypt.

Ḥanafiyya: Shams ad-dīn M. al-Ḥanafi, d. 847/1443.

Hāshimiyya: Egypt.

**Idrīsiyya*: Egypt. Possibly line of Aḥmad ibn Idrīs.

Jawhariyya: Egypt, eighteenth century.

**Khawāṭiriyya*: ʿAlī ibn Maimūn al-Idrīsī, 854/1450–917/1511. Organized as a Syrian *ṭā'ifa* by ʿAlī b. M. b. ʿAlī Ibn ʿArrāq, d. 963/1556.

Makkiyya: Egypt.

Muṣṭāriyya: Muḥammad al-Murābiṭ b. Aḥmad al-Miknāsī al-Muṣṭārī.

Qāsimiyya: Egypt, nineteenth century.

**Qāwuqjiyya*: Muḥammad b. Khalīl al-Mashīshī al-Qāwuqjī at-Tarābulsī, 1225/1810–1305/1888. In Egypt. Nickname comes from Turkish *qawuq* (= *ṭaraṭīr*), high conical cap worn by their dervishes.

Sabtiyya: Abu 'l-ʿAbbās Aḥmad b. Jaʿfar as-Sabtī, d. 901/1495–6 in Cairo.

**Salāmiyya.*

* Surviving in 1940.

**Shaibāniyya.*

Sha'rāniyya or *Sha'rāwiyya*: Cairo: 'Abd al-Wahhāb ash-Sha'rānī, 897/1492–973/1565.

Wafā'iyya: Syro-Egyptian. Muḥammad b. Aḥmad Wafā', d. 1358.

**Yashruṭiyya*: 'Alī Nūr ad-dīn al-Yashruṭī, b. Bizerta, 1793, d. Acre in 1891. Darqawiyya–Madaniyya, al-Madanī (d. 1846) being his initiator.

* Surviving in 1940.

APPENDIX H

Rifā'ī *Tā'ifas* in the Arab World[1]

A. 1. *'Ajlāniyya.*

2. *A'zabiyya*: Muḥyī 'd-dīn Ibrāhīm Abu Isḥāq al-A'zab, grandson of uncle of A. ar-Rifā'ī.

3. *'Azīziyya.*

4. *Ḥarīriyya*: Abu M. 'Alī al-Ḥarīrī of Buṣra in Ḥawrān, d. 645/1248. Adherents in Ḥawrān, Shām, Ḥalab, Ḥamāh, etc. A notable follower was Najm ad-dīn b. Isrā'īl, d. 1278.

5. *'Ilmiyya* or *'Alamiyya*?

6. *Jabartiyya*: Yemen. Aḥmad Abu Ismā'īl al-Jabartī.

7. *Jandaliyya*: Homs: Jandal ibn 'Alī al-Jandalī.

8. *Kiyāliyya.*

9. *Nūriyya.*

10. *Qaṭanāniyya*: Ḥasan ar-Rā'ī al-Qaṭanānī ad-Dimishqī.

11. *Sabsabiyya.*

12. *Sa'diyya* or *Jibawiyya*: Sa'd ad-dīn al-Jibāwī b. Yūsuf ash-Shaibānī, d. at Jiba, near Damascus, 736/1335.

13. *Ṣayyādiyya*: 'Izz ad-dīn Aḥmad aṣ-Ṣayyād (Ḥafīd A. ar-Rifā'ī), d. 670/1273.

14. *Shamsiyya.*

15. *Ṭālibiyya*: Damascus. Ṭālib ar-Rifā'ī, d. 683/1284.

16. *Wāsiṭiyya*: various groups with this name.

17. *Zainiyya.*

B. 18. *Bāziyya*: Egyptian.

19. *Ḥaidariyya*: a Turk, Quṭb ad-dīn Ḥaidar az-Zāwujī, thirteenth century (d. after 617/1220).

20. *'Ilwāniyya* (or *Awlād 'Ilwān*, see E. W. Lane, p. 248): Ṣafī ad-dīn Aḥmad al-'Ilwān.

21. *Ḥabībiyya*: nineteenth century. Egyptian. Muḥammad al-Ḥabībī. *Zāwiya* in Cairo built 1247/1831.

22. *Malakiyya.*

[1] 1–17 are mentioned by name without indication of founder in Abu 'l-Hudā M. aṣ-Ṣayyādī's collection of Rifā'ī biographies called *Tanwīr al-abṣār fī ṭabaqāt as-sādat ar-Rifā'iyya*, Cairo, 1306/1888, p. 25. They presumably all existed in the nineteenth century.

23. *Shunbukiyya-Wafā'iyya*: associated *ṭarīqa.* Abu Muḥammad 'Abdallāh Ṭalḥa ash-Shunbukī: tenth century, with Abu 'l-Wafā' Tāj al-'Ārifin (M. ibn M.), 417/1026–501/1107. A *zāwiya* of Aḥmad ash-Shunbukī was founded in Cairo in 933/1526.

24. *'Uqailiyya*: associated *ṭarīqa.* 'Uqail al-Manbajī al-'Umarī b. Shihāb ad-dīn Aḥmad al-Baṭā'iḥī al-Hakkārī. Syrian 'Umariyya, see al-Wāsiṭī, *Tiryāq*, pp. 44–6.

BIBLIOGRAPHY

THIS bibliography is intended to be comprehensive, since I cannot see any advantage to be gained by segregating works in oriental languages from those in European languages, or articles in journals from books. Arabic names are given under the most common designation, and names to which the definite article *al-* is prefixed will be found under the initial letter, e.g. -Hujwīrī. As throughout the text of the book, where only one date is given Hijriyya dates are preceded by A.H., but frequently both datings are indicated, thus 623/1226.

ʿAbd al-Jalīl, M, see ʿAin al-Quḍāt al-Hamadānī.

Abdel Kader, A. H., *The life, personality and writings of al-Junayd*, *G.M.S.* xiv, London, 1962.

ʿAbd al-Qādir al-Jīlānī, *Al-Fatḥ ar-rabbānī*, Cairo, A.H. 1302.

—— *Futūḥ al-ghaib*, text on margin of Shaṭṭanawfī's *Bahja*, tr. W. Braune, Leipzig, 1933.

—— *Al-ghunya li ṭālibī ṭarīq al-Ḥaqq*, Cairo, 1322/1905, etc.

—— *Sirr al-asrār wa naẓhar al-anwār*, Cairo, n.d.

Abu 'l-Faḍl al-ʿAllāmī, *Ā'īn-i Akbarī*, vol. i, tr. H. Blochman, Biblio. Indica, N.S., Calcutta, 1873; vols. ii and iii, tr. H. S. Jarrett, 1893–6. Repr. and ed. Jadu-nath Sarkar, Calcutta, 1948.

Abu Dharr 'Sibṭ ibn al-ʿAjamī', *Les Trésors d'or*, tr. J. Sauvaget, Beirut, 1950.

Abu Madyan Shuʿaib, *Dīwān*, ed. Damascus, 1938.

Abun-Nasr, J. M., *The Tijaniyya*, London, 1965.

Abu Nuʿaim al-Iṣbahānī (d. A.D. 1038), *Ḥilyat al-awliyā' wa ṭabaqāt al-aṣfiyā'*, 10 vols., Cairo, 1351/1932–1357/1938.

Abu Ṭālib al-Makkī (d. A.D. 998), *Qūt al-Qulūb* ('Food of hearts'), 2 vols., Cairo, 1310/1892 (last edn., Cairo, 1961).

ʿAfīfī, Abu 'l-ʿAlā', *Al-Malāmatiyya wa 'ṣ-Ṣūfiyya wa ahl al-futuwwa*, Cairo, 1364/1945.

—— *The mystical philosophy of Muḥyid Dín-Ibnul ʿArabí*, Cambridge, 1939.

—— *At-taṣawwuf: ath-thawrat ar-rūḥiyya fi 'l-Islām* ('Mysticism: the spiritual eruption in Islam'), Cairo, 1963.

-Aflākī, Shams ad-dīn Aḥmad, *Manāqib al-ʿārifīn* ('The meritorious works of the gnostics'), ed. T. Yaziji, 2 vols., Ankara, 1959–61, tr. C. Huart, *Les Saints des derviches tourneurs*, 2 vols., Paris, 1918 22.

Aḥmad, ʿAzīz, *Studies in Islamic culture in the Indian environment*, Oxford, 1964.

—— 'Religious and Political Ideas of Shaikh Ahmad Sirhindi', *R.S.O.* xxxvi (1961), 257–70.

Aḥmad Bābā at-Tunbuktī, *Nail al-ibtihāj bi taṭrīz ad-Dībāj*, lith. Fez, 1317/1899; and on margin of Ibn Farḥūn, *Dībāj*, Fez, 1329/1911.
Aḥmad ibn Idrīs al-Fāsī, *Majmūʿa aḥzāb wa awrād wa rasāʾil*, Cairo, 1359/1940.
—— *Kanz as-saʿāda wa ʾr-rashād*, Khartoum, 1939.
Aḥmad ibn Mubārak al-Lamṭī, *Adh-dhahab al-ibrīz fī manāqib ʿAbd al-ʿAzīz* [*ad-Dabbāgh*], Cairo, n.d.
Aḥmad ibn Muḥammad ibn ʿAbbād, *Al-mafākhir al-ʿaliyya fī ʾl-maʾāthir ash-Shādhiliyya*, Cairo, A.H. 1327.
ʿAin al-Quḍāt al-Hamadānī, 'Shakwā ʾl-gharīb ʿan al-awṭan ilā ʿulamāʾ al-buldān', ed. and tr. with introd. and notes by M. ʿAbd al-Jalīl, *J. Asiat.* ccxvi (1930), 1–76, 193–297.
—— *Resāle ye Lavāʾeḥ*, ed. and tr. F. Farmanesh, Tehran, A.H. 1337.
—— *Aḥvāl va athār-e ʿAin al-Quḍāt*, ed. F. Farmanesh, Tehran, A.H. 1338.
Aïnî, Mehmmed Ali, *Abd-al-Kadir Guilâni*, Paris, 1938.
ʿAlī ibn Ḥusain al-Wāʿiẓ, *Rashaḥāt ʿain al-ḥayāt* ('Sprinklings from the fountain of life'), Cawnpore, 1912.
ʿAlī Mubārak, *Al-Khiṭaṭ al-jadīda at-tawfīqiyya*, 20 vols., Bulaq, A.H. 1306.
ʿAllāl al-Fāsī, *Ḥadīth al-Maghrib fi ʾl-Mashriq*, Cairo, 1956.
Allen, H. E., *The Turkish transformation*, Chicago, 1935.
Amedroz, H. F., 'Notes on some Sufi lives', *J.R.A.S.* (1912), 551–86.
ʿAmmār, ʿAlī Sālim, *Abu ʾl-Ḥasan ash-Shādhilī* (1st edn., 1951), Cairo, 2 vols., 1962.
Anawati, G. C., and Gardet, L., *La Mystique musulmane*, Paris, 1961.
Anderson, S., 'Dervish orders of Constantinople', *M.W.* xii (1922), 53–61.
Andrews, G. F., 'Islam and the Confraternities in French North Africa', *Geog. Journ.* xlvii (1916).
-Anṣārī, Abu Ismāʿīl ʿAbdallāh al-Harawī, *Manāzil as-sāʾirīn* ('The stages of the pilgrims'), ed. and tr. S. de Beaurecueil, Cairo (Institut français d'archéologie orientale du Caire), 1962.
-Anṣārī, Zain ad-dīn Abu Yaḥyā Zakariyā (A.H. 826–910), 'Al-futūḥāt al-ilāhiyya fī nafʿi arwāh adh-dhawāt al-insāniyya', ed. A. H. Harley, *J. Roy. Asiat. Soc. Bengal*, N.S. xx (1924), 123–42.
Arberry, A. J., *An introduction to the history of Sufism*, Oxford, 1942.
—— *Sufism*, London, 1950.
—— *Revelation and reason in Islam*, London–New York, 1957.
Arnakis, G. G., 'Futuwwa traditions in the Ottoman Empire: Akhis, Bektashis, Dervishes and Craftsmen', *Journ. of Near Eastern Studies*, xii, no. 4 (Oct. 1953).
Arnaldez, R., *Ḥallâj ou la religion de la croix*, Paris, Plon (Coll. La Recherche de l'absolu), 1964.
-ʿArūsī, Muṣṭafā M., *Natāʾij al-afkār al-qudsiyya* (commentary on al-Qushairī's *Risāla*), Bulaq, A.H. 1290.
Asín Palacios, M., *Vidas de santones andaluces: la 'Epistola de la santidad' de Ibn ʿArabi de Murcia*, Madrid, 1933.
—— 'Šadhilies y alumbrados', *Al-Andalus*, ix (1944), 321–45; x. 1–52;

xi. 1–67; xii. 1–25, 245–65; xiii. 1–17, 255–73; xiv. 1–28, 253–72; xv. 1–25, 275–88; xvi (1951), 1–15.

Assad-Éfendi, Mohammed, *Précis historique de la destruction du corps des janissaires par le sultan Mahmoud, en 1826*, ed. and tr. A. P. Caussin de Perceval, Paris, 1833.

-ʿAṭṭār, Farīd ad-dīn, *Tadhkirat al-awliyā'* ('Memoirs of the saints'), ed. R. A. Nicholson, 2 vols., London, 1905–7.

—— *Manṭiq aṭ-ṭair* ('Speech of the birds'), ed. G. de Tassy, 1864.

-Attas, M. Naguib, *Rānīrī and the Wujūdiyya of seventeenth century Acheh*, Singapore, 1966.

Aubin, J. *Deux Sayyids de Bam au XVᵉ siècle: contribution à l'histoire de l'Iran timouride*, Wiesbaden, 1956.

—— *Matériaux pour la biographie de Shāh Niʿmatu-'llāh Valī Kirmānī*, Bibliothèque Iranienne, vol. vii, Tehran–Paris, 1956.

—— 'Un santon quhistānī de l'époque timouride', *R.E.I.* xxxv (1967), 185–216.

Babinger, F., 'Das Bektaschi-Kloster Demir Baba', *M.S.O.S.* xxxiv (1931).

—— 'Der Islam in Kleinasien', *Z.D.M.G.* lxxvi, 126–53.

—— 'Schejch Bedr ed-Dīn', *D. Isl.* xi (1921), 1–106; xvii (1928), 100–2.

—— 'Zur Frühgeschichte des Naqschbendī-Ordens', *D. Isl.* xiii (1923), 105–7, 282–3; xiv (1925), 112–14.

Badawī, ʿAbd ar-Raḥmān, *Rasā'il Ibn Sabʿīn*, Cairo, 1956.

—— *Shaṭḥāt aṣ-Ṣūfiyya*: I. *Abū Yazīd*, Cairo, 1949.

—— 'Les points de rencontre de la mystique musulmane et de l'existentialisme', *Studia Islamica*, xxvii (1967), 55–76.

-Bādisī, ʿAbd al-Ḥaqq, *Al-Maqṣad* (Vies des saints du Rîf), tr. G. S. Colin, *Archiv. Maroc.* xxvi (1926), 1–254; xxvii. 1–113.

-Bakrī, M. Tawfīq, *Bait aṣ-Ṣiddīq*, Cairo, 1323/1905.

—— *Bait as-sādāt al-Wafā'iyya*. Cairo, n.d.

Bannerth, E., 'La Khalwatiyya en Égypte', *M.I.D.E.O.* viii (1964–6), 1–74.

Barclay, H. B., *Buuri al Lamaab*, Ithaca, N.Y., 1964.

Barkan, O. L., 'Les derviches colonisateurs turcs de l'époque de la conquête et la zaviye', *Vakiflar Dergisi*, Ankara, ii (1942), 279–386.

Barthold, W., *Turkestan down to the Mongol invasion*, 2nd edn., London, 1928.

Bausani, A., 'Note su Shāh Walīullāh di Delhi', *Annali* (Naples), N.S. x (1960), 93–147.

Beaurecueil, S. de Laugier de, 'Un opuscule de Khwāja ʿAbdallāh Anṣārī concernant les bienséances des Soufis', *B.I.F.A.O.* lix (1960), 203–39.

—— *Khawādja ʿAbdullāh Anṣārī*, Beirut, 1965.

Bel, A., La Religion musulmane en Berbérie, Paris, 1938.

—— 'Le ṣûfisme en Occident musulman au XIIᵉ et au XIIIᵉ siècle de J.-C.', *A.I.E.O.* i (1934–5), 145–61.

—— 'Sidi Bou Medyan et son maître Ed-Daqqaq à Fez', *Mélanges R. Basset*, i (Paris, 1923).

Bennigsen, A., and Lemercier-Quelquejay, C., *Islam in the Soviet Union*, Eng. tr., London, 1967.
Berque, J., 'Un mystique moderniste, le cheikh Ben Alioua', *IIe Congrès des sociétés savantes de l'Afrique du Nord*, 1936, 691–776.
Beveridge, H., 'The Rashaḥāt-i 'Ain al-Ḥayāt', *J.R.A.S.* (1916), 59–75.
Bhatnagar, Ishwar Chandra, 'Mystic monasticism during the Mughal period', *Islamic Culture*, xv (1941), 79–90.
Birge, J. K., *The Bektashi order of dervishes*, London, 1937.
Bisbee, E., *The New Turks*, Philadelphia, 1951.
Bliss, F. J., *The religions of modern Syria and Palestine*, New York, 1912.
Blochet, M.E., 'Études sur l'ésotérisme musulman', *J. Asiat*, sér. IX, xix (1902), 489–521; xx. 49–111.
Borrell, E., 'La confrérie d'Ali Baba à Tchankiri', *R.E.I.* (1936), 309–32.
Bousquet, G. H., 'Introduction à l'étude de l'Islam indonésien', *R.E.I.* (1938,) 133–259.
Bouyges, M., *Essai de chronologie des œuvres d'al-Ghazālī*, ed. M. Allard, Beirut, 1959.
Braune, W., *Die Futūḥ al-Ġaib des 'Abd al-Qādir*, Leipzig, 1933.
Brockelmann, Carl, *Geschichte der arabischen Literatur*, 1897–1902.
Brown, J. P., see Rose, H. A.
Browne, E. G., *A literary history of Persia*, 4 vols., London and Cambridge, 1902–24.
—— 'Notes on the literature of the Ḥurūfīs and their connection with the Bektashī dervishes', *J.R.A.S.* 1907, 533–81.
Brunel, R., *Essai sur la confrérie religieuse des 'Aissaoua au Maroc*, Paris, 1926.
Brunschvig, R., *La Berbérie orientale sous les Ḥafṣides*, 2 vols., Paris, 1940 and 1947.
Burckhardt, T., 'Extracts from the letters of Shaikh al-'Arabi ad-Darqāwī', *Studies in Comparative Religion*, i (1967), 13–21.
—— *An Introduction to Sufi doctrine*, tr. D. M. Matheson, Lahore, 1959.
Burton, Sir Richard F., *Personal narrative of a pilgrimage to al-Madinah and Meccah* (1st edn., 1855), 2 vols., London, 1898.
-Būṣīrī, M. b. Sa'īd, *Qaṣīdat al-burda* ('The mantle ode': poem in praise of the Prophet), tr. and comment. R. Basset, *La Bordah*, Paris, 1894, Eng. tr. by J. W. Redhouse in Clouston, W. A., *Arabian poetry for English readers*, Glasgow, 1881, 319–41.
Busse, H., 'Abd al-Ġanī an-Nābulsīs Reisen im Lebanon 1100/1689–1112/1700', *D. Isl.* xliv (1968), 71–114.
Canaan, T., *Mohammedan saints and sanctuaries in Palestine*, London, 1927.
Carra de Vaux, B., *Les Penseurs de l'Islam*, 5 vols., Paris, 1921–6.
—— 'La philosophie illuminative d'après Suhrawardī Meqtoul', *J. Asiat.* sér. IX, xix (1902), 63–94.
Carson, W. M., 'The social history of an Egyptian factory', *M.E.J.* xi (1957).

Castagné, J., 'Le culte des lieux saints de l'Islam au Turkestan', *L'Ethnographie*, 1951, 46–124.

Choublier, M., 'Les bektachis et la Rouméli', *R.E.I.* i (1927), 427–50.

Corbin, H., *Suhrawardi d'Alep*, Paris, 1939.

—— *L'Imagination créatrice dans le soufisme d'Ibn 'Arabî*, Paris, Flammarion, 1958.

—— *Histoire de la philosophie islamique*, with the collaboration of S. H. Nasr and O. Yahya, vol. i, Paris, 1964.

—— 'L'intériorisation du sens en herméneutique soufie iranienne', *Eranos-Jahrbuch*, xxvi (Zurich, 1958), 137–73.

Cour, A., 'Recherches sur l'état des confréries religieuses musulmanes', *Revue Africaine*, 1921.

Creswell, K. A. C. *The Muslim architecture of Egypt*, vol. ii, Oxford, 1959.

-Dabbāgh, Abu Zaid 'AR. b. M. al-Anṣārī (d. 696/1296), *Mashāriq anwār al-qulūb*, ed. H. Ritter, Beirut, 1379/1959.

D'Alverny, A. 'La prière selon le Coran', *Proche-Orient chrétien*, Jerusalem, 1961, 3–16.

-Dardīr, Aḥmad, *Mawlid an-Nabī*, with commentary by Ibrāhīm al-Bayjūrī, Cairo, 1921.

—— *Tuḥfat al-ikhwān fī adab ahl al-'irfān*, Cairo, 1964.

Dawlatshāh, *Tadhkirat ash-shu'arā'* ('Memoirs of the poets'), ed. E. G. Browne, London–Leiden, 1901.

Deladrière, R., 'Abu Yazīd al-Bisṭāmī et son enseignement spirituel', *Arabica*, xiv (1967), 76–89.

Depont, O., and Coppolani, X., *Les Confréries religieuses musulmanes*, Algiers, 1897.

Dermenghem, E., *Le Culte des saints dans l'Islam maghrébin*, Paris, 1954.

—— *Vies des saints musulmans*, Algiers, 1942.

D'Ohsson, Mouradgea, *Tableau général de l'empire ottoman*, 5 vols., Paris, 1788–91.

Douglas, E. H., 'Al-Shādhilī, a North African Sufi, according to Ibn Ṣabbāgh', *M.W.* xxxviii (1948), 257–79.

Drague, G., *Esquisse d'histoire religieuse du Maroc: confréries et zaouias*, Paris, 1951.

Edmonds, C. J., 'The Kurds and the revolution in Iraq', *M.E.J.* xiii (1959), 1–10.

Evans-Pritchard, E. E., *The Sanusi of Cyrenaica*, Oxford, 1949.

Evliya Chelebi, *Narrative of Travels in Europe, Asia and Africa by Evliya Efendi*, tr. J. von Hammer-Purgstall, 2 vols., London, 1834–50.

Farrūkh, 'Umar, *At-taṣawwuf fī 'l-Islām*, Beirut, 1947.

Fauque, L. P., 'Où en est l'Islam traditionnel en Algérie?', *L'Afrique et l'Asie*, no. 55 (1961), 17–22.

Flügel, G., 'Scha'rānī und sein Werk über die muhammadanische Glaubenslehre', *Z.D.M.G.* xx (1866), 1–48; xxi (1867), 271–344.

Garcin, J. C., 'Index des Ṭabaqāt de Sha'rānī', *Annales islamologiques* (Institut français d'archéologie orientale du Caire), vi (1966), 31–94.

Garcin de Tassey, J. H., *Mémoire sur les particularités de la religion musulmane dans l'Inde*, 1874.

Gardet, L. *Expériences mystiques en terres non-chrétiennes*, Paris, 1953.
—— *Thèmes et textes mystiques. Recherche de critères en mystique comparée*, Paris, 1958.
—— 'La langue arabe et l'analyse des états spirituels', *Mélanges Louis Massignon*, ii. 215–43.
Gardet, L., and Anawati, G. C., see Anawati.
Gaudefroy-Demombynes, M., *La Syrie à l'époque des mamelouks*, Paris, 1923.
-Ghaiṭī, Najm ad-dīn, *Qiṣṣat al-miʿrāj al-kubrā.*
-Ghazālī, Abu Ḥāmid M., *Iljām al-ʿawām ʿan ʿilm al-kalām*, Cairo, A.H. 1351.
—— *Al-munqidh min aḍ-ḍalāl* ('That which delivers from error'), Damascus edn., 1358/1939.
—— *Iḥyā' ʿulūm ad-dīn* ('Revivification of the religious sciences'), Cairo, A.H. 1272, etc., see M. Murtaḍā az-Zabīdī.
-Ghazālī, Abu 'l-Futūḥ Aḥmad, *Sawāniḥ al-ʿushshāq* ('Intuitions of the lovers', a treatise on love, the lover, and the beloved), paraphrased in Persian by ʿAin al-Quḍāt al-Hamadānī as *Lawā'iḥ*, ed. H. Ritter, *Aphorismen über die Liebe*, Istanbul-Leipzig, 1942 (Bibliotheca Islamica, Bd. 15).
—— *Bawāriq al-ilmāʿ*, ed. and tr. J. Robson, *Tracts on listening to music*, London, 1938.
—— (attribution?), *Risālat aṭ-ṭair*, ed. L. Cheikho, *Al-Mashriq*, iv (1901), 918–24.
—— *Kitāb at-tajrīd fī kalimat at-tawḥīd*, Cairo, 1325/1907, *G.A.L.S.* i. 756.
Giacobetti, A., *La Confrérie de la Raḥmānīya*, Algiers, 1950.
Gibb, H. A. R., and Bowen, H., *Islamic society and the West*: I. *Islamic society in the eighteenth century*, London, 2 vols., 1950 and 1957.
Gilsenan, M. D., 'Some factors in the decline of the Sufi orders in modern Egypt', *M.W.* lvii (1967), 11–18.
Gobineau, J. A., *Les Religions et les philosophies dans l'Asie centrale*, 2nd edn., Paris, 1866.
Gramlich, R., *Die schiitischen Derwischorden Persiens. Erster Teil: Die Affiliationen*, Wiesbaden, 1965.
Guys, H., *Un Derviche algérien en Syrie*, Paris, 1854.
Haas, W. S., 'The zikr of the Rahmaniya order in Algeria', *M.W.* xxxiii (1943), 16–28.
-Ḥabshī ʿAlī b. M. *Simṭ ad-durar* ('String of pearls'), known as *Mawlid al-Ḥabshī*, Cairo, 1355/1936, etc.
Hadj-Sadok, M., 'Le *Mawlid* d'après le mufti poète d'Alger Ibn ʿAmmār', *Mélanges Louis Massignon*, ii. 269–92.
Ḥaidar, Muḥammad, *Ta'rīkh-i Rashīdī*, tr. E. D. Ross, London, 1895.
Ḥājjī Khalīfa, *Kashf aẓ-ẓunūn. Lexicon bibliographicum et encyclopædicum.* Arabic text and Lat. tr. G. Flügel, 7 vols., Leipzig–London, 1835–58.
Ḥājjī Sulṭān, *Das Vilâjet-nâme des Hâdschim Sultan*, ed. and tr. by Rudolf Tschudi, Berlin, 1914.

Hammer-Purgstall, J. von., *Geschichte des osmanischen Reiches*, 10 vols., Pest, 1827–35 (reimpression, Graz, 1963).
——*Histoire de l'empire othoman*, tr. J. J. Hellert, Paris, 1835–43.
-Harawī, ʿAlī b. Abī Bakr, *Guide des lieux de pèlerinage* (*Kitāb az-ziyārāt*), tr. J. Sourdel-Thomine, Damascus, 1957.
-Ḥarāzimī, Abu 'l-Ḥasan ʿAlī, *Jawāhir al-maʿānī wa bulūgh al-amānī fī faiḍ Abī 'l-ʿAbbās Aḥmad at-Tijānī*, 2 vols., Cairo, 1348/1929.
Hartmann, R., 'As-Sulamī's *Risālat al-Malāmatīja*', *D. Isl.* viii (1918), 157–203.
—— *Al-Ḳuchairīs Darstellung des Ṣufitums*, Türk. Biblio. 18, Berlin, 1914.
—— 'Futuwwa und Malāma', *Z.D.M.G.* lxxii (1918), 193–8.
Hasluck, F. W., *Christianity and Islam under the Sultans*, 2 vols., Oxford, 1929.
Ḥasrat, Bikramājīt, *Dārā Shikūh: His life and works*, Visvabharati, Santiniketan, 1953.
Hekmat, A. A., 'Les voyages d'un mystique persan de Hamadan au Kashmir', *J. Asiat.* ccxl (1952), 53–66.
Horten, M., *Lexikon wichtigster Termini der islamischen Mystik*, Heidelberg, 1928.
Huart, Cl., see Aflākī.
—— *Textes persans relatifs à la secte des Houroufis*, *G.M.S.*, Leiden, 1909.
—— *Konia, la ville des derviches tourneurs*, Paris. 1897.
Hughes, T. P., *Dictionary of Islam*, London, 1885.
-Hujwīrī, Abu 'l-Ḥasan ʿAlī al-Jullābī, *Kashf al-maḥjūb*, abridged tr. R. A. Nicholson, *G.M.S.*, London, 1936.
Huri, Sofi, 'Yunus Emre: In Memoriam', *M.W.* xlix (1959), 111–23.
Ḥusain, Yūsuf, *L'Inde mystique au moyen âge*, Paris, 1929.
—— 'Les Kâyasthâs ou "scribes", caste hindoue iranisée et la culture musulmane dans l'Inde', *R.E.I.* (1927).
—— '*Ḥawḍ al-Ḥayāt*: la version arabe de l'Amratkund', *J. Asiat.* ccxiii (1928), 291–344.
Husaini, Ishaq Musa, *The Moslem Brethren*, Beirut, 1956.
Ibn ʿAbbād, Aḥmad b. M., *Al-mafākhir al-ʿaliyya fī 'l-maʾāthir ash-Shādhiliyya*, Cairo, A.H. 1327.
Ibn ʿAbbād ar-Rundī, *Lettres de direction spirituelle* (*Ar-rasāʾil aṣ-ṣughrā*), ed. P. Nwyia, Beirut, 1958.
Ibn Abī Uṣaibiʿa, *ʿUyūn al-anbāʾ fī ṭabaqāt al-aṭibbāʾ* ('Classes of the physicians'), Cairo, 1299/1882; Beirut, Maktaba al-Ḥayāt, 1965.
Ibn Abī Zarʿ, *Rawḍ al-Qirṭās*, tr. A. Baumier, Paris, 1860.
Ibn al-Aḥmar, *Rawḍat an-nisrīn*, ed. and tr. Gh. Bouali and G. Marçais, Paris, 1917.
Ibn al-ʿArabī, Muḥyiddīn, *Tarjumān al-ashwāq* ('Interpreter of longings'), mystical odes ed. and tr. R. A. Nicholson with tr. of Ibn al-ʿArabī's own commentary, London, 1911; text of the poems and commentary, Dār Ṣādar, Beirut, 1386/1966.
—— *Al-asfār ʿan risālat al-anwār fīmā yatajallā li ahl adh-dhikr min al-anwār*, with commentary by ʿAbd al-Karīm al-Jīlī, Damascus, 1348/1929.

—— *Al-amr al-muḥkam al-marbūṭ fī mā yalzam ahl ṭarīq Allāh min ash-shurūṭ*, Istanbul, 1315/1897; Beirut, 1330/1912.

—— *Fuṣūṣ al-ḥikam* ('Bezels of wisdom'), ed. Abu 'l-ʿAlā' ʿAfīfī, Cairo, 1946.

—— *Kunh mā lā budda minhu li 'l-murīd*, Cairo, A.H. 1328.

—— *Al-futūḥāt al-Makkiyya* ('Meccan revelatory disclosures'), Cairo, A.H. 1329.

—— *At-tadbīrāt al-ilāhiyya fī iṣlāḥ al-mamlaka al-insāniyya*, Kleinere Schriften, ed. H. S. Nyberg, Leiden, 1919.

Ibn al-ʿArīf, Abu'l-ʿAbbās Aḥmad, *Maḥāsin al-majālis*, ed. and comment. M. Asin Palacios, Paris, 1933.

Ibn ʿAskar, *Dawhat an-nāshir*, tr. A. Graulle, *Archiv. Maroc.* xix (1913), 1–342.

Ibn ʿAṭā' Allāh al-Iskandarī, Tāj ad-dīn Aḥmad, *Laṭā'if al-minan fī manāqib Abī 'l-ʿAbbās al-Mursī wa shaikhihi Abī 'l-Ḥasan ash-Shādhilī*, on the margin of Shaʿrānī's *Laṭā'if al-minan*, Cairo, A.H. 1357, i. 2–ii. 88.

—— *Kitāb miftāḥ al-falāḥ wa misbāḥ al-arwāḥ*, on margin of Shaʿrānī's *Laṭā'if*, Cairo, 1357, ii. 89–234.

Ibn Baṭṭūṭa, *Voyages d'Ibn Batouta*, text and tr. C. Defrémery and B. R. Sanguinetti, 4 vols., Paris, 1853–8.

—— *Riḥla Ibn Baṭūṭa*, ed. Aḥmad al-ʿAwāmirī and M. Aḥmad Jād al-Mawlā, 2 vols., Cairo, 1939.

—— *Riḥla Ibn Baṭūṭa*. Cairo edn., al-maṭbaʿat al-Azhariyya, 1346/1928.

—— *Travels of Ibn Battuta*, tr. H. A. R. Gibb, Hakluyt Society, i. 1958; ii. 1962.

Ibn (Wad) Ḍaif Allāh, M. b. M. (A.H. 1139–1224), *Kitāb aṭ-ṭabaqāt fī khuṣūṣ al-awliyā'* wa *'ṣ-ṣāliḥīn wa 'l-ʿulamā' wa 'sh-shuʿarā fi s-Sūdān*, (*a*) ed. Ibrāhīm Ṣidaiq, Cairo, Maḥmūdiyya Press, 1930; (*b*) ed. Sulaimān Da'ūd Mandīl, Cairo, Muqtaṭaf Press, 1930.

Ibn al-Fuwaṭī, ʿAbd ar-Razzāq b. Aḥmad, *Al-Ḥawādith al-jāmiʿa*, ed. H. Jawād, Baghdad, 1351/1932.

Ibn Ḥajar al-ʿAsqalānī, Shihāb ad-dīn A. b. ʿAlī, *Ad-durar al- kāmina fī aʿyān al-mi'at ath-thāmina*, 2nd edn., M. Sayyid Jād al-Ḥaqq, Cairo, 1966.

Ibn Hudhail, ʿAlī b. ʿAR, *L'Ornement des âmes* (*Tuḥfat al-anfus*), tr. L. Mercier, Paris, 1939.

Ibn al-ʿImād al-Ḥanbalī (Abu 'l-Futūḥ ʿAbd al-Ḥayy, d. 1089/1678), *Shadharāt adh-dhahab fī akhbār man dhahab*, Cairo, 8 vols., A.H. 1350–1.

Ibn Iyās, *An account of the Ottoman conquest of Egypt*, tr. W. N. Salmon, London, 1921.

Ibn al-Jawzī, ʿAbd ar-Raḥmān, *Naqd al-ʿilm wa 'l-ʿulamā' aw Talbīs Iblīs*, Cairo edn., 1928; tr. D. S. Margoliouth, 'The Devil's Delusion' in *Islamic Culture* (Hyderabad), ix (1935)–xxii (1948).

Ibn Jubair, Abu 'l-Ḥusain M., *Riḥla* (Travels), 2nd edn., ed. W. Wright and M. J. de Goeje, G.M.S. V, Leiden–London, 1907; tr. R. J. C. Broadhurst, *The travels of Ibn Jubayr*, London, 1952; tr. M. Gaudefroy-Demombynes, 3 vols., Paris, 1949–56.

Ibn Kathīr, ʿImād ad-dīn Ismāʿīl, *Al-bidāya wa 'n-nihāya*, 14 vols., Cairo, 1351–8.

Ibn Khaldūn, *Kitāb al-ʿIbar* (Universal history), Bulaq, 7 vols., 1284/1868; Beirut 1956–9.

—— *The Muqaddimah*, tr. F. Rosenthal, 3 vols., New York–London, 1958.

—— *At-taʿrīf bi 'bni Khaldūn* (Autobiography to Dhū 'l-Qaʿda 807), ed. M. b. Tāwīt aṭ-Ṭanjī, Cairo, 1370/1951.

—— *Shifā' as-sā'il li tahdhīb al-masā'il* ('Satisfaction for the searcher after the elucidation of problems' in Sufism), edn. with intro. and vocab. by Ignace-Abdo Khalifé, Beirut, 1959; ed. M. b. Tāwīt aṭ-Ṭanjī, Ankara, 1958.

Ibn Khallikān, Aḥmad, *Wafayāt al-aʿyān wa anbā' abnā' az-zamān* ('Obituaries of the famous', a biographical dictionary), Cairo, A.H. 1275, 1299; tr. Baron MacGuckin de Slane, 4 vols., Paris, 1842–71; repr. 1961.

Ibn Marzūq, *Musnad*, ed. and tr. E. Lévi-Provençal in *Hespéris*, v. 1925.

Ibn al-Munawwar, M., *Asrār at-tawḥīd fī maqāmāt ash-Shaikh Abī Saʿīd* ('Mysteries of the divine unity as related to the stations of Abu Saʿīd b. Abī 'l-Khair), ed. Dhabīḥallāh-i Ṣafā, Tehran, A.H. 1332; ed. V. A. Zhukovsky, St. Petersburg, 1899; Arab. tr. by Qandīl Isʿād ʿAbd al-Hādī, Cairo, Dār at-Taʿlīf, 1966.

Ibn an-Nadīm, M. b. Isḥāq, *Fihrist* ('Index'), ed. G. Flügel, Leipzig, 1871–2.

Ibn Sabʿīn, 'Correspondance du philosophe soufi Ibn Sabʿīn Abd oul-Haqq avec l'empereur Frédéric II de Hohenstaufen', tr. A. F. Mehren, *J. Asiat.*, sér. VII, xiv (1880), 341–454.

Ibn Shākir al-Kutubī, *Fawāt al-Wafayāt* ('Omissions from *The Obituaries*' of Ibn Khallikān), Bulaq, 1283/1866, Cairo 1951.

Ibn ash-Shiḥna (d. 890/1485), *Ad-durr al-muntakhab fī ta'rīkh mamlakat Ḥalab*, ed. V. Sarkīs, Beirut, 1909; see Sauvaget.

Ibn Sīnā (Avicenna), Abū ʿAlī al-Ḥusain. *Risālat aṭ-ṭair*, ed. L. Cheikho, *Al-Mashriq*, iv (1901), 882–7.

—— *Traités mystiques*, ed. A. F. Mehren, Paris, 1891.

Ibn Taghrī-birdī, Abu 'l-Maḥāsin Y., *An-nujūm az-zāhira fi mulūk Miṣr wa 'l-Qāhira*, ed. W. Popper, Berkeley–Leiden, 1908–36.

Ibn Taimiya, *Majmūʿat ar-rasā'il wa 'l-masā'il*, 2 vols., Cairo, A.H. 1341–5.

—— *Majmūʿ fatāwī*, Cairo, A.H. 1326–9, Riyāḍ, A.H. 1381.

Ibn az-Zayyāt = Abu Yaʿqūb Yūsuf b. Yaḥyā at-Tādilī, *At-tashawwuf ilā rijāl at-taṣawwuf*, Rabat, 1958.

Iqbāl, Muḥammad, *The reconstruction of religious thought in Islam*, Oxford, 1934.

—— *The development of metaphysics in Persia*, London, 1908.

-Irbillī, al-Ḥasan b. Aḥmad, *Madāris Dimishq*, ed. Tawfīq M. A. Dahān, Damascus, 1366/1947.

Ismāʿīl b. ʿAbdallāh, *Al-ʿuhūd al-wāfiya fī kaifiyyat ṣifat aṭ-ṭarīqat al-Ismāʿīliyya*, Cairo, n.d. (1937?).

—— *Al-Mawlid ash-sharīf* (completed in A.H. 1240), Cairo, 1358/1939.
—— *Kitāb mashāriq shumūs al-anwār*, Cairo, 1357.
Ismāʿīl b. M. Saʿīd, *Al-fuyūḍāt ar-rabbāniyya*, Cairo, A.H. 1353.
Ivanow, W., *Ismaili literature: a bibliographical survey*, Tehran, 1963.
—— *Studies in early Ismailism*, Leiden, 1948.
—— 'The sources of the *Nafaḥāt*', *J.R.A.S.* 1922, 385–91.
-Jabartī, ʿAbd ar-Raḥmān, *ʿAjā'ib al-āthār fī 't-tarājim wa 'l-akhbār*, 4 vols., Cairo, 1322/1904; ed. Ḥasan M. Jawhar, Cairo, 1958.
Jabre, F., 'La biographie et l'œuvre de Ghazali reconsidérées à la lumière des *Ṭabaqāt* de Sobki', *M.I.D.E.O.* i (1954), 73–102.
—— *La Notion de la maʿrifa selon Ghazālī*, Beirut, 1958.
—— *La Notion de la certitude selon Ghazālī*, Paris, 1958.
Jaʿfar b. M. ʿUthmān al-Mirghanī. *Quṣṣat al-miʿrāj* or *Al-ʿuqūd al-fā'iqat ad-durriyya fī bathth quṣṣat al-asrā' bi sayyid Walad ʿAdnān*, Cairo, A.H. 1348.
Jāmī, ʿAbd ar-Raḥmān, *Kitāb Nafaḥāt al-uns* ('Breaths of divine intimacy'), ed. W. Nassau Lees, Calcutta, 1859; ed. M. Tawḥīdīpūr, Tehran, 1337/1919; tr. Silvestre de Sacy, *Not. et extr. des mss. Biblio. Nat.*, xii (1831), 287–436.
—— *Lawā'iḥ* (Light-shafts), tr. E. H. Whinfield and Mīrzā Muḥammad Qazvīnī, Or. Tr. Fund, 1906, 1928.
Jaussen, J. A., *Coutumes palestiniennes*, Paris, 1927.
-Jawsqī, M. ʿAlwān, *As-sirr al-abhar fī awrād Aḥmad at-Tijānī*, in M. b. ʿAbdallāh aṭ-Ṭaṣafāwī, *Al-fatḥ ar-rabbānī*, Cairo, n.d.
-Jazūlī, Abū ʿAbdallāh M., *Dalā'il al-khairāt* ('Proofs of the excellencies'), multiple printings.
-Jīlī, ʿAbd al-Karīm, *Al-Insān al-kāmil*, in R. A. Nicholson, *Studies in Islamic mysticism*, Cambridge, 1921.
Johns, A. H., 'Muslim mystics and historical writing', *Historians of South-east Asia*, ed. D. G. E. Hall, London, 1961.
-Junaid of Baghdad, Abu 'l-Qāsim, *The life, personality and writings of al-Junayd*, ed. Ali Hassan Abdel-Kader, *G.M.S.* London, 1962.
-Junaid Shīrāzī, Muʿīn ad-dīn Abu 'l-Qāsim, *Shadd al-izār fī khaṭṭ al-awzār ʿan zuwwār al-mazār* ('On places of visitation of dead Shirazi worthies'), ed. M. Qazvīnī and ʿAbbās Iqbāl, Tehran, 1328/1910.
-Kalābadhī, Abu Bakr, *Kitāb at-taʿarruf li madhhab ahl at-taṣawwuf* ('Book of inquiry into the tenets of the Sufis'), ed. (Cairo, 1934) and tr. (Cambridge, 1935) by A. J. Arberry.
Karpat, K. H., 'Social themes in contemporary Turkish literature', *M.E.J.* xiv (1960), 29–44, 153–68.
-Kattānī, M. b. Jaʿfar, *Salwat al-anfās*, 3 vols., lith. Fez, 1316/1898.
Kedourie, E., *Afghani and ʿAbduh*, London, 1966.
Khurd, Amīr, *Siyar al-awliyā'* (lives of early Chishtī shaikhs), Delhi, A.H. 1309.
-Kindī, *Quḍāt Miṣr*, ed. R. Guest, London, 1912.
Kissling, H. J., 'Die Wunder des Derwisches', *Z.D.M.G.* cvii, Heft 2, N.F. 32 (1957), 348–61.

Kissling, H. J., 'The sociological and educational role of the dervish orders in the Ottoman empire', *Memoirs of the American Anthropological Assn.*, no. 76 (1954), 23–35.
—— 'The role of the dervish orders in the Ottoman empire', *Studies in Islamic Cultural History,* ed. G. E. von Grunebaum, Chicago, 1954, 23–35.
—— 'Zur Geschichte des Derwischordens der Bajrāmijje', in *Südostforschungen,* xv (1956), 237 ff.
—— 'Aus der Geschichte der Chalvetijje-Ordens', *Z.D.M.G.* cii (1953), 233–319.
—— 'Die islamischen Derwischorden', *Zeitschrift für Religions- und Geistesgeschichte,* xii (1960), 1–16.
—— 'Ša'bān Velî und die Ša'bânijje', in *Serta Monacensia,* F. Babinger *zum 15. Januar 1951 als Festgruß dargebracht,* Leiden, 1952.
—— 'Āq Šems ed-Dîn: Ein türkischer Heiliger aus der Endzeit von Byzans', *Byzantinische Zeitschrift,* xliv (1951).
—— 'Einiges über den Zejnîje-Orden im osmanischen Reiche', *D. Isl.* xxxix (1964), 143–79.
Köprülüzade, Meḥmed Fu'ād, 'Abu Isḥāq Kāserūnī und die Isḥāqī-Derwische in Anatolien', *D. Isl.* xix (1931), 18–26.
—— *Influence du chamanisme turco-mongol sur les ordres mystiques musulmans,* Istanbul, 1929.
—— 'Les origines du bektachisme', *Actes du Congrès international d'histoire des religions,* 1925, ii. 391–411.
—— *Türk edebiyatenda ilk muteṣavviflar* ('The first mystics in Turkish literature'), pt. i, Istanbul, 1919 (Ankara, 1966); summarized by L. Bouvat in *R.M.M.* xliii (1921), 236–82.
Kremer, A. von, 'Notice sur Sha'râny', *J. Asiat.* sér. VI, xi (1868), 253–71.
—— 'Mollâ-Shâh' [= Mullah Shāh Badakhshī's life by Tawakkul Beg Kulalī]. *J. Asiat.* sér. VI, xiii (1869), 105–59.
Kubrā, Najm ad-dīn, *Die Fawā'iḥ al-jamāl wa fawātiḥ al-jalāl des Najm ad-dīn al-Kubrā,* ed. F. Meier, Wiesbaden, 1957.
—— *Ādāb al-murīdīn,* tr. F. Meier, 'Ein Knigge für Ṣūfī's', *R.S.O.* xxxii (1957), 485–524.
-Kutubī, see M. b. Shākir.
Lahhabi, Mohamed Aziz, *Le Personnalisme musulman,* Paris, 1964.
Lane, E. W., *The manners and customs of the modern Egyptians* (1st edn., 1836); Everyman edn., from 1908.
Lawrence, W. R., *The valley of Kashmir,* London, 1895.
Lebedew, O. de, *Traité sur le soufisme par Kochaïri,* Rome, 1911.
Le Chatelier, A., *Les Confréries musulmanes du Hedjaz,* Paris, 1887.
Leroy, J., *Monks and monasteries of the Near East,* Eng. tr., London, 1963.
Lévi-Provençal, E., *Les Historiens des Chorfa,* Paris, 1922.
Lewis, I. M., 'Sufism in Somaliland', *B.S.O.A.S.* xvii (1955), 581–602; xviii (1956), 146–60.
Lings, M., *A Moslem saint of the twentieth century: Shaikh Aḥmad al-'Alawī,* London, 1961.

Littmann, O., *Aḥmed il-Bedawī: ein Lied auf den ägyptischen Nationalheiligen*, Wiesbaden, 1950.
MacCallum, F. L., *The Mevlidi Sherif*, London, 1943.
Macdonald, D. B., 'Emotional religion in Islam as affected by music and singing', *J.R.A.S.* 1901, 195–252, 705–48; 1902, 1–28.
—— 'The life of al-Ghazzālī', *J. Amer. Or. Soc.* xx (1899), 71–132.
—— *Aspects of Islam*, New York, 1911.
—— *The religious attitude and life in Islam*, Chicago; 2nd edn., 1912.
—— *Development of Muslim theology, jurisprudence and constitutional theory*, New York, 1903.
McPherson, J. W., *The Moulids of Egypt*, Cairo, 1941.
-Maqdisī (-Muqaddasī), Shams ad-dīn Abū ʿAbdallāh M., *Aḥsan at-taqāsīm* (*Descriptio imperii moslemici*), ed. M. J. de Goeje, 2nd edn., Leiden, 1906.
-Maqrīzī, Taqī ad-dīn Aḥmad, *Al-Khiṭaṭ. Al-mawāʿiẓ wa 'l-iʿtibār bi dhikr al-khiṭaṭ wa 'l-āthār*, 4 vols., Cairo, A.H. 1326.
Marçais, G., 'Note sur les ribats en Berbérie', *Mélanges d'histoire et archéol. de l'occident musulman*, Algiers, i. 23–36.
Margoliouth, D. S., 'Contributions to the biography of ʿAbd al-Qādir of Jīlān', *J.R.A.S.* 1907, 267–310.
—— 'An Islamic saint of the seventh century A.H.' (= Taqiyyaddīn M. al-Yūnīnī by his son Quṭb ad-dīn Mūsā), *Islamic Culture*, xiii (1939), 263–89.
Massignon, Louis, *La Passion d'al-Ḥosayn Ibn Manṣour al-Ḥallāj*, 2 vols., Paris, 1922.
—— *Essai sur les origines du lexique technique de la mystique musulmane*, 2nd edn., Paris, 1954.
—— *Recueil de textes inédits, concernant l'histoire de la mystique en pays d'Islam*, Paris, 1929.
—— 'Les saints musulmans enterrés à Bagdad', *Revue de l'histoire des religions*, 1908; repr. in *Opera Minora*, Beirut, iii (1963), 94–101.
—— Art. 'Ṭarīḳa', in *E.I.*[1] iv. 667–72.
—— Art. 'Taṣawwuf', in *E.I.*[1] iv. 681–5.
Meier, F., 'Soufisme et déclin culturel', in *Classicisme et déclin culturel dans l'histoire de l'Islam*, Paris, 1957, 217–45.
—— *Firdōs al-murshidiyya: Die vita des Scheichs Abu Isḥāq al-Kāzerūnī*, Leipzig, 1948 (Bibliotheca Islamica, 14).
—— 'Stambuler Handschriften dreier persischer Mystiker: ʿAin al-quḍāt al-Hamadhānī, Najm ad-dīn Kubrā, Najm ad-dīn ad-Dāja', *D. Isl.* xxiv (1937), 1–42.
—— 'Die Welt der Urbilder bei Ali Hamadani', *Eranos-Jahrbuch*, xviii (1950), 115–73.
Michaux-Bellaire, E., 'Les confréries religieuses au Maroc', *Arch. Maroc.* xxvii (1927).
—— 'Les Derqaoua de Tanger', *R.M.M.* xxxix (1920), 98–118.
Miḥrābī, *Mazārāt-i Kirmān*, Tehran, A.H. 1330.
Miller, W. McE., 'Shīʿah mysticism: the Ṣūfīs of Gunabad', *M.W.* xiii (1923), 343–63.

-Mirghanī, M. ʿUthmān, *Mawlid an-Nabī*, Cairo, A.H. 1348, etc.
—— *Majmūʿ awrād aṭ-ṭarīqat al-Khatmiyya*, Cairo, A.H. 1344, etc.
Mokri, M., 'Le soufisme et la musique', in *Encyclopédie de la musique*, ed. Fasquelle, Paris, 1961, tome iii.
Molé, M. *Les Mystiques musulmans*, Paris, 1965.
—— 'Autour du Daré Mansour: l'apprentissage mystique de Bahā' ad-dīn Naqšband', *R.E.I.* (1959), 35–66.
—— 'Les Kubrawiya entre sunnisme et shiisme aux huitième et neuvième siècles de l'hégire', *R.E.I.* xxix (1961), 61–142.
—— 'Traités mineurs de Nağm al-dīn Kubrā', *Annales Islamologiques*, Cairo, iv (1963), 1–78.
Montet, E., 'Les confréries religieuses de l'Islam marocain', *Rev. hist. religions*, xlv (1902).
Moreno, M. M., 'Mistica musulmana e mistica indiana', *Annali Lateranensi*, xii (1948).
Mubārak, ʿAlī, *Al-khiṭaṭ al-jadīda at-tawfīqiyya*, 20 vols., Bulaq, 1306/1888–9.
Muḥammad al-ʿAbdarī, *Al-mudkhal ash-Sharʿ*, 3 vols., Alexandria, A.H. 1291.
Muḥammad b. Aḥmad al-Fāsī, *Shifā' al-gharām fī akhbār al-balad al-Ḥarām*, Cairo, 1956.
Muḥammad b. Ḥamza Ẓāfir al-Madanī, *An-nūr as-sātiʿ*, Istanbul, 1301/1884.
Muḥammad al-Mahdī al-Fāsī, *Mumattiʿ al-asmā fī dhikr al-Jazūlī wa 't-Tabbāʿ*, tr. in *Archiv. Maroc.* xix.
Muḥammad b. Mukhtār ash-Shinqīṭī (Wad al-ʿAliya), *ʿUnwān maṭāliʿ al-jamāl fī mawlid insān ʿain al-kamāl*, 1st edn., Maṭbaʿa Maḥmūdiyya, Cairo, 1353/1934.
Muḥammad ibn Shākir b. A. al-Kutubī, *Fawāt al-wafayāt* ('Omissions from the obituaries'), 2 vols., Bulaq, 1283/1866.
-Muḥibbī, M., *Khulāṣat al-athar fi aʿyān al-qarn al-ḥādī ʿashar*, Cairo, 1384.
Mujeeb, M., *The Indian Muslims*, London, 1967.
Mujīr ad-dīn al-ʿUlaimī, *Al-uns al-jalīl bi ta'rīkh al-Quds wa 'l-Khalīl*, 2 vols., Cairo, A.H. 1283; tr. H. Sauvaire, *Histoire de Jérusalem et d'Hébron*, Paris, 1876.
Murādī, M. Khalīl, *Silk ad-durar fī aʿyān al-qarn ath-thānī ʿashar* (biographical dictionary of the famous of the 12th/18th century), 4 vols., Cairo, 1874–83.
-Murtaḍā, M. b. M. b. al-Ḥusain az-Zabīdī (d. 1205/1790), *Itḥāf as-sāda* (commentary on Ghazālī's *Iḥyā'*), 10 vols., Cairo, A.H. 1311.
Nāṣirī, Aḥmad b. Khālid, *Kitāb al-istiqṣā li akhbār duwal al-Maghrib al-aqṣā*, 4 vols., Cairo, 1312/1894; tr. in *Archiv. Maroc.* ix–x, xiv, xvii, xxv–xxxiv.
Nasr, Sayyid Husain, *Three Muslim sages*, Harvard Univ. Pr., 1964.
Nicholson, R. A., *The idea of personality in Sufism*, Cambridge, 1923.
—— *The mystics of Islam*, London, 1914.
—— *Studies in Islamic mysticism*, Cambridge, 1921.

—— 'A historical inquiry concerning the origin and development of Ṣūfīism', *J.R.A.S.* 1906, 303–48.
—— 'The goal of Muhammadan mysticism', *J.R.A.S.* 1913, 55–68.
—— 'Sufis', *E.R.E.* xii (1921), 10–17.
—— *Selected odes from the Dīwān-i Shams-i Tibrīz*, Persian text and Eng. tr. by H. A. N., Cambridge, 1898.
—— 'The lives of ʿUmar Ibnul-Fāriḍ and Ibnul-ʿArabī', *J.R.A.S.* 1906, 797–824 (as given in Ibn al-ʿImād's *Shadharāt*).
Nikitine, B., 'Essai d'analyse du Ṣafvat-uṣ-Ṣafā', *J. Asiat.* ccxlv (1957), 385–94.
Nizami, K. A., *Religion and politics in India during the thirteenth century*, Bombay, 1961.
—— *The life and times of Shaikh Farīd ad-Dīn Ganj-i Shakar*, Aligarh, 1955.
—— 'Some aspects of khānqah life in medieval India', *Studia Islamica*, viii (1957), 51–69.
—— 'Naqshbandi influence on Mughal rulers and politics', *Islamic Culture*, xxxix (1965), 41–52.
—— Arts. 'Čishtī' and 'Čishtiyya' in *E.I.*[2] ii. 49–56.
Nwyia, P., *Ibn ʿAbbād de Ronda (1332–90)*, Beirut, 1956.
—— *Les Lettres de direction spirituelle d'Ibn ʿAbbād de Ronda (ar-rasāʾil aṣ-ṣughrā)*, Beirut, 1958.
Oliver Asín, J., 'Origen árabe de rebato', *Boletín de la Real Academia Española*, Madrid, 1928.
Oman, G., 'Uno "specchio per principi" del'Imām ʿAlī ibn Abī Ṭālib', *Annali*, N.S. x (1960), 1–35.
Padwick, Constance E., *Muslim devotions*, London, 1961.
Paret, Rudi, *Symbolik des Islams*, Stuttgart, 1958.
Perron, A., 'Balance de la loi musulmane ou esprit de la législation islamique et divergences de ses quatre rites jurisprudentiels par le cheikh El-Charani', *Revue Africaine*, xiv (1870), 209–52, 331–48.
-Qalqashandī, Aḥmad, *Ṣubḥ al-aʿshā*, 14 vols., Cairo, 1913–19.
Quatremère, É. Raschid-eldin, *Histoire des Mongols de la Perse*, Paris, 1836; reimpression Amsterdam, 1968.
Quelquejay, Ch., 'Le "vaïsisme" à Kazan. Contribution à l'étude des confréries musulmanes chez les Tartares de la Volga', *Die Welt des Islams*, N.F. vi, 1959.
-Qushairī, Abu 'l-Qāsim, *Ar-risālat al-Qushairiyya*, Cairo, A.H. 1319.
-Qushairī, ʿAbd al-Karīm al-Hawāzin, *Kitāb al-miʿrāj*, ed. ʿAlī Ḥasan ʿAbd al-Qādir, Cairo, 1964.
Rahim, A., 'The saints in Bengal: Shaikh Jalal al-Din Tabrezi and Shah Jalal', *J. Pakistan Hist. Soc.* vii (1960), 206–26.
Ramsaur, E., 'The Bektashi dervishes and the Young Turks', *M.W.* xxxii (1942), 7–14.
Rashīd ad-dīn, *Geschichte Ġāzān Khāns*, ed. K. Jahn, Leiden, 1940; see É. Quatremère.
Reed, H. A., 'Revival of Islam in Secular Turkey', *M.E.J.* viii (1954), 267–82.

Report by H.B.M.'s Government to the Council of the League of Nations on the Administration of Iraq, 1927.

Riazul Islam, 'A survey in outline of the mystic literature of the sultanate period', *J. Pakistan Hist. Soc.* iii (1955), 201–8.

Richard, Jean, 'La conversion de Berke et les débuts de l'islamisation de la horde d'or', *R.E.I.* xxxv (1967), 173–84.

-Rifāʿī, Aḥmad b. ʿAlī b. Yaḥyā, *K. rahīq al-kawthar min kalām ar-Rifāʿī*. Beirut, 1887.

Rihani, Ameen, *Around the coasts of Arabia*, London, 1930.

Rinn, Louis, *Marabouts et Khouan. Étude sur l'Islam en Algérie*, Algiers, 1884.

Ritter, H., *Das Meer der Seele, Mensch, Welt und Gott in den Geschichten des Fariduddîn ʿAttâr*, Leiden, 1955.

—— 'Autographs in Turkish libraries', *Oriens* (Leiden), vi (1953), 63–90.

—— 'Al-Bīrūnī's Übersetzung des Yoga-Sūtra des Patañjali', *Oriens*, ix (1956), 165–200.

——'Die Mevlânafeier in Konya vom 11.–17. Dezember 1960', *Oriens*, xv (1962), 249–70.

—— 'Philologika IX. Die vier Suhrawardī. Ihre Werke in Stambuler Handschriften', *D. Isl.* xxiv (1937), 270–86; xxv (1939), 35–86; xxvi (1940), 116–58.

—— 'Neue Literatur über Maulānā Calāluddīn Rūmī und seinen Orden', *Oriens*, xiii–xiv (1961), 342–54.

Rizvi, Athar Abbas, *Muslim revivalist movements in northern India in the sixteenth and seventeenth centuries*, Agra, 1965.

Robson, James, *Tracts on listening to music*, London, 1938.

Rose, H. A., *The dervishes*, A new edition of J. P. Brown's *The dervishes* (Istanbul, 1868), London, 1927.

Rubinacci, R., 'Un antico documento di vita cenobitica musulmana', *Annali* (Naples), 1960, 37–78.

-Rūmī, Jalāl ad-dīn, *Mathnawī*, ed., tr., and annotated by R. A. Nicholson, 8 vols., London, 1925–40 (*G.M.S.*, New Series, iv. 1–8).

—— *Discourses of Rūmī*, tr. A. J. Arberry, London, 1961.

Russell, Dorothea, *Medieval Cairo*, London, 1962.

-Ruṭbī, Aḥmad b. ʿAbd ar-Raḥmān, *Minḥat al-aṣḥāb*, in the collection *Ar-rasāʾil al-Mirghaniyya*, Cairo, 1358/1939, 69–98.

Rûzbehân Baqlî Shîrâzî, *Shar-e Shatîyât. Commentaire sur les paradoxes des soufis*, texte persan publ. avec une introd. en franç. (Bibl. Iran. 12), 1966.

—— *Le Jasmin des fidèles d'amour* (= *Kitāb-i ʿAbhar al-ʿāshiqīn*), ed. H. Corbin and M. Moʿīn. Tehran–Paris, 1958.

Saʿdī of Shīrāz, *Gulistān* ('Rose-garden'), ed. Platts, London, 1874.

—— *Bustān*, ed. K. H. Graf, Vienna, 1850.

Sadler, A. W., 'Visit to a Chishtī Qawwālī', *M.W.* liii (1963), 287–92.

-Ṣafadī, Ṣalāḥ ad-dīn Khalīl (d. A.D. 1363), *Al-wāfī bi 'l-Wafayāt* (a biographical dictionary), ed. H. Ritter, Leipzig–Istanbul, 1931, ed. Cairo, 1958.

-Sanūsī, M. b. ʿAlī, *As-salsabīl al-maʿīn fī 'ṭ-ṭarā'iq al-arbaʿīn*, On margin of the same author's *Al-masā'il al-ʿashar* (or *Bughyat al-maqāṣid fī khalāṣat al-marāṣid*). Cairo, 1353/1935.

-Sarrāj, Abu Naṣr ʿAbdallāh b. ʿAlī. *Al-lumaʿ fī 't-taṣawwuf*, ed. R. A. Nicholson, *G.M.S.* xxii, Leiden–London, 1914.

Sauvaget, J., '*Les Perles choisies' d'Ibn ach-Chihna* (a partial tr. of Ibn ash-Shiḥna's history of Aleppo), Beirut, 1933.

—— 'Inventaire des monuments musulmans de la ville d'Alep', *R.E.I.* v (1931), 59–114.

Sauvaire, H., 'Description de Damas', *J. Asiat.*, sér. IX, iii–iv (1894), v–vi (1895), vii (1896).

Savory, R. M., 'The office of Khalīfat al-Khulafā under the Ṣafawids', *J. Amer. Or. Soc.* lxxxv (1965), 497–502.

-Ṣayyādī, M. Abu 'l-Hudā, *Tanwīr al-abṣār fī ṭabaqāt as-sādat ar-Rifāʿiyya*, Cairo, A.H. 1306/1888.

—— *Dāʿī 'r-rashād*, Constantinople, n.d.

—— *Daw' ash-shams*, Constantinople, A.H. 1301.

Schimmel, Annemarie, 'Sufismus und Heiligenverehrung im spätmittelalterlichen Ägypten', *Festschrift Werner Caskel*, ed. E. Gräf, Leiden, 1968.

Sell, E., *The faith of Islam*, 4th edn. Madras, 1920.

Shabistarī, Saʿd ad-dīn Maḥmūd, *Gulshan-i rāz* ('Rosegarden of mystery'), a Sūfī *mathnawi*, ed. and tr. E. H. Whinfield, London, 1880.

Shaibī, Kāmil Muṣṭafā, *As-sila baina 't-taṣawwuf wa 't-tashayyuʿ*, 2 vols., Baghdad, 1382/1963–1383/1964.

-Shaʿrānī (-Shaʿrāwī), ʿAbd al-Wahhāb, *Aṭ-ṭabaqāt al-kubrā* or *Lawāqiḥ al-anwār fī ṭabaqāt al-akhyār*, 2 vols., Cairo, A.H. 1343/1925; 1355/1936.

—— *Al-yawāqīt wa 'l-jawāhir*, Cairo, A.H. 1307, 1321.

—— *Al-baḥr al-mawrūd*, Cairo, n.d.

—— *Kashf al-ghumma ʿan jamīʿ al-umma*, Cairo, A.H. 1317.

—— *Al-mīzān al-kubrā ash-Shaʿrāniyya*, Cairo, A.H. 1321, tr. A. Perron, Algiers, 1898.

—— *Al-mīzān al-Khiḍriyya*, on the margin of Ṣadr ad-dīn M. b. ʿAR, *Raḥmat al-umma fi 'khtilāf al-a'imma*, Cairo, 1304.

Sharif, M. M. (ed.), *A history of Muslim philosophy*, 2 vols., Wiesbaden, 1963.

-Shaṭṭanawfī, ʿAlī b. Yūsuf, *Bahjat al-asrār wa maʿdin al-anwār*, Cairo, A.H. 1304.

-Shinqīṭī, Aḥmad b. al-Amīn, *Al-wasīṭ fī tarājim udabā' Shinqīṭ*. Cairo, 1329/1911.

Sirajul Haq, 'Samā and Raqs of the dervishes', *Islamic Culture*, 1944, 111–30.

Smith, Margaret, *Rābiʿa the mystic and her fellow-saints in Islam*, Cambridge, 1928.

—— *An early mystic of Baghdad. A study of the life and teaching of Ḥārith b. Asad al-Muḥāsibī*, London, 1935.

—— *Studies in early mysticism in the Near and Middle East*, London, 1931.

—— *Al-Ghazālī the mystic*, London, 1944.

Smith, W. Cantwell, *Islam in modern history*, Princeton, 1957.

Snouck Hurgronje, C., *Mecca in the latter half of the nineteenth century*, tr. J. H. Monahan, Leiden, 1931.

—— 'Les confréries religieuses, La Mecque et le panislamisme', *Verspreide geschriften*, Bonn–Leipzig–Hague, iii (1923), 189–206.

Stein, M. Aurel, *Innermost Asia*, 2 vols., London, 1928.

Subhan, J. A., *Sufism: its saints and shrines*, 1938; revised edn., Lucknow, 1960.

Subkī, Tāj ad-dīn, *Aṭ-ṭabaqāt ash-Shāfiʿiyya al-kubrā*, 6 vols., Cairo, 1324/1906.

-Suhrawardī, Shihāb ad-dīn Abu Ḥafṣ ʿUmar, *ʿAwārif al-maʿārif* ('Bounties of divine knowledge'), ʿAlāmiyya Press, Cairo, 1358/1939; and on edns. of Ghazālī's *Iḥyā'*, e.g. A.H. 1334 edn.

Sulaimān Chelebi, *The Mevlidi Sherif*, tr. F. Lyman MacCallum, London, 1943.

-Sulamī, Abu ʿAbd ar-Raḥmān, *Kitāb ādāb aṣ-ṣuḥba*, ed. M. J. Kister, Jerusalem, 1954.

—— *Ṭabaqāt aṣ-Ṣūfiyya* ('Classes of the Sufis'), ed. J. Pedersen, Leiden, 1960.

—— *Risālat al-malāmatiyya*, ed. ʿAfīfī, *Malāmatiyya*, q.v.

Surūr, Ṭāhā ʿAbd al-Bāqī, *At-taṣawwuf al-Islāmī wa 'l-Imām ash-Shaʿrānī*, Cairo, 1952.

—— *Min aʿlām at-taṣawwuf*, 2 vols., Cairo, 1956.

—— *Al-Ghazālī*, Cairo, 1945.

—— *Muḥyiddīn Ibn al-ʿArabī*, Cairo, n.d.

-Suyūṭī, ʿAbd ar-Raḥmān, *Ḥuṣn al-muḥāḍara fī akhbār Miṣr wa 'l-Qāhira* (a history of old and new Cairo), Cairo, A.H. 1327.

—— *Ḥuṣn al-maqṣid fī ʿamal al-mawlid*, Cairo manuscript.

-Ṭabbākh, M. Rāghib, *Iʿlām an-nubalā' fī ta'rīkh Ḥalab ash-shahbā'*, 7 vols., Aleppo, 1923–6.

Taeschner, F., 'Eine Schrift des Šihābaddīn Suhrawardī über die Futūwa', *Oriens*, xv (1962), 277–80.

—— 'As-Sulamī's *Kitāb al-futuwwa*', ed. in *Studia Orientalia Joanni Pedersen . . . dicata*, Copenhagen, 1953.

-Tahānawī, *Kashshāf iṣṭilāḥāt al-ʿulūm wa 'l-funūn*, ed. A. Sprenger and W. N. Lees, Calcutta, 1862.

Tāj ad-dīn b. Mahdī Zamān ar-Rūmī, *Risālat fī sunan aṭ-ṭā'ifat an-Naqshabandiyya*, Cambridge, Add. MS. 1073.

Takle, J., 'The approach to Muslim mysticism', *M.W.* viii (1918), 249–58.

-Ṭaṣafāwī, M. b. ʿAbdallāh b. Ḥasanain, *Al-Fatḥ ar-rabbānī fīmā yaḥtāj ilaihi al-murīd at-Tijānī*, Cairo, n.d. (completed 1328/1910); other tracts in same volume.

-Ṭawīl, Tawfīq, *At-taṣawwuf fī Miṣr ibbān al-ʿaṣr al-ʿUthmānī*, Cairo, 1946.

—— *Ash-Shaʿrānī imām at-taṣawwuf fī ʿaṣrihi*, Cairo, 1945.

Teufel, J. K., *Eine Lebensbeschreibung des Scheichs ʿAlī-i Hamadānī, gestorben 1385* (die *Xulāṣat ul-manāqib* des Maulānā Nūr ud-dīn Caʿfar-i Badaxšī), Leiden, 1962.

Thorning, H., *Beiträge zur Kenntniss des islamischen Vereinswesens auf Grund 'Basṭ madad at-taufīq'*, Türkische Bibliothek, 16, Berlin, 1913; re-ed. H. Pérès, Algiers, 1948.
-Tirmidhī, al-Ḥakīm, *Kitāb khatm al-wilāya*, ed. and annotated by ʿUthmān Ismāʿīl Yaḥyā, Beirut, 1965.
Toynbee, A. J. and Kirkwood, K. P., *Turkey*, London, 1926.
Trimingham, J. S., *Islam in the Sudan*, London, 1949.
—— *Islam in Ethiopia*, London, 1952.
—— *Islam in West Africa*, Oxford, 1959.
—— *The Influence of Islam upon Africa*, London–Beirut, 1968.
Ubicini, M. A. *Letters on Turkey*, tr. Lady Easthope, London, 1856.
ʿUmar ibn Saʿīd al-Fūtī aṭ-Ṭūrī, *Rimāḥ ḥizb ar-raḥīm ʿalā nuhūr ḥizb ar-rajīm*, on margin of ʿAlī Ḥarāzim's *Jawāhir al-maʿānī*, Cairo, 1348/1929.
ʿUmarī, Ibn Faḍl Allāh, *At-taʿrīf bi 'l-muṣṭalaḥ ash-sharīf*, Cairo, 1312.
—— *Masālik al-abṣār fī mamālik al-amṣār* (*L'Afrique, moins l'Égypte*), tr. M. Gaudefroy-Demombynes, Paris, 1927.
Vámbéry, H., *Travels in central Asia*, New York, 1865.
Veccia Vaglieri, L., 'Sul "Nahj al-balāğah" e sul suo compilatore aš-Šarīf ar-raḍī', *Annali*, N.S. viii. 1–46.
-Wansharīsī, Aḥmad b. Yaḥyā, *Al-miʿyār*, lith. Fez, A.H. 1314, 12 vols.
-Wāsiṭī, Taqī ad-dīn ʿAbd ar-Raḥmān, *Tiryāq al-muḥibbīn fī ṭabaqat khirqat al-mashā'ikh al-ʿārifīn*, Cairo, 1305/1888.
Weir, T. H., *The Shaikhs of Morocco in the sixteenth century*, Edinburgh, 1904; an adaptation of Ibn ʿAskar, *Dawḥat an-nāshir*.
Westermarck, E., *Ritual and Belief in Morocco*, 2 vols., London, 1926.
Wittek, P., *The Rise of the Ottoman empire*, London, 1938, reprint, 1958.
Wüstenfeld, F., *Die Çufiten in Süd-Arabien*, Göttingen, 1883.
Yāfiʿī, ʿAbdallāh b. Asʿad. *Mir'āt al-janān* ('Mirror of time'), 4 vols., Haidarabad, A.H. 1337–9.
—— *Khulāṣat al-mafākhir fi 'khtiṣār manāqib ash-shaikh ʿAbd al-Qādir* [al-Jīlānī].
Yakan, Waliyyaddīn, *Al-maʿlūm wa 'l-majhūl*, 2 vols., Cairo, A.H. 1327–9.
-Yaʿqūbī, *Kitāb al-buldān*, ed. M. J. de Goeje, *Bibliotheca Geographorum Arabicorum*, vii., 1892.
Yāqūt, *Muʿjam al-buldān* (A geographical dictionary), ed. F. Wüstenfeld, 6 vols., Leipzig, 1866–73.
-Yashruṭiyya, Fāṭima, *Riḥlat ilā 'l-Ḥaqq* ('Pilgrimage to the Real'), Beirut, n.d. (1955?).
Zhukovsky, V. A., 'Persian Sufism', *B.S.O.A.S.* v (1928–30), 475–88.
Ziadeh, Nicola A., *Sanūsīyah*, Leiden, 1958.

GLOSSARY OF ARABIC TERMS

THIS glossary has been made fairly comprehensive since the translations of frequently employed Arabic words like *ṭarīqa* and *dhikr* are not necessarily repeated, whilst certain terms have varying usages in different contexts. The words are Arabic where no specific indication is given. Arabic broken plurals which appear in the text are given either with a reference to the singular or with a translation, especially if differing from the singular.

a'alem, 188 = Ar. *'alam*. A standard, flag
abdāl, pl. of *badal*. Substitutes, a category of saints, 164, 165
abdāl (Turk.). A dervish, 68
abrār, pl. of *bārr*. The dutiful ones, a category of saints, 164, 264
adab, pl. *ādāb*. Manners, the conduct and discipline of the Sufi in relation to his shaikh and associate Sufis, 5, 29, 34, 56, 146; *ādāb az-ziyāra*, ritual of approach to a saint's tomb, 179
'adhaba. Turban tassel, 189
ādhān. The call to prayer, 195
adhkār, pl. of *dhikr*. Recollection-formulae, the phrases used in the *dhikr* and *awrād*, 3, 29, 88, 115, 196, 215
aflāk. Celestial spheres, 190
'ahd. Compact; *'ahd al-yad/al-khirqa*, swearing allegiance by the hand (-clasp) or by investiture with the habit. Often extended to the whole initiation ceremony, 108, 182, 186, 187
ahl al-ma'rifa. The theosophists, 264
ahl as-silsila. The links in the chain of (spiritual) descent, 151
aḥwāl, see sing. *ḥāl*. 4, 35, 41, 139, 151
aḥzāb, pl. of *ḥizb* but in the sense of a single form of devotion, e.g. a prayer, 29, 72, 88, 114, 146, 186, 215, 216
akh. Brother, see pl. *ikhwān*
akhawiyya. Fraternity, 176
akhdh al-yad/khirqa/wird/'ahd. 'Taking the compact/habit/rule/oath' of allegiance to the shaikh, 182, 184, 215, 261
akhī. Member of a Turkish craft-guild or corporation, 24, 25, 39, 80
akhyār. The choice ones, (*a*) a saint-category, 164; (*b*) a Sufi attainment grade, 264
'ālam. World, 152, 154, 157, 160, 164; see *nāsūt*, *malakūt*, *jabarūt*, *lāhūt*, *arwāḥ*, *ghaib*
'ālim, pl. *'ulamā'*, q.v. One trained in the religious sciences, 42, 90, 221, 248
Allāhu akbar. God is greatest, 201
amīn. Master of a craft-guild, 25
ammāra, see *nafs*
amrad, pl. *murd*. A 'beardless' youth, 193, 212
anāshīd, s. *nashīd*. Songs, hymns, 205
'aqīqa. Naming ceremony on the eighth day after birth, 226
aqṭāb, see *quṭb*. 108, 115, 161, 164
arba'īniyya. The forty-day retreat or quadragesima, 30, 187, 190
'ārif, pl. *-īn*. Gnostic, adept, one who has been given mystical knowledge, 6, 60, 70, 194
'arīf. (*a*) Initiate, gnostic, pl. *'irfān*, *'urafā'*, 243; (*b*) master of a craft guild, 25
arkān, s. *rukn*, *'ālam al-*. World of the supports, principles, 152
arwāḥ, s. *rūḥ*, *'ālam al-*. World of the spirits, 152
asānīd, s. *sanad*. Ascription, chain of authorities (tradition term), 117
asātidha, pl. of *ustādh*. Master, 150
'āshiq. Lover, 175, 176

asmā', pl. of *ism*, name. *Al-asmā' al-ḥusnā*, 'the (ninety-nine) names most beautiful' (Qur'ān, vii. 180), 217
'aṣr. The afternoon prayer, 170
assa, 188 = Ar. *'aṣā*. Staff
ata (Turk.). A father, dervish or holy-man title, 54
'awālim, s. *'ālima*. Singing and dancing girls (Egypt), 234
āward-burd (Pers.). Controlling of the breath, a Sufi exercise, 202
awlād aṭ-ṭarīqa. Children (i.e. affiliates) of the order, 176
awliyā', pl. of *walī*, q.v. 26, 70, 134, 163, 165, 224
awqāf, see *waqf*. 7, 123, 125, 168, 169, 242
awqāt, pl. of *waqt*, time. *Dhikr al-awqāt*, the *dhikr* prescribed for specific 'hours', 201
awrād, pl. of *wird*. Litanies compounded of strung-together *adhkār* or remembrance formulae, 30, 37, 43, 49, 96, 115, 187, 190, 191, 192, 196, 215, 216, 230
awtād, s. *watad*. Stakes, supports; a category of saints, 164, 165
aynicem. A Bektashi ritual, 188
'azīzān (Cent. Asia). Affiliates of an order, 176

bābā (Turk.). Missionary or popular preacher, shaikh, 24, 54, 68, 70, 74, 81, 174, 232, 240, 267
badal, pl. *abdāl*, *budalā'*. Substitute, a category of saints of 'permutation', 164, 165. In Turkish *abdāl* was employed as a singular for a dervish, 68
badāwīn. Nomads, 80
bai'a. Vow of allegiance, 14, 137, 182, 186, 187
ballūṭ. Acorns, 6
baqā'. Abiding (in God), 152, 155, 156, 189, 202
baraka. Holiness, virtue as inherent spiritual power, 7, 26, 27, 34, 42, 45, 50, 72, 84, 85, 86, 88, 92, 104, 105, 108, 111, 159, 172, 180, 183, 192, 201, 224, 225, 226, 227, 234, 236, 249, 257, 271
barzakh, *'ālam al-*. The world of the isthmus, the purgatorial world, intermediary dark region, 152
ba-shar' (Persia, India). Orders within the Law, 233
basmala. The opening phrase of all Qur'ānic suras except one: *bismi'll-āhi 'r-raḥmāni 'r-raḥīm*, In the name of God the compassionate, the merciful, 28, 206
basṭ. Expansion, a spiritual state, 90
bāṭin. Interior, hidden (knowledge), 63; *bāṭin al-kawn*, the depths of the cosmos, 160
bāṭinī. Esoteric, 106, 142
bāz. Kettledrum, 247
bāz gasht (Pers.). Restraint, 203
bid'a, pl. *bida'*. A (blameworthy) innovation, 27, 51, 58, 148, 149, 246, 247
bisāṭ. Carpet, 173
bī-shar' (Persia, India). Outside the Law, 65, 97, 233
burda. Mantle, title of a celebrated poem in praise of the Prophet, 207

chelebi (*çelebì*.). Turk. title given heads of certain orders, 83, 174, 179, 189
chillā (Pers.). Forty-days retreat = *arba'īniyya*, 190

daerah. In India a Sufi institution, 177
dā'ira. (*a*) A *dhikr* 'circle', 205; (*b*) 'cycle', *dā'irat an-nubuwwa*, the cycle of prophesy, 133, 134; *dā'irat al-wilāya/walāya*, 133–4
dakka. A tribune or platform, 169
Dalā'il al-khairāt. 'Proofs of the excellencies or good deeds', title of al-Jazūlī's famous incantatory poem-prayer, 28, 70, 84, 85
ḍarb. Section of *dhikr*, one formula, 210, 211
dargāh (Pers.). A court, term for a Sufi convent, shrine or tomb, 177
darwīsh (Pers.), pl. *darāwīsh*. A dervish, 23, 24, 27, 68, 175, 243, 264
dawsa, coll. *dōsa*. Lit. a trampling. Sa'dī ceremony in which the shaikh of the order rode on horseback over the prostrate forms of his dervishes, 73, 125, 231, 246, 247
dede (Turk.). Shaikh, dervish, 75, 83, 174

dhākir. Mentioner, recollector, or commemorator, i.e. one engaged in 'mentioning' (*dhikr*) the name of God, 201, 203, 207, 210

dhāt ash-Sharī'a. The essence/reality/being of the revealed Law, 152, 153

dhāt al-kull. The essence/ground of the Whole, 152, 153

dhawq. Taste, tasting; with various technical mystical senses: e.g. sensitivity to, perceptivity between, antipodes like truth and falsity by the light of divine grace, 203

dhikr (√remember, recollect). 'Recollection', a spiritual exercise designed to render God's presence throughout one's being. The methods employed (rhythmical repetitive invocation of God's names) to attain this spiritual concentration, 2, 6, 12, 13, 19, 21, 28, 38, 50, 55, 58, 62, 67, 84, 89, 90, 96, 98, 104, 106, 108, 111, 113, 116, 119, 131, 136, 139, 146, 154, 155, 158, 165, 170, 174, 186, 188, 194, 196, 198, 200–7, 213, 214, 230, 244, 245, 248, 250, 255, 265; *dhikr al-awqāt*, the set daily repetitions, 72, 201; *dhikr al-ḥadra*, the communal exercise, 201; *dhikr jahrī* or *jalī*, vocal recollection, 194; *dhikr khafī*, mental, occult, recollection, 194, 201, 202, 203, 211, 266; *dhikr minshārī*, saw dhikr, 197; *dhikr* as the Logos, 161

dhu'āba. Turban-tassel, 189

dirāya. Teaching with the aim of reaching understanding, 189

diya. Blood wite, 237

dosa. 125, 231, 246, 247; see *dawsa*

du'ā'. A supplication. *Du'ā' li'l-insān*, prayer for mankind, 211

faiḍ, pl. *fuyūḍ*, *fuyūḍāt*. Outpouring, emanation, divine grace, 213

fallāḥ, pl. *-ūn*. Cultivator, peasant, 45, 223, 231

fanā'. 'Passing away', i.e. of the attributes of the *nafs*, 3, 152, 155, 156, 157, 161, 165, 202, 213; dying to self by transmutation, 224; *fanā' fi 't-tawḥīd*, *fi 'l-Ḥaqq*, union with the Unity, the Real, 189

faqīh, pl. *fuqahā'*. One trained in *fiqh*, a jurisconsult, 37, 42, 118, 176

faqd al-iḥsās. 'Loss of consciousness' in the ecstatic union, 200

faqīr, pl. *fuqarā'*. A poor one (in need of God), a general term for a dervish, 7, 97, 118, 127, 170, 175, 232, 264, 267; *faqīrāt*, women dervishes, 176

faqr. Poverty, 50

farā'iḍ, s. *farīḍa*. Obligatory religious duties, 266, 267

fard, pl. *afrād*. Category of saints of lowest rank, 'troops', 165

farīḍa. Obligatory ritual prayer, 193

fatā, pl. *fityān*. Lit. 'a young man'; a member of organizations known as *futuwwa*, 24, 184

Fātiḥa, al-. 'The Opener', the chapter with which the Qur'ān opens, 142, 180, 186, 205, 211

fātiḥat adh-dhikr. Opening prayer to a *dhikr* session, 205

fatwā, pl. *fatāwī*. A legal opinion issued by a *muftī*, 27, 35, 46, 76, 125, 198, 242, 247, 264

fiqh. Religious law, the *sharī'a* formulated, the juridico-canonical system of Islam, 34, 37, 42, 50, 53, 71, 170, 222, 241

fu'ād. Heart, 152

fuqahā', see *faqīh*. 51, 198, 222, 224, 225, 243, 248, 264

fuqarā', see *faqīr*. 10, 15, 21, 27, 38, 39, 40, 42, 82, 116, 168, 169, 172, 175, 198, 199, 222

furū', s. *far'*. Branches, 36

fūṭa. Waist-wrapper, 7

futuwwa. Chivalrous qualities of a young man (*fatā*), so ideal of chivalry. Term given to certain organizations, artizanal and chivalrous, 14, 24, 25, 34, 35, 184, 262. In Sufism: an ethical (rather than mystical) ideal which places the spiritual welfare of others before that of self, altruism, 24, 167

fuyūḍāt, emanations, 213, 221; see *faiḍ*

ghafla. Negligence. In Sufi senses: preoccupation with self, so inattention along the Way and forgetfulness of God, 145 *ghaib*. (*a*) Absense, what is hidden, 'mystery'; *'ālam al-ghaib*, the world of mystery, 152, 157, 161; (*b*) the divine mystery, *ahl al-ghaib*, partakers of the divine mystery, the saints, 164

ghalaba. Rapture, 4

ghawth, pl. *aghwāth*. Helper (of the Age), 115, 160, 164

ghazāwī or *ghawāzī*, s. *ghāziya*. Dancing girls, 234

ghāzī, pl. *ghuzāt*. Raider, but designating frequently warrior in the way of religion, 24, 68, 80, 100, 240

ghuzāt, see *ghāzī*. 100

ḥabīb aṭ-ṭulba. Patron saint of the law students (Morocco), 234

ḥabs-i dam (Pers.). Regulation of the breath, 62

ḥadīth. Tradition going back to the Prophet, based on an *isnād* or chain of transmitters, 7, 144, 151, 170, 171, 176, 180, 189, 212, 221, 241. *Ḥadīth qudsī*. A tradition in which God speaks in the first person, 26

ḥaḍra. Lit. 'presence', a Sufi gathering for song recitals and *dhikr*, 47, 79, 80, 88, 90, 113, 132, 176, 193, 201, 204–7, 216; *al-Ḥaḍrat ar-Rubūbiyya*, the divine presence, 204

ḥafīd. Grandson, and commonly 'descendant', 40

hailala, see *tahlīl*

ḥaira. State of stupefaction, bewilderment, 152, 155

ḥairān, s. *ḥuwār* (Sudan). Disciples, 176

ḥajj. Ritual pilgrimage to Mecca, 48, 96

ḥāl, pl. *aḥwāl*. A transitionary spiritual 'state' of enlightenment or 'rapture', associated with passage along the Sufi path, 23, 57, 115, 139, 140, 200, 201

ḥalqa. (*a*) 'Circle' around a spiritual director, 166; (*b*) circle of *dhikr* devotees or of students, and so a recital or a course of study, 96, 204, 211

ḥamdala. The act of saying *al-ḥamdu li'llāh*, 'praise is due to God (alone)', 201, 206

ḥaqīqa, al-. The Reality, 1, 4, 135, 142, 143, 145, 149, 152, 153, 159, 160, 161; *al-Ḥaqīqat al-Muḥammadiyya*, the Muhammadan Idea or Reality, 154, 161, 163

Ḥaqq, al-. The Real; Sufi term for God, and as distinguished from *ḥaqīqa*, like *shar'* from *sharī'a*, 1, 63, 158, 190, 203, 206

ḥaram. Sacred, 179

ḥāris. A superintendant, 169

ḥawliyya. Anniversary of a saint's death (*ḥawl* = year), 180, 235

ḥawqala. The phrase: *lā ḥawla wa lā quwata illā bi 'llāh*, 'there is no power and might save in God,' 206

ḥayy. Living, as *dhikr* ejaculation, 156, 190, 202, 206

ḥaẓẓ. Mystical apprehension, 196

ḥikam. Wise sayings or maxims, 146

ḥikma. Wisdom, 158; *ḥikma ilāhiyya*, divine wisdom, theosophia, 133, 146

ḥirfa, pl. *ḥiraf*. Trade-, craft-guild, 24, 25

ḥizām. Girdle, 184–5

ḥizb, pl. *aḥzāb*. (*a*) a division (one sixteenth) of the Qur'ān; (*b*) a prayer composed of formulae (similar to a *wird*), but one that has acquired special power (like *ḥizb al-baḥr* of ash-Shādhilī, pp. 28, 192, 216), and frequently with special conditions governing its recitation. 211, 214, 215–6; (*c*) the 'office' of an order, 205, 216; (*d*) the order itself, 216

ḥōliyya, see *ḥawliyya*

hōsh dar dam (Pers.). Awareness while breathing, 203

ḥulūl. Indwelling, infusion of God (the divine essence really) in a creature; in the literature of the orders it has the general meaning of 'a spiritual transformation', 11, 162

ḥuqūq aṭ-ṭarīq. Regulations governing the pursuit of the Way, 146

Ḥurūfis. 'Literalists' (from *ḥurūf*, 'letters'), an heretical sect, 68, 82

Huwa. 'He', the great pronoun of the divine Ipseity, one of the recollection names, 190, 206 *'ibāda*, pl. *-āt*. The canonical rites through which the relationship of the worshipper (*'abd*) is expressed. With Sufis = devotion expressed in the traditional *ẓāhirī* way, 142

'īd. Festival, 25

iḥlīl. 'Orifice', used as an euphemism for the membrum virile, 268

iḥtifāl. A celebration or commemoration, 256

ijāza. Licence or diploma, 86, 122, 174, 192–3, 227; *Ijāzat-nāma-simā'*, licence given to singers in India, 192; *ijāza irāda*, a novice's diploma, 192; *ijāza 't-tabarruk*, diploma testifying to the holder's link with the *ṭarīqa*-founder, 192

ijmā'. Consensus of the Muslim community as represented by the doctors of law, 105, 115, 119, 225

ikhwān, s. *akh*. Brethren, fellow members of an order, 20, 27, 116, 120, 146, 175, 176, 230

ikrār āyīnī (Turk.). 'Appointing ceremony', Bektāshi initiation ceremony, 188

ilāhī, *ilāhiyya*. Divine, 133, 146

ilhām. The quickening of the personal human soul by universal Spirit, generally translated by (personal) 'inspiration', 145, 224

'ilm, pl. *'ulūm*. Knowledge, science, of divine things; (*a*) Islamic, 151; (*b*) Sufi. 130, 151; *al-'ilm al-ladunnī*; Knowledge direct from on high which is the fruit of *ilhām* (q.v.). 'Knowledge possessed by the saints enters their hearts direct from the creative Truth Itself' (Ghazali (A.H.), *Kīmiyā' as-sa'āda*, pp. 16–17). 136, 221; *'ilm an-naẓar*, 'rationalism' in general, Mu'tazilism in particular, 53; *'ilm bāṭinī*, esoteric knowledge, 148; *'ilm ẓāhirī*, external knowledge, 148

imām. (*a*) 'Leader' in public worship, pl. *a'imma*, 265; (*b*) the spiritual and temporal leader of the Shī'īs, 99, 133, 135, 136, 137, 163, 211. Adj. *imāmī*, 164

imtizāj. Incorporation, 11

inkār al-kasb. Severing the acquisitive bonds, 265

inkisār. Contrition, 203

al-insān al-kāmil. The perfect man, 161

intamā. To trace one's (spiritual) descent to, to belong to (a *ṭarīqa*), 11, 20

intasaba. To trace one's (spiritual) lineage (*nisba*), to affiliate, ascribe oneself to, 11, 42

intisāb, see *intasaba*. 188

iqtadā (*iqtidā'*). To follow the example of, to be guided by, 182

irāda. The aspiration of the *murīd* (same root) to undertake the journey of the soul on the road to God; then, his rule of life on the road, his novitiate, 150, 182, 185

'irfān. Gnosis (*ahl al-'irfān*, gnostics), 140

'ishā', *ṣalāt al-*. The evening ritual, 202

īshān. Persian pronoun 3rd pers. pl. has in Central Asia the significance of 'master', 'guide', 172

'ishq. Passion, 152, 155

ishrāq. Illumination, 140; *Ishrāqī*, name of a Sufi school of intellectual esotericism, 140

ism. Name, see *asmā'*; *al-ism al-a'ẓam* or *ism al-jalāla*, 'the greatest Name' (of God), 158, 216

isnād. Ascription (of a prophetical or mystical tradition), chain of transmitters authenticating a tradition (cf. *ḥadīth*), 5, 10, 12–13, 71, 104, 143, 149, 163, 198

isrā'. Nocturnal journey (of the Prophet), 208

istiftāḥ adh-dhikr. Opening prayer at a *dhikr* session, 205

istighfār. Lit. 'forgiveness-asking'. The repetition of the formula, 'I ask forgiveness of God', 191, 206

istighrāq. 'Immersion', absorption in God, 194

istinbāṭ. Mystical interpretation, i.e. 'drawing out' the inner sense, 140

istiqrār. Enduring, 134

i'tikāf. Spiritual 'withdrawal' in an *'uzla*, 'retreat', without the true clausura (*khalwa*), 30

i'tiqād. Bond of allegiance to a shaikh, 11

i'tizāl. Seclusion, retreat, 30

ittiḥād. Identification of the divine and human natures. Various types, e.g. *al-ittiḥād al-'āmm al-muṭlaq* is that of the Hindu pantheists, identification of divinity and universe, 162

ittikā', from *ittaka'a*, 'to recline'. A refectory, 177

īwān. A hall, open on one side; a portico along the side of the court of a mosque or *madrasa*, 21, 169, 170

jabarūt, *'ālam al-*. The world of power, 160–1

jadhb. Attraction, 43, 148, 165

jadwal. Chart, 152

jāgīr (Pers.). A form of fiefship given as a reward for services rendered or as support, 23

jalaba. Party, group, 6

jalsa. Poses, Yoga-type, 198

jamā'at-khāna. Assembly-hall or a Sufi convent, 166, 177

jāmi'. A Friday mosque, 178, 232

jawharat al-kamāl. The chief prayer in the Tijānī cycle, 191, 208, 217

Jāwīdān-i kabīr. 'The great Eternal', title of a Ḥurūfī book, 82

jihād. (*a*) War 'in the way of religion', 105; (*b*) 'striving' along the mystical Path = *al-jihād al-akbar*, the greater warfare; cf. *mujahāda*; 139, 155, 168

jinn. A category of spirits, 165, 224

jubba. A long gown with full sleeves, 7

jūjiyya. Yoga, 98, 198

kabbara, v.n. *takbīr*. To repeat the phrase *Allāhu akbar*, 'God is greatest', 6

kafan. A winding-sheet, 181

kaimās. A vein of importance in Indian-type *dhikr* posture (*jalsa*), 202

kalām, *'ilm al-*. Scholastic theology, 71

al-kalimat aṭ-ṭayyiba. 'The blessed phrase', *the* word, i.e. the first phrase of the *shahāda*, 203

kamar-i ṣuḥbat/waḥdat (Pers.). Girdle of companionship/unity, 185

karāma, pl. *-āt*. Grace, thaumaturgic, charismatic gifts, 26, 51, 104, 141, 145, 228, 265

kasb. Acquisition, personal initiative, 221

kashf. Uncovering, disclosure, revelation in its literal meaning, re-velation—the taking away of the veil. Synonym: *fatḥ* or *futūḥ*, thus *'ilm al-futūḥ*, the technique of mystical revelation = *taṣawwuf*, 139, 151

kathra. Multiplicity, plurality, 152, 154

khādim. Servant, 201

khadīm. Steward, 171

khalīfa, pl. *khulafā'*, Vicar, deputy; the initiating leader of a branch of an order, nominated by the shaikh, 22, 27, 54, 55, 56, 62, 65, 72, 81, 95, 101, 113, 122, 124, 174, 175, 179, 191, 192, 206, 209, 235, 271

khalq, *al-*. The creation, 63

khalwa (√*khalā*, to be alone). Seclusion, retreat; place of seclusion or retreat, 5, 18, 30, 35, 60, 75, 89, 116, 151, 158, 169, 203, 213, 230, 250, 272

khalwat dar anjuman (Pers.). Solitude in a crowd, 203

khānaqāh, pl. *khawāniq* (Pers.). A religious hostel, cloister, Sufi centre, 5, 6, 7, 8, 9, 10, 17–23 *passim*, 32, 33, 39, 44, 46, 55, 57, 64, 65, 67, 69, 91, 92, 101, 128, 166, 168–72, 175, 214, 227, 230, 236, 238, 239, 242, 261

khātim al-anbiyā'. Seal of the prophets, 133

khatm al-wilāya. The seal of sanctity, 134

khatmat al-Qur'ān. 'Sealing the Qur'ān' = chanted recital of the whole book, 170

Khatm-i Khawājagān. 'The Seal of the Masters', the prayer-sequence obligatory upon Naqshabandī initiates, recited after the *'aṣr*, *'ishā'* and *ṣubḥ* prayers, consisting of the following with the minimum repetitions: (1) *istighfār*: 7 times, (2) *taṣliya*: 7 times, (3) *sūra* Fātiḥa: 7 times, (4) *sūra* Inshirāḥ (xciv): 9 times, (5) *sūra* Ikhlāṣ (cxii): 9 times, (6) *taṣliya*: once, (7) prayer embodying the *silsila* of the *ṭarīqa* (once), 202

khawāṣṣ. Elect, privileged, 264

khawātāt. Women dervishes, 176

khidma. Service, 183

khilāfa. Vicarship, see *khalīfa*, 95

khirqa. Lit. 'rag'. A dervish's patched garment, symbol of his vows of obedience to the rule of his order. Term is used also as equivalent to *silsila* or *ṭarīqa*. Grades: *khirqat al-irāda/ ṣuḥba/ khidma/ ta'līm/ tarbiya*: novitiate/ companionship/ diaconate/ teaching/ guidance. 12, 15, 29, 36, 37, 39, 41, 42, 48, 49, 50, 54, 55, 80, 89, 143, 181–5, 187, 261, 263, 265

khudāwand-gār (Pers.). A lord, a king, 175

khuddām, pl. of *khādim*. Helpers, term in certain orders for affiliates, 176

khulafā', see *khalīfa*

khulla. Friendship, 149

khuṭba. The homily delivered at the Friday and festival prayers, 8, 109

kufr. Infidelity, 53, 162, 224

kulāh (Pers.). A conical hat of black lambswool worn by dervishes, 184

kunnab. Hemp, 199

kunya. A patronymic, a name compounded with *abū*, *umm*, *ibn*, *bint*, 47

lāhūt. Divinity, *'Ālam al-lāhūt*, the world of divinity, 154

lailiyya. Term by which a *dhikr* session is called in certain orders, 206, 209

laqab. A sobriquet or honorific, 46, 228

laqqana, v.n. *talqīn*. To teach by dictation, by word of mouth, 182

laṭīf. (God's) essence, 163

lawā'iḥ, s. *lā'iḥa*. Shafts of illumination, 140

lawāmi', s. *lāmi'*. Gleams, 140

lawḥ, pl. *alwāḥ*. A tablet, 210

lawwāma, see *nafs*

libs (or *talbīs*) *al-khirqa*. Investiture with the habit of a Sufi, 182

lithām. A man's face veil, 45

ma'ānī, s. *ma'nā*. Esoteric things, 136

madad. (Supernatural) help. A phrase used during the *dhikr* out of joy or as an encouragement, 211

madā'iḥ, s. *madīḥ* and *madḥa*. Term applied to *dhikr* praise-songs, 206, 210

madār. Pivot, 158

madhhab, pl. *madhāhib*. (*a*) Sunnī juridical school, 242; (*b*) a school of thought, as *madhhab al-malāmatiyya*; (*c*) a method of traversing the Path, 3, 11, 12, 43

madrasa. A higher religious school, college, seminary, a collegiate mosque, 8, 9, 21, 32, 42, 50, 69, 98, 170, 176, 223, 238, 241, 269

maḥabba. Reciprocal love between God and His spiritual creation, 152, 155

Maḥbūb, al-. The Beloved, 213

maḥzam. Girdle or shawl, 185

majānīn, s. *majnūn*. One possessed by a spirit, 231

majdhūb (√*jadhaba*). An enraptured one, 15, 150, 165; pl. *majādhīb*, illuminati, 231

majlis, pl. *majālis*. (*a*) Gathering, assembly, 50; *majlis adh-dhikr*, gathering for recollection of God, 6, 176; (*b*) collection of a saint's sayings, 70.

makhzan. The state (Morocco), 85, 246

maktūbāt. Writings, collections of correspondence (India), 35, 70

malakūt. Royalty, *'Ālam al-malakūt*, the world of sovereignty, or the world of intelligible substances, 160–1

malāma. Blame, censure, 4, 265, 267

malāmatī. One who incurs censure, 13, 16, 40, 63, 69, 75, 125, 158, 175, 264–7, 272; *Malāmatiyya*, Sufi school, 50, 52, 89, 264–7

malfūẓāt. Collection of a saint's 'utterances', 70

ma'nā, pl. *ma'ānī*, q.v. Essence, significance, 142, 145, 241; *ma'nawī*, spiritual, essential, 212

manām, pl. *-āt*. Dream(s), 159

manāqib. (*a*) Virtues, works of merit (of saints), 209; (*b*) hagiographies, 37, 60, 70, 159, 221, 232 *maqām*, pl. *-āt*. (*a*) Stage or degree on the Sufi Path, 3, 4, 139, 156, 165, 200, 201; (*b*) place of manifestation where a saint has revealed his occasional presence and at which he can be communicated with, 26, 43, 234

maqbūl. Approved, 11

Maqtūl, al-. 'The Slain', epithet given to the theosophist, Shihāb ad-dīn Yaḥyā ibn Ḥabash as-Suhrawardī, 9, 53, 140, 141

marātib, s. *martaba*. Stages in the organized *dhikr* sessions, 205

mardūd. Condemned, refuted, 11

ma'rifa. (*a*) Mystical intuitive knowledge; (*b*) revealed knowledge of spiritual truth, 3, 140, 145, 147, 152, 153, 161, 264

marḥaban. A welcoming phrase, 209

mashdūd al-wasṭ. Girded (v. *shadd*) around the middle, 171

mashyakha. The function or office of a shaikh, 37, 38, 123; *mashyakhat ash-shuyūkh*, office of the chief shaikh, 19

mathnawī. Poem in 'doublets', 56, 61, 78

mawāsim. See *mawsim*. 38, 235

mawlā, pl. *mawālī*, Turk. *mōlā*, *mevla*, N. Africa *mulay*, French *mouley*, English *mulla(h)*; (*a*) Lord, master, patron, 135; *mawlānā*, 'our lord', 20, 61; (*b*) Client, 135, 261; Turk. *mevlānā hunkiàr*, a title of the head of the Mawlawiyya, 175

mawlid, pl. *mawālid*, coll. *mūlid*; Turk. *mevlid* and *mevlūt*, in the Maghrib *mulūd*. Birthday, expecially that of a saint or the Prophet. A liturgical recital in honour of saint or Prophet, 27, 47, 70, 75, 77, 78, 89, 162, 163, 174, 180, 204, 206–11, 226, 230, 231, 235, 245, 247, 254, 255, 257, 274

mawsim, pl. *mawāsim*. 'Season' for some celebration and so the celebration itself, 38, 108, 168, 235, 255

mazār. Place of visitation or shrine. 230

miḥrāb. A niche in the wall of a mosque indicating the *qibla* or direction of prayer, 169, 170

minna. Grace, 141

mi'rāj. Ascension, with reference to the Prophet Muḥammad's night-journey (*isrā'*), 98, 208, 210

mizāḥ. Jesting, 193

mu'allim. (*a*) Teacher, 118; (*b*) master-craftsman (guild), 25

mu'āmala. (*a*) Religious duties, as contrasted with *'ibādāt*, 142; (*b*) the technique of moral and spiritual self-purification (Ghazālī, *Iḥyā'*), contrasted with *mukāshafa*, 151

mu'āshara. Community life, 29

mubāya'a. Oath of initiation, 183, 186

mubtadi'. Postulant, apprentice, 25

mudhakkir. Remembrancer, 6

muftī. A canon lawyer authorized to promulgate a *fatwā* or formal legal opinion, 242

muḥibb. Lover, 175, 188; *muḥibbān* (Central Asia), affiliates to an order, 176

mujaddid al-alf ath-thānī. Reformer or renewer of the second millennium, 95

mujāhada. 'Striving' along the mystical Path, 139, 149, 151; *mujāhadat an-nafs*, mortification, striving with the unregenerate soul, 149, 189, 221, 222

mujerret āyīnī (Turk.). Bektāshī initiation ceremony for the celibate dervish, 188

mu'jiza. A prophetical miracle, 26, 145

mujtahid. The highest grade of Twelver Shī'ī divines, 99, 101, 164, 243

mukāshafa. Revelation, 151

mukhālafa. Difference, 223

mulaththam. Muffled, from *lithām*, muffler, 45

mulhama. Inspired, 152, 156

mūlid, see *mawlid*

mulk, *'ālam al-*. World of sovereignty, 160

munājāt. Meditations, 53

munshid, A singer at a *dhikr* circle, 205, 207, 209, 210, 211

muntasib. Lay 'affiliate' (Bektāshiyya), see *intasaba*; 175

muqaddam. A sectional leader in a Sufi order, 86, 107, 108, 109, 110, 111,

113, 120, 123, 126, 174, 175, 191, 192, 271, 276

muqaddama. A woman circle-leader, 114, 232

muqtadā. Exemplary, guide along the Way, 182

murābiṭ (Fr. *marabout*). Originally, inhabitant in a *ribāṭ*, a warrior for the faith which has become in N. Africa a general term for any kind of professional religious man, 167, 168

murāqaba. Awareness, watching. Spiritual communion with a saint or spiritual guide (*murshid*), 26, 146, 211–12, 213

muraqqaʿa. Patched frock, 17, 114, 181, 182, 184

murīd. An 'aspirant', disciple, novice, see *irāda*; 3, 29, 34, 45, 61, 80, 96, 116, 137, 148, 151, 158, 175, 184, 185, 186, 194, 213, 215, 216

murshid. Sufi guide or director, 3, 13, 14, 33, 45, 52, 53, 99, 136, 137, 148, 157, 158, 174, 187, 193, 201, 212, 213, 220

muṣāfaḥa. Handclasp (initiation rite), 171, 182, 186, 187, 188

muṣallā. Prayer-room, oratory, 166, 176

mushāhada. Contemplation, 139, 149, 189; *mushāhadāt ar-rubūbiyya*, visions of divine power, 142

muṣṭafā. 'The chosen one' = the prophet Muḥammad, 209

mustaʿrib. Adherent or assimilated to Arabism, 169

mustawā 's-sirr. The level or covert ('the ground') of the mystery, 152

mutajarridīn. Devotees, 143

mutashabbih. Affiliate, 185

mutawakkil. Quietist, 266, see *tawakkul*

muṭmaʾinna. Tranquil, state of the soul that has found peace, 152, 156

muwashshaḥ, pl. *āt*. A form of popular poetry, 47

muzamzim. Chanter, 196

nabī, pl. *anbiyāʾ*. A prophet, 133, 134, 206, 209, 241, 245

nafī wa ithbāt, 'Negation and affirmation', the term used for the first part of the *shahāda*: 'no god except God', 201

nafs. The lower 'self', the animal-spirit 'soul', 139, 151, 154, 155, 194, 197, 224

an-nafs al-ammāra, the 'head-strong', unregenerate, soul, 152, 155

——*lawwāma*, the reproachful, admonishing, soul, 152, 156

——*ṣāfiya* or *ṣafiyya*, the clarified soul, 155

——*mulhama*, the inspired soul, 152, 156

——*muṭmaʾinna*, the tranquil soul, 152, 156

——*rāḍiya*, the contented soul, 152, 156

——*marḍiyya*, approved soul, 152, 157

——*kāmila*, perfected soul, 152, 155, 157

mujāhadat an-nafs, striving with the soul, 149, 189

nafsiyya. Carnal, 197

naḥāʾir, s. *naḥīr*. Blood sacrifice, 255

nāʾib. Deputy, 123, 174, 175

naqīb. (*a*) Guardian of the liturgy in a Sufi order, 174; (*b*) member of a saint category, see *nuqabāʾ*, 164

nasab. (Spiritual) lineage, genealogy, 41, 182

nasip (Ar. *nasab*). Initiation rite (ascription) in the Bektāshī order, 175

nāsūt, *ʿālam an-*. The world of humanity, 160

nawāfil, s. *nāfila*. Acts (gen. *ṣalāts*) of supererogation, 266

nawshāh (Pers.). Bridegroom, 273

naẓar. Speculation, 53; *ʿilm an-naẓar*, rationalism, 53

naẓar bar qadam (Pers.). Watching one's steps, 203

naẓar ilā 'l-murd. Tranquil contemplation of the faces of novices (lit. 'beardless youth'), 193, 212

nazīl. Immigrant, 54

nigāh dāsht (Pers.). Watchfulness, 203

nisba. Epithet of origin, etc., 9, 34, 45, 48, 55, 60, 63, 71, 189, 261, 271; *nisbat al-khirqa*, initiatory filiation, 34 *nubuwwa*. Prophetship, prophesy, 133, 134, 136, 163

nujabā', s. *najīb*. Preeminent ones, a saint category, 165

nuqabā', s. *naqīb*. Chiefs, a saint category, 164

Nūr Muḥammadī. The primal pre-creation 'Muhammadan Light' from which all, angels, prophets, saints and ordinary humans, were created, 134, 161, 209

nussāk, s. *nāsik*, ascetics, 2

pálehenk (Turk.), *palahang* (Pers.). Halter, 188

pīr (Pers.). Elder, used for the Sufi director in Iranian and Indian spheres, 44, 74, 75, 83, 98, 147, 174, 178, 181, 182; *pīr-evi*, the superior in Turkish orders, 83, 174; *pīr-i ṣuḥbat*, the master who trained and initiated into 'companionship', 182; *pīr-i khirqat*, the master who invested with the habit, 182

pishtimāl, *peştamàl* (Turk.), *pusht-māl* (Pers). Waistcloth, 184

pōstakī (Turk.). Sheepskin, the 'throne' of a convent or order-head, 173

pōst-nishīn (Pers.). He who sits on a sheepskin, 174

qā'a. A large hall, 169

qabḍ. A (spiritual) contraction, a period of desolation, used frequently in association with its opposite *basṭ*, 89–90

qahhār. Subduer, 157, 190, 206

qalansuwa (Pers.). A high-crowned cap, 183

qalandar (Pers.). A dervish type that disregards appearance and flouts public opinion, 16, 22, 23, 30, 39, 53, 68, 98, 173, 264, 267–9

qalb. Heart, 152, 213 222; *qalb ṣanawbarī*, pineal heart, 148, 202

qarāfa. City of the dead (Egypt), 224

qarawī (from *qarya*, village). A villager, a rustic, and (met.) a dolt, 231

qaṣā'idīn. In Morocco a class of praise-singers, 208

qaṣīda, pl. *qaṣā'id*. A poetical form, 27, 90, 114, 208, 210

qawm. 'The folk'. In Sufi usage means the Sufis, i.e. the mystic people, 265

qāwuq, *kavùk* (Turk.). Wadded head-gear worn by dervishes, 278

qawwāl. The one who chants, 192, 196; *qawwālī* in India = 'recital' and itinerant singer and musician, 178

qayyūm, al-. The Eternal, a name for God, 190, 206

qibla. The direction a worshipper faces during ritual prayer (see *miḥrāb*), 213

qibliyya. An oratory, 169

qiyās. Analogical deduction, a process employed in *fiqh*, 119

qizil-bāsh. 'Red-head', Turkish term applied to redcapped dervishes, 68, 82, 100, 101, 188

qubba. A dome, and so, a domed building, 170, 171, 179, 230

quṣṣāṣ, s. *qāṣṣ*. Pious story-tellers, 6

quṭb. Lit. axis, pivot. (*a*) Head of the hierarchy of *awliyā'*, 42, 48, 99, 108, 137, 157, 161, 163–5, 209; (*b*) a grade of *awliyā'*, pl. *aqṭab*, 115, 163–5, 193

rābiṭa. (*a*) Hermitage, cf. *rābiṭ*, 'monk', 18, 170; (*b*) a Sufi technique, e.g. *ar-rābiṭa bi 'sh-shaikh*, 'union with one's guide', 211, 212–13, 248

rabṭ. Binding, 213; *rabṭ al-maḥzam*, binding of the girdle, 185

raḍī Allāh 'anhu. 'May God be pleased with him', phrase said after mentioning the name of someone who is dead, 81

rāḍiya. Contented (of the *nafs*), 152, 156

rak'a. The cycle of word and act surrounding a prostration in ritual prayer, 186

raqṣ. Dancing, 193

rasūl, Apostle, 134, 202

rātib, pl. *rawātib*. A fixed office prescribed by the director to his disciple, 216

ri'āya. A method for the pursuit of the mystical life, 3

ribāṭ. (*a*) A strong-point, frontier-post, 4, 46, 119, 167; (*b*) a religious hostel, hospice, 7, 24, 42, 94, 168; (*c*) a Sufi centre, 9, 17, 20, 21, 34, 35, 37, 49, 84, 167–8, 171, 241, 242
risāla, pl. *rasā'il*. Treatise, 35, 94, 119
riwāq. Cloisters around a court, 169.
riwāya. Tradition: chain of transmission, 189
rubūbiyya. Divine power, lordship, 53, 196
rūḥ. Spirit, 152, 197
rukhṣa, pl. *rukhaṣ*. Concession, dispensation, indulgency, 11, 193, 202
rushd. Right guidance, 136
ru'yā. Dream, 158, 159; *'ilm ta'bīr ar-ru'yā*, science of the interpretation of dreams, 158

ṣadr. Breast, 152
ṣafā. See *ṣafwa* (*b*)
safar dar waṭan (Pers.). Journeying in one's homeland, 203
ṣafwa. (*a*) Élite, 141; (*b*) purity from all existing things, 155
ṣāḥib. (*a*) Companion (in an order) pl. *aṣḥāb* = the circle of initiates, but *aṣ-Ṣaḥāba* = the companions of the Prophet, 168; (*b*) possessor of, *ṣāḥib al-ḥāl*, one subject to trances, 115; *Ṣāḥib az-Zamān*, the master of the age, 133, 137
sahn. The open court of a mosque, *khānaqāh*, or *zāwiya*, 169
sahr. Vigil, 30
ṣaḥw. Sobriety, the antithesis of *sukr*, 4
sā'iḥ. Itinerant (dervish), 49, 55
sajjāda. A prayer carpet or rug, 73, 169, 173; *shaikh as-sajjāda* or *sajjāda-nishīn* (Pers.), 'master of the prayer-mat' (of the founder of an order), the present head of the order 80, 123, 173, 224; *sajjādat al-irshād*, throne of spiritual direction, 37
Salafiyya. An end-of-nineteenth-century 'return to sources' school, 250, 255
salaka 'ṭ-ṭarīq (v.n. *sulūk*, 140). To traverse the (Sufi) Path, 1
ṣalāt. Ritual prayer, 119, 193, 194, 201, 216, 266
aṣ-ṣalāt 'alā 'n-nabī or *taṣliya*. The formula *ṣallā 'llāh 'alaihi wa sallam*, calling down blessings upon the Prophet, 206
ṣalāt al-fātiḥ. 'Prayer of the Opener' [Muḥammad], a Tijānī *taṣliya*-type prayer, 191
sālik. Pilgrim on the Way, 151, 203
samā', pl. *-āt*. Spiritual concert, recital, 9, 10, 56, 66, 178, 193, 195–6, 200, 202, 204, 207, 265; *samā'at-khāna*. Music-hall, 166
sanad, pl. *isnād*, q.v. Support, 12, 55, 90, 98, 149
ṣāni'. Companion-grade 'craftsman', 25
shadd. Girding, a part of the initiating ceremony sometimes extended to the whole, 'initiation rite', 35, 171, 185
shahawāt. The thoughts and desires of natural man, 152, 155
shahāda. (*a*) Testimony, 201; (*b*) the 'witness' of Islam, i.e. the profession of faith, 169, 191, 201, 203; (*c*) *'Ālam ash-shahāda*, the evidential world (of the senses), 152, 157, 160
shaikh al-ḥirfa. Master of a craft-guild, 25
shaikh as-sājjada. Occupier of the prayer-rug of the founder of an order, i.e. the present incumbent, 80, 123, 173
shaikh ash-shuyūkh. Title given by secular authority to a representative order-shaikh, 18, 77, 123, 162, 240, 242
shaikh aṣ-ṣuḥba. 'Head of the companionship', director of a Sufi circle, 33, 37, 192
shar'. The revealed law, as distinguished from *sharī'a*, 128, 133, 135, 142, 162
sharī'a. (*a*) The path to be followed = the exoteric revelation; equivalent to *shar'*, 1, 58, 136, 142, 143, 151, 152, 159, 160, 219, 220, 221, 230, 241; (*b*) jurisprudence, 104
sharīf, pl. *shurafā'*. One who claims descent from the Prophet, 46, 84
shaṭḥ, *shaṭḥiyyāt*. Ecstatic utterances, 150, 209
shurafā', see *sharīf*. 117, 122

shuṭṭār, s. *shāṭir*. A category of spiritual attainment according to some authors, 264

sibḥa. A rosary, 201

silsila. A chain, and so a lineage, chain of spiritual descent, 10, 11–16, 22, 28, 30, 32, 34, 36, 37, 42, 49, 50, 53, 54, 55, 57, 63, 64, 65, 72, 73, 74, 78, 80, 95, 96, 100, 103, 106, 108, 119, 136, 142, 149, 186, 192, 261–3, 267, 271, 275; *silsilat al-baraka*, chain of benediction, 149, 183; *silsilat al-wird* or *irāda*, chain of initiation, 150, 183; *silsilat adh-dhahab*, chain of gold, 150; *silsilat at-tarbiya*, chain of upbringing, 62, 150

ṣinf, pl. *aṣnaf*, *ṣunūf*. A craft-guild, 24

sirr. Mystery (rather than 'secret'), the 'ground' of the soul, 53, 152, 195, 211

sirwāl. Trousers, 184

ṣiyām. Fasting, 30

ṣubḥ. Dawn prayer, 216

subḥān Allāh. Glory be to God, 201, 206

ṣūf. Wool, 1, 181

ṣūfī. A Muslim mystic, *passim*

ṣuḥba. Companionship, fellowship, discipleship. (*Ṣāḥib* may mean 'disciple' or 'companion' in Sufi contexts), 4, 5, 29, 32, 37, 182, 185, 192, 212, 250

sukr. Intoxication, 4

sulūk. Traversing (the Sufi Way), 3, 140, 196

sunna. Custom, tradition of a custom of the Prophet, 8, 72, 115, 162, 253

sūra. A chapter of the Qur'ān, 28, 158, 216

ta'abbud. Devotion (in the way to God), 6

ta'ayyun. Individualization, 155

ṭabaqa, pl. *ṭibāq*. A dervish cell, 169

ṭabaqāt. 'Categories', biographies; *ṭabaqāt al-awliyā'*, biographies of the saints, 70

li 't-tabarruk. For the purpose of absorbing *baraka*, 55, 115, 180, 183, 185

ta'bīr ar-ru'yā. Interpretation of a dream, 158

tābi'ūn. Successors of the 'companions' (*aṣ-Ṣaḥāba*) of the Prophet, 261

tadrīb. Training, 189

tahdhīb. Instruction, 189

taḥiyya. An act of greeting as in ritual *ṣalāt* (end of second *rak'a*) or during a *mawlid* recital on the Prophet's spiritual arrival, 210

taḥkīm. Sufi discipline, 16, 183

tahlīl. The act of saying, 'there is no god but God', 187, 201, 205, 206, 210

taḥmīd. The act of praising God with the words, 'Praise (*ḥamd*) is due to God alone', 206

ṭā'ifa, pl. *ṭawā'if*. Lit. part, portion. Association, organization; the word used throughout for a Sufi 'order', 5, 15, 19, 20, 24, 36, 38, 43, 47, 51, 56, 65, 67, 71, 72, 73, 80, 85, 86, 88, 96, 102, 103, 126, 148, 158, 171, 173, 174, 179, 183, 201, 205, 223, 225–6, 234, 237, 239, 250, 251, 258

tāj (Pers.). Crown, term used for the high-crowned hat of a Persian dervish and extended to other types (esp. investing) of headgear, 100, 184, 185, 188

tajallī. Theophany, illumination, irradiation, 190; pl. *tajalliyāt*, epiphanies, 140

Tājīk. An Iranian, especially as opposed to a Turk. Term applied to Iranian settled population of central Asian regions after their occupation by the Turks, 63

takmīl as-sulūk. Completion of the course, 190

takhmīs. A quintain, four new hemistiches added to each hemistich of the poem of an earlier author, 70

takiyya, pl. *takāyā*. Centre of a Turkish order, see *tekkē*

ṭālib, pl. *ṭullāb*, *ṭulba*. A law-student, 234; candidate, a stage in initiation (Turkish orders), 175

ta'līm. Teaching, instruction, 108, 183, 192

talqīn (v.n. of *laqqana*, to prompt). 'Giving (secret) instruction', which becomes a synonym for 'initiation', 51, 80, 96, 182, 188, 189, 191, 215 *tamzīq*. Rending of garments during ecstasy, 115, 193

tanzīh. The doctrine of 'exemption' (*a*) according to which God is, by virtue of His essence, in no way at all like the creatures He has created, 143–4, 190, 223; (*b*) in Sufi usage corresponds to a *via remotionis*, a purging of one's being of all images and preconceived ideas of God, especially associated with the negative *lā ilāha* of the *tahlīl* formula, 144.

ṭāqiya. Skull cap or other headgear, 183

taqiyya. Lit. 'guarding oneself', precautionary dissembling, *pia dissimulatio*, 102, 137

taqrīr. Licence of appointment, 123

ṭarāṭīr, s. *ṭarṭūr*. The high conical cap worn by dervishes, 278

tarāwīḥ. Supererogatory prayers especially associated with Ramaḍān, 266

tarbiya. Guidance, 108, 150, 183, 192

ṭarīq and *ṭarīqa*, pl. *ṭuruq*. A way, the term for the Sufi path; a mystical method, system, or school of guidance for traversing the path, *passim* throughout; *ṭarīqa mujāhada*, via purgativa, 139, 149, 151, 189, 221, 222; *ṭarīqa mushāhada*, via illuminativa, 139, 149, 189; *Ṭarīqat al-Khawājagān*, the Way of the Masters, the proper name for the Naqshabandī Way, 14, 62, 92

tark. Gore or fold of a turban, 100

tasammā. To designate oneself (e.g. a Shādhilī), to claim (spiritual) relationship with (a saint), 11

taṣawwuf. Mysticism; English formation Sufism, derived from *ṣūf*, 'wool', 1, 6, 19, 20, 29, 32, 34, 37, 42, 44, 50, 71, 128, 136, 141, 143, 195, 222, 238, 241, 243, 250, 251, 252, 265, 266

taṣawwur. Apprehension visualization, 213

tasbīḥ. (*a*) The saying of the phrase *subḥān Allāh*, '(I proclaim) the glory of God', 201, 206; (*b*) a rosary, 201

tasbiḥa. A rosary, 80, 187, 201

taṣfiyat al-qalb. Purification of the heart, 222

taslīm-ṭāsh. Emblem or stone worn on a dervish's halter or breast, 188

taṣliya, see *ṣalāt*

tathqīb, v.n. of *thaqqaba*, to perforate, 268

ṭawā'if, pl. of *ṭā'ifa*, q.v., 85, 229, 242, 250, 258

tawajjuh. Confrontation (from *wajh*, face). A technique of contemplation, concentrating one's being upon someone, 58, 148, 157, 211, 213–14, 248

tawājud. An induced ecstasy. Vb. *tawājada*, to induce ecstasy (*wajd*) by means of the *dhikr*, 212

tawakkul. Trust (in God), mystic state of abandonment into God's hands, 4, 29, 156, 253, 265, 266

tawba. Repentance, turning to God, conversion, 145, 157; repetition of the phrase, 'I repent before God', 206

tawḥīd. The unity and unicity of God, 135, 141, 142, 186, 189; *'ilm at-tawḥīd* = synonym of *'ilm al-kalām* or dogmatic theology

ta'wīl. Allegorical interpretation, 140

tekkē, *tekyē*, *tekiyē* (see *takiyya*). Turkish order-centre, monastery, or hospice, 44, 60, 62, 69, 75, 76, 81, 83, 95, 126, 171, 175, 177, 178, 230, 234, 238, 253–4

thawb. A gown, 183, 185

ṭullāb, s. *ṭālib*. Law students, 223

'ubbād, s. *'ābid*. Worshippers, 265

'udhrī. Platonic doctrine of Eros; also Sufi exercise of contemplation of beauty, *naẓar ilā 'l-murd/ward*, 193, 212

'ulamā', s. *'ālim*. Those who are trained in the religious sciences, 8, 9, 29, 47, 48, 66, 67, 69, 79, 80, 82, 98, 106, 109, 115, 117, 118, 119, 121, 122, 125, 128, 133, 139, 162, 198, 222, 224, 230, 231, 238, 241–4, 245, 247

'ulūm, pl. of *'ilm*. *'Ulūm al-wahb* or *al-'ulūm al-wahabiyya*, gifted knowledge, 221, 222; *al-'ulūm al-kasbiyya*, acquired knowledge, 221

umma. A community, 241
ummī. Illiterate, untrained, 221
'uqda. 'Knot', covenant with a shaikh, 11
'urs. 'Wedding', term frequently used in India for the festival commemorating the death of a saint, 23, 178
uṣūl. Roots, fundamental principles, 34, 115; *uṣūl ad-din*, sources of religion (= *uṣūl al-fiqh*), 34
'uzla. Withdrawal, 30, 193

vakfi vucut (Turk.). A Bektashi oath ceremony, 188

wādī. Valley, 184
waḥda. Unicity, 152, 154; *Waḥdat al-wujūd*, the unicity of Being, existential monism, 58, 128, 131, 161, 162, 243; *Waḥdat ash-shuhūd*, unity of the witness or phenomena, 58, 95
waḥī. Exoteric, impersonal 'revelation' given to prophets through the mediumship of an angel, 145
Wāḥid, al-. The Unique, 163, 205
wajd. Ecstasy, 145, 150, 200; *wajada* (to find, to know), to fall into an ecstasy
wajh. Face, 212, 213; see *tawajjuh*
wakīl. Custodian, administrative officer of a mosque or a Sufi order, 174.
walāya. (*a*) Spiritual office or territory of spiritual 'jurisdiction', 48, 225; (*b*) rightful allegiance: Shī'ī sense, 133, 164
walī, pl. *awliyā'*. A 'protégé' of God, a saint; 'Surely, those under God's care (*awliyā' Allāh*) have no ground for fear, nor for grief', Qur'ān, x. 63; 13, 26, 82, 84, 100, 104, 108, 133, 134, 135, 137, 141, 158, 172, 179, 191, 220, 224–5, 232, 234
waqf, pl. *awqāf*. Pious foundation, 7, 18, 20, 21, 169, 241
waqfa. (*a*) Pause between two *maqāmāt*; (*b*) cessation of search, through transmutation of soul, 204
wāqif. One whose search is ended through having 'passed away' in the Sought, 204
wāridāt. Revelations in the broad sense of mystical enlightenments, 33, 196
wāsiṭa. Medium, 213
waṣiyya, pl. *waṣāyā*. Testamentary directives given by a shaikh to his successor or disciples, 18, 193
waẓīfa, pl. *waẓā'if*. A duty, an office. In the orders it is the daily office prescribed to the *murīd* by his shaikh, 191, 205, 216
wazīr. Minister, 15, 20, 112
al-wilāda 'l-ma'nawiyya. Spiritual sonship, 212
wilāya. Saintship, state of being under the protection of God (see *walī*), concept of sanctity, consecration, 26, 38, 58, 104, 133, 134, 136, 139, 140, 141, 143, 148, 152, 153, 159, 163, 224, 225, 228, 243
wirātha. Inheritance (mystical), 159
wird, pl. *awrād*. (*a*) a phrase-patterned devotion, a 'collect', 10, 13, 72, 75, 86, 107, 150, 159, 183, 191, 192, 193, 198, 206, 214–15, 217; (*b*) the 'office' of an order, 196, 214; (*c*) the order itself, 51, 184, 214
wuḍū'. Ritual ablution, 28, 187
wujūd. (*a*) God as pure Being (not a Being in a world of beings), the All of all (see *waḥda*), 161; (*b*) on the Path = the stage beyond *wajd* (q.v.), 'knowing', 'perceptivity', 195, 212
wuqūf-i zamānī (Pers.). Temporal pause, 203
wuqūf-i 'adadī (Pers.). Numerical pause, 203
wuqūf-i qalbī (Pers.). Heart pause, 203
wuṣla. Union, coupling, 152, 155
wuṣūl. Union, 191

yād kard (Pers.). Remembrance, making mention, 203
yād dāsht (Pers.). Recollection, 203

zaffa. Procession, 209
zāhid, pl. *zuhhād*. One who practises *zuhd* (q.v.), devotee, ascetic, 220
ẓāhir. Exterior, 63
ẓāhirī. Exoteric, -ist; literalist, formalist, 97, 106

zāwiya, pl. *zawāyā*. Lit. a corner. A small mosque, a saint's tomb, a small Sufi centre. In N. Africa, a comprehensive order-centre, 5, 9, 10, 15, 16, 17, 18, 19, 20, 38, 39, 40, 47, 49, 50, 69, 71, 76, 84, 86, 87, 88, 107, 110, 111, 112, 116, 118, 119, 120, 121, 122, 126, 168, 170, 171, 172, 175–7, 179, 205, 223, 226, 228, 230, 234, 238, 255, 267, 269

zindīq. Properly, a Manichaean, but in general usage = an atheist, infidel, 160

ziyāra, pl. *-āt*. Visitation (holy place, shrine), 26, 45, 108, 179, 230, 272

zuhd. Devotion, self- and world-denial, renunciation, 6, 75, 107

zuhhād, see *zāhid*, 2, 181

zwāya (*zawāyā*). Maraboutic tribes in the Sahara, 110, 235

GENERAL INDEX

(Both the Arabic definite article *al-* and *b.* (for *ibn*, 'son of') have been disregarded in indexing)